NEW DIRECTIONS IN GLOBAL ECONOMIC GOVERNANCE

The G8 and Global Governance Series

Series Editor: John J. Kirton

The G8 and Global Governance Series explores the issues, the institutions, and the strategies of the participants in the G8 network of global governance, and other actors, processes, and challenges that shape global order in the twenty-first century. Many aspects of globalisation, once considered domestic, are now moving into the international arena, generating a need for broader and deeper international co-operation and demanding new centres of leadership to revitalise, reform, reinforce, and even replace the galaxy of multilateral institutions created in 1945. In response, the G8, composed of the world's major market democracies, including Russia and the European Union, is emerging as an effective source of global governance. *The G8 and Global Governance Series* focusses on the new issues at the centre of global governance, covering topics such as finance, investment, and trade, as well as transnational threats to human security and traditional and emerging political and security challenges. The series examines the often invisible network of G8, G7, and other institutions as they operate inside and outside established international systems to generate desired outcomes and create a new order. It analyses how individual G8 members and other international actors, including multinational firms, civil society organisations, and other international institutions, devise and implement strategies to achieve their preferred global order.

Also in the series

New Directions in Global Economic Governance

Managing globalisation in the twenty-first century

Edited by
JOHN J. KIRTON
University of Toronto

GEORGE M. VON FURSTENBERG
Fordham University, New York

Ashgate

Aldershot • Burlington USA • Singapore • Sydney

Published by
Ashgate Publishing Limited
Gower House
Croft Road
Aldershot
Hants GU11 3HR
England

Ashgate Publishing Company
131 Main Street
Burlington, VT 05401-5600 USA

Ashgate website: http://www.ashgate.com

British Library Cataloguing in Publication Data
New directions in global economic governance : managing
    globalisation in the twenty-first century. - (The G8 and
    global governance series)
    1. Globalisation 2. International economic relations
    I. Kirton, John J. II. Von Furstenburg, George M., 1941-
    337

Library of Congress Control Number: 2001090007

ISBN 0 7546 1698 3

Printed and bound in Great Britain by MPG Books Ltd, Bodmin, Cornwall

Contents

PART II: NEW DIRECTIONS IN GLOBAL FINANCIAL GOVERNANCE

PART III: NEW DIRECTIONS IN GLOBAL TRADE GOVERNANCE

PART IV: CONCLUSION

APPENDICES

Figures

Contributors

Sir Nicholas Bayne, KCMG, is a Fellow at the International Trade Policy Unit of the London School of Economics and Political Science. As a British diplomat, he was High Commissioner to Canada from 1992 to 1996, Economic Director at the Foreign and Commonwealth Office from 1988 to 1992, and Ambassador to the Organisation for Economic Co-operation and Development from 1985 to 1988. He is author of *Hanging In There* (Ashgate, 2000), as well as co-author, with Robert Putnam, of *Hanging Together: Cooperation and Conflict in the Seven Power Summits* (Harvard University Press, 1987).

Theodore H. Cohn is a Professor of Political Science at Simon Fraser University in Vancouver. He received his Ph.D. from the University of Michigan and was Chair of Simon Fraser's Political Science Department from 1982 to 1987. His main research and teaching areas include international political economy, the politics of international trade, and global cities and cross-border relations. Among his books are *Global Political Economy: Theory and Practice* (Longman, 2000), *The International Politics of Agricultural Trade: Canadian-American Relations in a Global Agricultural Context* (University of British Columbia Press, 1990), and *Canadian Food Aid: Domestic and Foreign Policy Implications* (University of Denver, 1979). He is co-editor of, among others, *Power in the Global Era: Grounding Globalization* (St. Martin's Press, 2000) and *Innovation Systems in a Global Context: The North American Experience* (McGill-Queen's University Press, 1998). He has also published widely on international trade, the North American Free Trade Agreement and agricultural trade policy, as well as on his areas of research. He is currently writing a book on international institutions and global trade policy, and is co-authoring a textbook on international organisation.

Sébastien Dallaire is a doctoral student in International Relations at the Department of Political Science of the University of Toronto. His area of research is international political economy, particularly the impact of globalisation on domestic politics. He is co-author, with Jean-Philippe Thérien, of 'Nord-Sud: Une vision du monde en mutation', published in *La revue internationale et stratégique* (winter 1999–2000).

Kunihiko Ito is Associate Professor of Monetary Economics at the University of Tokushima in Japan. He was a Visiting Research Fellow of the Centre for International Studies and Economist-in-Residence of the G8 Research Group at the University of Toronto in 1998–99.

Saori N. Katada is Assistant Professor at the School of International Relations of the University of Southern California. She is the author of *Banking on Stability: Japan and the Cross-Pacific Dynamics of International Financial Crisis Management* (University of Michigan Press, 2001) and has published several journal articles on Japanese foreign economic policy toward countries in the Pacific Rim. Her current research focuses on the issue of policy coherence among Asian members regarding the regional financial structure.

John J. Kirton is Director of the G8 Research Group, Associate Professor of Political Science, Research Associate of the Centre for International Studies, and Fellow of Trinity College at the University of Toronto. He has advised the Canadian government on G7 participation, international trade, and sustainable development, and has written widely on G7/8 summitry. He is co-author of *Environmental Regulations and Corporate Strategy: A NAFTA Perspective* (Oxford University Press, 1999) and co-editor of *The G8's Role in the New Millennium* (Ashgate, 1999), *Shaping a New International Financial System* (Ashgate, 2000), and *Guiding Global Order: G8 Governance in the Twenty-First Century* (Ashgate, 2001).

Thomas C. Lawton is MBA Director and Lecturer in European Business and Corporate Strategy at Royal Holloway School of Management at the University of London. He holds a B.A. (Hons.) from the National University of Ireland in Cork, an M.Sc. (Econ.) from the London School of Economics and Political Science, and a Ph.D. in International Political Economy from the European University Institute in Florence. Dr. Lawton has previously been a Visiting Scholar at the University of California at Berkeley, a European Union Human Capital Mobility Fellow at the University of Essex, and a Research Fellow at INSEAD in France. He is the author of *Technology and the New Diplomacy* (Ashgate, 1997) and editor of *European Industrial Policy and Competitiveness* (Macmillan Business, 1999) and *Strange Power: Shaping the Parameters of International Relations and International Political Economy* (Ashgate, 2000). His writings have appeared in journals such as *International Business Review, Long Range Planning, European Business Journal,* and the *Journal of Public Policy.*

Michele Mastroeni is a doctoral candidate in Political Science majoring in International Relations and a Connaught Fellow at the University of Toronto. His current research interest is on innovations in the electronic economy and their effects on relations between developed and developing countries.

Heidi K. Ullrich is a temporary lecturer in the Department of Politics at the University of Southampton. She is completing her doctorate at the London School of Economics and Political Science, where she has also taught. She has worked as a research assistant at both the U.S. Mission to the World Trade Organization and the European Parliament. Her research interests include international political economy, relations between the U.S. and the European Union, European Union and U.S. trade and agricultural policies, and the impact of policy networks.

George M. von Furstenberg holds the Robert Bendheim Chair in Economic and Financial Policy at Fordham University in New York. He was previously Rudy Professor of Economics at Indiana University in Bloomington, Indiana. The president of the North American Economics and Finance Association, he has published widely on international and finance issues, including chapters on 'Transparentising the Global Money Business: Glasnost or Just Another Wild Card in Play?' in *Shaping a New International Financial System,* edited by Karl Kaiser, John Kirton, and Joseph Daniels (Ashgate, 2000), and on 'U.S. Dollarization: A Second-Best Form of Regional Currency Consolidation' in *Guiding Global Order: G8 Governance in the Twenty-First Century*, edited by John Kirton, Joseph Daniels, and Andreas Freytag (Ashgate, 2001).

Preface and Acknowledgements

This book, the sixth in Ashgate Publishing's series on the 'G8 and Global Governance', continues a tradition begun in 1998 of using the annual G8 Summit as a catalyst for an edited volume that explores the central themes in the emerging dynamic of global governance. The first volume, *The G8's Role in the New Millennium,* was produced on the basis of the 1998 Birmingham G8 Summit. The book focussed on the role of the G8 as it began its new era with Russia as a virtually full member, with a rapidly expanding array of ministerial-level institutions, and with a new, highly domestic agenda that included such new challenges of globalisation as financial supervision, employment, and crime. The 1999 Cologne Summit, which took place as the 1997–99 global financial crisis and the 1999 war to liberate Kosovo were coming to an end, inspired two volumes. The first, *Shaping a New International Financial System,* took an economic and political-economy approach to the central issue confronting the global economic community. The second, *Guiding Global Order: G8 Governance in the Twenty-First Century,* continued this economic exploration but extended the concern to embrace a wide range of political and international institutional issues and perspectives, including the defining highest political questions of war and peace.

This volume continues that pattern, while broadening the coverage in three important ways. First, in keeping with the series' emphasis on global governance in general, as well as on the G8 system in particular, it takes as its starting point the changing international economic order as a whole and the efforts by a wide range of actors to determine the content and impact of the G8's agenda. It thus gives central attention to the traditional international political-economy pillar of finance, both in its global dimensions and in the critical Asian region. It also takes an in-depth look at the international trade system in the wake of the failed attempt at Seattle in late 1999 to launch a new 'Millennium Round' of multilateral trade negotiations. And, above all, it begins with a close examination of the new digital economy that is transforming national societies and international systems alike.

Second, this volume focusses on new directions in the global economy and its governance by directly addressing the major transformational forces currently at work. The first of these is indeed the digital revolution, which affects the real economy profoundly, and raises the question of how the international community can govern the many dimensions of this new and unprecedented force. These new directions extend from hardware and channels to software and content, including the core question of whether the previous embedded liberalism and long-reigning neoliberal ideology are giving way to a new consensus, and what future such a consensus might have. And, most generally, the concern with new directions deals with the ultimate issue of whether the present process of proliferating globalisation can be effectively governed and, if so, by whom, how, and to what end.

Third, this book takes up the question of international order and the broad array of international institutions that are competing and co-operating to shape it in ways that respond to the needs of the international community in the twenty-first century. It examines the adjustments taking place in long-established institutions such as the International Monetary Fund (IMF) and the challenges facing the much newer World Trade Organization (WTO). It also explores emerging institutions, both those on a regional scale as seen in Asia and those representing a new approach to institutionalised global governance, as seen in the new 'Dot-Force' launched by the G8 at its Okinawa Summit. It explores how institutions old and new are moving to establish order in such essentially ungoverned areas as the global digital economy and society. And it analyses how the G7 and G8 are themselves working with newer bodies such as the G20 and the IMF's International Monetary and Financial Committee (IMFC) to govern the global economy in this new age. Thus the full global economy, the new directions transforming that global economy, and the efforts to create a new order on the part of new and reforming international institutions are the three linked pillars on which this book is built.

This volume has its origins in several activities. The first is an academic symposium that took place in Okinawa, Japan, on July 19–20, 2000, soon after the early July gathering of G7 finance ministers in Fukuoka and just before the July 21–23 Summit of the G7 and then G8 leaders in Okinawa itself. The symposium, sponsored jointly by the G8 Research Group based at the University of Toronto and the University of the Ryukyus, took as its theme 'New Directions in Global Governance? The G8's Okinawa Summit'. More than a dozen scholars from Japan, North America, and Europe assembled in front of an audience of 100 for an in-depth look at the central issues confronting the global economy and the G7 leaders themselves. The chapters by Nicholas Bayne (Chapter 2), Sébastien Dallaire, Kunihiko Ito, Michele Mastroeni,

Heidi K. Ullrich, and George M. von Furstenberg are extensively revised versions of their papers delivered at that symposium.

The second source consists of the set of papers and presentations given at a public policy conference held in Tokyo on July 17, 2000. That conference, co-sponsored by the G8 Research Group, the United Nations University, and Japan's Foundation for Advanced Studies in Development (FASID), dealt with the theme 'The Kyushu-Okinawa Summit: A G8-Developing Country Dialogue.' Senior representatives of developing countries from all global regions and major international development institutions participated with developed country experts close to the G7/G8 process in a day-long exchange before an audience of 250 interested individuals. The chapters by Nicholas Bayne (Chapter 2), John J. Kirton (Chapter 9), and George M. von Furstenberg (Chapter 5) reflect their contributions to that conference.

The third source for this volume was the Citizens' Forum held at the Nippon Press Centre in Tokyo on July 12, 2000. Here, John J. Kirton presented a paper entitled 'Prospects for the Okinawa-Kyushu Summit'. The forum, which was co-sponsored by the G8 Research Group and the London School of Economics and Political Science Forum, brought together an audience of 125, largely members of the Tokyo policy community as well as media representatives from across Japan, for a thorough examination of the issues and diplomacy at the centre of the forthcoming summit. Chapter 9 by John J. Kirton reflects his presentation and the discussion at the Forum.

The fourth source consists of specially invited contributions, designed to deal with critical components of the global economy and the ongoing effort to govern it, and to broaden the geographic and disciplinary base of the analysis. We are grateful to Theodore H. Cohn, Saori N. Katada, and Thomas C. Lawton for contributing in this way.

The fifth source is the ongoing work of the G8 Research Group on issues closely related to the evolution of the G7/8 system of international institutions and the broader issues of global order. John J. Kirton's chapter on the G7, G20, and the IMFC flows from this ongoing work.

This volume contains some of the research produced by or related to the University of Toronto's Centre for International Studies' project on 'Securing Canada's Environmental Community Through International Regime Reform' (EnviReform). Financed by the Social Sciences and Humanities Research Council of Canada, through its strategic grant programme on 'Globalization and Social Cohesion in Canada', the EnviReform project identifies effective ways for Canadians to participate more cohesively and directly in the international trade systems that affect their natural environment, food, health, and safety. It analyses the social and environmental impacts of existing trade liberalisation on Canadians and explores new strategies for regulation and risk assessment, environmental information, voluntary standards setting, and participation by civil society. These strategies aim at allowing Canadians to participate in a more unified manner in shaping trade and finance regimes in more socially and ecologically sustainable ways.

New Directions in Global Economic Governance explores its subject from several vantage points. It contains contributions from those based in all of the G8's constituent regions of North America, Europe, and Japan, and from half of its constituent countries. The contributors come from the disciplines of economics, the international political economy field of political science, and management studies, and from leading universities in the United States, Britain, Canada, and Japan. Many of the authors have had experience within many of the core governmental and intergovernmental institutions at work in the international economy, or through service in an advisory capacity to those institutions. They thus bring a broad array of perspectives, analytical approaches, and judgements to bear. The collection combines the insights of established veteran scholars of the international economy and the G7 with a new generation of younger scholars writing on their specific topics within a G8 and global governance context for the first time.

Given the rich diversity of views contained within these chapters, therefore, no effort has been made to impose a single theoretical tradition, interpretative framework, or even a simple consensus. Rather, this volume maintains its alternative perspectives as it moves through its sections on the 'new economy', international finance, and international trade.

Acknowledgements

Producing this volume had left us with a large debt to those who have contributed in so many different ways to this enterprise. Our first debt is to those members of the G8 Research Group's Professional Advisory Council, notably Nicholas Bayne, who served as a speaker at two of our lead-up conferences, added a subsequent chapter on trade, and worked tirelessly throughout the process of getting this book done.

We owe much to our partners at the University of the Ryukyus, the United Nations University, and FASID for their indispensable assistance. This debt begins with Professor Junichi Takase, of the Nagoya School of Foreign Studies, who first saw the promise in a joint venture, and Professor Takayoshi Egami of the University of the Ryukyus, who generously agreed to serve as our academic partner, secured important financial assistance, and mounted a highly productive conference. Our debt extends to Dr. Kazuo Takahashi, Director, and Yoshitaro Fuwa, Senior Deputy Director, International Development Research Institute, FASID, and to professors Hideo Sato, Senior Advisor to the Rector, and Ramesh Thakur, Vice-Rector of the Peace and Governance Program at the United Nations University in Tokyo. And it importantly includes Shin-ichiro Uda, Director of the LSE Forum, for his immense energy, advice, and assistance. In addition, Ambassador Leonard Edwards and Deanna Horton at the Canadian Embassy in Tokyo, and Don Campbell, Jonathan Fried, Paul Heinbecker, Joy Kane, and Michael Martin in Ottawa provided constant support.

We are most grateful to those organisations that provided the resources, both financial and in kind, to make possible the activities on which this volume is based and the associated program of the G8 Research Group. The University of the Ryukyus, the Japanese Ministry of Education, and the Prefectural Government of Okinawa provided financial support for the Academic Symposium at the University of the Ryukyus, and the Department of Political Science of the University of Toronto assisted three of its members to give papers there. The LSE Forum mounted the Citizens' Forum. The Japanese Ministry of Foreign Affairs, through the United Nations University, provided support to the Public Policy Conference. Our financial sponsors for G8 Online 2000 and thus the G8 Research Group's field program include the Canadian Department of Foreign Affairs and International Trade and Nortel Networks, whose generous support we gratefully acknowledge. We are grateful, too, to Trinity College for the financial support given to make it possible for its students to participate in our field program. Our in-kind sponsors for the Academic Symposium and Public Policy Conference, and for the innovative webcasting program that broadcast them to the world, were eCollege.com and Sony, Canada's *National Post,* the *Toronto Star,* and the *Pasadena Star-Times.*

We are also grateful to Jeffrey Hart of Indiana University and the many other colleagues who offered insightful comments on draft versions of the chapters in the trade section of this volume, which were presented at the annual conference of the International Studies Association in Chicago from 20 to 24 February 2001.

We owe a special word of thanks to three individuals. The first is Paul Jacobelli, whose dedication, initiative, persistence, and skill were vital in drawing together the sponsorship consortium that made G8 Online, our other field events, and thus this volume possible. The second is Gina Stephens, for co-ordinating the G8 Research Group at the University of Toronto and raising the funds to assist doctoral students presenting papers at the Academic Symposium. The third is Madeline Koch, Managing Editor of the G8 Research Group, whose managerial and editorial skills were essential in ensuring that the initial thoughts and rough drafts offered in English and Japanese were transformed into a polished book.

More broadly, we note with deep appreciation the indispensable contributions of Cheryl Chandran, Director of Communications of the G8 Research Group, of Sandra Larmour, the Director of Development of the G8 Research Group, and of Nancy Scott and Allison Smith who served as legal advisors, as well as of Heidi K. Ullrich of the London School of Economics and Political Science.

We are further grateful to the members of the G8 Research Group, particularly those who were able to join us for the Academic Symposium and the Summit in Okinawa. While all contributed in so many ways, we must thank in particular Haruka Araki and Toshio Kodama for their devoted work in organising our Japanese operations, and Christine Lucyk, Colleen McShane, and Ralph Czychun. We also appreciate the efforts of those who were unable to join us in Japan, notably Helen Walsh and Michael Greenspoon.

At the University of Toronto, we are grateful for the continuing support of our colleagues at the Centre for International Studies: Professor Louis Pauly, its director, who oversees our research activities, and Professor Peter Hajnal, who assumed the onerous but essential task of securing the anonymous referees who reviewed our draft manuscript and collectively approved it for publication. We owe much to the comments of our reviewers, whose often trenchant but ultimately supportive comments have been taken fully into account. At Trinity College, we acknowledge the critical support of Provost Tom Delworth; Bursar Geoffrey Seaborn, who manages the G8 Research Group's accounts; Head Librarian Linda Corman, who oversees the development of the G8 Research Library Collection; and Professor Robert Bothwell, Co-ordinator of the International Relations Program. At the Department of Political Science, Professor Robert Vipond, the Chair, and professors Ronald Deibert and Larry LeDuc have provided constant encouragement. At the University of Toronto Library, Chief Librarian Carole Moore, Internet Director Sian Miekle, and Project Manager Marc Lalonde have been indispensable. At the Office of Public Affairs, Cheryl Sullivan has cheerfully and effectively assisted us with publicity and promotion.

Perhaps our greatest gratitude is reserved for our commissioning editor, Kirstin Howgate, and her colleagues at Ashgate. It was Kirstin who had the vision to see the virtue of producing this volume and who worked effectively to ensure a smooth production and publication of the manuscript.

Finally, we acknowledge the understanding, patience, and support of our families as we laboured to convert raw drafts into published text. We are also indebted to our students and the alumni of the G8 Research Group who provided constant inspiration as we pursued our work. It is to this next generation of scholars on the G7/8 and global governance that we dedicate this book.

John J. Kirton and George M. von Furstenberg, March 2001

Abbreviations

ADB	Asian Development Bank
AMF	Asian Monetary Fund
APEC	Asia-Pacific Economic Cooperation
ASEAN	Association of South-East Asian Nations
BIAC	Business and Industry Advisory Committee
BIS	Bank for International Settlements
B2B	business to business
B2C	business to consumer
CAP	Common Agricultural Policy
CCL	contingent credit line
CG18	Consultative Group of 18
COPA	Comité des Organisations Professionelles Agricoles
CSO	civil society organisation
DC	Developed Countries
DSA	Debt Sustainability Analysis
EC	European Community
ECB	European Central Bank
ERP	enterprise resource planning
ESAF	Enhanced Structural Adjustment Facility
EU	European Union
FATF	Financial Action Task Force
FBI	(U.S.) Federal Bureau of Investigation
FDI	foreign direct investment
FOGS	Functioning of the GATT System
FSAP	Financial Sector Assessment Program
FSF	Financial Stability Forum
G5	Group of 5
G10	Group of 10
G20	Group of 20
G22	Group of 22
G24	Group of 24
G48	Group of 48

G77	Group of 77
GAB	General Arrangements to Borrow
GATT	General Agreement on Tariffs and Trade
GDP	gross domestic product
GIIC	Global Information Infrastructure Commission
GNP	gross national product
HIPC	Heavily Indebted Poor Countries
HLIs	highly leveraged institutions
IBRD	International Bank for Reconstruction and Development
ICC	International Chamber of Commerce
ICT	information and communications technology
IFIs	international financial institutions
ILO	International Labour Organization
IMF	International Monetary Fund
IMFC	International Monetary and Financial Committee
IT	information technology
ITO	International Trade Organization
KIEO	keystone international economic organisation
LDCs	less developed countries
LLDCs	least of the less developed countries
LTCM	Long-Term Capital Management
MDBs	multilateral development banks
MNCs	multinational corporations
MTM	ministerial trade mandate
NGO	nongovernmental organisation
NICs	newly industrialised countries
NIEO	New International Economic Order
NMD	national missile defence
NTB	nontariff barrier
ODA	official development assistance
OECD	Organisation for Economic Co-operation and Development
OEEC	Organisation for European Economic Co-operation
OFC	offshore financial centre
OPEC	Organization of the Petroleum Exporting Countries
PC	personal computer
PGA	Peoples' Global Action
PRGF	Poverty Reduction and Growth Facility
R&D	research and development
ROSCs	Reports on Observance of Standards and Codes

SAF	Structural Adjustment Facility
SAP	structural adjustment programmes
TABD	Transatlantic Business Dialogue
TRIPs	trade-related aspects of intellectual property
TRIMs	trade-related investment measures
UN	United Nations
UNCITRAL	United Nations Commission on International Trade Law
UNCTAD	United Nations Conference on Trade and Development
UNCTC	United Nations Centre on Transnational Corporations
UNESCO	United Nation Educational, Scientific, and Cultural Organization
UNICEF	United Nations Children's Fund
WIPO	World Intellectual Property Organization
WTO	World Trade Organization

Introduction

1 New Directions in Global Economic Governance: Challenges and Responses

JOHN J. KIRTON AND GEORGE M. VON FURSTENBERG

The New Challenges of Global Economic Governance

As the twenty-first century opens, the global economy is caught in the throes of several major forces that together promise to transform its very foundation, operation, and impact. The first force is the information technology (IT) revolution. In its North American heartland, and increasingly in Europe and Japan, the adoption of new, internet-based systems and an infrastructure based on high-speed connections, fibre optics, and wireless networks is creating entire new industries, revitalising old ones, and changing the way businesses and consumers act throughout the economy. Fuelled by rapidly rising investments in the new technologies and companies based on them, this 'new economy' is bringing major increases in productivity, entrepreneurship, and consumer choice. Together these offer the prospect of sustained, non-inflationary growth at a level never previously achieved.

A second force, fuelled by the first, is the rapid move of finance into a single global market operating with a speed, connectedness, and complexity never before seen. The growing volume and share of international financial transactions conducted across international borders, the participation of more developed and emerging economies in this network centred in New York, London, and Tokyo, and the growing use of ever more sophisticated derivatives, hedge funds, and other highly leveraged instruments generate a global financial system increasingly disconnected from the familiar real economies operating within national boundaries. The advent of the single European currency, the Euro, on 1 January 1999 and the increasing use of the U.S. dollar through the Western Hemisphere are visible symbols of the movement toward a single system of fully global reach. The final years of the twentieth century were dominated by a global financial crisis that raised doubts about the desirability, controllability, and inevitability of the emerging system; the return of growth

1

in the crisis-affected economies, however, and stability in the international financial system, together with the construction of a new international financial architecture, allow many to start the new century with confidence that an improved global financial system is in place.

The third force is the intensification, global spread, and individual reach of international trade, the foreign direct investment (FDI), business alliances, and internationally integrated production that lie behind it, and the environmental, social, and cultural concerns now involved in it. The IT revolution allows an expanding array of Web-based business to market to a global audience and allows their equally wired consumers to shop directly and easily from firms around the world. The IT revolution makes order fulfilment easier and faster, even as it reaches back to determine which products are made when and how components are assembled and secured. Such changes reinforce the earlier advantages brought by IT in allowing managers to produce and assemble on a global basis, from an integrated network of locations where components and services can be produced at the lowest cost. With the attendant moves to the internet-based globalisation of services such as advertising, they bring the growing reality of international trade much more directly into the daily lives of people around the world.

None of these individual changes that flourish so prominently had, of course, arisen *ab initio* when the year 2000 began. Rather, it is the intensification and intersection of those changes that are are generating such a groundswell throughout the global economy. Yet, as the new century unfolds, there are profound doubts about where these new forces in the global economy will lead, and about how and by whom they will be controlled. The collapse of share prices in 'new economy' technology stocks on the U.S. and other markets during 2000, the rapidly slowing growth in the once invincible U.S. economy as the year ended, and even the return of soaring energy prices suggest that the benefits brought by the new economy might be less certain than initially thought; indeed, this 'new' economy might also be subject to the great economic cycles that Americans and others endured in decades before the 'Goldilocks' 1990s arrived. The return of financial crises, first in Argentina, then in Turkey, and prospectively in a half dozen other countries, constrain the confidence of those who assumed that the recent construction of an improved international financial architecture had banished crises — and the immense costs they brought — for good. The failure to launch a new round of multilateral trade liberalisation in late 1999 and 2000, the similar failure to create a liberalising multilateral agreement on investment a few years before, and the reductions in trade growth that a slowing U.S. economy brought imply that the new directions in international trade itself might be subject to pauses and even reversal.

The debates that arise from these conflicting trends, the uncertainties surrounding them, and the very pace and extent of these transformations in the global economy bring to the fore the question of governance — how, by whom, and to what end these new forces should and can be controlled. At the heart of the governance question, and the international communities' concern as the twenty-first century opens, lie four priority concerns.

The first and most basic is about power. Can and should the emerging global economy be controlled by governments, acting individually or collectively? Alternatively, does the revolutionary nature of IT and the new economy, as it transforms finance, trade, and other domains, mean that powerful multinationals, anonymous markets, or technologically empowered individuals as consumers are destined or should be encouraged to prevail? Under the former scenario, the international community is ripe for a new generation of building international institutions. This could involve the creation of a comprehensive centre of governance for the only fragmentarily regulated domain of the new IT and economy, the strengthening of the central finance and trade institutions — the International Monetary Fund (IMF) and World Trade Organization (WTO) — to deal with the new forces, the establishment of similarly powerful institutions to govern the global ecology and protect social values, and to ensure the mutually reinforcing integration of these economic, ecological, and social domains. Under the latter scenario, governments and their international institutions should be redesigned to deliver the reliable transparent information that markets require, should retreat from resource provision and regulation, should entrench property rights and private actors' prerogatives, and should help countries adapt to a reliance on private sector capital flows.

The second concern, closely related to the first, is about principles. Will the neoliberal consensus that flourished in the 1990s, with its emphasis on the liberalisation of finance and trade, the privileging of the private sector, and the strengthening of property rights, continue to prevail in an economy that is fully global in ways that will permit the full advantages of the IT revolution to be secured? Will neoliberalism be revised, rather than reinforced and reaffirmed, in ways that return to a central place the values of distributive justice and social protection of the embedded liberalism at the core of the grand bargain that brought about the order constructed in 1945 (Ruggie 1998; Ikenberry 1998)? Will any revisions add new elements that were absent from the 1945 edifice but central to the twenty-first century world, notably ecological enhancement, cultural and linguistic diversity, and citizens' direct rights in international regimes (Kirton, Daniels, and Freytag 2001)? Will the effort represent a reformist revision of the old or its replacement by a new order in which these principles have pride of place?

The third concern is about participation and procedure. Which countries and national communities will be granted consequential places in the new system of global economic governance and how will its institutions be designed to secure the effectiveness and legitimacy now lacking in the edifice largely constructed in 1945? Will the United States, which some see as being as predominant in the new economy of 2000 as it had been in that old economy of 1945, play a pre-eminent a role in managing the new system and providing the model that the rest of the world will adopt? Will its closest Anglo-American associates have a consequential, catalytic role in offering leadership when the U.S. is unable or unwilling to lead? Will the other major market democracies of continental Europe and Japan, with their distinctive histories and internal structures, have an equal place? Will rapidly if unevenly growing transition and emerging economies be brought to the centre of the new system? And will the traditional tension between globalism and regionalism be resolved, in both the old and new institutions, in ways that offer improved representativeness, effectiveness, and legitimacy in both the procedures employed and the underlying principles they affirm?

The fourth and final concern is about people, both as objects and subjects in the new order. In their role as recipients of the impacts of the globalising forces of the new economy, finance, and trade, there is a basic question about who will be privileged by these new forces and their governance, and how those left out can be changed from victims to victors in the new order. In their role as citizens of the new global order, there is an equally important question of how they can be given effective rights — of information, accountability, and transparency — in the international institutions that are constructing and managing the new order. Whether the 1945 edifice constructed on the Westphalian model with its monopoly for sovereign states will yield, whether people will become direct participants through the nongovernmental organisations (NGOs) that claim most loudly to represent civil society, or whether a new way can be found remain open but highly contested questions.

At the centre of coping with these new forces in the global economy and addressing the concerns of the global community for their governance lie the world's major international economic institutions — the IMF, the WTO, and, above all, the G7 major industrial democracies. Even as these institutions look outward to the challenges of the new world, each is in the midst of important internal change. The IMF is moving toward completing a process, launched amidst the global financial crisis of 1997–99, to reconstruct itself to serve as the centre of a new international financial architecture to govern global finance (Kaiser, Kirton, and Daniels 2000). The WTO is moving to begin its built-in agenda of negotiations on agriculture and the expanding sphere of services, experimenting with ways to incorporate environmental and labour concerns and constituencies, and searching for formulae to launch and conduct a comprehensive new round of liberalisation, involving a much broader array of values and communities. The G7 itself, having just celebrated its 25th anniversary in 1999, is defining its relationship with its new partner, Russia, devising ways to incorporate rising powers such as China, and pioneering new fora, such as the G20 and the Financial Stability Forum (FSF), both established in 1999, to meet the needs for broader participation in the new generation of global economic governance.

Each of these institutions and their leading country members confront the challenge of constructing their interests and identities to meet the uncertainties and complexities of the new age. With the European-centred cold war long gone, with the market democratic model firmly entrenched throughout many regions of the world, and with globalisation the central reality rather than an invigorating novelty, it is clear that a new era has begun and that a new order is rapidly taking shape. As the crisis years of 1997–99 recede, however, the outstanding questions remain of just what powers, principles, participants, and procedures it will have at its core and which people will benefit most from its operation.

The Approach

This book explores these questions through a detailed examination of how the world's central international institutions and powers are confronting them during the opening years of the twenty-first century. It embraces the major issues at the centre of debates among specialists in the analytic and policy communities about how the new information economy, the globalised world of finance, and the deepening world of international trade, investment, and production should be managed and governed. Yet it focusses on the distinctive question of how the significant changes at work in these three central domains of the global economy come together to define an emerging new order, both in the real world of the market economy and in the political and social world that seeks to govern it.

This volume makes three contributions to the ongoing debate among students of international economics and international political economy about these issues. First, it takes as its starting point the changing international economic order as a whole and the efforts by a wide range of actors to determine its content and impact. It thus gives central attention to the traditional international political economy pillar of finance, both in its global dimensions and in the critical Asian region. It also takes an extensive and in-depth look at the international trade system in the wake of the failed attempt at Seattle in December 1999 to launch a new 'Millennium Round' of multilateral trade negotiations. Above all, it begins with a close examination of the new digital economy that is transforming national societies and the international system alike.

Second, this volume focusses on new directions in the global economy and its governance by directly addressing the major transformational forces currently at work. The first of these is the digital revolution, which is profoundly affecting the real economy and raising questions about how the international community can best govern the many dimensions of this new and unprecedented force. Here the challenges extend from hardware and channels to software and content, including the core question of whether the previous embedded liberalism and successor neoliberal ideology are giving way to a new consensus, and what its future might be. And, most generally, the concern with new directions centres on the ultimate issue of whether the present process of proliferating globalisation can be effectively governed and, if so, by whom, how, and to what end.

Third, this book takes up the question of international order and the broad array of international institutions that are competing and co-operating to shape it in ways that respond to the needs of the international community in the twenty-first century. Here it examines the adjustments taking place in long-established institutions such as the IMF and the challenges facing the much newer WTO. It also explores emerging institutions, both on a regional scale as seen in Asia, and those representing a new approach to institutionalised global governance, as seen in the new Dot-Force launched by the G8 at its summit in Okinawa. It probes how institutions old and new are moving to establish order in such essentially ungoverned areas as the global digital economy and society. And it analyses how the G7 and G8 themselves are working with newer bodies such as the G20 and International Monetary and Financial Committee (IMFC) to govern the global economy in this new age. Thus the full global economy, the new directions transforming that economy, and the efforts to create a new order on the part of new and reforming international institutions are the three integrated pillars on which this book is built.

In taking up this broad *problèmatique*, this volume has four specific purposes. The first is to provide a detailed description of the significant underlying but often otherwise obscure changes taking place in the global economy and inside the core institutions of global economic governance during 2000 and early 2001. The second is to assess, on this foundation, the actual degree, depth, direction, and impact of these changes, both in the important domain of discourse and in the real world of observable behaviour. The third is to identify, amidst the broad phenomenon of 'globalisation', the underlying drivers that propel these changes in the global economy and its management by governments and citizens. The fourth is to offer recommendations, to those governments, to civil society actors, and to the constituents of each, about desirable policies they might pursue to push the global economy and global economic governance toward more desirable ends. In each case, the aim is not to provide definite answers at still early stages of processes that are often without precedent; rather, it is to offer confident descriptions of the primary patterns that are currently emerging as dominant at a point when they are still open to change through policy action.

To accomplish these tasks, this work examines in turn the major changes taking place within the three primary domains of the global economy: the new information economy, finance, and trade. In each case, the emphasis is on the pace, path, process, and products of change in the real economy and in the efforts of political leaders through established and emerging international institutions to manage these changes in a rapidly globalising age. Thus, this exploration begins with the central but still ill-understood process of the IT revolution. It examines how managers of global firms create a new economy based on it, how the U.S. government is pioneering a new international regime to govern it, and how the G7 is seeking to shape that regime through processes and principles very different than those that flourished before. It includes a searching scrutiny of the principle of transparency thought to be so central to the new economy and the regime it demands. Here some new directions are apparent. Yet given the revolutionary nature of the new IT and the lack of a single international institution or regime that can claim a central role in the governance of this sphere, the emphasis is on the challenges that exist and await, rather than the effectiveness of any established edifice now in place.

This book then proceeds to examine international finance. Here it begins by calling into question whether the new principles pioneered by the IMF and the G7 in the immediate wake of the 1997–99 global financial crisis are genuinely new in terms of content, in the light of past efforts at revision and in their practical effect. It highlights how the emerging new international financial architecture, with familiar Anglo-American principles and practices at its core, remains contested by those, led by Japan and its Asian neighbours, that prefer a different approach. It further shows how newer international institutions, notably the G20 and IMFC, have succeeded in giving these voices, and those of emerging markets and the global community beyond, a consequential place in shaping and managing the new global economic order.

This volume then addresses the domain of international trade. Here it focusses in particular on how plurilateral institutions and groups, led by the G7 but including the Organisation for Economic Co-operation and Development (OECD) and other bodies that cross the old north-south divide, can lead the process of liberalisation in the new age. It details the past success of the G7 in this domain, and the disappointments that have come in recent years. It explores how the effective functioning of the broadly multilateral General Agreement on Tariffs and Trade (GATT) and WTO depends on the leadership brought by plurilateral bodies such as the G7. And it looks ahead to how the G7 can shape the process of trade liberalisation and the WTO in the twenty-first century, in part by bringing in civil society actors from the outside.

The volume explores these subjects from a wide variety of vantage points. It contains contributions from authors based in all of the G8's constituent regions of North America, Europe, and Japan, and from half of its member countries. The contributors come from the disciplines of economics, the international political economy field of political science, and management studies, and from leading universities in the United States, Britain, Canada, and Japan. Many of the authors have had experience within, or through service in an advisory capacity to, some of the core governmental and intergovernmental institutions at work in the international economy. The collection combines the insights of established veteran scholars of the international economy and the G7 with a new generation of largely younger scholars, writing on their specific topics within the context of globalisation, global governance, and the G7 for the first time.

Given the rich diversity of views contained within these chapters, no *a priori* effort has been made to force all to follow a single theoretical tradition, interpretative framework, methodological approach, or concluding consensus. Rather, the common foundation has been that each contributor pursue a close empirical analysis of recent events and do so within the context of historical understanding, the major concepts in the fields of international economics and international political economy, and a concern with their relevance to current policy debates and citizens' concerns. Although many chapters draw on the theories of the established liberal-institutionalist tradition in international political economy, the contributions of realists, critical approaches, and constructivist insights have a legitimate and substantial place (Keohane 1989; Cox 1996; Wendt 1999). The result is a rich menu that includes those that see both much and little change, that applaud and critique the unfolding directions, and that pursue both a reformist problem-solving and more radical critical orientation. In this diversity they reflect the debate, the uncertainty, and the intellectual passion at work in the real world.

The Analyses

This volume begins in Part I with the 'New Challenges in Global "New Economy" Governance'. In Chapter 2, on 'Managing Globalisation and the New Economy: The Contribution of the G8 Summit', Nicholas Bayne sets the broad foundation for the book by examining the process of globalisation and the effort of the G8 to manage it from 1994, when it first singled out the phenomenon in its Naples Summit communiqué, to the present, when the subject has come to dominate its agenda. Bayne analyses the response to globalisation by the G7 and G8, focussing on the new message from the Okinawa Summit in July 2000. To do so, he examines the record of the G7 and G8 at their annual summits in Birmingham 1998, Cologne 1999, and Okinawa, under the four categories of domestic penetration, the international financial system, international development, and helping the good spirits of IT, trade, and the environment.

Bayne concludes that Okinawa continued the response to globalisation begun at Birmingham, but shifted priorities to reflect the emergence of the new information economy. With G7 economies buoyant, earlier domestic anxieties about jobs and crime in retreat, and calm returned to the financial system, the G7 turned its attention to the plight of the poorest countries. But it was frustrated over debt relief and made little progress on trade and aid, despite a promising advance in improving health. The G7 and G8 at Okinawa were most innovative in their treatment of IT and the new economy, which they identified as the key to many of the benefits of globalisation. They failed, however, to advance the advantages available from the trading system or to resolve differences over the environment. Thus, even as they turned their attention in 2000 to the positive aspects of globalisation, the G8 leaders made only selective, promising beginnings, rather than the decisive, broad-based breakthroughs that would set convincing new directions for the years ahead.

In Chapter 3, entitled 'The New Global Electronic Economy: Consensus, Confusion, Contradictions', Thomas C. Lawton deals with the corporate foundations of, and governmental response to, this 'new economy'. He begins by noting that over the past decade, the number of global citizens accessing the internet has grown from 3 million to more than 300 million and that approximately one quarter make purchases online from electronic commerce sites. The resulting transformation of the old economy, the rise of the new economy, and the broader economic, social and technological ramifications of these changes generate significant debate about the role of government in the new global electronic 'marketspace'. The first part of this chapter examines the driving forces facilitating the transformation of contemporary organisational structure in the global electronic economy. It charts the transformation of the corporate value chain from vertical to virtual and how this transition makes knowledge and business relationships increasingly important strategy variables. The second part of the chapter discusses governance in the era of the global electronic economy and the consensus, confusion, and contradictions surrounding regulation and control of the internet and e-commerce. It assesses the various policy initiatives that have emerged and efforts made by the G8 and other international actors to shape the emerging international regulatory regime.

Lawton concludes that the evolution of the organisational and industry value chain, facilitated by enterprise resource planning (ERP) and the internet, results in dramatic time and cost efficiencies and in increased customer satisfaction levels. The resulting virtual value chain is a highly flexible and extremely competitive structure that privileges both knowledge and relationships and demands a more open, less secretive process for creating a common corporate strategy embracing all members of the value chain. Yet the revolutionary productivity-enhancing impact of this new electronic business system on the global economy will only emerge if the international regime governing e-commerce develops in supportive ways. Although considerable international consensus has already emerged over the creation of rules and a dispute-settlement procedure for the electronic economy, large differences remain, particularly between the U.S. and the European Union (EU), over the extent to which government should be involved in governance of the electronic economy. However, amidst these disagreements and emerging doubts that an all-embracing global regulatory framework is desirable or even possible, influential international actors in the WTO, the OECD, and the G8 are joining with business to create a regulatory agenda centred on key issues such as authentication, consumer protection, privacy, encryption, and even taxation. The unresolved question remains: Who or what will emerge as the chief regulatory authority for the global marketspace?

In Chapter 4, 'Creating Rules for the Global Information Economy: The United States and G8 Leadership', Michele Mastroeni looks in detail at the origins and success of the U.S. approach to fashion this new regime. He begins with the most notable and dominant initiative regarding regulation — the U.S.-proposed three-year moratorium on new taxation of electronic commerce that is being upheld by developed countries at present. He questions the motives for embracing this policy and considers the broader political, social, and economic issues. He then broadens the analysis to look beyond economic gains to consider the other issues that will arise in the near future.

Mastroeni challenges the easy judgement that the moratorium is a positive first step in ensuring the open nature of an emerging and important market and affirming the principle of open trade. He suggests that maintaining a moratorium on new taxes without an in-depth analysis would be a mistake, as it would lead to a loss of new sources of revenue for states, damage to other sectors of the economy through lack of regulation and 'tax bias', a potential deterioration of state sovereignty, and a resulting breakdown in co-operation among states. Rather than a moratorium on new taxes and tariffs on the new economy as the centrepiece of the emerging international e-commerce regime, he calls for harnessing the current high level of international co-operation to insure a proper infrastructure and regulatory framework. Such a framework would guarantee fruitful interaction between the new economy and older sectors or markets, as well as maintain the political and social structures necessary to ensure justice and maintain order.

In Chapter 5, 'Transparent End-Use Technology and the Changing Nature of Security Threats', George M. von Furstenberg critically examines the meaning and implications of transparency, the concept at the core of the new internet-based economy, and the new international financial architecture alike. He notes that changing transparency relations — who or what is exposed to penetrating scrutiny to whom for whose purpose — can have revolutionary societal implications. These are ignored by those official bodies that keep calling for more transparency in many areas. Transparency relations can be changed not only by political influence and through shifting rules and conventions but also through technological developments. He thus examines in turn the logic of transparency, the political purposes behind calls for greater transparency, the distributional consequences of greater transparency, and the revolutionary impact of the new internet-based transparency technologies in the economic and security domains.

Von Furstenberg asserts that a momentous leap is now occurring and bringing entirely new invasive and interactive capabilities to people outside established hierarchies. Because this empowerment is indiscriminate, it increases the risks to the information and communications technology (ICT) systems on which the world increasingly relies. Technologically driven changes in transparency have thus become a major security issue. Technological transparency has a dark side that is ignored in upbeat assessments, such as that issued by the G8 at Okinawa, that credit ICT with many of the same beneficial effects as political, social, and legal transparency. While a public good in some respects, in many others transparency is divisive, as with power and monitoring: the more transparency the powerful are able to compel from others, the less they need to provide themselves. Hence transparency must be finely balanced, not maximised wherever possible, for the common good.

Part II, 'New Directions in Global Financial Governance', examines the impact of the IT revolution and other unfolding forces of international finance more directly. In Chapter 6, 'Continuity and Change in the Global Monetary Order', Sébastien Dallaire challenges a common view that over the last decade, particularly in the wake of the 1997–99 global financial crisis, there was a marked shift in the international community's vision of development, with the earlier 'Washington Consensus' replaced by a more socially oriented approach integrating economic, political, and social needs. He examines the discourse and policies over the past 20 years of the G7 and the IMF, the two most influent actors in the international development debate. He notes that the discussions held at the G7 summits shape the international discourse on development and are reflected in the language and policies of the IMF, where G7 countries dominate the decision-making process.

Dallaire concludes that while a change in the international development discourse has taken place, the core of the previous 'consensus' remains essentially intact. Actors in international economic fora such as the IMF and the G7 summits may increasingly discuss social issues and political problems involved in development, but their economic beliefs remain unchanged. They continue to see liberalisation as the key to sustainable growth, and internal adjustments to international pressures as the only way out of poverty. They assume that the external environment is fundamentally 'good' and that countries must learn to turn it to their advantage. At the same time, the increased insistence on the importance of social issues within the discourse and policies of the G7 at Cologne 1999 and onward and of the IMF in response imply that modification of their respective vision of international development is possible. Yet much remains to be done to achieve a genuine and necessary transformation in the development discourse of the G8 and the IMF. A start can be made by reconstructing globalisation and by having the wealthy industrial democracies pursue more effective policies and put more money behind their promises.

In Chapter 7, 'Japan's Approach to Shaping a New International Financial Architecture', Saori N. Katada explores how Japan has approached the task of modernising the mechanisms of global financial governance to meet the needs of the new age. She examines how the G7 summits have been important for the Japanese government in this task and how Japan's position changed from the initial debate at the 1994 Naples Summit through those summits — at Birmingham, Cologne, and Okinawa — taking place after the Asian crisis had begun. She then assesses how Japanese leaders used the G7 as a forum for agenda setting and Japan's alleged role as a 'bridge' between Asia and the Western democracies.

Katada concludes that G7 summits have been a place for high-profile diplomacy, where Japanese leaders have sought to go beyond the constraints of the U.S. Japanese bilateral relationship in which Japan's agenda-setting ability and influence are limited. The Japanese government hoped to use the G7 economic forum in the aftermath of the Asian financial crisis to reshape an international financial structure seen by Japan as threatening the viability of relatively healthy economies in South-East and East Asia. The Japanese government needed a plurilateral forum such as the G7 to circumvent the U.S., with its insistence on an IMF-led solution to the crisis that limited Japan's ability to resort to regional responses. Japan saw the cause of the crisis lying in the flaws associated with the prevailing international financial structure, especially the adverse effects of highly leveraged institutions (HLIs) such as hedge funds. The Japanese government looked to the G7 summit (and elsewhere) to assert the need for certain regulations in the global financial market (especially of the HLIs) and for IMF reform. With European attitudes changing after the 1998 Russian crisis, by the time of Cologne in 1999 there was a solid consensus on the need to regulate some activities in international financial markets. Japan thus accomplished more than it could have hoped for on a bilateral basis with the United States. In so doing it operated effectively as a representative of broader Asian positions and as a bridge between Asia and the West.

In Chapter 8, 'Japan, the Asian Economy, the International Financial System, and the G8: A Critical Perspective', Kunihiko Ito continues this exploration of the Japanese and Asian approach to international financial system reform. He considers in turn the calls for greater Asian regional co-operation in the finance field, the flaws in the G7's response to international crisis and system reconstruction from 1996 onward, the Asian approach to these issues, and the progress made in Asian regional co-operation. He ends with a close examination of Japan's role during its hosting of the G7 in 2000.

Ito looks sympathetically on the calls for progress toward Asian regional co-operation in international finance, but envisages a community open to the entire Asian community, including Australia and New Zealand. He recommends the establishment of an Asian Monetary Fund (AMF) in the short run and the formation of an Asian currency bloc in the long run, as the institutional anchors of the Asian approach in the twenty-first century. He does so even while acknowledging that the past reform programs led by the annual G7 and G8 have generally been positive. Yet he argues that the pace has been too slow, and that the results are compromised as a consequence of large differences among members in interests, philosophy, thought, society, and culture. It will take a very long time for the G7/8 members to agree upon the grand design of the international financial system and to undertake a drastic reform of that system. It is thus necessary to build regional co-operative systems as a supplement to the G7/8 and IMF processes for stabilising the international financial system to cope with crises that could erupt at any time.

In Chapter 9, 'Guiding Global Economic Governance: The G20, the G7, and the International Monetary Fund at Century's Dawn', John J. Kirton asks 'in the rapidly globalising world of the twenty-first century, where will the centre of global economic governance effectively lie?' He addresses this question by focussing on the new institution of the G20, created by the G7 in 1999 as a forum for G7 countries to join with the major emerging market economies to shape a new international financial architecture and confront the larger challenges of globalisation. He assesses the G20's role and relevance in relationship to another new international institution created in 1999 to help govern global finance, the IMFC, and their parent institutions, the G7 and IMF respectively. He offers a detailed empirical account in turn of the G7, IMFC, and G20 during 2000. In each case, he focusses on the coalition diplomacy within the institution, its accomplishments, the role it secured in international financial and economic governance, the relationship it forged with its institutional colleagues and competitors, and the causes of the different paths each pursued.

This analysis reveals that the G20 at its Montreal meeting in 2000 proved to be an effective and legitimate institution that delivered significant achievements. These achievements lay primarily in the new principles and directions it set, but also in some of the specific decisions it reached and in the institutional processes it put in place. These considerable achievements compare favourably with those of its old and new institutional competitors. They flow from the advantages the G20 has in its particularly powerful and representative membership, flexible mandate and procedure, and skilful chairmanship. Together these factors enabled the G20 to put at the forefront of its work the broad, integrative agenda of globalisation that preoccupies citizens of the global community, and to set genuinely new directions in how the process of globalisation should be governed in the world of the twenty-first century. More generally, the operation of the G20, in comparison with that of the IMFC, G7, and IMF, demonstrates that international institutions matter, in ways well embraced within the liberal-institutionalist and realist traditions. These institutions do so even in a rapidly changing world where rampant globalisation is leading countries and international institutions alike to reconstruct or reaffirm their interests and identities.

Part III, 'New Directions in Global Trade Governance', broadens the focus to examine the second traditional domain of the global economy — international trade — where the process of globalisation is bringing similarly large transformations. In Chapter 10, 'The G7 and Multilateral Trade Liberalisation: Past Performance, Future Challenges', Nicholas Bayne reviews the contributions made by the G7 and G8 summits thus far to strengthening the international trading system. He examines in turn the summit record on trade matters through four stages: the Tokyo Round of 1975–78, between the rounds from 1979 to 1986, the Uruguay Round from 1987 to 1993, and from Marrakech to Seattle from 1994 to 2000. For each stage, he judges the summit's performance against the criteria of leadership, effectiveness, durability, acceptability, and consistency.

Bayne concludes that the summits have displayed decisive leadership when they committed themselves to complete international trade negotiations and took steps to make good those commitments. They were effective when they clearly resisted domestic pressures for protectionism, but their reputation suffered when their actual policies did not match their summit undertakings. To have durable effect, the G7 had to agree among themselves and ensure their commitments were followed through. The results finally achieved in both the Tokyo and Uruguay rounds proved acceptable to the international community, but subsequent dissatisfaction among developing countries has raised the standard of acceptability that the summits must now meet. Inconsistent macroeconomic or sectoral policies have on occasion undermined trade commitments, while weak trade performance has frustrated other summit efforts in areas such as development. In the light of this record, recent summits, including Okinawa in 2000, have not performed well on trade and have contributed to the failure to launch a new trade round in the WTO. The summits must thus repair nearly eight years' neglect of trade by exerting themselves to regain the initiative. This will require a series of actions: clear G7 agreement on the agenda for a new round, with greater openness to proposals from developing countries; mobilisation of the Quadrilateral of Trade Ministers meeting, or Quad, under summit direction; resistance to domestic pressures for protection and an end to distracting transatlantic disputes; convincing deadlines to ensure that the round, once started, is concluded; implementation in full of commitments made to improve trade access and 'capacity building' for poor countries; encouraging the Quad to develop more inclusive consultations; and consistent policies elsewhere, both in economic management and in development.

In Chapter 11, 'Securing Multilateral Trade Liberalisation: International Institutions in Conflict and Convergence', Theodore H. Cohn examines the important role played in multilateral trade relations by the OECD, the G7, and the Quad, and the relationship of these institutions to the GATT/WTO. Covering the period from the GATT Tokyo Round negotiations in the 1970s to the establishment of the WTO in 1995, the chapter begins by discussing one of the three factors explaining institutional involvement in global trade policy: the constrained nature of the GATT/WTO as an international organisation. It then proceeds to trace the role of the G7, the Quad, and the OECD in the context of northern dominance and U.S. relative decline, from the Tokyo Round through the 1979–86 interregnum to the Uruguay Round of 1986–94. It concludes by looking ahead to the formidable protests these three bodies will face from less developed countries (LDCs) and civil society and the responses they should make to these new demands.

Cohn argues that the G7, the Quad, and the OECD played an important role in multilateral trade liberalisation during this period as a result of three factors: the dominance of the North over the South, the relative decline of U.S. trade hegemony, and the constrained nature of the GATT/WTO as an international organisation. In contrast, institutions such as the G77 and the United Nations Conference on Trade and Development (UNCTAD), which identify with the interests of LDCs, have been far less important. The LDCs gained some influence in the 1980s and 1990s, because they were more involved in the Uruguay Round than in previous GATT rounds. Nevertheless, developed country (DC) institutions such as the G7, the Quad, and the OECD continue to have predominant influence in the WTO and global trade regime. In the years ahead, however, they need to share power with disaffected and disadvantaged groups.

In Chapter 12, 'Stimulating Trade Liberalisation after Seattle: G7/8 Leadership in Global Governance', Heidi K. Ullrich explores the role of the G8 in stimulating trade liberalisation in the post-Seattle environment. She begins with a brief background of G7/8 activities in the multilateral trading system, with particular emphasis on multilateral trade negotiations and the evolution of the Quad involving the trade ministers from the U.S., the EU, Japan, and Canada. She then describes the events leading up to the Seattle ministerial, the sources of stalemate in Seattle, and what the WTO has done in the aftermath. She next addresses the newly active civil society participants and the potential for G8 involvement. She concludes with recommendations on how the G8 can stimulate the post-Seattle multilateral trading system and the challenges of the 2001 Genoa Summit and its successors.

Ullrich contends that the G7/8 has to date provided adequate leadership in the area of multilateral trade through supporting the institutions and activities that encourage liberalisation. There is now a pressing need for the G8 to serve as a firm advocate of the benefits deriving from an open trading system. The G8 must take the political risk to speak with a strong and united voice in supporting the next round of multilateral trade negotiations if its leadership is to be effective rather than merely adequate. In order to stimulate further trade liberalisation in the post-Seattle, WTO-led multilateral trading system, the G8 must increase its credibility and courage in communicating with its members' citizens. It should enter into a structured dialogue with NGOs and business, nonprofit and for-profit groups. Such dialogue must be carried out in a transparent manner allowing for an open and mutually beneficial exchange of information and opinions.

The Answers

As outlined in detail in the concluding chapter of this volume, these analyses reveal that there are indeed important new directions underway in the global economy and in the efforts of governments and their citizens to govern it. These new directions focus on the revolutionary potential of information technology to create a new economy, a new society, and new security threats, on the rapid emergence of an integrated global financial system with inherent instabilities and complex risks, and on the new dominance in the global economy of trade, the international investment and production that underlie it, and the environmental, social, and cultural demands now integrally involved. Although many in civil society and governments around the world protest and ponder the pace, path, and impact of these forces, they are unfolding with the power and the potential to provide major net benefits. This strongly suggests they are here to stay.

Far less advanced, however, and far more controversial, are the emerging and desirable directions in global economic governance that have arisen in response to these defining realities of a rapidly globalising world. While there is a shared sense that these profound forces of economic globalisation can be governed by the conscious, co-operative international actions of national governments and their citizens, there remain much disappointment and disagreement about how this is being done. Although the world's major multilateral institutions are responding to these new forces, their adaptations thus far have been partial and problematic. The new information economy still lacks a defined, comprehensive global governance structure and institution to provide the coherent regulatory framework it may need to serve the economic, social, political, and security needs of members of the international community. Despite the important advances of recent years in building a new international financial architecture, global financial governance still centres on an IMF wedded to its core mission of 1945, even with its new IMFC. Its efforts to move beyond a neoliberal consensus remain largely rhetorical, while those of the G20 and G7 to produce a broader and more balanced response to globalisation have just begun. And in the trade system, the WTO, even with the support of plurilateral institutions such as the G7/8, the Quad, and the OECD, has yet to take up the new demands of the world of services and e-commerce, foreign investment, integrated production, and business alliances, and of the pressing demands for environmental and social sensitivity and democratic accountability.

In short, important new directions are underway in both the global economy and the institutions that seek to govern it. But they have not yet congealed into an integrated new order. Many of the responses to this newly globalised economy are in fact tentative beginnings, false starts, or even unwelcome retreats. All the analyses in this volume share an underlying optimism that the economic processes and political efforts now underway are capable of being shaped into an order that is more efficient and equitable for all. The forces of globalisation are neither inevitable nor beyond the point where they are capable of being fundamentally changed. And while many have much to do in propelling this change into more desirable new directions, there is a premium on the leadership that has been and can be offered by the G7, the broader community of the G20, and civil society organisations eager to play their part.

References

Cox, Robert, with T. Sinclair (1996). *Approaches to World Order*. Cambridge University Press, Cambridge.

Ikenberry, John (1998). 'Institutions, Strategic Restraint, and the Persistence of American Postwar Order'. *International Security* vol. 23, Winter, pp. 43–78.

Kaiser, Karl, John J. Kirton, and Joseph P. Daniels, eds. (2000). *Shaping a New International Financial System: Challenges of Governance in a Globalizing World*. Ashgate, Aldershot.

Keohane, Robert (1989). *International Institutions and State Power: Essays in International Relations Theory*. Westview Press, Boulder, CO.

Kirton, John J., Joseph P. Daniels, and Andreas Freytag, eds. (2001). *Guiding Global Order: G8 Governance in the Twenty-First Century*. Ashgate, Aldershot.

Ruggie, John (1998). *Constructing the World Polity: Essays on International Institutionalisation*. London, Routledge.

Wendt, Alexander (1999). *A Social Theory of International Politics*. Cambridge University Press, Cambridge.

Part I
New Challenges in Global 'New Economy' Governance

2 Managing Globalisation and the New Economy: The Contribution of the G8 Summit

NICHOLAS BAYNE

The Okinawa G7/8 Summit, held on 21–23 July 2000, was the 26th such summit in an unbroken sequence going back to 1975. The first summit had only six members — the United States, Japan, Germany, France, the United Kingdom, and Italy. Canada and the European Union (EU) were soon added, forming the G7. Russia made it up to G8 at the Birmingham Summit of 1998.

The summits were created for three purposes, which remain just as valid today as they were at the beginning:

- To provide collective management of the world economy, with Europe, Japan, and Canada sharing responsibility with the United States;
- To reconcile the tensions of what began as interdependence but is now recognised as globalisation. These tensions arise because external factors increasingly interact with domestic economic policy;
- To generate political leadership, where heads of state and government take co-operation further than their officials and ministers can.

This chapter examines progress against the second of these objectives.[1] For almost two decades after the foundation of the G7 in 1975, globalisation was not in the summit vocabulary. Instead, the key concept was interdependence. When the G7 leaders held their third meeting in Japan, at Tokyo in 1993, they did not recognise the advance of globalisation; the first reference to it was in their communiqué from Naples in 1994. Despite this slow start, however, the recognition of globalisation and the response to it came to dominate the summits of the 1990s. It was still top of the agenda at Okinawa 2000, at the start of a new decade.

This chapter analyses this response to globalisation by the G7 and G8, focussing on the new message from the Okinawa Summit. The main findings are as follows:

- Okinawa continued the response to globalisation begun at Birmingham in 1998, but with a shift in priorities to reflect the emergence of the new economy.
- With the G7 economies so buoyant, domestic anxieties about jobs and crime were in abeyance, while calm had returned to the financial system.
- The problems of the poorest countries caused the greatest concern. But Okinawa was frustrated by debt relief and made little progress on trade and aid. The most promising advance was in improving health.
- Okinawa was most innovative in its treatment of information technology (IT) and the new economy, which it identified as the key to many of the benefits of globalisation. But it failed to advance the benefits available from the trading system or to resolve differences over the environment.

Okinawa marked a further evolution in the G8's treatment of globalisation. After giving priority to the international consequences and to domestic anxieties, in 2000 the G8 leaders turned their attention to the beneficial aspects of globalisation.

Globalisation at the Summits of the 1990s

The summits of the mid 1990s, starting with Naples 1994, thought that globalisation held no fears for the G7 member countries themselves. After all, they had been dealing with the tensions of interdependence since 1975 and even earlier; they thought that globalisation was all gain for them. However, they doubted whether the international economic system could stand the strains generated by globalisation; for four years, up to the Denver Summit in 1997, they concentrated on the reform of multilateral institutions. This had intrinsic value, since it involved the G7 leaders more closely in the institutions, replacing their earlier aloof attitude. This was a necessary response, and work on the international system continues today. But it was not a sufficient response.

As those years passed, the G7 leaders came to realise that globalisation placed new demands on them at home, as well as internationally. To harvest the benefits of globalisation, they needed dynamic and competitive market economies — but that was not enough. They also needed to intervene to set and implement the rules for those markets and to help the weak that fell behind and were marginalised by globalisation. Above all, they had to counter public fears about globalisation, as their populations worried about becoming vulnerable to external forces beyond their control.

So Birmingham 1998 marked a turning point in the summit's treatment of globalisation, and not only because it was the first G8 summit with the Russians as full members, and the first where the heads of government met on their own, without supporting ministers. For Birmingham, the leaders chose an agenda focussed on four themes. These might be called the four evil spirits of globalisation, as they are the issues that generate the strongest public concern about globalisation. They are loss of jobs, crime and internal disorder, financial panic, and world poverty. None of these is a new subject for the G8; many of them go back to the dawn of summitry. But globalisation requires the summits to tackle them in a new way.[2]

Cologne in 1999 and Okinawa in 2000 expanded the definition of these themes, but the four evil spirits still form the foundation of the G8 agenda. The G8 response to globalisation so far, as reflected in the record of Birmingham and Cologne and augmented by Okinawa can be analysed under four broad headings:

- Domestic Penetration;
- The International Financial System;
- International Development;
- Helping the Good Spirits — IT, Trade, and the Environment.

This chapter examines each in turn, concentrating on the contribution from Okinawa.

Domestic Penetration

The first pair of topics — jobs and crime — draws the G8 deeper and deeper into domestic policy issues. This is as expected — globalisation requires more international action on issues formerly considered domestic. The discussion of employability at Birmingham expanded to cover education and social protection at Cologne. It was further expanded in the preparations for Okinawa to encompass policies for older citizens. In these discussions, the leaders learn from each other and develop standards of good practice. The treatment of crime has also spread to cover conflict prevention. This topic involves strengthening justice, human rights, and public order within countries. But it also means fighting international criminal movements. Regrettably, globalisation and new technology facilitate these, just as they encourage more honest activities.

These topics are well chosen, because they merit persistent attention from heads of state and government. But they have two pitfalls. First, even with the attentions of the heads, progress toward their objectives of higher employment levels for all and lower crime rates is bound to be slow. There is a danger of creating expectations of quick results, which will later be disappointed. Second, when G7 economies are buoyant and prosperous, the political salience of these issues declines and momentum is lost.

This could be observed at Okinawa, where the exchanges among the heads on these topics were lively but fairly inconclusive. Ageing, featured earlier by the Japanese hosts in the preparations, was barely touched. The discussion on crime and drug smuggling concentrated on various international events, such as the United Nations Convention on Organised Crime and another conference on high-tech crime, to be held later in the year.[3] The heads endorsed the substantial work done on conflict prevention by the G8 foreign ministers meeting in Miyazaki a week before. There was also interest, among the G7 heads, in the laundering of the proceeds of crime, a subject considered under the next heading.

The International Financial System

The second pair of themes — financial panic and world poverty — focusses more on the international system. The summits' work on the international response to globalisation, begun in 1994, is far from complete. Some measures agreed on earlier have proved insufficient or the problems they addressed have returned in a different form. On these issues, the summits conduct an iterative dialogue with international institutions. This iteration is necessary because the summits do not always find the best solution in their first attempt. After all, only the most intractable problems come up to the heads of state and government — easy ones are resolved at lower levels.

This applies very clearly to the international financial architecture. The reforms to the financial system, agreed at Halifax in 1995 in response to the Mexican crisis, did not suffice to prevent the more serious speculative crises of 1997–98, in Asia, Russia, and Brazil.[4] For nearly three years, after the outbreak of the Asian crisis in 1997, the G7 gave high priority to creating a new international financial architecture. The summits at Birmingham in 1998 and again at Cologne in 1999 devoted much attention to devising the necessary reforms. By the time of Okinawa, most of these were in place at the International Monetary Fund (IMF) and the World Bank, and calm had returned to the world financial system. But the new systems had yet to be tested under stress and no one knew if they would be robust enough to deter or to withstand future crises.

The exact division of roles between the IMF and the World Bank also remained in debate. The work rather lost momentum once the crisis atmosphere receded, especially as large parts of the world economy — notably the U.S. — remained dynamic and even those areas hit hardest were recovering strongly.[5]

The G7 leaders addressed these issues when they met, without Russia, for two hours on the first afternoon at Okinawa. Their discussion covered the following:

- The world economy: The exchange on world economic prospects revealed everyone as very confident, apart from some worries over oil prices.
- Financial architecture: The leaders endorsed a report agreed by their finance ministers in Fukuoka ten days earlier, adding nothing of their own. This document was essentially a progress report on action to implement the measures agreed at Cologne, especially in the reform of the IMF and the multilateral development banks. There was little new, except for a positive reference to regional arrangements, in recognition of recent Japanese moves.
- Money laundering and related issues: The leaders again endorsed a report prepared by their finance ministers, adding nothing substantial. This report, called 'Actions Against Abuse of the Global Financial System', contained more original elements, as it picked up and brought together the work done by the Financial Action Task Force (FATF) on money laundering, by the Organisation for Economic Co-operation and Development (OECD) on harmful tax competition and by the Financial Stability Forum (FSF) on offshore financial centres. In each area, delinquent countries had been identified and named. The G7 offered to help them mend their ways, identifying eight areas of improvement, but hinted at sanctions if they did not reform.

Although serious work was done on the latter two issues by the finance ministers, none of these issues was central to the exchanges at the Okinawa Summit itself.

International Development

The low-profile treatment at Okinawa both of the domestic concerns provoked by globalisation, such as jobs and crime, and of the international financial system, reflected a sense that these issues, for the moment at least, were not a source of major preoccupation. This was not true of the fourth of the evil spirits — world poverty. This provided the main source of anxiety at Okinawa.

Since the late 1990s, the summits had paid growing attention to the issues concerned with development. French president Jacques Chirac started this, when the Lyon Summit of 1996 took the reform of development institutions as its main theme. The heads of the institutions — the World Bank, the IMF, the World Trade Organization (WTO), and the United Nations (UN) — were invited there to meet the G7 leaders. The next year U.S. president Bill Clinton devoted much of the Denver Summit to the problems of Africa. British prime minister Tony Blair at Birmingham 1998 and German chancellor Gerhart Schroeder at Cologne 1999 both chose debt relief as a key topic. Okinawa addressed a wide range of development issues. This priority reflected the explicit recognition by the G8 of two important consequences of globalisation. First, any international economic measures they proposed must benefit all countries, developing as well as developed. Second, the poorest countries risked being marginalised, without special efforts to enable them to share in the advantages of globalisation.

The most valuable contribution of the previous summits to helping the poorest countries had been in debt relief. This again illustrates the practice of iteration. From the Toronto Summit of 1988 onward, the summits launched a succession of debt relief programmes, each more ambitious than the last, as the leaders came to realise the extent of the debt burdens that weighed on poor countries. The leaders engaged their own reputations on this issue and were ready to override their finance ministers, if needed. The Cologne Summit of 1999 made a major advance, promising both faster and deeper debt relief for eligible poor countries, linked to programmes to direct more funds to development purposes. This raised the hopes of Jubilee 2000, a world-wide group of nongovernmental organisations (NGOs) campaigning for debt relief to release funds for education and health.[6]

But as the Okinawa Summit approached, it became clear that both on debt relief and on other issues of concern to poor countries, the G8's intentions were good but its performance was sluggish or inadequate. For example:

- Since Cologne the movement toward the targets set for debt relief had been too slow and not enough countries were benefitting. Jubilee 2000 was very disappointed.
- At Birmingham, the G8 promised to work on untying bilateral aid. But the members failed to agree on the necessary measures at a meeting of the OECD a month before the summit.
- The measures to help Africa pledged by the U.S. at Denver were only endorsed by Congress early in 2000, after nearly three years' delay.
- Duty-free trade access for the exports of the poorest countries, first proposed at the Lyon Summit in 1996, was promised by G7 members at

the WTO ministerial meeting in Seattle in late 1999. But the G7 made so many exceptions as to remove most of the value of this pledge.
- Over the 1990s, total aid spending had shrunk in real terms. As reports published in 2000 showed, efforts to reduce poverty had fallen short of targets set during the 1990s. As many people still lived in deep poverty as a decade ago, although this was a smaller share of world population.

These failures to honour its own pledges were deeply damaging to the G8's reputation.[7]

Debt Relief for the Poorest Countries

This was the most difficult subject for the G7 leaders at their meeting on the first afternoon at Okinawa. Blair led off, stressing the extent of public feeling on the topic. He had received 150 000 postcards and 100 000 e-mail messages during the previous three months. The problem for the G7 was that, despite some considerable efforts, their major initiative from Cologne in 1999 was falling behind schedule. Bilaterally, the G7 had in fact gone beyond its Cologne commitments, since all members had agreed to give 100 percent reduction of commercial debt, instead of the 90 percent reduction promised a year before. But the multilateral aspects were the source of obstacles. The requirement for beneficiary countries to conclude 'poverty reduction strategies' was slowing things down. There was doubt whether pledges made to compensate the World Bank would be met. Many eligible countries in Africa were being undermined by conflict, either internal or external, so that they could not meet the conditions required.

The Cologne Summit had set a target of getting three quarters of the 41 eligible countries to their 'decision point', when the scale of debt relief was agreed, by the end of 2000. This target, which had been added by the heads of state and government themselves, would clearly not be met. Only nine countries had qualified so far, and 11 more should have made it by the end of the year. The leaders were clearly frustrated by this. But the G7 could not offer any radical measures to speed things up and made clear their anxiety about conflict in Africa (see Appendix B). For this they were bitterly denounced by Jubilee 2000, which said it was 'totally dismayed' by the statement issued after the G7 meeting.[8]

Blair and Chirac returned to this subject in the G8 meeting the next day, urging greater efforts to show that the summit leaders cared about the poorest countries. The G8 Communiqué contained extended provisions on development, discussed below. But it could not offer more on debt relief, beyond aiming to get a total of 20 countries to decision point by the end of the year.

Other Development Issues

There was wide-ranging discussion of development among the G8 heads at their meeting on the second morning at Okinawa, reflected in the long development section of the G8 Communiqué (see Appendix B). This went some way to recognise the scale of the problem — 'there are still 1.2 billion people living on less than one dollar a day' (paragraph 13) — and the inadequacy of earlier G7/8 measures. But it still fell short of a satisfactory response on several points.

Aid Okinawa, like earlier communiqués, had provisions for improving aid effectiveness. But, unlike Cologne 1999, it made no commitment to increase aid volume. However, after the failure to agree to untie aid at the OECD in June, the G8 set a new and more precise target, to untie aid for least of the less developed countries (LLDCs) by the beginning of 2002.

Trade The incentives offered to the poorest countries were disappointing. The G8 admitted in paragraph 35 of the Communiqué that its earlier offers on market access and capacity building were not good enough: 'We recognise the need to go further with greater urgency in this area. And we will do so.' But a long passage on capacity building contained only rhetorical commitments, while nothing more was said in the Communiqué about better market access at all. The European Commission made a separate commitment to give duty- and quota-free access to 'almost all' of the products of less developed countries (LDCs) by 2005, but this may not be endorsed by the member states.[9]

Health This was the most encouraging area, to which several leaders gave priority. Japanese prime minister Yoshiro Mori focussed on the fight against infectious diseases, pledging US$3 billion over three years in aid from Japan, plus a fund to support nongovernmental organisations (NGOs). Clinton spoke of U.S. action to subsidise the cost of drugs for poor countries. In the Communiqué, the leaders committed themselves to a partnership 'to deliver three critical UN targets' for reducing the prevalence of AIDS, tuberculosis, and malaria (paragraphs 29–30). They called for a strategy conference in the autumn and a UN conference on AIDS the following year. The aims of the partnership included 'mobilising additional resources', access to drugs and vaccines, and stimulating research, but there were no details on how these aims could be met.

Helping the Good Spirits — Information Technology, Trade, and the Environment

Recent summits, as explained above, have come to concentrate on the evil spirits or problem areas of globalisation. But they have not hitherto given much attention to the good spirits, which help to harvest the benefits of globalisation. The Japanese hosts took the welcome decision in 2000 to focus the summit on the diffusion of information and communications technology (ICT) and the implications of the new economy.

Information and Communications Technology

There is no doubt that ICT is a driving force behind globalisation. It has grown and spread so strongly because of its accessibility and openness to enterprise and innovation. But that does not mean that governments can treat it with benign neglect. There are issues of privacy, fraud, public morals, and consumer protection where rules are necessary. There are areas such as education, where public encouragement and standards are needed. Above all, the benefits of ICT must not simply accrue to the rich, but must be spread so as to contribute to development, especially of the poorest. Okinawa was intended to yield some useful guidance on all these issues.

ICT was the most substantial subject covered in the G8 heads' discussion. They issued an extensive document: the Okinawa Charter on Global Information Society (see Appendix C). Work on this provided a major focus for the summit preparations, including a conference with leading private sector figures just before the summit. The charter offered a vision of 'an information society ... that better enables people to fulfil their potential and realise their aspirations' (paragraph 2).

The document falls into three sections:
- Digital Opportunities;
- Digital Divide;
- Global Participation.

The Digital Opportunities section focussed on economic activities and their regulation in developed countries. It struck a reasonable balance between the leading role of the private sector and the responsibility of government 'to create a predictable, transparent and non-discriminatory policy and regulatory environment' (paragraph 7). It sought to reconcile transatlantic differences of approach. A long set of principles began with recognisable U.S. objectives, for example on e-commerce in the international trading system, and ended with more European concerns about consumer trust and privacy. The Digital Divide section dealt with social policies in developed countries, including wider network access and opportunities in education. These first two parts of the Charter represented a fair synthesis of much current discussion of the role and potential of ICT and the new economy in developed countries.

The Global Participation section focussed on ICT for developing countries. After welcoming contributions from other institutions and the private sector, it created the Digital Opportunity Task Force (the Dot-Force), with a wide range of tasks, to report to the Genoa Summit in 2001. This was the critical part of the Charter, which would largely be judged on how it helped developing countries benefit from ICT, especially the poorest. Here there were many uncertainties. The composition and powers of the Dot-Force were not defined in the Communiqué and subsequent progress was slow. Though the Charter recognised (in paragraph 13) the 'gaps in terms of basic economic and social infrastructures' in poor countries — that is, no electricity, no telephones, and low education — it did not say much about how these gaps could be filled. The resources required were not identified nor did the document contain commitments, although Japan separately pledged US$15 billion over five years.

Trade

Regrettably, earlier summits had neglected another good spirit of globalisation — trade liberalisation. Successful globalisation depends on international trade rules that encourage competitiveness and are extended to cover new sectors of the economy as these develop. But at both Birmingham and Cologne the G8 failed to resolve their differences about what the next round of WTO negotiations should do. This contributed to the failure to launch a new round at Seattle in December 1999.

There were divided views among the leaders on whether the G8 should call for a new trade round to start by the end of 2000. But Mori, in summing up the discussion, said that all could agree the round should start by the end of the year, if possible. The Communiqué duly committed the G8 'to try together with other WTO members to launch such a round during the course of this year' (paragraph 36). The round should have an 'ambitious, balanced and inclusive agenda', including market access, WTO rules, support for developing countries, and making trade compatible with social and environmental policies. While this looked like a slight move toward the European Union/Japanese position, it was not clear that G8 members had resolved their internal differences or worked out how they could persuade developing countries to agree to the nontrade items. The end of 2000 passed with no decision to start a new round, leaving a heavy responsibility to the Genoa Summit of 2001.[10]

Environment

Protecting the environment becomes more effective with the advance of globalisation, in principle, as world-wide agreements become feasible. The recent record of the summits, however, has not been very positive. The 1997 Denver Summit was unable to agree on G7 commitments to climate change, despite the approach of the Kyoto conference later that year. However, agreement was reached, with difficulty, at Kyoto itself. At Birmingham 1998 and Cologne 1999, the environment received little attention, except that Cologne introduced the sensitive topic of food safety.

At Okinawa, the G8 heads discussed bringing into force the Kyoto Protocol on Climate Change. But, as in 1997, they did not resolve their transatlantic differences and later in the year these frustrated agreement at the climate change conference at The Hague.[11] They made more progress on forest management, including illegal logging, and on encouraging the use of renewable energy in developing countries, where the leaders set up a task force to report before the Genoa Summit in 2001. The exchanges on food safety were inconclusive. There was the usual division between those who would rely on scientific evidence (Clinton, Blair, and Canada's Jean Chrétien) and those advocating the precautionary principle (the other Europeans). The matter was not resolved and the Communiqué (paragraphs 55–59) contains language giving comfort to both camps. The proposal to create 'an independent international panel' was only noted, not adopted, because of differing views about its composition.

Conclusion

The G8 Communiqué from Okinawa set out aspirations for the twenty-first century and a wide-ranging response to the demands of globalisation and the new economy. In this, the Okinawa Summit continued the process begun at Birmingham in 1998. But the conditions prevailing at the beginning of the 2000s prompted a shift in the summit's priorities.

Three out of the four evil spirits of concern at Birmingham and Cologne — job loss, crime, and financial panic — seemed to be quiescent, if not wholly tamed:

- There was general satisfaction with the performance of the G7's own economies, with even Japan recovering. Domestic worries about globalisation, for example over jobs, no longer needed attention. There were few contentious issues between the G8 themselves that had to be resolved at Okinawa.
- Political anxieties about crime and conflict prevention were major topics for the G8 foreign ministers, but did not take up much of the time of the leaders themselves.
- The leaders endorsed two reports from their finance ministers on the international system. But the report on financial architecture was largely work in progress, while the report on money laundering and related issues pulled together work done elsewhere.

So the main focus of Okinawa was always likely to be on world poverty and economic subjects of concern to developing countries. Recent summits, since Lyon in 1996, had shown increasing concern that the poorest countries were being left behind by globalisation. But they had found it hard to match their good intentions with effective measures, which laid them open to criticism. The Okinawa Summit was an opportunity for the G8 to regain the initiative and to show themselves responsive to the needs and concerns of developing countries, especially the poorest. The topics chosen were, in principle, very suitable for this purpose. But the treatment of them, though often full of detail, was not very satisfactory.

In particular:

- The Cologne Debt Initiative, which should have been a major asset, had clearly run into problems. Although there were some good reasons for the slow progress, the failure to meet the Cologne timetable undermined confidence in summit commitments.
- Offers of trade access for poor countries were recognised as being inadequate — but the summit did not agree on new ones.
- In the absence of any commitment to increase aid volumes, the various promises of assistance scattered throughout the documents lacked conviction. The new target on untying aid, although welcome, still had to be met.

The most promising commitments were in the field of health and the fight against infectious diseases. But success would depend on the G8 mobilising the intellectual, human, and financial resources required from all available quarters — governments, business, and NGOs active in the field.

Okinawa's greatest innovation was in its focus on information and communications technology, one of the good spirits of globalisation. The G7 had addressed this topic before and stimulated two meetings of the Global Information Society in 1995 and 1996.[12] But the work was not sustained. The achievement of Okinawa was to recognise the central contribution of IT and the new economy to the beneficial effects of globalisation and its potential in accelerating development.

The commitments in the Okinawa Charter on Global Information Society did not break new ground as regards the strategies of developed countries, although the divergent approaches of Americans and Europeans were skilfully reconciled. But the programme laid out by the G8 could be enormously beneficial for developing countries, if properly implemented. This would depend on the G8 recognising the scale of the measures needed to enable the poorest countries to have access to these benefits. It would also need commitments of the necessary funds. The private sector must be involved as much as possible, but this could not substitute for government action. So the results of Okinawa could only be judged in the light of the achievements of the Dot-Force and the follow-on action pursued in the run-up to the Genoa Summit, as well as at lower levels.

On other good spirits, notably trade and the environment, the Okinawa Summit was less successful, although there were some advances on illegal logging and renewable energy.

Okinawa suggests a further evolution in the G8's response to globalisation. In their first recognition of globalisation, from Naples in 1994, the leaders focussed on reshaping the international system, while regarding globalisation itself as essentially a benign force. From Birmingham in 1998, they became concerned with the darker aspects of globalisation, domestic as well as international. By Okinawa in 2000, some of the domestic concerns about globalisation were in abeyance, especially as the G7 economies were buoyant. So the problems of the poorest countries occupied the centre of attention — and proved as intractable as ever. But alongside these evil spirits, the summit could also give some attention to the good spirits, which generate the benefits of globalisation. In particular, the G8 started an innovative process in its treatment of IT, which should help countries at all stages of development. Although it failed to make progress on international trade, it should have another chance at Genoa in 2001.

The G8 had thought the institutional review was complete by Denver 1997. In fact, it had to embark on a new cycle of international reforms, beginning with financial architecture. Domestic concerns, most active from Birmingham 1998, were muted at Okinawa, but could well revive again. In the G8's successive response to different aspects of globalisation, the practice of iteration remains fundamental to the summit process. Where agreement is reached and commitments are made, it is essential for the G8 to ensure that the targets and deadlines are met and the necessary resources are mobilised. Where agreement is not reached or the commitments prove inadequate, the G8 must keep on trying until it achieves an effective result. The summits should not be discouraged when they are attacked for agreeing on a solution that fails to solve the problem. But they should look to their reputation when they are criticised for making commitments and then failing to honour them.

Notes

1   This chapter matches Chapter 2, 'The G8 Summit and Global Governance: The Message of Okinawa' (Bayne forthcoming), in the parallel volume called *New Directions in Global Political Governance*. In brief, this chapter looks at summit issues — what the G8 does. The other chapter looks at the summit process — how the G8 does it — and concentrates on the first and third objectives. Both chapters are based on papers delivered at conferences in Tokyo and Okinawa in July 2000 and on impressions gathered at the summit itself. Accounts of what happened in the leaders' meetings are taken mainly from official press briefings. Texts of the G7 and G8 documents are available on the Web site of the University of Toronto G8 Research Group at <www.g7.utoronto.ca> and in the Appendices to this volume.

2   For an analysis of the summits' response to globalisation up to 1999, see Bayne 2000b, especially pp. 200–208. In that passage, the image of the 'four horsemen' (from the Book of Revelation in the Christian Bible) are applied to the fears about globalisation. Here, the more neutral term of 'evil spirits' is used. This permits more than four of them, if necessary, and it permits the ability to contrast them with 'good spirits'.

3   A successful conference on cyber-crime took place in October 2000 in Berlin. A further conference is planned for Tokyo in May 2001.

4   See Kenen 1996 for a series of post-Halifax assessments, most of which did not anticipate future crises.

5   Recent analyses of the G7's contribution to designing a new international financial architecture are in Bayne 2000a and Kirton 2000, both chapters in the fourth volume in the G8 and Global Governance series.

6   On the G7 and debt relief for the poorest, see Bayne 2000b, pp. 179–186, and Bayne 2000b. A historical analysis, from 1987 onward, is in Evans 1999.

7   On the OECD meetings on untying aid, see Beattie and Jonquières 2000 and Beattie 2000. On Congressional approval for help to Africa, see McGregor 2000. On trade access for the poorest, see Chote and Jonquières 1996 (the first proposal), and Chapter 10 in this volume. The report on world poverty by the World Bank and others is assessed in 'The Poor Who Are Always With Us' 2000, and is the source of the figure of 1.2 billion people living on less than one dollar a day quoted in the G8 Communiqué. For an analysis of the progress toward international development targets, see *Eliminating World Poverty* (United Kingdom 2000), especially figures 1.1 and 1.2.

8   As reported, for example, in Fidler, Green, and Tett 2000.
9   The European Commission's formal proposals were reported in Smith 2000. For subsequent difficulties, see Jonquières 2000.
10   This issue is the subject of Chapter 10 in this volume.
11   For reports of the unsuccessful Hague conference to agree on commitments under the Kyoto Protocol, see Lean 2000, and Houlder 2000.
12   Accounts of the earlier meetings of the Global Information Society are in Hajnal 1999, pp. 38, 60–61.

References

Bayne, Nicholas (2000a). 'The G7 Summit's Contribution: Past, Present, and Prospective', in Karl Kaiser, John J. Kirton, and Joseph P. Daniels, eds., *Shaping a New International Financial System: Challenges of Governance in a Globalizing World*, pp. 19–35. Ashgate, Aldershot.

Bayne, Nicholas (2000b). *Hanging In There: The G7 and G8 Summit in Maturity and Renewal*. Ashgate, Aldershot.

Bayne, Nicholas (forthcoming). 'The G8 Summit and Global Governance: The Message of Okinawa', in John J. Kirton, and Junichi Takese, eds., *New Directions in Global Political Governance*. Ashgate, Aldershot.

Beattie, Alan (2000). 'OECD Meeting Fails to Agree to End Tied Aid'. *Financial Times*, 23 June, p. 14.

Beattie, Alan and Guy de Jonquières (2000). 'Tied Aid Plan at Risk: OECD, France, Denmark, and Japan Seek to Change Terms of Accord'. *Financial Times*, 19 June, p. 3.

Chote, Robert and Guy de Jonquières (1996). 'Tariff Plea to Aid Poor Countries' Exports'. *Financial Times*, 1 July, p. 4.

Evans, H. P. (1999). 'Debt Relief for the Poorest Countries: Why Did It Take So Long?', *Development Policy Review*, vol. 17, no. 3, pp. 267–279.

Fidler, Stephen, Brian Groom, and Gillian Tett (2000). 'Charities in Attack on "Obscene" G8 Spending'. *Financial Times*, 22 July, p. 5.

Hajnal, Peter (1999). *The G7/G8 System: Evolution, Role, and Documentation*. Ashgate, Aldershot.

Houlder, Vanessa (2000). 'US and EU Swap Blows on Climate Talks: Some Optimism amid Recriminations for Collapse of Agreement to Combat Global Warming'. *Financial Times*, 27 November, p. 1.

Jonquières, Guy de (2000). 'Altruism with a Bitter Taste: Brussels Is Being Forced to Rethink Plans to End Trade Barriers for the Poorest Countries'. *Financial Times*, 19 December, p. 23.

Kenen, Peter B., ed. (1996). *From Halifax to Lyon: What Has Been Done about Crisis Management? Essays in International Finance*, no. 200. Princeton University Press, Princeton.

Kirton, John J. (2000), 'The Dynamics of G7 Leadership in Crisis Response and System Reconstruction', in Karl Kaiser, John J. Kirton, and Joseph P. Daniels, eds., *Shaping a New International Financial System: Challenges of Governance in a Globalizing World*, pp. 65–94. Ashgate, Aldershot.

Lean, Geoffrey (2000). 'World Climate Talks Collapse in Chaos — And We Are All the Losers'. *Independent*, 26 November, p. 1.

McGregor, Deborah (2000). 'Way Clear For Us — Africa Trade Bill'. *Financial Times*, 4 May, p. 14.

'The Poor Who Are Always With Us' (2000). *Economist*, 1. July.

Smith, Mike (2000). 'EU May End Duty for Poor Nations'. *Financial Times*, 21 September, p. 15.

United Kingdom (2000). 'Eliminating World Poverty: Making Globalisation Work for the World's Poor'. British Government White Paper on International Development <www.globalisation.gov.uk> (March 2001).

3 The New Global Electronic Economy: Consensus, Confusion, Contradictions

THOMAS C. LAWTON

At the beginning of the 1990s, fewer than 3 million people world-wide used the internet and its commercial application was non-existent. A decade later, the number of people with access to the internet had grown to more than 300 million and approximately one quarter of users made purchases online from electronic commerce sites, worth in excess of US$110 billion (Organisation for Economic and Co-operation and Development [OECD] 2000, 3). Although it is difficult to quantify, this figure is expected to leap to more than US$730 billion by 2004. This would represent about 5 percent of total global business-to-business (B2B) and business-to-consumer (B2C) sales.[1] Conservative estimates expect fivefold growth in e-commerce and e-business during the first half of this decade and the most optimistic forecasts are for a tenfold increase (p. 25). Modern managers cannot ignore such figures. The electronic economy has therefore forced a transformation in the structure and strategy of many so-called 'old economy' companies, as well as stimulating the emergence of a wide range of 'new economy' companies. Moreover, the economic significance of the 'electronic economy', or e-conomy, together with its social and technological ramifications and its transborder nature, has generated significant debate about the role of government in the new 'marketspace'. These twin challenges — to business and to government — form the focal point of this chapter.

The first part of this chapter examines the driving forces facilitating the transformation of contemporary organisational structure in the global electronic economy. The transformation of the corporate value chain is charted from vertical to virtual and the way in which, as this transition occurs, knowledge and business relationships become increasingly important strategy variables is outlined (see Figure 3.1).

The second part of the chapter discusses governance in the era of the global electronic economy and the consensus, confusion, and contradictions surrounding regulation and control of the internet and e-commerce. The various policy initiatives that have emerged are considered and efforts by the G8 and other international actors to shape the emerging international regulatory regime are assessed.

Before proceeding, some of the terminology that will be employed throughout this chapter should be clarified. E-commerce is, according to the U.S. *Internet Tax Freedom Act of 1998*:

> any transaction conducted over the Internet or through Internet access, comprising the sale, lease, license, offer, or delivery of property, goods, services, or information, whether or not for consideration, and includes the provision of Internet access.

The terms 'e-commerce' and 'e-business' are often used interchangeably, particularly in public discourse. In management parlance, e-commerce is often taken to mean business-to-business (B2B) transactions and e-business refers to business-to-consumer (B2C) sales. E-commerce can also be seen as the more generic of the two terms, in effect encapsulating all forms of electronic commercial transaction. It is this latter interpretation that is employed in this chapter. The terms 'supply chain' and 'value chain' are often used interchangeably in this chapter. There are, however, subtle differences between the two concepts. Philip Evans and Thomas Wurster (2000, 10) argue that 'supply chains link supplier and customer corporations together. They are shaped by the same kind

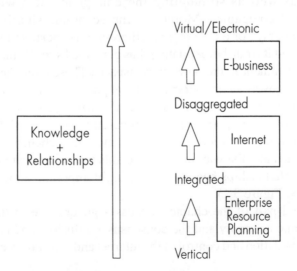

Figure 3.1. Value Chain Stages of Transition

of information logic as the value chains within companies, but in a weaker form'. Another way of distinguishing between the two concepts is that the supply chain should be conceptualised as the physical transport of goods, typically associated with logistics, manufacturing, and so forth. The value chain, by distinction, incorporates supply chain operations as well as knowledge activities such as research and development (R&D) and administration. Thus, the term 'value chain' is broader and more inclusive. However, given the general ambiguity in management literature, the terms are used interchangeably here.

The Transformation of Firm Structure in the Electronic Economy

The pace of change in the new global economy is likely to accelerate to the point where only the most flexible organisational structures will be able to withstand the stress. Intensifying competition from 'giants around the globe and knowledge-based entrepreneurs around the corner' will drive corporations to seek out new sources of competitive advantage and new allies in the struggle to survive (Economist Intelligence Unit and Arthur Andersen 1997, 1). The outer limits of every corporate structure will be stretched by outsourcing arrangements and strategic alliances and will ultimately create inter-firm networks or even 'virtual' organisational forms. This trend toward 'smaller' corporations reflects the growing uncertainties and the realisation that central control may not add enough value. Flexible organisational structures are seen to be a core driver of competitive advantage in the twenty-first century.

B2B e-commerce constitutes more than three quarters of all electronic sales transactions. This is due in large part to a phenomenon referred to as the 'disaggregation of the value chain', facilitated by developments in information and communications technologies. The past decade has witnessed many changes related to international production, caused both by political factors and by technological factors. On the political side, the successful completion of the Uruguay Round of the General Agreement on Tariffs and Trade (GATT), the emergence of the World Trade Organization (WTO), and a general trend toward deregulation and privatisation by governments around the world have created a favourable environment for global production and international trade. Technology has also shaped international production as a result of falling transport and communications costs, the onset of the internet and e-commerce, and the emergence of a new breed of service sector multinational corporations (MNCs): global logistics suppliers. While the changes in international production are numerous, the emphasis here is on the disaggregation or 'explosion' of the production value chain. A major trend in international production is the growing physical separation of activities defining the value chain of the firm. M. E. Porter (1985, 36) describes the value chain as a collection of activities that are performed by the firm to design, produce, market, deliver, and support a product or service. The configuration of a firm's value chain — the decisions relating to the technology, process, and location, and to whether to 'make or buy' for each of these activities — is the basis of competitive advantage. The value chain is, in turn, part of a larger value system that incorporates all value-added activities from raw materials to components and final assembly through buyer distribution channels. For much of the twentieth century, the value systems of many sectors were influenced by mass-production techniques pioneered by Henry Ford in the 1920s. These techniques emphasised scale, standardisation, and vertical integration to increase automobile production productivity. The epitome of 'Fordist' production was the River Rouge production facility in Michigan, which was co-located with a port and steel foundry. Most value-added activities were confined to a single facility to improve co-ordination and reduce the transportation costs of intermediate goods.

A direct challenge to this production model emerged in the 1950s and 1960s from the Toyota Motor Company in Japan (Womack, Jones, and Roos 1990). In place of standard products with long production runs by self-reliant vertically integrated firms, Toyota emphasised rapid product innovation, flexible production, and just-in-time inventory systems. Rather than vertical integration, Toyota emphasised strong relations with suppliers clustered near final assembly facilities. The productivity advantages of this lean production approach were significant, as Toyota could produce an automobile with fewer than half the labour hours of its American and European competitors. The Toyota model continued to evolve with falling transportation and communications costs in the 1970s and 1980s and soon it became feasible to co-ordinate large, extended supply chains on a global basis.[2] This production model, which some scholars have dubbed 'post-Fordist', spread to other manufacturing sectors beyond automotive and facilitated ever-greater movement of intermediate goods and components across national borders.[3]

As Figure 3.1 illustrates, the growing use of information technology (IT) in the 1990s brought further innovation to the post-Fordist model. The introduction of enterprise resource planning (ERP) software improved intra-firm co-ordination between frequently disparate functions as conceptualised in Porter's value chain. Prior to ERP, key functions of the value chain — such as inbound logistics, operations, outbound logistics, and marketing — frequently had separate organisations, with separate information systems that did not easily share information with each other. Each function was, in effect, in a 'silo' performing its own task but not optimising overall operations. ERP created an 'electronic nervous system' to link each function together, improve decisions, and increase overall productivity. An example is the impact on the operations and inbound logistics functions of a typical manufacturing firm. Historically, the operations (manufacturing) function demanded high inventory levels to ensure smooth production and avoid costly production shutdowns. At the same time, the inbound logistics function focussed on minimising transportation costs. The result was excessive inventory levels that were replenished periodically in large batches by slow, inexpensive transportation alternatives. ERP broke down information barriers between 'functional silos' to shed light on the relationship among transportation costs, inventory levels, and operations. In some cases, firms found that they could eliminate most inventories by shifting to faster but more expensive transportation alternatives (for example, air cargo) that replenished supply just-in-time. Simply put, ERP allowed information to replace inventory.

Revolutionary advances in communications technology spurred further evolution of the production model in the late 1990s. The emergence of the internet as a low-cost conduit for sharing vast quantities of data facilitated more and more information sharing between firms, extending the benefits of ERP from the value chain of an individual firm to the entire value system of firms and their suppliers and customers. If implemented correctly, ERP can be a vital component in controlling complex supply chains and in the fast developing world of e-business and B2B electronic exchanges. Dell Computer's phenomenal success in squeezing out inefficiencies establishes it as a model for many other companies, both within the computer industry and beyond.

The Dell Model

One of the early pioneers of the ERP model and of its value-system advantages was Dell Computer. Along with the likes of Coca Cola and Wal-Mart, Dell's success is based on realising the strategic power of the supply chain (Evans and Danks 1998, 20). The core of the Dell model is to deal directly with and sell directly to the customer and build products to order. In so doing, Dell collapses the value chain and eliminates two significant cost components: the retailer's mark-up and the costs and risks associated with carrying large inventories of finished goods.

Texas-based Dell is the world's second largest maker of personal computers. Founded in the early 1980s by a university student, Michael Dell, the company leads the sector with annual growth rates of 30 percent to 40 percent. Dell has achieved its success in large part due to its highly efficient value-chain integration approach, supported by ERP and — more recently — by the internet. Dell produces custom-made computers 'just in time' for orders received directly from the customer via telephone or the internet. As Dell received an order, it shared production requirement information electronically with its suppliers world-wide for immediate delivery to a Dell production facility, where the computer was assembled and shipped directly to the customer within a week. The Dell model relied on 'demand-side pull' rather than 'supply-side push' — no computer was produced unless there was corresponding demand in the marketplace. Thus, the massive queues of inventory usually sitting idle within retail stores, distributors, and factories were essentially eliminated. The productivity advantages of this production model were profound. Dell was able to operate with half the number of employees and one tenth of the inventory of its traditional computer competitors. Return on invested capital reached 195 percent in 1999 compared to 10 percent to 20 percent for traditional manufacturing firms.[4] Soon, companies from around the world were flocking to Austin, Texas, to understand the Dell production model, much as firms had flocked to Tokyo and River Rouge earlier in the century. The opportunity for productivity improvement was enormous; in the United States alone, the cost of goods in inventory of all value systems was nearly US$1 trillion in 1997.[5] As the decade closed, the Dell model (see Figure 3.2) began to spread from high technology to traditional

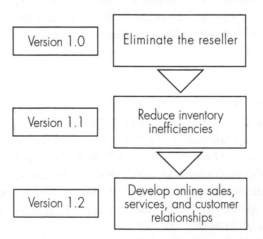

Figure 3.2. The Dell Direct Model: Stages of Development
Based on Dell (1999, 21–22, 78–79, 91).

manufacturing sectors such as automobile production. In late 1999, General Motors and Ford announced they were moving to electronic supply-chain management systems similar to Dell Computer. If successful, the Dell model could be every bit as revolutionary to the production structure as Ford's vertical integration and Toyota's lean production models were in earlier eras.

The direct model employed by Dell is not original. Cutting out the retail chain — the intermediary — and selling directly to the customer was a tried and tested business approach long before Dell was founded. In the late nineteenth century in the United States, Sears and Roebuck Company supplanted many clothing and hardware retailers with the launch of its mail order catalogue. Evans and Wurster (2000, 70) describe Dell's approach as 'disintermediation' and assert that bankers used the term in the 1970s to describe how securities markets displaced corporate banking. Dell's innovativeness was that it was the first personal computer manufacturer to sell personal computers (PCs) directly to the consumer, eschewing dealer networks. Dell's originality therefore lay in the approach that it adopted in implementing the direct business model. In particular, unlike other computer manufacturers, Dell sells directly to all their customers and not just to large corporate clients. By developing a direct relationship with all of their individual clients and building their computers to order, Dell was able to build a highly efficient just-in-time process, eliminating most of its inventory in the process. A further advantage to the Dell approach is the instant, current, and continuous market research that it produces. In knowing exactly what individual customers want in a personal computer or computer network, Dell is able to anticipate market demand and shape the technological and competitive parameters of the computer industry. Terry Austin (1998, 198) argues that the direct model creates the most compressed PC supply chain by eliminating all intermediaries. Moreover, compared to a traditional supply chain structure, the direct model can reduce inventory investment by 50 percent to 70 percent.

The concept behind Dell's drive to reduce inventory inefficiencies 'has nothing to do with stockpiling and everything to do with information' (Dell 1999, 80). Due to its made-to-order approach, Dell is able to see on a daily basis if, for instance, customer preference is shifting to larger PC monitors. The company can also discern whether this is happening for certain customer segments or across the market. Dell immediately relays its assessment of this information to its suppliers, allowing them to adjust their inventory accordingly and rapidly meet demand. It stands to reason that the more information a company has about what a customer wants and how much he or she requires, the less inventory the company needs to maintain. Less inventory means less inventory depreciation. In an industry such as computer manufacturing, component prices are constantly falling — typically 15 percent to 25 percent per annum. Six days of inventory (Dell's norm) compared with 34 days (standard at Compaq) can therefore result in significant cost savings on inputs. Furthermore, reduced stockpiles can offset the risk of being caught with large amounts of obsolete inventory if technology shifts and there is a transition to a next-generation product — as often happens in high-technology sectors. It therefore comes as no surprise to learn that Dell's competitors such as IBM and Compaq are constantly striving to cut their inventory levels but have yet to match Dell's success in this area.

The Dell Direct Model and Virtual Value-Chain Integration

The notion of linkages between supply chain participants is not new. It was traditionally referred to as 'vertical integration'. Unlike the Dell model though, vertical integration implies ownership of both upstream suppliers and downstream distributors. Firms such as Ford habitually controlled all elements of the value sequence, vertically integrating the information, decision, financial, and operational dimensions of the strategic supply chain (Evans and Danks 1998, 31).

The spread of internet-based commerce during the 1990s resulted in the emergence of 'virtual' supply-/value-chain linkages. This approach was perceived by many companies as a way of realising the benefits of supply chain integration while avoiding the perceived negative impact of integrating vertically (Evans and Danks 1998, 31). By seamlessly integrating supply chain suppliers, manufacturers, distributors, and retailers into a single virtual enterprise serving the customer, companies achieve huge competitive advantages. Companies such as Federal Express, Proctor & Gamble, and Wal-Mart have used the networked supply chain to dramatically transform the competitive landscape of their markets.

In addition to the previously discussed inventory and disintermediation cost savings, there are other advantages associated with the direct business model. In particular, as Michael Dell states, 'you actually get to have a relationship with the customer' (Magretta 1998, 73). A direct link to the individual customer provides a manufacturer such as Dell with a wealth of marketing and product development information. This information enables the company to build a position of strength relative to both its customers and its suppliers. When that information is combined with the technology of the internet, it allows a company to develop a revolutionary new value chain infrastructure and business model. This is what Dell has done through its 'virtual integration of the value chain' approach. 'Virtual integration' means a blurring of the conventional value-chain boundaries and roles among suppliers, manufacturers, and end users. Michael Dell (1999, 185) defines virtual integration as 'the idea of interweaving distinct businesses so that our partners are treated as if they're inside our company'. This results in gains of efficiency and productivity, as well as in significant gains in return to investors. Higher returns on investment are achieved by concentrating resources on activities where value can be added for the customer and not in activities that simply need to be done (Magretta 1998, 74). By this logic, Dell argues that a computer company, for instance, does not actually have to make computers. If fabricating semiconductor chips or even placing them on motherboards does not result in significant profit margins, then the computer company should consider outsourcing such activities. In Dell's case, this meant focussing instead on its distinct core competency — delivering solutions and systems to customers.

Douglas Aldrich (1999) refers to Dell's virtual integration model as 'the digital value chain'. By this, he means the use of technology/the internet to create a faster, more efficient, and more flexible version of the traditional supply chain. Within a digital value chain, one company serves as the 'anchor', that is, 'the power player around which the digital value chain is organized and often optimized' (p. 93). The power player is identified as such because it either provides the major share of the value delivered to the customer, is the dominant supplier, or is the owner of a product or service that cannot be replicated by any other member of the value chain. Dell is a classic digital value-chain anchor. Through its control of the consumer relationship, it establishes the rules and shapes the competitive dynamics of the value chain.

Cisco Systems employs a similar structure to the Dell model that it calls 'networked supply chain management'. The Cisco solution fuses supply chain constituents — suppliers, distributors, retailers, and customers — into what Cisco (2000) refers to as 'a networked extension of a single enterprise to serve the customer'. Cisco Systems saves US$75 million annually as a direct result of its networked supply chain. As with Dell, Cisco's supply chain starts with the customer — more than 80 percent of Cisco product orders are now placed via the internet. This results in more US$35 million in business per day (up from US$10 million in the late 1990s). Customer satisfaction ratings have soared since the company implemented this online ordering process.[6]

Nortel Networks has also developed strategic supplier partnerships with a number of manufacturing and logistics service companies to provide those functions previously carried out internally (Elwood and Holland-Fox 2000, 5).

Nortel moved from being a vertically integrated company, where almost everything was manufactured and controlled in-house, to a virtually integrated organisation that takes maximum advantage of its supplier capabilities.

As John Mangan and Kevin Hannigan (2000, 241) argue and as these examples illustrate, management of the supply chain has emerged as a key source of competitive advantage for firms vis-à-vis their rivals. Managing a supply chain more cost efficiently and with greater strategic effectiveness than competitors can ensure sustainable market leadership for companies such as Dell, Cisco, and Nortel. Thus, success in modern markets is increasingly premised on the performance of a network of companies, rather than on the performance of an individual corporation. As a senior manager at Oracle puts it: 'The battle taking place in today's market is no longer company against company ... what we're seeing now is supply chain competing against supply chain'.[7]

Thus, the virtual value-chain structure — based on a knowledge-sharing strategic network of integrated activities — transforms the fundamental premises of strategic management and market competition. With supply chains operating constantly and interactively to move vast volumes of goods, services, and information across international boundaries on a global basis, it raises the compelling question of what regime shall be shaped to govern this revolutionary world of global e-commerce.

Governance in the Electronic Economy

John Braithwaite and Peter Drahos (2000, 112) argue that the process of consumers and traders participating in global markets by means of digital technologies has led in recent years to a wide variety of governance initiatives on e-commerce. In addition to national government schemes, international organisations such as the Organisation for Economic Co-operation and Development (OECD), the WTO, and the United Nations Commission on International Trade Law (UNCITRAL), as well as businesses, nongovernmental organisations (NGOs), and regulators such as the Basle Committee on Banking Supervision and the European Union (EU), are writing reports and formulating discussion papers and policy proposals on regulating and governing the global electronic economy. The WTO, for instance, has begun to tackle e-commerce taxation issues. The approach pursued has been to consider e-commerce as another medium for exchange and thus subject to the same rules and regulations as conventional transactions: the principle of equivalent treatment (OECD 2000, 18). In May 1998, WTO members agreed on a temporary moratorium against the imposition of customs duties on electronic transactions. The U.S. and a number of other countries favour extending this moratorium indefinitely.

The International Chamber of Commerce (ICC) is very concerned about the proliferation of potential global regulators of e-commerce. It claims that at least 18 international organisations are working on e-commerce issues. It wants to rationalise this situation and create space to develop a global business self-regulatory approach. Consequently, the ICC has developed a global action plan to sell a business perspective on which international or supranational organisations should do what. This agenda is based on the U.S. National Information Infrastructure of 1993, the Global Information Infrastructure Initiative of 1995, and the 1997 White House report titled 'A Framework for Global Electronic Commerce' (Braithwaite and Drahos 2000, 112). The U.S. initiative on global e-commerce is driven by the concept of facilitation of private-sector e-business. For now, U.S. ideology and policy initiatives drive the development of a regulatory framework for global e-commerce. However, the reality is that consensus and co-ordination must emerge between and among governments and supranational regulators in many areas, including customs, taxation, electronic payments systems, and model contracts for e-commerce (p. 112).

In addition to key countries such as the U.S., five international and supranational organisations are determining the governance discourse and shaping the regulatory agenda for the global electronic economy. These are:
- The United Nations system (Centre on Transnational Corporations [UNCTC], Conference on Trade and Development [UNCTAD], and especially the Commission on International Trade Law [UNCITRAL]; UNCITRAL was established by the United Nations General Assembly to promote the harmonisation and unification of international trade law (Tayeb 2000, 77), which are key considerations in the international policy dialogue surrounding e-commerce).
- The WTO (which serves as the driving force behind the global reduction — if not removal — of both tariffs and nontariff barriers, such as quotas and local content requirements; with regard to e-commerce, it has issued an important declaration not to impose customs duties on electronic transmissions).
- The G8 of industrialised democracies.
- The EU.
- The OECD.

The extraordinary growth of e-commerce is still in its embryonic stage. As global information networks do not respect geographically defined borders, governments are naturally concerned about issues of sovereignty and jurisdiction. Law enforcement, the potential erosion of tax revenue and regulatory control all become key areas of contention and policy challenge for governmental authorities. This growth also leads to debates about the interoperability on a global scale of national law and governance and the identification of appropriate supranational initiatives. It should be stressed that cyberspace is not a lawless frontier — a complex array of laws do, in fact, exist for the regulation of internet-based commerce and other activities. The real issue for governments is the lack of jurisdiction. Thus, the main issue under discussion is whether a global system of e-commerce regulation is needed. At the moment, the prime example of supranational regulatory co-ordination is the EU. The EU is working on aspects of e-commerce and the information and communications society in the context of the single market programme. The EU's Directive on Electronic Commerce (Council of the European Union [CEU] 2000) argues that the development of e-commerce is an important instrument in the ongoing struggle to eliminate internal market barriers. E-commerce is also seen by the EU as a means to stimulate employment and small enterprise development and to promote innovation and competitiveness among European companies more generally. In terms of regulation, the EU's first objective is to ensure a high level of legal integration across the jurisdiction in order to remove existing obstacles to an e-commerce single market. This is an effort both to eradicate differences in legislation affecting e-commerce across Europe and to remove the uncertainty surrounding national legal jurisdiction in e-commerce. An important point to note is that the EU directive on e-commerce 'does not aim to establish rules on fiscal obligations nor does it pre-empt the drawing up of Community instruments concerning fiscal aspects of electronic commerce' (p. 7).

The key issue of taxing e-commerce transactions is therefore excluded from the directive's remit. Nonetheless, the harmonisation of European e-commerce legislation and the clarification of legal jurisdiction are both important steps toward simplifying and improving the regulatory environment of e-commerce in the EU.

On the issue of global regulatory co-ordination, the 2000 EU directive explicitly states that its mandate does not extend to services supplied by providers established in non-EU states. However, it does acknowledge the global dimension of e-commerce and the consequent need to ensure that EU rules are consistent with international rules (CEU 2000, 20). In this respect, the directive is 'without prejudice' to the results of discussions on legal issues within international organisations such as the WTO and OECD. No contradiction or conflict of interests is perceived between efforts to develop a global regulatory regime and the co-ordination of national regulatory measures within the EU and the related creation of a European regulatory framework. This approach reflects the wider debate about whether the twin phenomena of regionalisation and globalisation are mutually exclusive or mutually reinforcing. On the issue of e-commerce regulation, the EU clearly supports consensus between countries, regions, and the global community. At the same time, the EU is moving toward the creation of an internal regime for e-commerce regulation. This may result in confusion and even conflict if legislative contradictions emerge in global fora.

In a joint statement issued in 1998, the U.S. and Australia concurred with the EU's calls for the co-ordination and harmonisation of e-commerce legislation, both domestically and internationally (primarily through the WTO) (White House 1998). The two countries argued for a 'light touch' regulatory environment for e-commerce, allowing self-regulation wherever and whenever possible. Business supports this approach, as evidenced in the 1998 Global Action Plan for E-Commerce produced by the ICC and the Business and Industry Advisory Committee to the OECD (BIAC), in association with numerous other private sector organisations. This document argues that 'the pace of change and nascent state of electronic commerce have heightened the risks associated with premature or unnecessary government regulation' (BIAC et al. 1998, 8). The action plan calls for a hands-off approach by government on most e-commerce issues, with the exception of matters such as intellectual property rights, taxation, and the removal of barriers to competition. This differs significantly in tone and text from the 2000 EU directive, which placed considerable emphasis on the role of government as internet regulator and e-commerce promoter. This divergence reflects what Colin Turner (2000) describes as an 'EU-U.S. culture clash' on matters relating to internet regulation. At the core of this disagreement is the EU's tendency to place less confidence than the U.S. places in the ability of the market to regulate itself (p. 142). The clash may also be summarised as a U.S. preference for some form of governance and a European preference for actual government. J. N. Rosenau and E.-O. Czempiel (1992) have argued that there can be governance without government — a scenario that is clearly manifest in the modern global electronic economy. For R. A.W. Rhodes, governance is about managing self-organising, interdependent networks of public and private actors (1996, 658). Government, by comparison, refers to direct state control where regulation of a specific activity will follow centralised governmental goals (Gould 2000, 194). This divergence of approach reveals the wider industrial policy differences between the EU and the U.S. in particular. It casts some doubt on the creation and maintenance of a global consensus on the governance of the internet and e-commerce.

The approach in Japan appears similar to that of the U.S., with official documentation indicating that the public sector's main role is to encourage e-commerce through ensuring nondiscriminatory treatment, reducing trade restrictions and harmonising regulations for e-commerce (Ministry of International Trade and Industry 2000). The extent to which Japan favours e-commerce self-regulation over public regulation is implicit, if not explicit, in official position papers and policy statements. Most significantly though, Japanese policy makers accept the need for global policy co-ordination and the creation of a global consensus on internet/e-commerce governance. Since 1997, Japan's Ministry of International Trade and Industry has been co-ordinating government policy on e-commerce governance. In May 1997, the Ministry produced a draft document titled 'Towards the Age of the Digital Economy' that outlined several principles of government policy for the digital economy. These principles included an emphasis on international policy co-ordination, acknowledging the global characteristics of a network-based digital economy and the need to promote the rigorous exchange of information. The Ministry's 2000 proposal for a WTO e-commerce initiative, 'Towards eQuality', stresses the need to ensure the international harmonisation of regulations and standards for e-commerce that 'reflect market realities' (Ministry of International Trade and Industry 2000, 4). In the event that such harmonisation may not be feasible or desirable, the document argues in favour of the recognition of equivalence of foreign regulatory measures. In this paper, the Ministry (2000, 6) again asserts the need to garner international agreement, arguing for the promotion of 'bilateral, plurilateral or multilateral cooperation programmes' to achieve global policy consensus on e-commerce governance.

In line with the aforementioned 1998 ICC/BIAC Global Action Plan for E-commerce, the private sector in Japan also favours self-regulation whenever and wherever possible. A 1999 policy proposal for the promotion of e-commerce, produced by the Keidanren (Japan Federation of Economic Organizations), contends that the private sector should play an active and leading role in the development of global e-commerce frameworks. It further argues that the role of government is to create an open and fair market environment in which e-commerce can flourish.

The U.S. and Australia have also taken a clear joint stance on the issue of internet and e-commerce taxation, arguing that governments should consult and co-operate — both bilaterally and in international fora — to prevent tax evasion and avoidance. Furthermore, both countries support the indefinite extension of the WTO declaration of May 1998 not to impose customs duties on electronic transmissions. The U.S. Congress's Advisory Commission on Electronic Commerce (2000), reporting in April 2000, further supports the WTO declaration and also backs the 1998 U.S.-Australia joint statement, arguing that 'an international consensus for the taxation of e-commerce should be developed'. The commission goes on to reason that the OECD is the appropriate forum to sponsor the required international dialogue, which will require input from both business and non-OECD countries. Moreover, it contends that existing, internationally accepted tax rules should apply to e-commerce and that no new taxes are required. Finally, in concurrence with international opinion, the commission supports the goals of simplification, neutrality, and the avoidance of double taxation for e-commerce.

In 1998, an OECD ministerial conference was held in Ottawa on the theme of 'A Borderless World: Realising the Potential of Global Electronic Commerce'. The conference brought together not only OECD ministers but also observers from non-OECD countries, business leaders, labour representatives, and consumer and social interest groups. The objective was to articulate their joint plans to promote the development of global electronic commerce. The conference concluded that first, public policy for e-commerce should be a co-operative and inclusive process (involving all interested governmental, private sector, and civil society players); second, policy and regulatory actions should strive to be internationally compatible whenever possible; third, governments should promote a pro-competitive environment and work to eliminate barriers to trade (OECD 1998, 4–5). Significant emphasis was placed on ensuring legal clarity and consistency for global e-commerce. Agreement was also reached on the role of government vis-à-vis firms in the development and control of e-commerce: the private sector should take the lead in e-commerce development and should continue to extend self-regulation mechanisms. On taxation, it was agreed that business would continue to work with the OECD to ensure that neutrality is the guiding principle and that taxes are not imposed in a discriminatory manner.

The 1998 conference was followed by an OECD action plan for e-commerce and important ministerial declarations on e-commerce issues, including consumer protection, protection of privacy and authentication.

The G8 and the Global Electronic Economy

Carol Charles (2000) argues that the G8 can and should play a key role in the creation of a global framework for e-commerce. This framework should address issues such as privacy, cross-border dispute settlement, and recognition of electronic contracts. The first significant G7 initiative emerged in Brussels at a pre-summit ministerial meeting in 1995, with the creation of the Global Information Infrastructure Commission (GIIC). The GIIC, an independent, nongovernmental organisation, attempts to ensure that developing countries are constantly engaged with the global e-commerce dialogue. It works with national governments, industry groups, and international organisations to advance the dialogue on the rules needed for the global information economy. The GIIC has been encouraging the removal of barriers to e-commerce in countries such as India, China, and Venezuela. It has also been working with a coalition of businesses in 140 countries to urge governments to rely on e-business self-regulation. The GIIC argues that the G8 should work with the private sector and with international organisations such as the WTO, the World Intellectual Property Organization (WIPO), the OECD, and UNCITRAL to create co-operative systems for e-commerce regulation and promotion. This approach is strongly supported by Japan, which argues that each forum should work on issues of electronic economy governance as they relate to specific areas of expertise (Ministry of International Trade and Industry 2000, 6). Japan believes that in addition to the G8 and the WTO, regional groupings such as APEC (Asia-Pacific Economic Cooperation) should play a lead role in e-commerce policy harmonisation and regulatory enforcement.

At the July 2000 Okinawa Summit, the leaders of the eight major industrialised democracies and the president of the European Commission agreed on the Okinawa Charter on Global Information Society (see Appendix C). The main thrust of this charter was an agreement to work together in maximising the benefits and the global dissemination of IT. In practical terms, this meant the establishment of the Digital Opportunity Task Force (Dot-Force), charged with formulating recommendations on global action to bridge the international information divide. The leaders also agreed in paragraph 4 to exercise their leadership in advancing governmental efforts to foster an appropriate policy and regulatory framework to stimulate competition and innovation and fight abuses that undermine the integrity of the internet. The key objectives of e-commerce governance emerging from the Charter include the following:

- Continue to promote competition in and open markets for the provision of IT and telecommunication products and services;

- Protect intellectual property rights for IT-related technology;
- Renew commitment to using software in full compliance with protection of intellectual property rights;
- Prioritise the improved efficiency of telecommunications, transportation, and package delivery as critical services within the information society;
- Facilitate cross-border e-commerce by promoting further liberalisation and improvement in networks and related services and procedures in the context of a strong WTO framework, continued work on e-commerce in the WTO and other international fora, and the application of existing WTO trade disciplines to e-commerce;
- Maintain a consistent approach to the taxation of e-commerce based on the conventional principles including neutrality, equity, and simplicity;
- Continue the practice of not imposing customs duties on electronic transmissions;
- Promote consumer trust in the electronic marketplace and provide consumer protection in the online world, as well as explore options to resolve cross-border disputes for consumers;
- Develop effective and meaningful privacy protection for consumers;
- Encourage further development and effective functioning of electronic authentication and cryptography.

The consensus achieved within the G8 on these ten objectives may prove vital to ensuring the consolidation of a global framework for e-commerce governance. As already mentioned, differences of approach and of emphasis persist, particularly between the U.S. and the EU. However, these differences may be marginalised and even eliminated if the G8 consolidates its leading role in shaping the regulatory and policy environment of the global electronic economy.

Conclusion

The virtual integration of the value-chain approach evolved out of Dell Computer's need to garner better information from its customers and to enhance logistics management with its suppliers. Therefore, through what Michael Dell describes as 'information partnerships' with both suppliers and customers, his company has gained the benefits of tightly co-ordinated supply chain management normally associated with vertically integrated companies. At the same time, Dell has accrued the benefits of speed and flexibility associated with a virtual integration structure. This is the essence of Dell's success and these are the lessons that can be learned from studying the Dell case.

On this basis, one may conclude that the evolution of the organisational and industry value chain, facilitated by ERP and the internet, has resulted in dramatic time and cost efficiencies and customer satisfaction levels for those companies willing and able to adapt. The resultant virtual value chain is a highly flexible and extremely competitive structure. To function effectively, it privileges both knowledge and relationships. Thus, an organisation's corporate strategy must also change, becoming a more open, less secretive process. Virtual value chains succeed only if information (about customers, technology, markets, etc.) flows freely among all of the associates and if the value-chain anchor firm keeps its partners within the strategic decision-making loop. Thus, although the core power player determines strategy, all members of the value chain network are tied into the value chain's common strategic purpose.

Yet the revolutionary productivity-enhancing impact of this new e-business system on the global economy will only become apparent if the international regime governing e-commerce develops in supportive ways. Considerable international consensus has already emerged over the creation of rules and a dispute settlement procedure for the electronic economy, or e-conomy. The two mainstays of the world trade, finance, and investment systems — the U.S. and the EU — have issued a joint statement on the governance of electronic commerce. Both agree on the essential issues that must be resolved. They also agree on the fact that self-regulation is important, with business establishing its own rules and practices for the operation of the electronic economy. However, as with so many other policy domains, they differ in their views on the way and extent to which government should be involved in e-conomy governance. In particular, the EU does not possess the same confidence as the U.S. in the ability (or willingness) of business to regulate itself. As Turner states (2000, 142), despite states having agreed upon the core issues to be addressed, they often differ upon the means of achieving these objectives. The world's third dominant economic power, Japan, supports the same governance agenda as the U.S. and the EU and strongly advocates international policy consensus and regulatory harmonisation for e-commerce. Japan has also indicated its support for a process of self-regulation and appears closer to the U.S. than to the EU in its level of confidence in the private sector to self-regulate.

There are emerging doubts that an all-embracing global regulatory framework for the internet and for e-commerce is possible or even desirable (Dryden 1999). Despite the advance of globalisation, national or at best regional policies and approaches are likely to remain for the foreseeable future. This is contrary to the wishes of business, which advocates international co-ordination, arguing that 'internationally incompatible laws create a fragmented global market with significant uncertainty as to what rules apply' (BIAC et al. 1998, 8). Influential international actors such as the WTO, the OECD, and the G8 support this perspective. This influential troika is working on various elements of a regulatory agenda that will be acceptable to all interested parties, both in the public domain and in the private. It will prove difficult for any country to defy such an influential coalition — particularly whilst it maintains the support of the U.S. Although national differences cannot be discounted, international consensus on key issues such as authentication, consumer protection, privacy, encryption, and even taxation appears likely in the near future. This will prove instrumental in the development, diffusion, and economic importance of e-commerce throughout the world economy. States may differ on the means to an end but such differences can be immaterial once the end objectives are the same. This is the situation vis-à-vis the governance and regulation of the electronic economy. The process of reaching policy consensus may be slower but it is not likely to be halted. The unresolved question is not therefore whether consensus will emerge on how to regulate and govern the electronic economy. It is, rather, who or what will emerge as the chief regulatory authority for the global marketspace. It is on this issue that contradictions and confusion persist.

Notes

1   The largest share of electronic commerce in fact takes place between businesses. In 1999, these transactions accounted for 70 percent to 85 percent of all electronic sales. This trend is likely to continue for the foreseeable future.
2   For a discussion of Toyota's lean production approach, see Womack, Jones, and Roos (1990).
3   For a discussion of post-Fordism, see R. Kaplinsky in Eden (1993), p. 112.
4   Data from speech by Michael Dell to Detroit Economic Club, 1 November 1999.
5   See 'Colography Group Examines 20 Years of U.S. Air Cargo Deregulation,' Colography Group, 22 November 1997.
6   Data are derived from the Cisco Systems Web site at <www.cisco.com>.
7   Lou Unkeless, Senior Director of Applications Marketing, Oracle, cited in Paul Mann's 'Delivering Value across the Internet Supply Chain', *Manufacturing Systems*, July 1999, p. iv.

References

Advisory Commission on Electronic Commerce (2000). *Report to Congress.* April <www.ecommercecommission.org/report.htm> (March 2001).

Aldrich, Douglas F. (1999). *Mastering the Digital Market Place.* Wiley, New York.

Austin, Terry (1998). 'The Personal Computer Supply Chain: Unlocking Hidden Value'. In J. Gattorna, ed., *Strategic Supply Chain Alignment: Best Practice in Supply Chain Management.* Cambridge University Press, Cambridge.

Braithwaite, John, and Peter Drahos (2000). *Global Business Regulation.* Cambridge University Press, Cambridge.

Business and Industry Advisory Committee to the Organisation for Economic Co-operation and Development, Global Information Infrastructure Commission, and International Chamber of Commerce. (1998). 'A Global Action Plan for Electronic Commerce: Prepared by Business with Recommendations for Governments'. <www.biac.org/position.htm> (March 2001).

Charles, Carol (2000). *New Global Rules for E-Commerce: Moving the Dialogue beyond the G8.* Global Information Infrastructure Commission, Washington DC.

Cisco Systems (2000). *Networking the Supply Chain for Competitive Advantage: An Overview of the Cisco Networked Supply Chain Management Solution.* <www.cisco.com/warp/public/779/ibs/solutions/supply/scm_ov.pdf> (March 2001).

Council of the European Union (2000). 'Directive on Electronic Commerce'. Interinstitutional file 98/0325 (COD), 28 February, Brussels.

Dell, Michael, with Catherine Fredman (1999). *Direct from Dell: Strategies That Revolutionized an Industry.* Harper Business, New York.

Dryden, John (1999). 'The Digital Economy in International Perspective: Common Construction and Regional Rivalry'. Paper presented at the University of California E-conomy Project, Washington DC.

Economist Intelligence Unit and Arthur Andersen (1997). *Vision 2010: Designing Tomorrow's Organisation.* Economist Intelligence Unit, London.

Eden, Lorraine, and Evan Potter, eds. (1993). *Multinationals in the Global Political Economy.* St. Martin's Press, New York.

Elwood, Larry, and Sheila Holland-Fox (2000). 'Nortel Networks: Competitive Advantage of Outsourcing'. Irish Academy of Management, annual conference, 7–8 September, Dublin.

Evans, Philip, and Thomas S. Wurster (2000). *Blown to Bits: How the New Economics of Information Transforms Strategy.* Harvard Business School Press, Boston.

Evans, Robert, and Alister Danks (1998). 'Strategic Supply Chain Management: Creating Shareholder Value by Aligning Supply Chain Strategy with Business Strategy'. In John Gattorna, ed., *Strategic Supply Chain Alignment: Best Practice in Supply Chain Management.* Gower, Aldershot.

Gould, Mark (2000). 'Locating Internet Governance: Lessons from the Standards Process'. In Christopher T. Marsden, ed., *Regulating the Global Information Society*. Routledge, London.

Keidanren (1999). *Proposal for the Promotion of Electronic Commerce*. Keidanren, Tokyo.

Magretta, Joan (1998). 'The Power of Virtual Integration: An Interview with Dell Computer's Michael Dell'. *Harvard Business Review* March-April, pp. 73–84.

Mangan, John, and Kevin Hannigan (2000). *Logistics and Transport in a Fast-Growing Economy: Managing the Supply Chain for High Performance*. Blackhall Publishing, Dublin.

Ministry of International Trade and Industry (1997). 'Towards the Age of the Digital Economy: For Rapid Progress in the Japanese Economy and World Economic Growth in the 21st Century'. Draft, Ministry of International Trade and Industry, Tokyo.

Ministry of International Trade and Industry (2000). 'Towards eQuality: Global E-Commerce Presents Digital Opportunity to Close the Divide between Developed and Developing Countries (MITI's Proposal for WTO E-Commerce Initiative)'. Second draft. Ministry of International Trade and Industry, Tokyo.

Organisation for Economic Co-operation and Development (1998). 'A Borderless World: Realising the Potential of Global Electronic Commerce'. Directorate for Science, Technology and Industry, SG/EC(98)14/Final. Organisation for Economic Co-operation and Development, Paris.

Organisation for Economic Co-operation and Development (2000). 'E-Commerce: Impacts and Policy Challenges'. Economics Department Working Papers No. 252 (Jonathan Coppel). Organisation for Economic Co-operation and Development, Paris.

Porter, M. E. (1985). *Competitive Advantage: Creating and Sustaining Superior Performance*. Free Press, New York.

Rhodes, R. A. W. (1996). 'The New Governance: Governing without Government'. *Political Studies*, vol. 44, pp 652–667.

Rosenau, J. N., and E.-O. Czempiel, eds. (1992). *Governance Without Government: Order and Change in World Politics*. Cambridge University Press, Cambridge.

Tayeb, Monir (2000). *International Business: Theories, Policies and Practices*. FT Prentice Hall, London.

Turner, Colin (2000). *The Information Economy: Business Strategies for Competing in the Digital Age*. Kogan Page, London.

United States (1998). *Internet Tax Freedom Act of 1998* (Reported in the House). H.R.3529.RH. <thomas.loc.gov/bss/d105/hot-titl.html> (March 2001).

White House, Office of the Press Secretary (1998). 'Joint Statement from Australia and the United States on Electronic Commerce'. 20 November.

Womack, J. R., Jones, D. T., and Roos, D., eds. (1990). *The Machine That Changed The World*. Ranson Associates, New York.

4 Creating Rules for the Global Information Economy: The United States and G8 Leadership

MICHELE MASTROENI

The 'new economy', which began in the United States, has created a flurry of activity in developed and developing countries in an attempt to harness its economic potential. Developed countries are currently searching for ways to develop the infrastructure needed to participate and succeed in this technological revolution. The question of regulating this new economy has also drawn attention, the most notable and dominant initiative regarding regulation being the U.S.-proposed three-year moratorium on new taxation of electronic commerce, which is being upheld by developed countries for the time being. At first glance, this may seem to be a very positive first step in ensuring the open nature of an emerging and important market; the principle of open trade — something that the G8 and most other countries that are members of the World Trade Organization (WTO) nominally support. However, maintaining a moratorium on new taxes without an in-depth analysis would be a mistake. It would lead to a loss of new sources of revenue for states, damage to other sectors of the economy through lack of regulation and 'tax bias', a potential deterioration of state sovereignty, and a resulting breakdown in co-operation among states. Rather than a moratorium on new taxes and tariffs on the new economy as the centrepiece of the emerging international e-commerce regime, the current high level of international co-operation should be harnessed in order to ensure proper infrastructure as well as a proper regulatory framework for the new economy. Such a framework is necessary to guarantee fruitful interaction between the 'new economy' and older sectors or markets, as well as to provide and maintain the political and social structures necessary to ensure justice and maintain order. The expansion of technology does not mean inevitability of use and lack of control; markets are opened and managed by political factors and not just the invisible hand, even if the latter has grown beyond Adam Smith's imagination.

These various issues are examined in this chapter using the current debate on internet taxation as a starting point. Motives for embracing certain policies will be questioned and broader political, social, and economic issues of interest to state politics will be considered. To remain focussed solely on specific issues and concerns coming from tax law would require expertise and an in-depth investigation beyond the scope of this chapter. However, after a consideration of the issue of taxation of electronic commerce, other related issues can be discussed. By analysing U.S. proposals and the temporary moratorium, the discussion can move on to the broader questions mentioned above. This chapter thus adds to what has been a discussion largely limited to looking at economic gains for the near future.

Although a strictly economic outlook seems to be commonly held by states involved in this new economy, an outlook that is insufficiently broad and focusses on the economic benefits of electronic commerce is not surprising. The U.S. position illustrates this well:

> The dramatic growth of the Internet and electronic commerce is creating jobs and economic growth, expanding customer choice, and making U.S. firms more competitive in global markets. We would not want duplicative, discriminatory or inappropriate taxation by 30,000 different state and local tax jurisdictions to stunt the development of what President Clinton has called "the most promising new economic opportunity in decades" (Summers 1998).

Lawrence Summers, then deputy secretary of the Department of the Treasury, goes on to expand upon the potential benefits of this new economy. In his statement before the Senate Committee on Commerce Subcommittee on Communications, Summers (1997) states that the internet and electronic commerce 'will provide an integrated collection of low-cost, reliable services to handle tremendous volumes of business and technical transactions and to amass, analyze, and control large quantities of data'. He also describes how the internet will increase efficiency, facilitate re-engineering, and increase overall productivity, as well as allow smaller firms to enter into markets previously unavailable to them. As a result:

> In order to encourage the growth of this technology and the resulting social and economic benefits, it is crucial that government take a responsible role toward regulating and taxing the Internet. In the realm of international taxation, the Administration's key objectives are: no new Internet taxes, neutrality in taxing electronic commerce as compared with economically similar transactions and

above all, no tax rules at the national, international, federal or subfederal levels which inappropriately impede the full developments of these exciting new technologies (Summers 1997).

Of course, the U.S. position does not imply no taxation whatsoever, but rather that old tax laws be adapted to work on the new electronic economy.

> At the same time, we must not allow the Internet to become a tax haven that drains the sales tax and other revenues that our states and cities need to educate our children and keep our streets safe. In conjunction with this moratorium, we need to establish a commission that will explore the longer-term tax issues raised by electronic commerce, and develop a policy framework that is fair to states and localities while allowing the Internet to earn its fair place in the ever-changing business world (Summers 1997).

Although the U.S. administration does not advocate new taxes, it states that the developed tax policy must address several issues. Indeed, the white paper touches upon the relevant economic and tax issues effectively (United States Department of Treasury 1996). One such issue is adherence to the principle of neutrality, which rejects the imposition of new or additional taxes on electronic transactions, but rather requires the tax system to treat similar income equally regardless of its source. The forces of digital money and their value must also be addressed by tax policy, as well as the issue of tracing transactions using such money and establishing a basis for taxation. Taxation policy must also accommodate the fact that this 'new economy' is 'radically decentralized' and has 'no central control'; users and intermediaries have no real power over whether the information they seek, use, or send travels within or across national boundaries, including information involved in commercial transactions. Furthermore, because of the increased case of excluding banks and other financial institutions from electronic business dealings, the lack of such intermediaries in transactions eliminates some of the 'reporting requirements' used to provide information for taxation. Another concern is that the physical location of a user and computer can be quite different from the domain or address of the user's Web site or e-mail address. There is no regulation or central control of access to the internet. Still another issue is that contents of messages or transactions are unknown until deciphered from their binary form, so that a letter is indistinct from a monetary transaction. Most of the remaining discussion in the white paper dealt with U.S. policy, the ascendancy of residence-based taxation over service-based taxation, and the important role played by international treaties in making this principle consistent.

The U.S. Treasury white paper was among the first serious attempts to address some of the major issues arising out of this new economy. As Reuven Avi-Yonah (1997, 523) states:

> Treasury should be commended for undertaking the extremely important task of being the first tax administration to set forth its views on the tax policy implications of global electronic commerce. Published in November 1996, the White Paper represents the best summary so far of the international tax issues raised by electronic commerce. It provides fewer answers than questions, but that is natural in a document officially labeled a 'discussion paper', and given the current state of the scholarship on this issue. As a framework for discussion, it is excellent.

Avi-Yonah points out that most of the issues are still unresolved and implies that many of the proposals should be challenged in seeking a legal framework for the new economy. Indeed, it would be a mistake to accept the proposals put forth by the U.S. administration without serious questioning. Charles McLure (1997, 274) points out that it may be difficult to accomplish the objective of no new taxes or tariffs on electronic commerce. Laws would have to be 'rethought' in order to apply to electronic commerce. Any current tax laws that could apply are inappropriate, even without the added dimension of electronic commerce. Furthermore, McLure states that 'no new taxes' is not the right answer, especially given that unilateral action will not be enough but would require international co-operation and treaties as well as intranational co-operation (that is, among the states in the United States) for practical taxation to take place (pp. 295–297).

McLure discusses many of the issues mentioned by the Treasury white paper and potential ways of addressing them from the perspective of tax law. For example, on the necessity of tax neutrality, he points out that differentiated taxation among sources delivering the same end results (whether information or more tangible products) would help to bias markets against one method over another, thus making the playing field uneven. However, McLure goes further by stating that electronic commerce makes a level playing field less feasible because of the jurisdictional issues relating to who collects taxes, who pays, and what requires payment. Using the current standard for taxation (that is, the U.S. standard, which uses nexus or physical presence) would make it difficult for small businesses to comply, as the complicated process of interpreting tax laws based on current standards favours larger corporations able to afford tax departments that could make sense of various tax jurisdictions and creates compliance problems for smaller business (McClure 1997, 295–296). This last point must be taken into consideration together with the fact that many aspects of the new economy are cross-border in nature, especially given that current technology facilitates the spread of production over various locations, thus rendering jurisdictional questions more problematic. It would seem, therefore, that 'it is essential that actions taken to address the taxation of electronic commerce be multilateral' and aware of the limitation of current standards and methods (p. 277).

The necessity of multilateral agreement on internet taxation is a direct result of the changing economic system among developed states. Thomas Lairson and David Skidmore (1997) offer a useful description of these changes, based on five major developments of ongoing change: rapid growth in financial transactions, rapid growth in trade among transnational firms, rapid growth in foreign direct investment (FDI), decline in market segmentation, and the global diffusion of technology and ideas — essentially the broader systemic transformation in which electronic commerce finds itself. Changes in markets and methods of production have meant production lines have spread out globally or across the 'operating zones' of multinational corporations (MNCs); this globalisation of production accompanies the post-Fordist methods of production such as just-in-time and small-batch production over mass production. These changes therefore mean greater integration of economies among states, which in turn suggests greater co-operation. The current co-operation on internet taxation could be considered part of such co-operation. However, it also results in more and more states and their respective economies competing for the same markets; thus competition and conflict also flow from this process. As Lairson and Skidmore state, with regard to financial markets the movement toward liberalisation was prompted mostly by competition for foreign capital and attempts to attract it rather than from efforts to improve the efficiency and smoothness of the system (pp. 96–105). The state's motivation for economic openness and co-operation is self-gain, which should be reflected in choices that obtain a beneficial result for all.

Co-operation on internet taxation and electronic commerce in general is needed to create benefit for all states involved, but there is the possibility of thwarting any co-operative attitude if certain issues and possibilities are overlooked. To the credit of the leading economies, multilateral co-operation is well underway; governments are seeking ways to facilitate the growth of an economy based on information technology (IT). As explained in *Electronic*

Commerce and the Role of the WTO (WTO 1998, 40), the Organisation for Economic Co-operation and Development (OECD) has set forth guidelines for internet taxation, as follows:

1. *The system should be equitable:* taxpayers in similar situations who carry out similar transactions should be taxed in the same way.
2. *The system should be simple:* administrative costs for the tax authorities and compliance costs for the taxpayers should be minimised as much as possible.
3. *The rules should provide certainty for the taxpayer:* the tax consequences of a transaction should be known in advance so taxpayers can know what is to be taxed and when, and where the tax is accounted for.
4. *Any system adopted should be effective:* the system should produce the right amount of tax at the right time and minimise the potential for tax evasion and avoidance.
5. *Economic distortions should be avoided:* corporate decision makers should be motivated by commercial rather than tax considerations.
6. *The system should be sufficiently flexible and dynamic:* the system must ensure that the tax rules keep pace with technological and commercial developments.
7. *The tax base should be shared among countries:* any tax arrangements adopted domestically and any changes to existing international taxation principles should be structured to facilitate fair sharing of the internet tax base, particularly among developed and developing countries.

However, although the OECD makes these suggestions, it acknowledges the problems that will face taxation of electronic commerce, especially in the area of value-added taxes across borders and the difficulty of assigning responsibility to the party who must pay. The OECD has found that services traded between countries lead either to no taxation or to double taxation; if no new methods or new taxes are devised, worse could happen with the spread of electronic commerce. Solutions have been proposed in light of the agreed moratorium on new taxes. The United Nations Commission on International Trade Law (UNCITRAL) is working on a 'model law' for electronic commerce in order to strengthen the framework for electronic commerce, and self-regulation and model contracts have also been proposed (WTO 1998, 33, 37).[1] Whatever the solution, it must not only meet the requirements of helping the new economy of electronic commerce grow, but must also look broadly into the future. States must not get caught up in the rhetoric of unlimited growth and lose sight of their sovereignty, healthy social and political development, and the health of the old economy and traditional engines of growth.

It sometimes appears that other developed countries feel the need to catch up to the United States and not let the U.S.-led IT bandwagon ride away without them. This attitude is partially reflected in their ready agreement to U.S.-influenced ideas of free competition and programs that expand the use of IT and keep emerging economies from being taxed or subject to tariffs. Thierry Vedel (1997), writing about France's 'information superhighway' policy, sees a notable difference between the U.S. and European approach to the information superhighway — the infrastructure necessary for the new economy. The U.S. view professes to take into consideration social and democratic considerations (or improvements emerging from the information superhighway — although not offering a real analysis of detriments) than the more commercially oriented European view. Also, the process in Europe has been more closed and technocratically driven than in the U.S. Its closed nature was exemplified by the fact that during a G7 meeting in Brussels in February 1995, labour organisations and some political parties held a counter-summit to denounce the lack of democratic input, the possible social costs, and the way future decisions would be made and who (technocrats, large business and industry) would influence those decisions. Vedel concludes that 'the diffusion of information services depends not only on technical infrastructure but also on social infrastructures' (p. 340). Discussions such as the taxation of electronic commerce must take place in light of such considerations. The issue of internet taxation determines not only the economic biases that will affect the development of e-commerce, but also whether the regulation will be imposed by the economy, insofar as it would further limit the political and social actions of individual states.

Individual states must consider serious questions about how to pursue the goals of this new economy. Government must provide or facilitate the construction of the infrastructure necessary for the new IT-based economy; aside from the private sector's direct participation, this infrastructure must receive funding to some extent (Kahin and Wilson 1997). Where does such funding come from? Government initiatives ultimately depend on tax revenue, but without effective (and potentially new) taxation on electronic commerce, the old economy will provide much of that funding. Although politicians and technophiles may state that the old economy will only benefit and be integrated into the IT-based economy, such a guarantee is not certain. This view represents a potential and troubling bias against more traditional economic sectors.

Furthermore, in most of the literature on economic development and growth-seeking economic policy, increases in technological content and the resulting increases in productivity do not necessarily translate into more employment opportunities. As seen in developing countries that expanded their manufacturing productivity through new technology, productivity increased per unit but lowered the amount of labour needed. Would such an outcome occur in an IT economy? What do the new economy and the accompanying tax proposals mean for the individual welfare state and its maintenance? If the welfare state is still considered a valid choice (and it would be difficult to see some of the European states relinquishing this idea), the framework of the new economy must be developed in such a way that preserves the ability of individual states to determine domestic policy. Would new taxation or altered taxation be needed to achieve those social and political goals that fall under government responsibility?

It is up to the state to maintain the stability of the economy, as much as possible within its power, under current and future systemic circumstances. The growth of the IT economy challenges this ability in a very direct way. As an example, Ellen Frost (1998) cites the 1997 Thailand banking crisis in 1997, which negatively affected financial markets world-wide. Frost points out that U.S. Federal Reserve chairman Alan Greenspan acknowledged that 'the new technology increases "systemic risk" by creating the mechanisms for mistakes to "ricochet" throughout the global financial system'. Another example of market instability made easier (although in the guise of econo-democratic access to markets) comes from South Korea. On-line day trading in South Korea has increased rapidly, in many cases undercutting stock brokers, but is considered akin to video-gaming or gambling rather than business transactions (*Economist* 2000, 85). The problem is not that more people participate, but that more uninformed people are participating, which renders profits more uncertain, speculation more likely, and the stock market 'herd mentality' more likely to cause peaks and falls. Would this not justify a new tax on stock market transactions or financial-market capital transactions, which could create a fund for compensation or at least stabilise market activity through a participatory cost? It seems unwise to leave a national economy vulnerable to the whims of internet day traders and financial speculators around the world in order to maintain maximum market openness.

The questions that states must consider with regard to the IT economy can be distilled into one of how much sovereignty must be forfeited for the benefit of developing these economic conditions. Stephen Kobrin (1998) sees the new economy or the 'third industrial revolution' (characterised by intensive application of information technology, along with post-Fordist production) pushing the international economic system away from the state-dominated system to a neo-medieval series of authorities and loyalties. In reference to electronic commerce and globalisation, national and domestic laws cannot capture the complexities of fast transactions, digital interaction, and cyberspace (which has no real geographical boundaries). In order to cope, the state-centric system (which Kobrin calls a historical outlier) must give way to a system along medieval lines where there are overlapping loyalties, a push for some central authority (with international organisations taking on the role of the medieval church), and the emergence of new actors that blur the lines between public and private. States must consider any alterations to the international system that weaken the state and weigh them against their own motivations for embracing the new economy, as is currently the fashion, in a manner that lets it run as freely as possible.

The possible motivations behind the Treasury white paper and the U.S. administration's desire to pursue open and tax-free (in regard to new taxation) electronic commerce offer a point of departure for comparing other nation-states' position on e-commerce. According to *Electronic Commerce and the Role of the WTO* (WTO 1998, 25), 70 percent of Web sites are located in the United States, 8 percent are in Canada, and 14 percent are in Europe.[2] More interestingly, the report states that 85 percent of internet-generated revenue world-wide in 1996–97 was generated in the United States, indicating a preliminary U.S. advantage in e-commerce. Frost (1998) discusses the U.S. trade advantage in high-technology products, which allows the United States to cut down its trade deficit in other sectors. Furthermore, she states, 'as of 1996, the surplus in U.S. services exports offsets about one-third of the deficit in merchandise trade, reducing the overall deficit from U.S. \$170.2 billion to U.S. \$111 billion'. She notes that the internet and its facilitation of commerce, especially in services in which the U.S. has advantages, could help further reduce the U.S. deficit. However, she also observes that U.S. policy is more careful in areas that could negatively affect U.S. interests such as copyright laws and security (as in encryption technology). U.S. policy makers do not hesitate in at least slowing the process down on these issues. Of course, this national advantage has not prevented conflict over tax jurisdiction within the United States between the state and federal governments. In an interview with the *Journal of International Affairs*, Ira Magaziner said the federal government is trying to dissuade state governments (which have protested the *Internet Tax Freedom Act* through the National Association of Governors) from creating new taxes on the internet, while the states reply that the Act infringes on their sovereignty (Cutter and Costa 1998). Magaziner's final statement on this question is relevant both specifically and in a broader sense internationally:

At the federal level, we have an easier job because we have an income tax-based system. So basically we have a corporate profit tax already: As electronic commerce grows, companies do more business, they make more money and the government automatically gets its share. But if you have a sales tax or a valueadded tax (VAT) system — as states and other countries do — then you need to find some way to develop a uniform, tax-neutral system (Cutter and Costa 1998).

The European VAT system may therefore have larger adjustment costs than the U.S. federal government.

In light of these potential problems, which introduce the possibility of conflict between states, what will happen to the current atmosphere of co-operation among developed countries on the development of the new economy? One behavioural view is that co-operation among nation-states is driven more by fear of loss rather than by potential for gain (Stein and Pauly 1992). Loss is felt more strongly and therefore compels co-operation. Fear of losing the benefits of electronic commerce and possibly stifling this new economy has prompted the current co-operation. Were it not for this fear, unilateral activities that more openly seek a competitive advantage, as in other sectors of the economy, would be pursued. The need to connect systems and develop a common infrastructure is necessary in order to avoid losing the benefits of the IT economy.

However, the current attitude toward the new economy, which only seeks economic growth and maximum stoking of this new economic furnace, may create further concerns. The potential consequences of this lack of peripheral vision or broader concerns could in fact squash the current spirit of co-operation. Individual countries or small groups of states might possibly reject a multilateral agreement on open access and electronic commerce, or they might refuse to co-operate and choose to assert themselves through unilateral policy; although it may be difficult or self-damaging to penalise electronic commerce through discriminatory taxes or tariffs, it would not prevent a unilateral backlash from other sectors of the economy. A second possibility is that the new facilitation of speculation and market fluctuation — the ease of instability — would invite a general backlash and multilateral over-regulation of the new economy that would overcompensate and penalise the positive aspects of the IT economy along with the negative ones. Again, there is no evidence of such a trend at present, but the possibility exists, as is illustrated the complaints by the U.S. states about their sovereignty and the recent G8 concerns over a technology gap. An atmosphere of co-operation prevails among the developed countries on developing this new economy and harnessing its potential, in other words to avoid the loss of its full potential if no action were taken. This spirit of co-operation must be tapped and used to its fullest benefit, not only to create economic growth but also to determine the social and political concerns and subsequently install the necessary systemic remedies.

Systemic remedies are indeed possible and the spirit of co-operation may be used fruitfully if one fundamental but often overlooked fact is kept in mind: the current features of the internet and electronic commerce 'are not indispensable parts of the operation of the internet, and some or all of them may be changed by government regulation if that is deemed necessary to achieve relevant goals of taxation' (Helleiner 1998). For example, problems arising from electronic money could be solved if states co-operate and allow only state-issued electronic legal tender to be used for the purpose of e-commerce. Furthermore, with regard to electronic money and the financial markets, although liberalisation decisions and technological advances have been occurring together, to say that they must co-exist is unconvincing. The sovereign state can and does regulate such markets and has done so more effectively than naysayers have thought possible, as illustrated by adequacy standards stipulated for the G10 by the 1988 Basle Capital Accord and regulation written by the OECD's Financial Action Task Force (FATF) to control cross-border financial flows to prevent money laundering. Although these examples exist because of international co-operation, sovereign states took the initiative and co-operated in order to enhance their control over activities within their territory. Electronic transactions leave more records and traces than do cash transactions because of the use of electronic clearing houses, or chokepoints, through which most transactions must pass. Consequently, effective regulation, along with enforcement, can occur in the IT economy. International co-operation could also facilitate tax collection by way of a mandatory membership, with or without a token payment, to a particular Web site or interface where a client conducts 'cyber-business'; becoming a member would require the registration of the client's residence or address substantiated by official documentation such as a driver's licence or business licence (Helleiner 1998).

There are a myriad of ways to solve or prevent the concerns about taxation of e-commerce. Acceptance of the 'no new taxes, no tariffs' moratorium without hesitation could well lead to some the problems expressed in this chapter becoming manifest, possibly resulting in a default position of 'no taxes' (in order to avoid difficulty). This would benefit no one. The U.S. administration's initiative deserves merit for putting forth issues stemming from the new economy as well as taking an initial policy stance. However, the initiative should be built upon. Current technological constraints and abilities for regulation and taxation should be weighed against the economic, political, and social merits of regulation and a resulting framework should be established so as to do justice to one of the most co-operative periods in international relations. Surely the G7/8 members, as a group and as individuals, could cut a path toward a fruitful, stable, and systemically integrated 'new economy.'

Notes

1   Canada has been experimenting with private tax collection, wherein it is the responsibility of the delivery or courier service to collect the required tax per transaction. This method allegedly makes logistics simpler; however, its success is unclear.
2   However, the criteria used by the WTO to determine geographical designation are not given.

References

Avi-Yonah, Reuven (1997). 'International Taxation of Electronic Commerce'. *Tax Law Review*, vol. 52, no. 3.
Cutter, Ann Grier, and Len A. Costa (1998). 'The Framework for Global Electronic Commerce: A Policy Perspective. Ira C. Magaziner'. *Journal of International Affairs* vol. 51, no. 2 (Spring), pp. 527–538 [electronic version cited].
Frost, Ellen L. (1998). 'Horse Trading in Cyberspace: U.S. Trade Policy in the Information Age'. *Journal of International Affairs* vol. 51, no. 2 (Spring), pp. 473–496 [electronic edition cited].
Helleiner, Eric (1998). 'Electronic Money: A Challenge to the Sovereign State?' *Journal of International Affairs* vol. 51, no. 2 (Spring), pp. 387–409 [electronic version cited].
Kahin, Brian, and Ernest Wilson, eds. (1997). *National Information Infrastructure Initiatives*. MIT Press, Cambridge, MA.
Kobrin, Stephen J. (1998). 'Back to the Future: Neomedievalism and the Postmodern Digital World Economy'. *Journal of International Affairs* vol. 51, no. 2 (Spring), pp. 361–386 [electronic version cited].
Lairson, Thomas, and David Skidmore (1997). *International Political Economy*. Harcourt Brace, Toronto.
McLure, Charles E. (1997). 'Taxation of Electronic Commerce: Economic Objectives, Technological Constraints, and Tax Laws'. *Tax Law Review* vol. 52, no. 3.
'Online, of Course' (2000). *Economist* 10–16 June.

Stein, Janice Gross and Louis W. Pauly (1992). 'Choosing to Cooperate: How States Avoid Loss'. *International Journal* vol. 47, no. 2 (Spring/Special Issue).

Summers, Lawrence H. (1997). 'Statement of Lawrence H. Summers Deputy Secretary Department of the Treasury before the Committee on Commerce Subcommittee on Communications United States Senate'. <www.treas.gov/press/releases/pr052297a.html> (March 2001).

Summers, Lawrence H. (1998). 'Letter to Speaker of the House', 23 June. <www.treas.gov/cc/062398.htm> (March 2001).

United States Department of Treasury (1996). 'Selected Tax Policy Implications of Global Electronic Commerce'. Office of Tax Policy, November. <www.treas.gov/taxpolicy/library/internet.txt> (March 2001).

Vedel, Thierry (1997). 'Information Superhighway Policy in France: The End of High Tech Colbertism?' In B. Kahin and E. Wilson, eds., *National Information Infrastructure Initiatives*. MIT Press, Cambridge, MA.

World Trade Organization (1998). *Electronic Commerce and the Role of the WTO*. World Trade Organization, Geneva.

5 Transparent End-Use Technology and the Changing Nature of Security Threats

GEORGE M. VON FURSTENBERG

Changing transparency relations — who or what is exposed to penetrating scrutiny to whom for whose purpose — can have revolutionary implications in society. These are ignored by those official bodies that keep calling for more transparency in many areas, including some under their own control, and for less decision making behind closed doors. Other participants in the public debate, such as nongovernmental organisations (NGOs) and protest groups, are not naive about these implications. When they shadow international meetings from Seattle to Singapore, and call for greater transparency in Davos, Washington, Okinawa, and Prague or wherever the world's most powerful meet, they know that changing transparency relations is not just a matter of procedure but of substance. This is the first point of this chapter.

The second point is that transparency relations can be changed not only by political influence and through shifting rules and conventions but also through technological developments. Indeed, there is just now a momentous leap that is bringing entirely new capabilities to people outside established hierarchies. Today's information technology (IT) offers smart end users consumption bundles to take off the shelf or to download, as well as interactive and invasive capabilities they never had before. Because this empowerment is indiscriminate — no security clearance or professional appointment or code of ethics required — it also increases the risks to the information and communications technology (ICT) systems on which the world increasingly relies. Technologically driven changes in transparency have thus become a major security issue.

Official international recognition of the threat to national security posed by cyber-terrorism has been slow. An Associated Press report by Angela Doland released over the internet on 5 July 2000, in advance of the Okinawa Summit, states that Interpol currently has a half-dozen investigators devoted to internet crime. The Okinawa Charter on Global Information Society (released 22 July

2000) contained only a passing endorsement of measures against cyber-crime 'as set out in the OECD Guidelines for Security of Information Systems' (paragraph 8; see Appendix C). The G8 Communiqué released the next day also welcomed 'the results and the momentum created by the Government/ Industry Dialogue on Safety and Confidence in Cyberspace in Paris' and looked forward to conferences on high-tech crime planned for Berlin and Tokyo (paragraph 44; see Appendix B). However, actions against excessive bank secrecy and money laundering, and not against cyber-terrorism *per se,* were the chief concern.

Transparency of high-powered applications of ICT enables end users by giving them an instant global reach and possible impact. Cyber-terrorists are empowered when they can wreak destruction on a massive scale *incognito* or with little fear of retribution. Hence technological transparency has a dark side, one that is ignored in upbeat assessments that credit IT with many of the same beneficial effects as political, social, and legal transparency. For instance, the Okinawa Charter referred only to calls for work to realise the potential of IT to 'strengthen democracy, increase transparency and accountability in governance, promote human rights, enhance cultural diversity, and to foster international peace and stability' (paragraph 2). This is not what cyber-terrorists, enabled by the new technological transparency, have in mind.

Strip Poker

People have all kinds of relations with each other and in society. Transparency is one of these relations, because it defines a condition not only of those who have this quality but also of how it appears to others who might use it. Technically, it is an interactive relation between a subject and an indirect object to whom the subject is transparent. This interaction, as between a central bank and the general public forming expectations about monetary policy, does not need to involve transactions, contracts, or other forms of direct dealings between the parties interested in each other's transparency. Even then, transparency relations may be so important that changing them shakes the foundations of power. This makes transparency a fighting word in the social sciences: altering who is transparent to whom and how much thus has revolutionary potential. As the game theorist Roy Gardner (1995, 74) has written: 'Many times in a game with imperfect information a player has information that might be valuable to an opponent and detrimental to the player if it were to be revealed. In such cases that player has a strong incentive to keep that information secret'. Even auction markets, which economists like to credit with efficient and impersonal market-clearing price formation, do not tell all. Big players who want to acquire major works of art at auction take elaborate steps to hide their interest from others precisely because the results of the bidding might be affected. For related reasons, there is a real question, as discussed by Robert Bloomfield and Maureen O'Hara (2000), of whether transparent dealers can survive when faced with direct competition from less transparent dealers.

For this reason, people choose to cover their tracks when stalking an objective and protect their privacy with a poker face. Learning to be unpredictable is a sustainable strategy against smart opponents in a number of areas. When people must submit to questions about their status and concerns or comply with generally accepted accounting standards or disclosure requirements in their business dealings, they try to confine their exposure to their lawyer, banker, or tax accountant, unless public disclosure is mandatory. When baring their bodies, minds, and souls to their doctors, psychiatrists, or even trusted journalists, patients and whistleblowers expect their confidences to be respected. There are protections against forced self-incrimination in a civilised society and, unlike show trials, trials are public to make the system of justice transparent and not to strip the accused of all defences. The biochemical production of transparency, for instance by the forced administration of 'truth serum', is an abomination.

Technological developments also may help break down information asymmetries by force of new technical capabilities even if there is no change in the cultural consensus about the proper limits of transparency. Such developments now contribute to making technologically unsophisticated individuals potentially more transparent without adequate compensation, that is, against their will. Because of the ICT revolution in the delivery of payment, ordering, and communication services and in a range of tests, individuals leave ever more records of where they go and stay, what they buy, rent, and click on, and how they are diagnosed, priced, rated, and evaluated. Too often, these records can readily be retrieved, aggregated, and disseminated to generate a variety of profiles for interested parties all over the world. Robert Scheer (2000) provides a vivid picture of our exposure from within the internet community. Any national law that inhibits profiting from unauthorised use of information that should by law be treated as confidential provides only limited comfort. First of all, targets for prosecution are difficult to identify and, second of all, injunctions tend to prove ineffective against rapidly multiplying and self-propagating foreign and domestic targets. Thus, opportunities for abuse are growing exponentially and without effective checks.

Instead of assuming uncritically that the more transparency there is in any one sector the better, attention should focus on large imbalances of transparency and its new technological foundations. Maintaining privacy through privileged information is not just aesthetically gratifying or indulging a peculiar human taste but is essential for physical and spiritual survival. For persons or organisations to be transparent means that they are conditionally predictable — faced with this, they will do that. Hence they are manipulable — an easy mark — as long as they are not aware of their exploitability and do not react to this sorry condition by ceasing to be quite so transparent.

Transparency is not the simple and seemingly costless public good that it appears to be when it is prescribed in ever higher doses against a broad spectrum of social ills. A fair sampling of the prescriptions, usually issued without regard to possible side effects, can be drawn from George Kopits and Jon Craig (1998), Felipe Larraín and José Tavares (1999), the Institute of International Finance (1999), G24 (2000), and the International Monetary Fund (IMF) (IMF 2000a, 2000b). Transparency's trendy indications, bordering on social quackery, are seemingly endless. They now include elitism everywhere, exclusivity, and bureaucratic secrecy, for instance in decision making by international organisations, and autocracy in government and in other organisations except, of course, the saintly NGOs. The list goes on with discrimination, corruption, injustice, and unpleasant surprises leading to financial crises. Indeed, the only metric for transparency used in empirical testing (see, for instance, Goldsmith 1999) is based on Transparency International's Corruption Perceptions Index rating countries by degree of corruption on a scale of 10 (highly clean) to 0 (highly corrupt). The list of indications, like that for Aspirin, keeps getting longer, making transparency appear just as cheap and well tolerated by those to whom it is administered.

Gorbachev's Lenin and God and Eve

Those who call for more transparency rarely also press for its more equal distribution or mutual provision. Far from being a broad-spectrum remedy that is easy to take for all, providing for greater transparency that is one-sided can be social dynamite. It empowers one party against the other, like American settlers intentionally giving smallpox-infected blankets to unwitting Indians. Mikhail Gorbachev gave centre stage to the transforming power of greater openness when he wrote in *Perestroika* (1987, 75–76) in a way that now appears in a new light (cf. von Furstenberg 2000):

> *More Light to Glasnost!* We want more openness about public affairs in every sphere of life ... Truth is the main thing. Lenin said: More Light!
>
> Let the Party know everything! ... People are becoming increasingly convinced that glasnost is an effective form of public control over the activities of all government bodies, without exception, and a powerful lever in correcting shortcomings.

What Gorbachev was hiding in this broken chain of reasoning was that Lenin and glasnost do not mix. A party that wants to know everything seeks to exercise complete control. So people must know little about the inner workings of the party lest they frustrate its control over them. By aiming a glaring light, disinformation, and propaganda at people, the party purposefully tries to keep them isolated and confused. Seeking to know one's government and what is really going on without being part of its inner circle may lead to being charged with treason. Knowing exactly what Big Brother is looking for, and why, might allow secret resisters to dissimulate effectively, hoping that Big Brother could be blindsided.

In an ideal democratic society based on civil liberties, by contrast, it is the political top, the agents, who are transparent to the bottom. The many principals would never be individually transparent to their collective agents. Rather these few key agents should be transparent to their many individual principals, and transparency would not all flow in the opposite direction as under Orwellian control. The secret ballot, for instance, is an institution under which election procedures and the determination of election outcomes and their consequences are perfectly transparent and binding on politicians while the ballot choices of individual voters are not transparent. Voters may have identified themselves or registered as members of particular parties, interest groups, or lobbies, but even then it is not possible for them to prove for whom they actually voted. Secrecy of the ballot is mandatory and inalienable for their own protection as a group.

It is not just communist socialism that has an obsession with transparency relations management. Rather, many belief systems and social or political ideologies are predicated on a grid of transparency relations to be disturbed only at one's peril. When forethinking Prometheus took back the fire of knowledge and civilisation from heaven, he ended up chained to a rock by Zeus and wrecked by the painful loss of his liver that was re-enacted daily. Likewise, when the symbols of the basic human quest, Adam and Eve, tried to seize knowledge from the tree to gain self-possession and empowerment, they, like Lucifer, suffered dearly for wanting 'to be like God'. As characterised by

Thomas More (1965 [1516]), the vast majority of believers, perhaps not only in *Utopia*, have since taken the much safer view that there is a single divine power, unknown, eternal, infinite, inexplicable, and quite beyond the grasp of the human mind.

No Giveaways

Asymmetric transparency relations, and their defence, may be as central to religion as they are to the institutional architecture and *modus operandi* of secular society. In the latter, all parties generally know what the prevailing transparency relations are and seek to change them to their own advantage. Any development that restructures these relations redistributes power and wealth, advantage and risks, making the field of transparency relations a battleground.

Sometimes a group voluntarily allows itself to become more transparent in its motives and operations in return for another group doing the same. A high level of transparency of principals tends to be voluntary only in those limited areas of equality where individuals are willing to trade greater mutual transparency with those who concern them by making full and complete disclosures to each other, particularly in areas of perceived strength. Building trust and thereby reducing information and transaction costs, and lowering risk premiums may be the reward, not to mention any comfort in sharing, empathy, and intimacy derived from the social part of human nature, which economic paradigms generally fail to grasp.

Horizontal transparency pacts also may occur between organisations and governments, for instance in the area of arms control verification or contract and treaty compliance. Even 'unilateral disarmament' may have its rewards in some areas. Thus agents may opt for truthfully and completely revealing their goals, procedures, and track record to acquire a good reputation and credibility with principals and other agents. However, the relation between a subject and the different parties that benefit from its transparency remains typically adversarial because their interests conflict. Accepted conventions or transparency codes are designed to arbitrate and to dull the edge of conflicts about moving in on any of the information asymmetries that are 'pervasive in markets and life', as Gardner (1995, 239) puts it.

Like so often in economics, where increasing opportunity costs and declining marginal benefits assure interior solutions, 'the more the better' does not hold for transparency. Rather, it has an interior optimum. Hence, there can be either too much or too little transparency, or transparency can be misdirected.

Transparency should not be pushed to the limit but should be supplied and consumed to the point of balance between its marginal costs and benefits, and between risk and return, in its different applications.

For example, the current Director General of the World Trade Organization (WTO), Mike Moore (2000a; 2000b; see also Chapter 12), like some other heads of international organisations, makes speeches about increasing transparency as if doing so was overdue and all to the good. He has promised to cut down on the use of the much-criticised 'Green Room' or to make the practice useless by lifting its exclusivity. With the Green Room widely used by NGOs as an ugly symbol of opaqueness and privilege, he vows to increase openness and equal access in an organisation that has 'no secrets'. Being asked to the Green Room used to mean that selected powerful members, principally the United States and the European Union (EU), were invited to negotiate among themselves and to come to terms on particularly sticky issues that could then be submitted to the rest of the membership. Presumably, the Director General's predecessors felt that granting a little privacy and exclusivity could be an efficient way to overcome stalemate. A director general may surely choose to dispense with the practice but not without some cost: Having more transparent stalemates, and more of them, perhaps is not of any great net benefit.

While calls for greater transparency are frequently echoed either in an uncritical or in a cowardly and pandering way by international agencies, some qualifications have begun to be asserted in the best of them. For instance, the Code of Good Practices on Transparency in Monetary and Financial Policies, which was adopted in 1999 by what is now known as the International Monetary and Financial Committee (IMFC), provides a useful definition of transparency. It also shows that giving away transparency can be problematic. In the document, agency transparency is defined as 'an environment in which the objectives of policy, its legal, institutional, and economic framework, policy decisions and their rationale, data and information ... and the terms of agencies' accountability, are provided to the public on an understandable, accessible and timely basis' (International Monetary Fund 1999, paragraph 3). While generally advocating such transparency, the code, developed by the International Monetary Fund (IMF), then proceeds to show awareness that there is a cost. For instance, granting transparency can lower decision-making quality and create problems of its own, if those to whom it is given choose to benefit improperly from this gift. They can do so by playing upon exploitable aspects of agency behaviour that has become conditionally predictable:

The rationale for limiting some types of disclosure arises because it could adversely affect the decision-making process and the effectiveness of policies ... For example, extensive disclosure requirements about internal policy discussion on money and exchange market operations might disrupt markets, constrain the free flow of discussion by policymakers, or prevent the adoption of contingency plans ... Additional concerns could be posed by some aspects of the transparency ... Moral hazard, market discipline, and financial market stability considerations may justify limiting both the content and timing of the disclosure of some corrective actions and emergency lending decisions, and information pertaining to market and firm-specific conditions. In order to maintain access to sensitive information from market participants, there is also a need to safeguard the confidentiality and privacy of information on individual firms (commonly referred to as "commercial confidentiality") (IMF 1999, paragraphs 8–9).

Charles Enoch, Peter Stella, and May Khamis (1997), Frederic Mishkin (1999), and Andrew Hughes Hallett and Nicola Viegi (2000) also consider different realms of transparency, such as transparency of final targets or economic transparency, and procedural and political transparency, of central banks. They find that central banks need not be bound by rules or conditionally predictable in every respect if they are to remain credible and effective managers in a world full of surprises whose citizens care about end results.

Implications of Technology Becoming Transparent to End Users

Because transparency is valued by each in others and is normally costly to provide oneself, it is valuable to withhold and not to give away without adequate compensation. Instead of providing such compensation, force is often used to require transparency of some for the benefit of others. Principals, in turn, may require their agents, such as institutions and governments, to be transparent and accountable lest they exercise undelegated powers over them. Transparency of technologies, as of agents, also empowers principals. For technologies that become transparent because they are based on publicly available knowledge, open access, and free use may have characteristics of public goods. Since the principle of exclusion does not apply to such goods, transparent high-powered technologies may also lend themselves to uncontrolled, indeed anarchic, abuse. They may be turned by individual private principals against others, or by small groups of terrorist principals against domestic or foreign societies and their vital institutions.

Public accountability, disclosure requirements, and the limits of information sharing often are a matter of law and social policy. But technology can also have dramatic implications for transparency. Two-way mirrors are a good example of transparency being asymmetric, and of subjecting some to the scrutiny of others in a way that may greatly affect their welfare. Such mirrors allow witnesses in a separate room to pick out criminals from a group without being seen to enable positive identifications to be made without undue stress. The latest ICT revolution may have turned tables: Now potential terrorists can look in at their leisure without being identified. Indeed, it appears that the use of high-powered technologies has become far less proprietary and much more easily appropriated, and for many more purposes than in former times. This development has radical implications, addressed in the remainder of this chapter, in both civilian and military spheres.

The lead industries in the late nineteenth and much of the twentieth century had a number of features in common. These features perhaps are best epitomised by the chemical industry and by the chemical engineering that was necessary to exploit chemistry on an industrial scale. Light and heavy chemistry are both famous for being highly capital and research intensive, and their output nearly always requires further processing before reaching the ultimate consumer. Because their output has so many actual and potential applications, producers of heavy chemicals at least, tend to be oriented toward sources of raw material rather than the ultimate consumers' preferences. For decades, oligopolies and cartels dominated the international market and enjoyed extensive patent protection in a number of basic chemicals and pharmaceuticals. Correspondingly, entry was difficult and applied knowledge closely held.

In other words, those physical and biological sciences that became the subject of chemical engineering, nuclear engineering, bioengineering, and genetic engineering generally did not produce anything that consumers could importantly transform or activate by themselves. Much of atomic and nuclear physics, some astrophysics, and broad elements of space science and satellite and radar surveillance technology now have huge investment and accumulation requirements. Because so much expensive capital and interlocking research organisation is required, the traditional defence science establishment naturally is somewhat closed. It is thus protected from easy penetration or outside appropriation of its fruits. Military secrecy acts as a further barrier to intruders.

Today's leading technology, ICT, functions very differently. Instead of producing something in a highly roundabout manner that is ultimately delivered or exported to a final destination for passive consumption, its product is the creation of consumer capabilities and instant global networking on the basis of equal access. In place of huge hardware requirements there are large software requirements. Instead of being protected behind walls of highly and secretively trained expertise, anyone can pitch in with new software, if not with an entirely new operating system. Britain for a time managed to keep India from manufacturing even such comparatively simple products as textiles a few steps up in the value chain, but the United States could not prevent software and internet applications from being developed and entered from anywhere in the world. Rather than maintaining a division between production and consumption and clear product identifications, the consumer becomes an interactive co-producer in multiple information environments. Instead of paying for what you actually get, payment is for access or capabilities more than for any of their realisations.

New Capabilities for Terrorism

Exposure to terrorism has also changed both qualitatively or quantitatively. Bombs and poison gas must be delivered to their target by freelance terrorists still mostly on foot, by vehicle, or by parcel post. Cyber-terrorism instead can use an instant global communication system with self-replicating and forward-proliferation features, like a global neutron cluster bomb, to incapacitate multiple sites indiscriminately without necessarily needing to preposition or to identify and select particular targets.

Making a bomb to blow up the Alfred P. Murray Federal Building in Oklahoma City or obtaining deadly sarin gas for the Tokyo subway riders may take about the same level of sophistication as designing and releasing a deadly computer virus. Twelve people died in the 1995 sarin gas attack and 5500 were injured. The 1993 World Trade Center bombing killed six and injured about 1000; the Oklahoma City bombing in 1995 killed 168 people and injured several hundred more. Partly as a result, from 1995 to 1997, law makers approved more than US$350 million for more than 1000 staff positions at the Federal Bureau of Investigation (FBI) mostly dedicated to fighting such low-tech domestic terrorism. Further suggestive of this mostly backward orientation, the 1996 *Anti-terrorism Act,* in addition to providing US$1 billion for counterterrorism activity, instituted new restrictions on the sale of explosives and made the use of chemical weapons in the United States a crime. From what little is publicly known about Carnivore, the internet wiretap system developed by the FBI, its designated targets are known criminal suspects and organisations, and not potential cyber-terrorists.

Those small groups of terrorists who have, on rare occasions, made active use of the earlier technologies for bomb and gas attacks did only limited damage and got caught. Those who inflict the latest acts of terror with home-made applications of ICT frequently can and have caused damage, due to disruption of essential systems and services, on an incomparably larger human and financial scale, and may well not get caught. They do so by aiming to disrupt a whole range of increasingly interdependent essential systems and services.

The time when industrial accidents like Chernobyl and Bhopal were prone to cause much greater human and material losses than terrorist attacks may well be drawing to a close. In the future, the latter will tend to dwarf the former sources of loss. In 1984, gas leaking from a tank of methyl isocyanate at a plant in Bhopal, India, owned and operated by Union Carbide India Limited, killed about 3800 people and left a roughly equal number with permanent total or partial disabilities. (Union Carbide, while accepting financial responsibility in the amount of almost US$0.5 billion, has disputed the description of the tragedy as an industrial accident since sabotage by a disgruntled employee may have been involved.) When an explosion ripped through reactor No. 4 of the Chernobyl nuclear power plant in Ukraine in 1986, only human error, compounded by a faulty design, could be blamed. Exposure to massive amounts of radiation immediately killed 32 plant workers and firefighters. Thousands more died later from effects of the accident and are still dying, especially in Belarus, while long-term genetic damage may extend the suffering to future generations. By contrast, one estimate has it that computer viruses and hacking will cost businesses world-wide about US$1.6 trillion in 2000 alone, or 2.5 percent of world gross domestic product.

Compared with bombs and intentional releases of poison gas, biological warfare provides a somewhat more applicable slow-motion picture of the massive, intended, and unintended consequences of which cyber-terrorism is capable. In what an encyclopaedia calls the most celebrated case of biological warfare, the siege of Caffa in the Crimea in 1347, the Mongols catapulted bodies of plague victims over the walls of the Genoese defenders. Genoese ships carried the bacillus to Europe, loosing the massive epidemic known as the Black Death, in which about one third of Europe's population perished. The mass of the expiring victims did not know where their deadly affliction had come from and who had willed it for what purpose. Those Mongols who had superior resistance to the plague they helped spread then lived to fight other bloody wars of aggression.

Implications for Defence Planning

It appears, therefore, that the growing reliance on open or penetrable internet technology has begun to change the direction of transparency very much in favour of terrorists, particularly 'private' organisations of terrorists that lack demonstrable support from any established government. Such terrorists are now able to gain anonymous access to advanced system-information resources and to avail themselves of relay and self-propagation mechanisms that allow them to impose significant civilian defence costs on the leading countries, in particular the United States. One of the foremost tasks of international co-operation would therefore be to contribute to the timely anticipation of the growing vulnerability to expert decentralised saboteurs who operate from multiple pseudo- or borrowed-host locations, particularly from within the United States, so as to deny retaliation from any identifiable target to which it could be directed.

Instead of taking the lead in directing more resources to that goal, the U.S. administration, with its reformulated national missile defence (NMD) programme, remains wedded to an obsolete concept of ICT threats. Implementation of this Maginot-line program would be wasteful for the United States because the costs are huge and completion far enough away for the currently envisaged constellation and delivery of threats to be superseded by something different against which antiballistic missile defences are inapplicable. William J. Broad (2000) gives an impression of some of the costs and time schedules:

> The scope of the proposed [national missile defence] project is both challenging and enormous, growing in four steps from an initial 20 missile interceptors in 2005 to a much larger system by 2011. By the time it is complete, the shield would require at least 2 launching sites, 3 command centers, 5 communication relay stations, 15 radars, 29 satellites, 250 underground silos and 250 missile interceptors.
>
> It would be based in Hawaii, Alaska, California, Colorado, North Dakota, Massachusetts, Greenland, Britain and possibly Maine. Two radars [radar stations] would be set up in Asia, possibly in Japan and South Korea. Building it would cost at least $60 billion and running it would take at least 1,455 people ... The first phase alone is supposed to take eight years, the government says, though most experts consider 12 to 16 years a safer pace and less risky.

It certainly is conceivable that any remaining rogue states would like to see acts of terrorism against the United States and other countries. But they cannot be seen as sponsoring such acts on a large scale or as actively providing terrorists with bases of operation for space missile attacks. For launching increasingly miniaturised but nevertheless hugely capital- and co-ordination-intensive traceable land- or sea-based missiles from identifiable platforms and locations against the United States would be a national suicide mission that no government in the world could rationally approve. It would be an extremely expensive and technically complex proposition, requiring decades of concerted preparation not sustainable by suicidal intent. Terrorists could not produce or operate such offensive systems without a significant degree of government co-ordination and complicity, leaving governments nowhere to hide.

Multi-point cyber and biological attacks launched preferably from within the United States, and using unwitting hosts and internet access and replication technology, are far more rational and thus likely. As long as there is a good chance that the perpetrators, or their hidden sponsors or contact organisations, cannot positively be identified and punished, they can settle for diffuse destruction with low expected payoff. The nature of threats changes fundamentally when attack-related new technologies become transparent from below and inexpensive while their potential abusers may know enough to make themselves invisible.

Conclusion

Transparency, like power, is distributive; like positions of power, it does not readily yield to pleas of equality for all. Nor should it yield as easily as many of its preachers demand. The ICT revolution has brought new vulnerabilities and new opportunities. It has added risks and rewards both by changing transparency relationships and by raising the actual and potential transparency services obtained from information systems and new storage, analysis, and communications technologies. While a public good in some respects, in many other respects transparency, like power and monitoring, is divisive: The more transparency the powerful are able to compel from others, the less they need to provide themselves. Hence transparency must be finely balanced, not maximised wherever possible, for the common good.

Any change in the balance, whether driven by new technology, political restructuring, or cultural change, has pervasive consequences for freedom from intimidation and for security. Abrupt changes in political or technical operating regimes and in their transparency requirements create exposure to unaccustomed risks and social stress. While ordinary citizens find their protections against transparency eroded through new technology, the technology itself offers much greater reach and stealth to potential terrorists at low costs. By starting cyber-gang attacks, associating hackers in a frenzy of destruction in which participants rush to play their spontaneously recognised, and not pre-planned or pre-assigned, parts, terror systems may acquire self-organising features while being bent on disorganising. Such self-organising systems, as the management-systems scientist Nikko Georgantzas (forthcoming) has pointed out, can be effective, indeed victorious, precisely because their articulations are inherently nontransparent to outsiders and unpredictable, in at least some respects, even from within.

Perhaps the earlier application to national defence shows how much the distribution and capabilities of intransparency have changed. In its proposed NMD programme, the United States is continuing to develop privileged technology and complex applications that are not transparent to others, including Congress, and whose performance characteristics and rationales are difficult to establish, let alone to scrutinise publicly. The setting therefore follows the cold war pattern of a government-to-government arms race where key officials and the military hold all the cards and no one else may look into them. The fact that no country will enter a contest with the United States when the winner is known beforehand must mean that this race is off, but not that deterrence is successful. It could mean that a different type of contest looms that can inflict deadly harm and great damage by disorganising networks and established systems with much more limited means and ends using technology that initially was a U.S. gift to the world.

The future technology that may be used to damage the United States and other G7 countries will have many inherently transparent, widely, and anonymously accessible and replicable elements, with legitimate and illegitimate, harmless and hostile, foreign and domestic instigators not distinguishable immediately in real time. Trojan-horse threats thus will be privatised, dispersed, proxied, and carried out by electronic infiltration into and from the territory of the party to be attacked. All or most explicitly military or particularly difficult targets will be bypassed. Attacks will aim at mass disruption and not at achieving lasting control, and they will have only diffuse political goals and low required payoff in those regards. Attacks that can be mounted at low cost may be induced by small benefits to 'the cause' of the attacker, but the collateral damage is huge. As with the plague that was sown in Caffa, the damage will be entirely disproportionate, indeed almost irrelevant, to any immediate goals sought. Self-appointed random terrorism will have emerged as the supreme threat to security by the time the NMD system is ready to start its pointless watch for the nation-to-nation ballistic threats that expired in President Ronald Reagan's era.

The new technology is phenomenally important also in another respect. This is perhaps illuminated by the fact that a student with only a little training from a Philippine computer college could cause an estimated US$7 to US$10 billion of damage world-wide from releasing the self-replicating ILOVEYOU virus in May 2000. The presumed perpetrator has not yet confessed or been charged with actually creating the virus and the exact nature of his involvement and culpability, beyond using an unauthorised access device, has yet to be determined at the beginning of 2001. Even so, the fact that a student from a country with generally still poor education infrastructure, with a little specialised instruction, could teach himself to use some aspects of the new technology effectively without needing to understand the technological basis, organisation, or design shows that a fundamental change is underway: Unlike earlier technological breakthroughs, say in metallurgy or the chemical industry, that marked the stages of industrial revolution in manufacturing, the new software-based technology does not offer extended protection for the innovator. It requires little physical capital to tap into, and it is driven by wide-open, end-use applications, and it is versatile. Just as with wireless access to communications and the capture of satellite signals by inexpensive devices, developing countries linking to the internet will be able to leapfrog several stages and levels of infrastructure development. There will be no enduring 'digital divide' between the capabilities for cyber-terrorism based in those countries and those based elsewhere.

Acknowledgements

I am indebted to Nikko Georgantzas, Roy Gardner, and Ernest Scalberg for comments on earlier drafts. Suggestions from participants in the 17 July 2000, Tokyo United Nations University Conference on The Kyushu-Okinawa Summit: The Challenges and Opportunities for the Developing World in the Twenty-First Century are also gratefully acknowledged.

References

Bloomfield, Robert, and Maureen O'Hara (2000). 'Can Transparent Markets Survive'. *Journal of Financial Economics* vol. 55, no. 3, pp. 425–429.

Broad, William J. (2000). 'The Nuclear Shield: Repelling an Attack; A Missile Defense with Limits'. *New York Times*, 30 June, p. A10.

Enoch, Charles, Peter Stella, and May Khamis (1997). 'Transparency and Ambiguity in Central Bank Safety Net Operations'. Working Paper WP/97/138-EAWP/97/138. International Monetary Fund.

G24 (2000). 'Intergovernmental Group of Twenty-Four on International Monetary Affairs Communiqué'. Intergovernmental Group of Twenty-Four on International Monetary Affairs Communiqué. April 15. <www.imf.org/external/np/cm/2000/041500.HTM> (March 2001).

Gardner, Roy (1995). *Games for Business and Economics*. Wiley, New York.

Georgantzas, Nicholas C. (forthcoming). 'Self-Organizing Systems (SOS)'. In M. Warner and J. Kotter, eds., *International Encyclopedia of Business and Management*. Thomson Learning, London.

Goldsmith, Arthur A. (1999). 'Slapping the Grasping Hand: Correlates of Corruption in Emerging Markets'. *American Journal of Economics and Sociology* vol. 58, no. 4, pp. 865–883.

Gorbachev, Mikhail (1987). *Perestroika: New Thinking for Our Country and the World*. Collins, London.

Hughes Hallett, Andrew J. and Nicola Viegi (2000). 'Credibility, Transparency and Asymmetric Information in Monetary Policy'. Prepared at the University of Strathclyde, Glasgow. March.

Institute of International Finance (1999). *Report of the Working Group on Transparency in Emerging Markets Finance. March*. Institute of International Finance, Washington DC.

International Monetary Fund (1999). 'Code of Good Practices on Transparency in Monetary and Financial Policies: Declaration of Principles'. International Monetary Fund, Washington DC.

International Monetary Fund (2000a). 'Recovery from the Asian Crisis and the Role of the IMF'. Recovery from the Asian Crisis and the Role of the IMF. <www.imf.org/external/np/exr/ib/2000/062300.htm> (March 2001).

International Monetary Fund (2000b). 'Report of the Acting Managing Director to the International Monetary and Financial Committee on Progress in Reforming the IMF and Strengthening the Architecture of the International Financial System'. 12 April. <www.imf.org/external/np/omd/2000/report.htm> (March 2001).

Kopits, George and Jon Craig (1998). 'Transparency in Government Operations'. *Occasional Paper No. 158*. International Monetary Fund, Washington DC.

Larraín B., Felipe and José Tavares (1999). 'Can Openness Deter Corruption?', Center for International Development, Harvard University, and Department of Economics, University of California.

Mishkin, Frederic S. (1999). 'International Experiences with Different Monetary Policy Regimes'. *Journal of Monetary Economics* vol. 43, no. 3, pp. 579–605.

Moore, Mike (2000a). 'Open Societies Do Better'. Statement by the Director-General of the World Trade Organization at the 11th International Military Chiefs of Chaplains Conference. 9 February. <www.wto.org/english/news_e/spmm_e/spmm22_e.htm> (March 2001).

Moore, Mike (2000b). 'The Post-Seattle Trade Agenda'. Speech Delivered at International Chamber of Commerce — 33rd World Congress, Budapest. <www.wto.org/english/news_e/spmm_e/spmm30_e.htm> (March 2001).

More, Thomas (1965 [1516]). *Utopia*. Penguin Books, London.

Scheer, Robert (2000). 'Nowhere to Hide'. *Yahoo Internet Life* vol. 6, pp. 100–102.

Von Furstenberg, George M. (2000). 'Transparentising the Global Money Business'. In K. Kaiser, J. J. Kirton, and J. P. Daniels, eds., *Shaping a New International Financial System: Challenges of Governance in a Globalizing World*, pp. 97–111. Ashgate, Aldershot.

Part II
New Directions in Global Financial Governance

6 Continuity and Change in the Global Monetary Order

SÉBASTIEN DALLAIRE

Many observers believe that over the last decade, particularly in the wake of the Asian financial crisis, a marked shift has taken place in the international community's vision of development. The so-called 'Washington Consensus' (Williamson 1990), characterised in part by a strong belief that market-friendly structural adjustment programmes (SAPS) were the only viable path to long-term development, has apparently been replaced by a more socially oriented approach, one that does not separate economics from political and social needs. This chapter argues that although a change in the international development discourse has indeed occurred, the core of the previous consensus remains the same. Actors in international economic fora such as the International Monetary Fund (IMF) and the G7 summits[1] increasingly discuss social issues and political problems involved in development, but their economic beliefs remain essentially unchanged. Effectively, liberalisation is still the key to sustainable growth according to the international financial institutions (IFIs) and the G7, while internal adjustments to international pressures remain the only way out of poverty. The rationale behind this reasoning is that the external environment is fundamentally 'good' and countries must learn to turn it to their advantage. This conclusion should obviously not be applied to every international institution, since the United Nations (UN) and its many agencies promote a very different view of international development (Thérien and Dallaire 1999). However, the dominant discourse is certainly embodied in the Bretton Woods institutions, which promote this vision, and not in the United Nations institutions (Thérien 1999, 725).

In order to demonstrate the validity of this claim, this chapter examines the discourse and policies of the G7 and the IMF over the last 20 years. These institutions are two of the most influent actors in the international development debate and clearly promote the 'Bretton Woods paradigm' (Thérien 1999). The discussions held at the G7 summits certainly influence and shape the international discourse on development. These talks are reflected in the discourse and policies of the IMF, an institution dominated by the G7 countries due to its decision-making process. The arrow of causation does not flow only in one direction, however. Both international institutions influence each other in the construction of the international discourse on economic development.

Methodological Considerations

Discursive analyses are not a popular approach in the field of international relations or international political economy, mainly due to the predominance of a strong positivist core in the discipline, particularly in the United States. Because discourse relates to ideas, not hard facts, most scholars have neglected it as a research tool. However, much recent research in these two fields has pointed to the importance of ideas in international politics. This body of research comes from diverse perspectives, emanating from either liberal institutionalism (Goldstein and Keohane 1993; Keohane 1984), social constructivism (Ruggie 1998; Wendt 1992, 1999), critical theory (George 1994), post-modernism (Ashley and Walker 1990; Der Derian and Shapiro 1989), the Gramscian perspective (Cox 1987; Gill 1993), or diverse feminist approaches (Peterson 1992; Tickner 1992). Leaving aside the enormous differences among each of these approaches to the study of international relations, they all point to a renewed interest in the importance of ideas in international politics.

From a more traditional standpoint, international regime theory was a step toward the inclusion of ideas in international relations theory. Regimes were defined as a set of 'implicit or explicit principles, norms, rules and decision making procedures around which actors' expectations converge in a given area of international relations' (Krasner 1983, 3). Ideational factors are certainly present in this definition, given the importance extended to principles and norms. However, most regime analysts cannot fully profit from the possibility of including ideas within international relations theorising because they maintain the same strong positivist epistemology that overlooks ideational factors that cannot be measured (Kratochwil and Ruggie 1986).

In order to avoid this problem, this chapter applies a more social constructivist approach to regime analysis. Although some social constructivist theorists often maintain a positivist premises for their analyses because of their adherence to a Lakatosian vision of social science, which emphasises the possibility and even necessity of progress, constructivism overcomes the limitations of regime theory when applied to the study of international discursive changes. It overcomes this limitation by allowing research to go beyond mere facts and look at ideas themselves. Ideas can have an existence of their own, and they can be studied without looking at their concrete manifestations in policies. Accordingly, institutions can play an important role in the creation and promotion of particular world views and ideas at the international level by acting as socialising and legitimating entities (Finnemore 1996; Kratochwil and Ruggie 1986). As such, the discourse of the G7 and the IMF is analysed in this chapter in order to see how these two institutions have changed their respective visions of economic development and how they construct international beliefs in that manner.

Although very often portrayed as inefficient and solely representing the interests of rich countries (Commission on Global Governance 1995; Ikenberry 1993), the G7 still constitutes an important forum of discussions among major actors in the world economy. Stating that the G7 is 'maligned, mistrusted and misunderstood', John J. Kirton (1999, 46) believes that on the contrary, 'the G7 and now Group of Eight (G8) is emerging as an effective centre, and is prospectively the effective centre, of global governance'. Whether the summitry process will become the effective centre of global governance remains to be seen; its importance, however, in shaping the international discourse on international issues can hardly be denied.

Having started primarily as an economic forum where the leaders of the seven countries exchanged views on economic co-operation among themselves, the G7 gradually expanded its horizons, with international poverty and development becoming more visible over time in the G7 documentation. The 1999 Summit of the Eight at Cologne showed a genuine concern for the plight of the poor. Upon returning home, British prime minister Tony Blair insisted that for him, the collective promise made to alleviate the debt burden of the poorest nations of the world was the most important commitment taken at the Cologne Summit (British Foreign and Commonwealth Office 1999). This is not an insignificant statement, given the numerous topics covered. Moreover, the fact that human suffering and poverty are treated as equal to the economic problems of developing countries shows that the group's view of development has changed.

Among the Bretton Woods institutions, the choice of the IMF rather than the World Bank or the World Trade Organization (WTO) for this study rests on two considerations. First, the IMF has seen its importance grow dramatically in this era of globalisation, and its leaders fully expect to see this trend continue as it becomes the key institution in the new international financial architecture (IMF 1996b, 243; 1998). Second, because the IMF was first created to ensure short-term equilibrium for both current and capital accounts and thus prevent any major international financial instability, it can be argued that the inclusion of social safety nets and poverty reduction objectives within the IMF's structural adjustment programmes in the last decade genuinely marks a break with the orthodoxy of the 1980s. The thesis of a pendulum swing within the international community's development discourse in the 1990s should thus be reinforced by any major modifications in the discourse and policies of the IMF.

The Evolution of the International Development Discourse

The 1960s and the 1980s can both be considered times of total reversals in the international development discourse. While the 1960s saw the plight of the poor become a major topic in the international arena, the 1980s saw the developing countries' demands being rejected by rich countries. However, at present the international development discourse of the G7 and the Bretton Woods' institutions appears to be shifting toward renewed interest in the social needs of developing countries and in international poverty more generally.

The massive decolonisation movement that started in the 1950s and continued in the 1960s brought new (mainly poor) countries into the international institutions and rapidly changed the face of international debates on development and poverty, especially within UN institutions. Due to the 'one nation, one vote' mechanism in the decision-making process of the United Nations, poor countries saw their weight increase dramatically within the institution, giving them a powerful new voice in this international arena. The creation of the United Nations Conference on Trade and Development (UNCTAD) in 1964 to discuss international trade and economic development issues within the UN institutional framework also increased the negotiating power of the South (Adams 1993). Taking advantage of this apparently favourable position, poor countries put together an ambitious program of reform of the international system: the New International Economic Order (NIEO). The NIEO explicitly demanded that the international economic system be reformed to give additional advantages to developing countries due to their unfavourable economic situations (Krasner 1985; Murphy 1984; Tinbergen 1978).

Unfortunately for developing countries, these demands were harshly rejected by the rich North in the 1980s, partly due to the mounting influence of the conservative right with the election of Ronald Reagan in the United States and Margaret Thatcher in Britain. Then ensued the boycott of the United Nations Educational, Scientific, and Cultural Organization (UNESCO) and other international discussion fora on development by the United States and Britain at the beginning of the 1980s, really marking the end of the north-south dialogue and the beginning of the 'lost decade' for development. The claims of the South fell on many more deaf ears than in the previous decades, despite the efforts of many.

In addition to the changing ideological stance of the North, the South itself lost some of its supposed homogeneity (Berger 1994). It quickly became apparent that some countries were profiting from the existing order, with the economies of the newly industrialised countries (NICs) growing at an extraordinarily fast rate. On the other hand, many extremely poor countries were simply unable to get out of their state of extreme poverty and felt more and more isolated from the international economic system. This loss of harmony in the South was devastating for those countries, which lost much of their bargaining power with the North. These extremely poor countries could not bring much to the negotiating table without the complicity of the 'wealthier' southern states.

Also during the 1980s, the United Nations became less important as a forum for economic discussion. It was superseded by the Bretton Woods institutions, namely the IMF, the World Bank, and the General Agreement on Tariffs and Trade (GATT) and later the WTO, where the decision-making process is not as democratic as at the UN, allowing for a much greater control over decisions by the richer nations. This changing locus of discussions on development had a major influence on the nature of the debate. Talks no longer sought to adapt the system to the needs of poor countries, but demanded a better adjustment to the system by those countries. In this new light, SAPs became the principal instrument for attempting to modify the economic conditions of the developing countries and integrate them into the international economy. Social needs and poverty alleviation were not important parts of adjustment packages, which often overlooked the societal impact of the reforms undertaken. Many scholars saw this insistence on strong macroeconomic adjustments as a strategy to force developing countries into the international capitalist system, thus helping the economies of rich countries more than those of poor countries (Wood 1986; 1996).

Some observers claim that there has been another major reversal in the international development discourse of the Bretton Woods institutions in the 1990s, which saw social problems and poverty coming back as major international issues (Shakow 1995; IMF 1997e, 28). Conversely, although there were undoubtedly major indications of change within the international development discourse of the G7 and the IMF, the very nature of the discourse remained the same. It is certainly true that poverty and the social aspects of adjustment policies have made a remarkable return in the language of the G7 and the IMF. On the other hand, one fundamental aspect has been maintained firmly, that is, that 'the primary responsibility for fighting poverty lies with the governments and the people of developing countries themselves' (World Bank 1996, vii). Thus, while the NIEO and the discussions of the 1960s and 1970s were oriented toward transforming the system in favour of poor countries, the discourse of the 1990s is similar to the orthodoxy of the 1980s in that the fault for underdevelopment lies within national barriers. But again, there were nonetheless some signs of discursive changes within both international institutions.

The Signs of Major Discursive Changes

Since the mid 1980s, the debates over international development have restored poverty and other social issues as important topics to discuss along with the economy. Within both the G7 and the IMF, it is clear that these issues have gained prominence in the last decade. Although development has been mentioned from the very beginning of the G7 process (Bayne 1999, 33), it gained considerable importance only after the 1988 Toronto Summit, where important decisions, known as the 'Toronto terms', were taken regarding poor countries' indebtedness. These terms were also accepted by the IMF and the Paris Club. From then on, the issue of developing countries' indebtedness became a recurring topic at each summit, culminating with the 1999 Cologne Debt Initiative. This initiative asks that creditor countries relieve up to 90 percent of the bilateral commercial debts of the poorest countries included in the Heavily Indebted Poor Countries (HIPC) framework. Although debt reduction and poverty reduction are different matters, both the G7 and the IMF see a very tight link between indebtedness and underdevelopment, making debt relief a major concern in any discussion of economic development.

But this increased emphasis on debt forgiveness is not the only area where the G7 has focussed its attention on international development issues. The Lyon Summit of 1996 may have been the most important turning point in this regard, with the implementation of the 'New Partnership for Development'. This new partnership, where rich and poor countries were assigned a list of responsibilities to ensure global prosperity and welfare, set many important goals, such as the 'reduction of poverty and social inequities, the respect of internationally recognized labour standards, protection of children, a strengthened civil society, protection of the environment, improved health and education' (G7 1996). There is no doubt that these objectives reflect more than a simple concern for macroeconomics and mark a change to more human sensitivity in the G7 discourse. It was also at Lyon that the G7 fully endorsed the HIPC Initiative. In Denver in 1997, African development was a major concern. Member countries asserted that they were 'committed to a results-oriented approach to development policy, with the particular goal of combating extreme poverty' (G8 1997).

At Birmingham in 1998, the same concern for the problems of the poorest was noticeable. However, the onset of the Asian financial crisis before the summit directed attention toward this region. Responding to the enormous social costs of the crisis, the G8 insisted that 'economic and financial reform needed to be matched with actions and policies by the countries concerned to help protect [the poor and most vulnerable] from the worst effects of the crisis' (G8 1998). In accordance with the visible changes of the previous summits, the final communiqué of the Cologne Summit of 1999 included an unprecedented number of developmental issues. A large part of the text relating to development emphasised the need to invest in people and social protection, reinforcing the previously identified trend.

The IMF also modified its discourse on international development during the same period. The 1987 publication of *Adjustment with a Human Face* (Cornia, Stewart, and Jolly 1987) by the United Nations Children's Fund (UNICEF) is often mentioned as a pivotal point, when social issues were inserted into the structural adjustment programmes of the IMF and the World Bank (Thérien 1999, 729). From then on, poverty alleviation and the social impact of adjustment policies gained salience in the discourse and the macroeconomic policies of both institutions.

On the discursive side, former managing director of the IMF Michel Camdessus recognised that the 'persistence of zones of extreme poverty is a scandal' (IMF 1995a, 35). He also insisted on the importance of increasing the equity of the economic reforms proposed to poor countries by the IMF (IMF 1997e, 29). In 1996, Eduardo Aninat, Deputy Managing Director of the IMF, stated that there was an 'urgent need for increased efficiency and better targeting of social spending as an effective means to improve social equity and to reduce poverty' (IMF 1996c, 9). The IMF has also been engaging in active dialogues with other international institutions possessing more expertise on poverty and other social issues, such as the World Bank and the UN (International Monetary Fund 1999c). The IMF participated in many international social policy forums, such as the 1995 World Summit for Social Development. It also organised the 1995 conference on income distribution and sustainable growth and another one on economic policy and equity in 1998, reflecting a more serious concern for equity issues (IMF 1999c, 9). In line with these international discussions, the IMF also started to publish more studies on the impact of its policies on the poor (Gupta et al. 1998; IMF 1995b). Considering the macroeconomic reasons behind the creation of the IMF and its policies in the 1970s and early 1980s, this increased attention to social issues is far from insignificant.

From a policy standpoint, the IMF has taken numerous steps to include social policy concerns in its adjustment packages. The establishment of the Structural Adjustment Facility (SAF) in 1986 was the first of these steps, followed by the Enhanced Structural Adjustment Facility (ESAF) in 1987 and finally the HIPC Initiative in 1996. In accordance with the new insistence on the maintenance or even increase of social spending by governments in periods of adjustment, the IMF also started to monitor more closely the level of public spending in countries subjected to SAPs (IMF 1999c). Moreover, following the demands of finance ministers for an enhanced framework for poverty reduction at the 1999 Cologne Summit, the IMF has increased its efforts at monitoring and increasing its attention to social issues (p. 7), with strengthened social safety nets presented as an 'essential element' of the IMF's programs (IMF 1999b, 6). Also, just prior to the Okinawa Summit, the new Managing Director of the IMF, Horst Köhler, affirmed that the IMF 'will continue to place a high priority on poverty reduction' (IMF 1999a, 229).

The Same Underlying Message

The previous section argued that important changes toward the inclusion of social issues such as poverty and social safety nets have occurred in the development discourse and policies of the G7 and the IMF. However, these changes remain superficial. The underlying message and beliefs of the discourse and policies have remained relatively unchanged. Thus, while there has been increased attention given to poverty and other social issues by both the G7 and the IMF, their leaders still maintain that it is the responsibility of poor countries to adapt to the international system, and not of the system to adapt to the needs of poor countries. So, while it is acknowledged that globalisation can have deleterious effects on some populations, the afflicted countries must assume full responsibility for their problems. This view is based on a 'consensus that global opening and integration offer the *only path* to worldwide prosperity' (IMF 1997a, 289, emphasis added). There is thus no viable alternative other than to accept the rules of the globalising free-market economy. Free markets and low government interventionism are presented as keys to sustainable development, because governments 'cannot be expected to play the dominant role in fostering growth. The most effective economic strategies are private sector led and outward oriented' (IMF 1997c, 10).

The G7 summits may have put more emphasis on poverty alleviation and social problems, but a strong belief in the goodness of economic liberalisation is still noticeable in every final communiqué over the last decade. Mentions of the 'benefits' of globalisation appear repeatedly in the summitry's official documents. However, on every occasion it is stressed that these benefits can only be reaped if countries accept the necessary economic and political reforms. Poor countries are thus deemed responsible for their own situations. The acclaimed 'New Partnership for Development' established at Lyon 'starts from the principle that it is the responsibility of the developing countries themselves to determine and pursue policies to reduce poverty and foster sustainable, job-creating, equitable and environmentally friendly development' (G7 1996). The Denver and Birmingham summits are not an exception to this rule, with the leaders emphasising the need to integrate developing countries better into the global economy. Even at the Cologne Summit, arguably the most favourable to the plight of the poor, the G7 leaders insisted that countries adapt to globalisation in order to reap the benefits. Contrary to the discussions in the 1960s and particularly in the 1970s, with the NIEO, there was and still is no real reform of the international system on the agenda. The burden of adjustment rests entirely with the developing countries.

For the IMF, the same notion of internal domestic adjustments to the needs of the international system reappears throughout its discourse in the 1980s and 1990s. As with the G7, globalisation is seen as fundamentally good and is an 'opportunity to seize' (IMF 1997b, translated by the author). Aninat stated in 2000 that the 'world economy is basically in good shape, giving us a much-needed opportunity to step up our efforts to spread the benefits of globalization to the disconnected' (IMF 1999a, 227). But to be able to seize this opportunity, countries must play by the rules, because they cannot 'compete for blessings of the global capital markets and refuse their discipline' (IMF 1997d, 292). Structural adjustments remain oriented toward cuts in government spending, privatisation, and liberalisation. Not only do countries need to make formidable adjustment efforts within a few years, but structural adjustment is also now presented as a permanent feature of the economic policies of developing countries (IMF 1996a, 259). Globalisation and structural adjustments can have deleterious short-term effects on the poorest of the poor, but both are deemed necessary for long-term growth and poverty reduction. There is not much of a difference with the discourse of the 1980s, except for the constant use of the word 'globalisation'.

Implications for International Development

This analysis of the discourse and policies of the G7 and the IMF has not rendered a judgement on the viability of the proposed developmental solutions. It has simply outlined how the fundamental nature of the discourse was maintained throughout the 1980s and 1990s. But the implications of these similarities for the development prospects of poor countries in the new millennium are great. Without flatly rejecting the many advantages brought about by democratic capitalism, some major caveats and contradictions can be pointed out in the language and policies of the G7 and the IMF.

First, the strong emphasis on the need for countries to adjust internally to the international environment is a cause for concern in an era of globalisation. The concern stems primarily from the great instability of the international economy due to the sheer amount of money that circulates around the world every day (McKenzie and Lee 1991; Solomon 1995; Strange 1986). The Mexican peso crisis of 1994 and the Asian financial crisis of 1997 are both clear examples of this fragility. Some countries can indeed be blamed for their problems. However, higher international instability increases the possibility of unjustified financial downturns, especially for extremely poor countries. If globalisation can be a threat to the possibility of domestic governance for rich and politically stable democracies (Cerny 1995; Martin and Schumann 1997; Schmidt 1995), one can imagine how destabilising it can be for the poorest developing countries, which lack political and economic stability. The G7 and the IMF are thus asking countries to adjust to a system that can punish them even if they do exactly what they are instructed. Moreover, by implementing the adjustments necessary according the G7 and the IMF, these countries increase their short-term vulnerability to political and social crises. The possibility of sustainable development thus depends on both the appropriateness of the reforms demanded and the good will of capital markets. The risks associated with increased globalisation and the structural reforms would be easier to accept if the affected countries were not the only imputable parties for the possible problems. But the development discourse of the two institutions implies that although countries can always be blamed for their problems (even when they have done nothing wrong), neither the international system nor globalisation can be blamed or modified to prevent domestic troubles. But if justice is to be served, individual countries should not be faulted for the mistakes of the system.

The first contradiction outlined above is amplified by a second one: the lack of funding for the poorest countries. Both organisations recognise that the poorest of the poor are not viewed favourably by financial markets. Although the macroeconomic reforms demanded from these countries have the objective of making them more attractive to private investors, the G7 and the IMF insist on the fact that public funds are essential for these countries because it takes time to gain the confidence of investors. Summit after summit, the G7 commits itself to support these poorer nations by furnishing sufficient official development assistance (ODA), as does the IMF each year. However, the ratio of aid to the gross domestic product (GDP) given by G7 countries is steadily declining since the end of the cold war, and the rest of the international community is not faring much better (Development Assistance Committee, various years). A slight increase in ODA figures was noticeable in 1998–1999, but the G7 countries gave on average 0.20 percent of their GDP, compared to 0.45 percent for the other donor countries (Development Assistance Committee 1999). Thus, G7 countries certainly do not make a very strong effort to respect their promises compared to the rest of the donor community. Tight budgetary conditions at the national level can probably be faulted for cuts in ODA, but why continue to insist on aid's centrality if rich nations refuse to commit to give the money needed? Poor countries are told to make their own efforts to make adjustments that are difficult (and risky in a context of globalisation), but the public money needed to compensate for the lack of private funding is simply not forthcoming.

This argument does not imply a total lack of responsibility for poor countries themselves. It would be too easy to say that the industrial states of the North need to bear all the blame for the situation of developing countries. Poor countries did and do make mistakes and take bad decisions. However, this chapter serves as a reminder that rich nations should be held accountable for their decisions and actions regarding their southern counterparts.

The two caveats presented here do not represent an exhaustive list of the reproaches that can be directed at both institutions, as critiques from the left and the right have always feasted on the discourse and policies of these two institutions. Moreover, this chapter does not enter into a discussion of the viability of the type of global capitalism promoted by the G7 and the IMF, but highlights the discursive incongruities in the vision of international development shared by these two institutions. The inconsistencies discussed here point to one major implication for the development possibilities of poor countries: the policies proposed increase the risk of domestic crises by implementing socially and politically costly adjustments and opening the economy to unstable international capital markets. This is not to say that this strategy will never bring about sustainable development or will always provoke major internal trouble. It can certainly have positive effects for many countries. However, the risks involved are great and rich countries must take the responsibility to make them less dangerous for poor countries engaging in the process of reform. Diminishing the risks means, among many other things, increasing the levels of ODA granted and also envisaging a modification of the international economic order so that it becomes more just for everyone.

Conclusion

The increased insistence on the importance of social issues within the discourse and policies of the G7 and the IMF is a sign that modification of their vision of international development is possible. The 1999 Cologne Summit and the reaction of the Bretton Woods institutions to the Asian financial crisis are solid signs of this possibility. In Cologne, the leaders of the G8 displayed greater concerns for the problems of developing countries than ever before. Also, the IMF and the World Bank admitted that they had made some mistakes in their interventions before and during the Asian financial crisis. But even the severity of this financial turmoil did not moderate their enthusiasm regarding the free movement of capital, as prospects were deemed to have been only 'temporarily set back' by the crisis (G8 1998). Much remains to be done to achieve a genuine and necessary transformation in the development discourse of the G8 and the IMF.

A good starting point for this change would be to follow the advice of Joseph Stiglitz (1998) and recognise that liberalisation and other economic reforms are only means to achieve an end, and not the end in itself. In other words, the end is development and the tools should not be reified as permanent or perfect. There is always room for change and improvement. Although a return to protectionism and trade wars would not be a solution for anyone, increased international co-operation to 'tame' capital markets (Porter 1996) and discipline them to the needs of the world's populations is necessary. Regaining some control over financial markets might be difficult, but it remains possible (Eichengreen, Tobin, and Wyplosz 1995; Kapstein 1994; Underhill 1991). Saying that it is impossible or that there is no other way is mostly an ideological statement.

Globalisation did not appear by itself, without the intervention of governments. On the contrary, the global economy was constructed over the years by political and economical decisions in rich countries and in international organisations devised by them. The creation of the Bretton Woods system and institutions was informed by the will to promote global trade while keeping capital markets under control (Goodman and Pauly 1993; Helleiner 1994). Thus, globalisation was constructed and as such can be deconstructed.

For many, globalisation might well be a buzzword without any substantial meaning, but it can nonetheless be used as a dangerous rhetorical tool (Krugman 1994, 1996). It thus becomes easy for governments to blame an 'uncontrollable' globalisation for domestic or international problems, allowing them to avoid taking responsibility for their own actions and decisions. But rich countries must face their responsibilities. Any simple revision of the ordering principles of the international economic syste, such as the creation of a new international financial architecture, is not sufficient to improve the plight of the poorest of the poor. Wealthy industrial democracies must add effective policies and more money to their promises, because words alone will not help.

Note

1   Because this chapter looks at the discourse of the G7 since its inception in 1975 and Russia only joined at Denver in 1997, Russia was absent from the process for more than 20 years. However, the use of the G7 rather than the G8 here is not intended to understate the importance of Russia in the Group's meetings and decisions.

References

Adams, Nassau A. (1993). *Worlds Apart: The North-South Divide and the International System*. Zed Books, London.

Ashley, Richard and R. J. B. Walker (1990). 'Reading Dissidence/Writing the Discipline'. *International Studies Quarterly* vol. 34, pp. 367–416.

Bayne, Nicholas (1999). 'Continuity and Leadership in an Age of Globalisation'. In M. R. Hodges, J. J. Kirton and J. P. Daniels, eds., *The G8's Role in the New Millennium*, pp. 21–44. Ashgate, Aldershot.

Berger, Mark T. (1994). 'The End of the "Third World"?' *Third World Quarterly* vol. 15, no. 2, pp. 257–275.

British Foreign and Commonwealth Office (1999). 'Blair Reports on Cologne G8 Summit: Statement by the Prime Minister, Mr. Tony Blair, House of Commons, London, 21 June 1999'. <www.fco.gov.uk/news/newstext.asp?2577> (March 2001).

Cerny, Philip G. (1995). 'Globalization and the Changing Logic of Collective Action'. *International Organisation* vol. 49, no. 4, pp. 595–625.

Commission on Global Governance (1995). *Our Global Neighbourhood: The Report of the Commission on Global Governance.* Oxford University Press, Oxford.

Cornia, Giovanni Andrea, Frances Stewart, and Richard Jolly (1987). *Adjustment with a Human Face.* Clarendon Press, Oxford.

Cox, Robert W. (1987). *Production, Power, and World Order: Social Forces in the Making of History.* Columbia University Press, New York.

Der Derian, James and Michael J. Shapiro (1989). *International/Intertextual Relations: Postmodern Readings of World Politics.* Lexington Books, Lexington, MA.

Development Assistance Committee (1999). Development Co-Operation: Efforts and Policies of the Members of the Development Assistance Committee. Organisation for Economic Co-operation and Development, Paris.

Development Assistance Committee (various years). Development Co-Operation: Efforts and Policies of the Members of the Development Assistance Committee. Organisation for Economic Co-operation and Development, Paris.

Eichengreen, Barry, James Tobin, and Charles Wyplosz (1995). 'Two Cases for Sand in the Wheels of Global Finance'. *Economic Journal* vol. 105, no. 1, pp. 162–172.

Finnemore, Martha (1996). *National Interests in International Society.* Cornell University Press, Ithaca, NY.

G7 (1996). 'Economic Communiqué: Making a Success of Globalization for the Benefit of All'. 28 June, Lyon. <www.library.utoronto.ca/g7/summit/1996lyon/communique/index.html> (March 2001).

G8 (1997). 'Communiqué'. 22 June, Denver. <www.library.utoronto.ca/g7/summit/1997denver/g8final.htm> (March 2001).

G8 (1998). 'Communiqué'. 15 May, Birmingham. <www.library.utoronto.ca/g7/summit/1998birmingham/finalcom.htm> (March 2001).

George, Jim (1994). *Discourses of Global Politics: A Critical (Re)Introduction to International Relations.* Lynne Rienner Publishers, Boulder, CO.

Gill, Stephen, ed. (1993). *Gramsci, Historical Materialism, and International Relations.* Cambridge University Press, Cambridge.

Goldstein, Judith and Robert O. Keohane (1993). *Ideas and Foreign Policy: Beliefs, Institutions, and Political Change.* Cornell University Press, Ithaca, NY.

Goodman, John B. and Louis W. Pauly (1993). 'Obsolescence of Capital Controls? Economic Management in an Age of Global Markets'. *World Politics* vol. 46, no. 1, pp. 50–82.

Gupta, Sanjeev, et al. (1998). 'The IMF and the Poor'. Pamphlet Series, no. 52. International Monetary Fund, Washington DC.

Helleiner, Eric (1994). *States and the Reemergence of Global Finance: From Bretton Woods to the 1990s*. Cornell University Press, Ithaca, NY.

Ikenberry, John (1993). 'Salvaging the G7'. *Foreign Affairs* vol. 72 (Spring), pp. 132–139.

International Monetary Fund (1995a). 'Presentation of the Fiftieth Annual Report by the Chairman of the Executive Board of the International Monetary Fund'. Summary Proceedings: Annual Meeting 1995. International Monetary Fund, Washington DC.

International Monetary Fund (1995b). 'Social Dimensions of the IMF's Policy Dialogue'. IMF Pamphlet Series 47. International Monetary Fund, Washington DC.

International Monetary Fund (1996a). 'African Prospects Tied to Courageous Adjustment Efforts'. *IMF Survey* vol. 25, no. 15, pp. 259.

International Monetary Fund (1996b). 'Concluding Remarks: Statement by the Chairman of the Executive Board and Managing Director of the International Monetary Fund, Michel Camdessus'. Summary Proceedings: Annual Meeting 1996. International Monetary Fund, Washington DC.

International Monetary Fund (1996c). 'Opening Address by the Chairman of the Boards of Governors and Governor of the Fund and the Bank for Chile. Eduardo Aninat'. Summary Proceedings: Annual Meetings 1996. International Monetary Fund, Washington DC.

International Monetary Fund (1997a). 'Annual Meetings: IMF Given Role in Fostering Freer Capital Flows; Quota Increase. SDR Allocation Agreed'. *IMF Survey* vol. 26, no. 18, pp. 289–292.

International Monetary Fund (1997b). 'La Mondialisation, une Chance à Saisir'. *Bulletin du FMI* vol. 26, no. 10 (2 June), pp. 153–155.

International Monetary Fund (1997c). 'Making the Most of Debt Relief, External Finance'. *IMF Survey* vol. 26, no. 1, pp. 10–11.

International Monetary Fund (1997d). 'Managing Director's Opening Address: Camdessus Calls for Responsibility, Solidarity in Dealing with Challenges of Globalisation'. *IMF Survey* vol. 26, no. 18 (6 October), pp. 292–294.

International Monetary Fund (1997e). 'Presentation of the Fifty-Second Annual Report by the Chairman of the Executive Board of the International Monetary Fund'. Summary Proceedings: Annual Meeting 1997. International Monetary Fund, Washington DC.

International Monetary Fund (1998). 'Speech to Economic Club: Participation in the IMF Is an Investment in World Stability and Prosperity'. *IMF Survey* vol. 27, no. 6 (23 March), pp. 88–90.

International Monetary Fund (1999a). 'ECOSOC Address: Aninat Outlines Ways to Integrate All Countries into Increasingly Globalized Economy'. *IMF Survey* vol. 29, no. 14 (17 July), pp. 227–230.

International Monetary Fund (1999b). 'IMF Annual Report 1999'. International Monetary Fund, Washington DC.

International Monetary Fund (1999c). 'Review of Social Issues and Policies'. IMF-Supported Programs. International Monetary Fund, Washington DC.

Kapstein, Ethan B. (1994). *Governing the Global Economy: International Finance and the State.* Harvard University Press, Cambridge, MA.

Keohane, Robert O. (1984). *After Hegemony: Cooperation and Discord in the World Political Economy.* Princeton University Press, Princeton.

Kirton, John J. (1999). 'Explaining G8 Effectiveness'. In M. R. Hodges, J. J. Kirton and J. P. Daniels, eds., *The G8's Role in the New Millennium*, pp. 45–68. Ashgate, Aldershot.

Krasner, Stephen D. (1983). *International Regimes.* Cornell University Press, Ithaca, NY.

Krasner, Stephen D. (1985). *Structural Conflict: The Third World against Global Liberalism.* University of California Press, Berkeley.

Kratochwil, Fredrich and John Gerard Ruggie (1986). 'International Organisation: A State of the Art on the Art of the State'. *International Organisation* vol. 40, no. 4, pp. 753–775.

Krugman, Paul R. (1994). 'Competitiveness: A Dangerous Obsession'. *Foreign Affairs* vol. 73, no. 2, pp. 28–44.

Krugman, Paul R. (1996). *Pop Internationalism.* MIT Press, Cambridge, MA.

Martin, Hans-Peter and Harald Schumann (1997). *The Global Trap: Globalization and the Assault on Prosperity and Democracy.* Zed Books, London.

McKenzie, Richard B. and Dwight R. Lee (1991). *Quicksilver Capital: How the Rapid Movement of Wealth Has Changed the World.* Free Press, New York.

Murphy, Craig (1984). *The Emergence of the NIEO Ideology.* Westview Press, Boulder, CO.

Peterson, V. Spike (1992). *Gendered States: Feminist (Re)Visions of International Relations Theory.* Lynne Rienner Publishers, Boulder, CO.

Porter, Tony (1996). 'Capital Mobility and Currency Markets: Can They Be Tamed?' *International Journal* vol. 51, no. 4, pp. 669–689.

Ruggie, John Gerard (1998). *Constructing the World Polity: Essays on International Institutionalization.* Routledge, London.

Schmidt, Vivien A. (1995). 'The New World Order Incorporated: The Rise of Business and the Decline of the Nation-State'. *Daedalus* vol. 124, no. 2, pp. 75–106.

Shakow, Alexander (1995). 'A Changing Institution in a Changing World'. In M. ul Haq, R. Jolly and P. Streeten, et al., eds., *The UN and the Bretton Woods Institutions: New Challenges for the Twenty-First Century.* St. Martin's Press, New York.

Solomon, Steven (1995). *The Confidence Game: How Unelected Central Bankers Are Governing the Changed Global Economy.* Simon & Schuster, New York.

Stiglitz, Joseph (1998). 'World Bank Conference on Development Economics: Speakers Explore Range of Development Issues and Appropriate Responses to Financial Crises'. *IMF Survey* vol. 27, no. 9 (11 May), pp. 146–148.

Strange, Susan (1986). *Casino Capitalism*. B. Blackwell, Oxford.

Thérien, Jean-Philippe (1999). 'Beyond the North-South Divide: The Two Tales of World Poverty'. *Third World Quarterly* vol. 20, no. 4, pp. 723–742.

Thérien, Jean-Philippe and Sébastien Dallaire (1999). 'Nord-Sud: une vision du monde en mutation'. *La revue internationale et stratégique* vol. 36, Winter 1999–2000, pp. 21–35.

Tickner, J. Ann (1992). *Gender in International Relations: Feminist Perspectives on Achieving Global Security*. Columbia University Press, New York.

Tinbergen, Jan (1978). *Nord-Sud, du défi au dialogue? Propositions pour un nouvel ordre international*. SNED-Dunod, Paris.

Underhill, Geoffrey R. D. (1991). 'Markets Beyond Politics? The State and the Internationalisation of Financial Markets'. *European Journal of Political Research* vol. 19, no. 1, pp. 197–225.

Wendt, Alexander (1992). 'Anarchy Is What States Make of It: The Social Construction of Power Politics'. *International Organisation* vol. 46, no. 2, pp. 391–425.

Wendt, Alexander (1999). *Social Theory of International Politics*. Cambridge University Press, Cambridge.

Williamson, John (1990). 'What Washington Means by Policy Reform'. In J. Williamson, ed., *Latin American Adjustment: How Much Has Happened?*, pp. 5–38. Institute for International Economics, Washington DC.

Wood, Robert Everett (1986). *From Marshall Plan to Debt Crisis: Foreign Aid and Development Choices in the World Economy*. University of California Press, Berkeley.

Wood, Robert Everett (1996). 'Rethinking Economic Aid'. In S. W. Hook, ed., *Foreign Aid toward the Millennium*, pp. 19–37. Lynne Rienner Publishers, Boulder, CO.

World Bank (1996). *Poverty Reduction and the World Bank: Progress and Challenges in the 1990s*. World Bank, Washington DC.

7 Japan's Approach to Shaping a New International Financial Architecture

SAORI N. KATADA

For the Japanese government, the G7 summit[1] is a place of high-profile diplomacy where Japanese leaders seek to go beyond the constraints of the United States–Japanese bilateral relationship, in which Japan's influence and agenda-setting ability are limited.[2] The Japanese government has hoped for an active 'use' of the G7 economic forum in the aftermath of the Asian financial crisis to reshape the international financial structure that, from the Japanese perspective, threatened the viability of relatively healthy economies in South-East and East Asia. The Japanese government needs a multilateral forum such as the G7 to circumvent U.S. opposition to Japan's preferred approach. The predominant Japanese understanding is that Japan's ability to resort to regional means at the height of the crisis in 1997–98 was limited by US. insistence on a solution led by the International Monetary Fund (IMF).

In the United States, the government and its financial sector are both the major shapers and the major beneficiaries of the international financial dynamics of the 1990s; they were therefore leading actors in diagnosing 'what went wrong' in the financial crisis that hit the (former) miracle economies in Asia. Despite some variations, the dominant and widely accepted explanation was that it was a crisis of the fundamentals led by mismanagement of Asia's financial sector under a false sense of security (due especially to fixed or near-fixed exchange rates).[3] Some even went further and blamed both the corrupt and often inefficient 'crony capitalism' of many Asian economies.[4] Japan, whose troubled economy and weak currency had hurt the Asian economies for the past few years before the crisis, had a different view. In the context of the international financial reform that emerged as a part of the G7 agenda since the middle of 1990s, the Japanese government insisted on the flaws associated with the prevailing international financial structure, especially the adverse effects of highly leveraged institutions (HLIs) such as hedge funds.

113

Because Japanese leaders have had difficulty in unilaterally putting issues on the international agenda that directly confront U.S. objectives, the series of G7 fora since the 1998 Birmingham Summit have become battlegrounds for Japan to shape the direction of the debate over the international financial architecture. This chapter examines the importance of the G7 summit in allowing the Japanese government to address significant issues regarding the future international financial structure. The Japanese government emphasises a new structure that not only increases international financial stability but also provides better opportunities for the Asian countries, including Japan, to compete. The chapter analyses Japan's position from the initial stage of the debate over the international financial architecture in 1994 at the Naples Summit and in the face of the Mexican peso crisis in 1995. This former position is contrasted with that of the three summits (Birmingham, Cologne, and Okinawa) that took place after the onset of the Asian crisis. The chapter concludes with an assessment of how the Japanese leaders took up the G7 forum as a place for agenda setting. It also discusses, as a part of the conclusion, Japan's alleged role as a bridge between Asia and the Western democracies.

Before the Asian Crisis: Naples, Halifax, Lyon, and Denver

In view of the 50th anniversary of the Bretton Woods system, at the 1994 Naples Summit the leaders of the G7 called for a 'thorough review of the institutional foundation of the international monetary system' (Bergsten and Henning 1996, 118), hoping that such review and reform would serve the need of developing countries for effective and beneficial economic co-operation. Several months later, in December 1994, the 'first financial crisis of the twenty-first century' struck Mexico. In the post–cold war world with a relatively stable domestic economic environment, in which the G7 sought an appropriate rationale for its existence (Ikenberry 1993), these events set the stage for the long debate over international financial architecture at the G7 summit.

As the major creditor governments faced the Mexican currency crisis in the early months of 1995, there was a definite sense of discord among the G7 members, particularly between the Western European countries (especially Germany and the United Kingdom) and the North American ones (the United States and, to a certain extent, Canada). The Clinton administration, wanting to restore confidence in the Mexican economy in the face of its own Congress stalling on the authorisation of a rescue package, assembled a bailout package of close to US$50 billion, including US$17.8 billion in stand-by credit from the IMF. Many of the European governments, in turn, criticised the U.S.-imposed decision. The Japanese government supported the U.S. initiative; however, it did so reluctantly.

Despite such discord, the G7 members shared the same sense of alarm about the emergence of Mexico-type financial crises, including contagion to different parts of the world. Thus, the Halifax Summit, held between 15 and 17 June 1995, became the venue for discussing how to prevent 'future Mexicos' along with an ongoing consideration of the reform of international financial institutions (IFIs) such as the IMF and the World Bank. The participating members acknowledged the problem of volatile financial markets, and recommended establishment of the following: an early-warning system to alert market participants of financial problems facing emerging market countries, an emergency financial mechanism that contained strong conditionality and larger up-front disbursement than before, a new IMF quota review to mobilise more funds for contingencies, and prudential standards for financial institutions.

The Canadian Prime Minister, Jean Chrétien, as the host of the Halifax Summit, played a major role in shaping the discussion. The Japanese representatives supported these initiatives. The Japanese government especially welcomed the review of the IMF quota, which was more likely to call for the increase and reallocation of voting power within the IMF. Although Japan had the second largest voting power along with Germany and next to the United States, its Ministry of Finance has long argued for the further increase of Japan's voting power within the institution to reflect Japan's contribution toward the solution of the debt crisis of the 1980s. The Halifax Summit, along with the challenges of the new financial crisis, provided the opportunity for the Japanese government to gain further ground on this matter.[5]

Although the Mexican crisis had stabilised by 1996, the issue of financial globalisation continued to be the central agenda of the G7 summits. At the 1996 Lyon Summit, the host Jacques Chirac emphasised that the leaders must address both the positive and negative sides of economic globalisation, and that international co-operation was essential in achieving equitable globalisation. The G7 leaders reached consensus on various issues related to international financial reforms, including prudential regulation and an increase in emergency funding. No Japanese initiatives on these matters were visible, except for some strong support for the development of Africa.

Japan's co-operative position toward the U.S. agenda continued into the Denver Summit, which took place just as the Thai government was frantically defending its currency against a market attack in June 1997. The strong U.S.

position continued to dominate and highlighted the positive side of financial globalisation (with caution). The G7 members praised the efforts taken by their governments individually and in concert on international financial reform, especially in preparing themselves to prevent and respond adequately to the new type of international financial crises. They also emphasised the importance of the upcoming World Bank/IMF annual meeting in Hong Kong in September 1997 in helping countries build long-term economic potential through trade and investment:

> By the time of the World Bank/IMF annual meetings in Hong Kong, we seek substantial agreement on key elements of an amendment to the IMF Articles to give the IMF the specific mandate to promote capital account liberalization to meet the new challenges in global capital market (G7 1997).

The Japanese government was much more concerned at Denver about the expected criticism by the United States and the other G7 members of the country's slow economic recovery and its continuing trade surplus, rather than about the future form of the international financial architecture. The Japanese government also took some leadership on global environmental issues by advocating an international conference on climate change to be held in Japan.

In sum, the Japanese government and its leaders supported a seemingly solid understanding of financial globalisation among the industrialised nations until the Denver Summit. The understanding was that financial liberalisation among the emerging market countries should continue, but that these countries should liberalise with adequate transparency, and the IFIs should be ready to monitor the situation, evaluate the process, and prevent crisis. In addition, the IFIs and the private financial sector should be prepared to respond as swiftly and as adequately as they could to curb the spread of a Mexico-type crisis. Given the volatile relationship of the Japanese yen with the U.S. dollar during the mid 1990s and the country's slow economic recovery (as well as the stable Asian economy), Japanese leaders spent more time worrying about how to promote their efforts to jump-start their economy through the usual fiscal measures. Despite a continuation of Japan's domestic economic problems and its foreign exchange rate volatility, however, the intensification of the Asian crisis and Japan's 'loss' in the battle against the 'Washington Consensus' led Japanese leaders to launch an offensive at the G7 level to include Japan's and, to certain extent, Asia's perspective on the international financial architecture debate after 1997.

After the Asian Crisis: Birmingham and Cologne

The Asian crisis ended Japan's receptive attitude toward G7 co-operation on international finance, particularly co-operation in accordance with the U.S. lead. For the Japanese government, dealing with the Asian crisis between its onset in July 1997 into the G7 Summit at Birmingham in May 1998 was a continuous uphill battle.

In the early stage of the Asian crisis, as Thailand urgently needed a rescue package,[6] U.S. involvement in the rescue effort was somewhat limited. Under these circumstances, the Japanese government, along with many Asian neighbours, stepped up its efforts to support Thailand.[7] Following this experience of a Thai rescue and supported by Asian governments, Japanese finance minister Hiroshi Mistuzuka unveilled the idea of a regional emergency fund — later dubbed the Asian Monetary Fund (AMF) — during the World Bank/IMF annual meeting in Hong Kong in September 1997. The IMF, the U.S. government, and the Europeans immediately opposed this proposal. Some elements were kept in the form of an agreement on the Manila Framework (via the IMF), but the idea of a regional fund was put on hold. The reason for the opposition by the U.S. and the IMF derived from the fear of creating a rival institution that might threaten the effectiveness of IMF conditionality. The Europeans opposed it for fear that such an additional fund (along with the IMF) would create added moral hazard in international finance.

Having lost the momentum for an Asian regional arrangement, and plagued by its own domestic financial turmoil after the collapse of two major financial institutions in November, the Japanese government retreated to a receptive position in dealing with the Asian crisis at the end of 1997. During this time, two important economies in Asia — Indonesia and South Korea — went into rescue arrangements led by the IMF and the U.S.[8] Of course, the IMF packages came with an explicit understanding that the recipient country's macroeconomic policies had to be modified to address the country's problems with balance of payments. During the Asian crisis, moreover, the packages also addressed the problems of their economic structures.

Various strong criticisms surged both in Japan and in other parts of the world regarding the assumptions made by the IMF analysts about the Asian crisis, particularly in terms of the IMF's involvement in structural adjustment of those crisis-ridden countries. The famous debate between the World Bank's chief economist, Joseph Stiglitz, and the IMF (and the U.S. Treasury) about 'a boat and an aeroplane' summarises the essence of the debate. Some saw the Asian countries as boats. A very rough sea hit these boats, and it did not matter how sturdily each boat was made, as all were swallowed by the overwhelming forces of the rough ocean — the volatile and often speculative international financial market embodied by hedge funds. On the other hand, others argued that it was crony capitalism and the mismanagement of financial sectors of the Asian countries that invited those very rare crises, not the forces of the financial market. If only the afflicted countries had put their fragile, aeroplane-like houses in order (like Taiwan), they would not crash (Stiglitz 1998). Based on this contrast in understanding, the Japanese government went on the offensive at the G7 summits that followed the Asian crisis. It took the approach that the problem of the international financial market should be addressed in the form of increased regulation on some financial activities.

On the other hand, many G7 governments, particularly the United States, were critical of the Japanese government for possibly being one of the causes of the Asian crisis, and for not having done enough to improve Asia's economic conditions. At the time of the G7 finance ministers meeting in February 1998, the Japanese government was declared to be the 'villain' in the Asian crisis (Sanger 1998).

The 1998 G7 Summit at Birmingham, from 15 to 17 May, was the first summit occasion to assert Japan's position on the emerging concept of a 'new international financial architecture'. At the meeting of finance ministers held a week before the Summit itself, the issue of international finance was at the top of the G7 agenda. The Japanese media emphasised the prospect that a certain level of regulation would be imposed on short-term monetary flows, including those by hedge funds ('Shihon Ido no Kanshi Kyoka, G7 Zoushoukaigou Kaimakuhe, Gouiann Go Koumoku — Ajia Kiki Saihatsu Boushi' 1998). The real focus of discussion, however, was not what the Japanese wished or expected. The G7 leaders, especially the United States, focussed on Japan's problematic financial reform as an essential threat to global economic stability, rather than the activities of the hedge funds ('Nichibei Shuno Kaidan, Shushou, "Kinyuu Mondai" Soukishori He — Keizai Saisei Bei Ga Aturyoku' 1998).

The G7 statement at the end of the summit emphasised that it was important for the G7 to maintain and expand the global economy (G7 1998). The statement also stressed that each country had to continue its effort to reform its economy in order for the global market to function smoothly. The statement was an explicit confirmation that the G7 governments were not about to regulate certain cross-border financial activities, although some efforts would be made to increase the efficiency and transparency of international financial activities. Furthermore, the G7 members confirmed that the IMF should continue to serve the central function of supporting and reforming those Asian economies that were experiencing the effects of the crisis.

A series of financial crises in the latter half of 1998, however, changed the attitudes of G7 members. They became more critical of an unregulated international financial market. As a partial contagion of the Asian financial crisis, Russia, which had already suffered from many difficulties in its transition to a market economy, devalued its currency and partially defaulted on its external debt in August. It did so despite the financial support of the IMF and other creditors, particularly since May of the same year. In addition, Brazil faced financial turmoil before and after its presidential election in October 1998. Despite the precautionary rescue package provided to Brazil in November, the country was later forced to abandon its currency peg to the dollars and devalue, triggering further capital outflow and a decline in its stock market in January 1999. Added to these international financial crises, the United States experienced a domestic financial crisis arising from a dramatic decline of its stock market in the late summer of 1998 and the failure and bailout of the Long-Term Capital Management (LTCM) hedge fund in the fall.

Consequently, Japan's argument for increased caution on certain types of international financial activities attracted sympathy, particularly from the Europeans. The leaders from major European countries, which had just launched the Euro in January 1999, emphasised the importance of stable exchange rates and the danger of HLIs such as hedge funds. This was because those institutions could impose tremendous pressure on the exchange rate and induce a large capital outflow from countries in distress. On the other hand, the United States, whose financial institutions dominate this type of financial activity, insisted on maintaining the principle of open market and financial liberalisation but with adequate supervision and transparency. The contrast in perspectives predominated at the G7 finance ministers meeting in October 1998.

Encouraged by increased support from both the Asians and the Europeans, however, the Japanese government promoted the idea of curtailing short-term capital flow reversals. Their proposal emphasised that countries in financial crisis should be allowed to suspend their external payments temporarily, and that non-national financial institutions would have to maintain a certain level of outstanding claims to those countries in crisis ('Hejji Fando Taisaku Kento Shyuyokoku Ga Kinyuu Antei Kyougikai: Ofushoa Shijou Kanshi Mo' 1999). The Japanese government promoted this idea at the G7 finance ministers meeting in April 1999. Although this plan was not taken up in the same form, the Japanese government saw it as progress when other G7 members (although not so much the United States) appeared sympathetic to the idea of checking and regulating short-term capital flows across borders.

The 1999 Cologne Summit became the place to address the direction of the new international financial architecture. The G7 finance ministries had already conducted the bulk of the discussion on the new international financial architecture in the newly created Financial Stability Forum (FSF) in February 1999 and during the meeting of the finance ministers two weeks before the leaders' summit. The division was always clear. Even after the events in October 1998, which U.S. president Bill Clinton called 'the biggest crisis of the past 50 years', the U.S. administration was reluctant to address the increased regulation of hedge funds. On the other hand, the Europeans and the Japanese were concerned about both the unregulated and volatile nature of those funds and the management of exchange rates (rather than total flexibility) for many countries.

What came out of the meetings of financial specialists were plans to strengthen the international financial system further through the participation of the private financial sector. The emphasis on the co-responsibility of the lenders (rather than just the borrowers) characterises the direction of these plans. Interviewed by the *Nihon Keizai Shimbun* on 8 June, Japan's Vice-Minister of Finance, Eisuke Sakakibara (nicknamed Mr. Yen), noted:

> There has been an increase in awareness regarding the crisis in global capitalism even in the United States as the Asian crisis spread to Latin America and Russia, and as the major American hedge fund failed. The United States, Europe, and Japan *now all agree* that the centre of the causes of these crises lies in capital movements. We have to strengthen our capacity to monitor short-term capital movement, in particular. In that context, the G7 members all acknowledge the possibility of regulating the movement (entrance and exit) of capital at the time of crisis ('Kokusai Kinyuu Kaikau Oosuji Goui He, Samitto. Sakakibara Zaimukan Kaikenn, Tankishihon No Kokusai Ido, Kanshi Kyouka' 1999, translated by author, emphasis added).

The redirection of the international financial system toward stability rather than growth was further helped by the host of that year's summit, German chancellor Gerhart Schroeder, who identified the aim of the meeting as achieving globalisation with a human face. Schroeder also stressed the need for regulating activities of institutional investors at the time of international financial instability. Taking up the opportunity, Japanese leaders cautioned against the predominant force of the U.S.-led 'market fundamentalism' (Kondo 1999). The Japanese government also insisted on the need to respect the values of other cultures when it came to the universal values promoted by the 'global standard'.

The resulting document on financial issues — the 'Report of the G7 Finance Ministers to the Köln Economic Summit' — included discussions on the adverse affect of policy biases in favour of short-term capital flows, caution on drastic capital account liberalisation, and the justifiability of the use of controls on capital inflows. Furthermore, the G7 members agreed to establish the International Monetary and Financial Committee (IMFC) within the IMF. They also agreed to set up the G20 consisting of the G7 members and emerging market countries 'to establish an informal mechanism for dialogue among systemically important countries within the framework of the Bretton Woods institutional system' (G7 Finance Ministers 1999, paragraph 7).[9]

These particular agreements came as a result of what the G7 members learned through their experience of volatile financial markets in the aftermath of the Asian crisis. Nevertheless, the Japanese government did accomplish at least part of what it had set out to do: It convinced the G7 members that the international financial system, particularly the activities of hedge funds (and other short-term capital flows), deserved partial blame, and increased the influence of developing countries, notably some from Asia, in the debate over the new international financial architecture.[10]

Japan's Challenge in International Finance and the Okinawa Summit

The Japanese government, on the initiative of the Ministry of Finance, prepared its position as the only Asian country among the G7 members and as the host government of the 2000 Okinawa Summit. In the process, and in the hope of advancing Asian regional interests in restructuring the international financial system, on 20 June 2000 the Council on Foreign Exchange and Other Transactions (a council of the Ministry of Finance) published a study that summarised the strategy for reinvigorating the Asian economy (Subcouncil of the Revitalization of the Asian Economy and Financial Markets et al. 2000). In the report, the council made two points clear. First, a regional framework is critical when the Asian economies address the possibility of continual and stable economic growth in the future. Second, Japan has to (or would like to) play a critical role in this regional strategy.

Furthermore, with the hope of reaching out to nonmembers of the G7 and building support for Japan's initiatives, the Ministry of Foreign Affairs took the unusual step of inviting leaders of (mostly) African countries for a meeting right before the Okinawa Summit, on 20 July. This encounter gave leaders from both developed and developing countries an opportunity to meet, exchange views, and build bridges between North and South on the variety of issues ranging from information technology and external debt to infectious diseases. Before this meeting, the Japanese government announced details of a US$18 billion aid package to be used to increase access to information technology among developing countries, particularly in Asia.

Among the G7 members, with the economic recovery of Asia and the continuing boom in the U.S. economy, the sense of crisis dissipated as their finance ministers arrived at Fukuoka, the site for the ministerial meeting two weeks prior to the leaders meeting in Okinawa. Yet the challenges of financial globalisation remained. The finance ministers presented two reports to the heads of state. In the first one, called 'Strengthening the International Financial Architecture', they reported on the progress of international financial reform to strengthen the global financial architecture since the Cologne Summit (see Appendix D). The second, 'Impact of the IT Revolution on the Economy and Finance', summarised the new focus of interest among the G7 finance ministers on the good governance of international financial activities, including combating money laundering and harmful tax competition (G7 Finance Ministers 2000). The G7 finance ministers also addressed abuse of offshore financial centres (OFCs) following the recommendations made by the FSF. In addition, the central problem of international finance seemed to have shifted from crisis prevention and management to debt forgiveness for Heavily Indebted Poor Countries (HIPCs).

Japan's goals at this summit were to show that the Japanese government had contributed immensely to the reform of the international financial architecture, would continue to commit to such reform (including the reform of the IMF) in order to reflect the Asian perspective, and was very sensitive to the importance of cultural diversity (that is, against 'global standardising' culture). As a part of such efforts, the leaders from Japan continued to push IMF reform.[11]

In sum, since the Asian crisis, Japanese leaders have used the summits as well as the support of the Europeans (as Russia was rattled by a financial crisis), to achieve their goal of establishing a consensus on the danger of unregulated short-term capital flows. This goal would never have been accomplished in a bilateral framework between Japan and the United States.

Conclusion

The Japanese government always considers itself as a bridge between Asia and the West. In particular, the Japanese government often poses as a representative of regional Asian interests (or even more widely the interests of non-Western peoples) at the time of G7 summit meetings, especially when it will help promote Japan's own interests. Because the G7 summit meetings have allowed Japan to go beyond the U.S.-Japan bilateral framework, the Japanese government has relied on this multilateral function when U.S. opposition has loomed over Japan's position on Asian matters.[12]

In the aftermath of the Asian crisis, that dynamic was overwhelmingly clear. When the Japanese government did not have a strong agenda of its own, before the Asian financial crisis and the IMF's involvement in it, Japan tended to be a mere supporter of U.S. initiatives. Although it did have an agenda of its own, such as increasing voting power, with regard to the reform of the IFIs proposed in 1994 the government tried to manage it by supporting U.S. initiatives. As the Asian crisis struck and the different perspectives on the appropriate direction of the international financial arrangements became clear, the Japanese government went to the G7 summit (and elsewhere) to assert the need for certain regulations in the global financial market (especially of the HLIs) and IMF reform. Concomitantly, the Japanese government, even with a sluggish economy, with a domestic financial crisis and tight budget, proposed and implemented on its own various initiatives to support the management of the Asian financial crisis and to hasten the recovery of Asian economies.

The changing attitudes of the Europeans, especially after the 1998 Russian crisis, weakened the U.S. position by the time of the 1999 Cologne Summit. Although a compromise was made so as not to single out the flaws of hedge funds, there was a solid consensus on the need for regulating some activities in international financial markets. This is not a full victory for Japan, but Japan still accomplished more than it could have hoped to bilaterally with the United States. By the time of the 2000 Okinawa Summit, the focus of the issue shifted somewhat from the Asian crisis to information technology, HIPCs, and money laundering. Yet the Japanese government continued to show full support and commitment to the G7/8 process. It is, indeed, one of a few global mechanisms for the Japanese government to show its independent initiatives in times of need.

Notes

1 Although Russia formally joined the Summit at the 1997 Denver Summit Group of Eight, most of the top-level discussions on G7 economic and financial issues are still carried out without the participation of Russia; thus the term 'G7' is used throughout this chapter.

2 In one of the few analytical works on Japan and the G7 by Japanese scholars, Kuniko Inoguchi (1994, 30–33) notes that for the Japanese, the major significance of the G7 is that it enables Japan to build strong substantive and political ties with major nations beyond the United States at the highest level. This expands Japan's scope for political manoeuvring and gives Japan more opportunity to shape rules in regard to international issues than would have been possible in the context of U.S.-Japan bilateral relations. The G7 also has helped strengthen Japan's position on its own foreign policy and provides a salutary 'deadline effect' on Japanese domestic decision-making.

3 Typical of such discussion is Alan Greenspan's testimony to the Senate Foreign Relations Committee in February 1998.

4 Especially in regard to Indonesia.

5 It is ironic that the reallocation of the IMF quota that gave Japan the sole second voting power was announced during the World Bank/IMF Annual Conference in September 1997 in the aftermath of the Thai crisis. At that conference, the Japanese government called for the establishment of the controversial Asian Monetary Fund.

6 The Philippines also requested help, but it has always been an exceptional case in Asia. The IMF had been involved in its debt restructuring since the 1980s.

7 A US$17.2 billion rescue package for Thailand, agreed on by the IMF and other contributing countries, did not include any bilateral contribution from the United States. Many U.S. policy makers note that at the time of this agreement in August 1997, Thailand seemed to be an isolated incident and U.S. domestic constraint made it difficult for its administration to commit funds.

8 The governments of both Indonesia and South Korea, as well as the government of Thailand, hoped to avoid IMF involvement at the onset of their respective financial crises for fear of the IMF's stringent conditionality. These governments turned to the IMF after being refused by Japan and other bilateral creditors.

9 The G7 finance ministers meeting on 25 September 1999 formally established the G20 forum of finance ministers and central bank governors. The forum is to include 'systematically important countries from the regions around the world', and has been chaired by Canadian finance minister Paul Martin for its first two years. The G20 was launched on 15 December 1999. Besides the G8 members, countries such as Saudi Arabia, Australia, Brazil, Argentina, China, Indonesia, and South Korea were invited. See Kirton 1999.

10 The Asian countries, including Thailand, South Korea, Malaysia, and China, welcomed the progress even though some urged further regulation in the capital market ('Ajia Kangeimo Ondosa: G-7 Hejji Fando Kanshi Kyoka ni Goui' 1999).

11 Vice-minister of finance Haruhiko Kuroda summarised Japan's three major objectives in reforming the IMF: the focus on surveillance and programs should respond to potentially abrupt large-scale cross-border capital movements, the involvement of the IMF in structural policies should be limited to cases directly related to crises, and its transparency and decision-making process should be improved (Kuroda 2000).

12   Inoguchi's (1994, fn 2) characterisation of Japan's concerns at the summit does not include this point. The typical case was at the time of the China's Tiananmen Square incident in 1989, when the Japanese government strove to, and partially succeeded in, mitigating the harsh criticism of China during the 1989 Paris Summit.

References

'Ajia Kangeimo Ondosa: G-7 Hejji Fando Kanshi Kyoka ni Goui' (Variation in Asia's Reception: A G7 Agreement on Tightened Regulations on the Hedge Funds) (1999). *Asahi Shimbun*, 19 June, p. 1.

Bergsten, C. Fred and C. Randall Henning (1996). *Global Economic Leadership and the Group of Seven.* Institute for International Economics, Washington DC.

G7 (1997). 'Confronting Global Economic and Financial Challenges. Denver Summit Statement by Seven'. 21 June, Denver. <www.g7.utoronto.ca/g7/summit/ 1997denver/confront.htm> (March 2001).

G7 (1998). 'G7 Chairman's Statement'. 15 May, Birmingham. <www.g7.utoronto.ca/ g7/summit/1998birmingham/chair.htm> (March 2001).

G7 Finance Ministers (1999). 'Report of the G7 Finance Ministers to the Köln Economic Summit'. 18 June, Cologne. <www.g7.utoronto.ca/g7/finance/ fm061999.htm> (March 2001).

G7 Finance Ministers (2000). 'Actions against Abuse of the Global Financial System'. Report from G7 Finance Ministers to the Heads of State and Government. 21 July. <www.g7.utoronto.ca/g7/summit/2000okinawa/abuse.htm> (March 2001).

'Hejji Fando Taisaku Kento Shyuyokoku Ga Kinyuu Antei Kyougikai: Ofushoa Shijou Kanshi Mo' (Considering Regulation of Hedge Funds, Key Countries Launch Financial Stabilization Committee Which May Include Surveillance of Off-Shore Market) (1999). *Nihon Keizai Shimbun*, 15 April, p. 3.

Ikenberry, John (1993). 'Salvaging the G7'. *Foreign Affairs* vol. 72 (Spring), pp. 132–139.

Inoguchi, Kuniko (1994). 'The Changing Significance of the G7 Summits'. *Japan Review of International Affairs* Winter, pp. 21–38.

Kirton, John J. (1999). 'What Is the G20?' <www.library.utoronto.ca/g7/g20/ g20whatisit.html> (March 2001).

'Kokusai Kinyuu Kaikau Oosuji Goui He, Samitto. Sakakibara Zaimukan Kaikenn, Tankishihon No Kokusai Ido, Kanshi Kyouka' (International Financial Reform Leading to General Agreement at the Summit: Vice-Minister Sakakibara Notes Increase in Surveillance on International Short-term Capital Movement) (1999). *Nihon Keizai Shimbun*, 8 June, p. 5.

Kondo, Seiji (1999). 'Kerun Samitto no Seika To Nihon' (The Results of the Cologne Summit and Japan). *Sekai Keizai Hyoron*, pp. 8–28.

Kuroda, Haruhiko (2000). 'Vice-Minister's Speech on the Future International Financial Architecture and Regional Capital Market Development'. Delivered at the Round Table on Capital Market Reform in Asia, Tokyo, 11 April. <www.mof.go.jp/english/if/if015.htm> (March 2001).

'Nichibei Shuno Kaidan, Shushou, "Kinyuu Mondai" Soukishori He — Keizai Saisei Bei Ga Aturyoku' (U.S.-Japan Leaders Meeting: Prime Minister Promised to Have Swift Solution to the 'Financial Problem' — U.S. Pressures Japan on Its Economic Recovery (1998). *Nihon Keizai Shimbun*, 16 May, p. 1.

Sanger, David E. (1998). 'U.S. Sees New Villain in Asian Crisis: Tokyo's Leadership'. *New York Times*, 22 February, p. 3.

'Shihon Ido no Kanshi Kyoka, G7 Zoushoukaigou Kaimakuhe, Gouiann Go Koumoku — Ajia Kiki Saihatsu Boushi' (Strengthening of Surveillance on Capital Movement: G7 Finance Ministers' Meeting Opens with Five Issues to Be Agreed Including the Future Prevention of Asian Crisis (1998). *Nihon Keizai Shimbun*, 8 May, p. 1.

Stiglitz, Joseph (1998). 'Boats, Planes, and Capital Flows: Personal View'. *Financial Times*, 25 March, p. 32.

Subcouncil of the Revitalization of the Asian Economy and Financial Markets, Council on Exchange and Other Transactions (2000). 'The Road to the Revival of the Asian Economy and Financial System: Sustainable Growth in the 21st Century and Building a Multilayered Regional Cooperative Network'. (Mimeograph.) Ministry of Finance, Tokyo.

8 Japan, the Asian Economy, the International Financial System, and the G8: A Critical Perspective

KUNIHIKO ITO

In 1999, Michio Morishima published a book provocatively titled *Why Do I Expect Japan to Collapse?* He asserted that the only way for Japan to avoid collapse in the near future was to form an Asian community consisting of Japan, China, North and South Korea, Taiwan, and a hypothesised independent Okinawa known as Ryukyu. At the centre of the Asian community, Ryukyu would serve as the capital. Furthermore, Japan must apologise to Asian victims and others for its past aggression and make an effort to consult them about Asia's future.

Most of Morishima's proposal is sound. Yet the Asian community need not be limited to North-East Asia. Rather, the Asian community should consist of all Asian countries including Australia and New Zealand. In the context of the reforming international financial system, this means the establishment of the Asian Monetary Fund (AMF) in the short run and the formation of an Asian currency bloc in the long run. Asian co-operation, as would be required by the AMF, would be the basic element of the Asian approach in the twenty-first century. However, there are two obstacles to this development. The first is that some Japanese political leaders have a faulty understanding of their history, especially the Emperor system and Japan's war of aggression. The second is the influence of the United States on Japanese policy.

Although this argument might appear to be that of a regionalist, past reform programs led by the annual G7/8 can be regarded as generally positive. The basic framework for such programs consists of four key ideas: market mechanisms, individual responsibility, surveillance, and safety nets. Yet the pace of these programs is too slow. They also tend to become compromised, because of major differences in interests, philosophy, thought, society, and culture among the G7/8 members, even if they share the slogan of democracy and market economy.

Although there is a possibility that a financial crisis will still break out, it will take a very long time for the G7/8 members to agree upon the grand design of the international financial system for the twenty-first century and to accomplish a drastic reform of the system. There are limits to surveillance by the International Monetary Fund (IMF). At present, the G7 and the IMF must work to bring the U.S. economy to a soft landing. As preventive measures for financial crises that might happen over the long term, there is a need to build regional co-operative systems. Such co-operation could supplement the G7/8 process and IMF attempts to stabilise the international financial system.

Furthermore, democracy is one of the fundamental principles of global governance, so the burden of global governance should not be borne only by taxes on people in the G7 countries. The current system of paying the costs of global governance has some adverse effects. Some member countries complain about using the resources of the IMF — that is, their taxes — to shore up the mismanaged economic policies of other countries. The current system encourages the G7 members, especially the U.S., to overreact to other countries' moral hazard. When the G7 members try to set their finances in order, it is difficult for them to agree on their respective share of the cost. The G7's large share of the financing of the international financial institutions (IFIs) and the United Nations (UN) is an incentive to its member nations that want to decrease such funding. The costs for global governance will continue to increase. One way to solve such a dilemma is to introduce a Tobin tax. If this is done, coping with offshore financial centres (OFCs), tax havens, and financial crimes will become more important. The information technology (IT) revolution also strengthens the feasibility of the Tobin tax.

At the Cologne Summit in 1999, the G7/8 leaders agreed to pursue globalisation with a human face. The Association of South-East Asian Nations plus Japan, China, and South Korea (ASEAN + 3) agreed to strengthen their financial co-operation in East Asia at Chiang Mai, Thailand, in May 2000. Many Asian countries support the notion of the AMF, a notion that China also does not oppose. Japan's task at the Okinawa Summit in 2000 was to express the Asian voice in the presence of the other G7/8 members and to participate in drawing the grand design for global management in the twenty-first century. The G7/8 also needs to discuss the relationship between globalism and regionalism. It is obvious that the Japanese government, as the host, gave the IT revolution too much single-minded importance. A further large problem facing the Asian approach is that the U.S. easily influences the diplomacy of the Japanese government. The mission of Japan, now the Japan of Asia, is very serious.

International Financial System Reform and G7/8 Process

Since the failure of the Bretton Woods system as a result of the so-called dollar shock in August 1971, the world monetary system had drifted along by the rules of the game only to respond to situations as they occurred, for example, with the Kingston Accord in 1976. When a financial problem developed, the main countries mended defective parts of the world monetary system after the fact. The European countries headed for monetary integration to avoid the influence of the U.S. dollar. The G5 countries formed a framework of international policy co-ordination to align exchange rates in September 1985.[1] The resulting Plaza Accord was a turning point. At the Tokyo Summit of 1986, the G5 leaders agreed to establish regular meetings of the G7 finance ministers and central bank governors, including those of Italy and Canada, and to strengthen multilateral surveillance in co-operation with the IMF. The G7 members then showed a strong interest in exchange rates and trade balances. However, the G7 did not discuss drastic reform of the international financial system.

After numerous currency and financial crises in the first half of the 1990s, the G7 leaders took up a review of the international institutions, that is, the UN and the IFIs, as one of the main subjects of the Halifax Summit in 1995.[2] On the issue of the international financial system, the G7 agreed to establish an early warning system that included improved and effective surveillance of national economic policies and financial market developments, to establish a new standing procedure known as the Emergency Financing Mechanism, and to enable the G10 to double the amount currently available under the General Arrangements to Borrow (GAB).[3] Carl-Johan Lindgren, G. G. Garcia, and Matthew Saal (1996) reported that the number of nations that faced banking crises between 1980 and 1995 totalled 133 out of the 181 IMF members. Germany was the only G7 nation never to face such a crisis. Nonetheless, it took considerable time for the G7 to broach the topic of reforming the Bretton Woods system. In 1992, the private sector launched the Bretton Woods Commission made up of international finance specialists in the U.S., European Union (EU), and Japan in order to hasten drastic reform of the international financial system. The commission completed a realistic but provocative report in 1994, copies of which were sent to the G7 governments so it could be discussed at the Naples Summit. However, at the summit, the leaders decided to bring up the matter of reform of the international financial system at Halifax the next year.

The main theme at the Lyon Summit in 1996 was economic globalisation. Kazuo Ogura, the Japanese sherpa, reported on the leaders' discussion of reform of the international institutions. The U.S. and the UK asserted that increasing economic globalisation enabled them to reduce their role and that private investment and technology transfers should take a major role in the world economy. With the exception of Japan and France, the G7 members displayed a negative attitude toward increasing resources or sharing expenses of the multilateral financial institutions because of financial difficulties in their own countries. Some leaders suggested that donors not increase their IMF quota, but that the IMF should dispose of its stockpile of gold in order to facilitate the financing of the Enhanced Structural Adjustment Facility (ESAF). Germany strongly opposed this suggestion, which could have opened the way to a sale of gold held by the Bundesbank. This episode shows the obstacles to reaching agreements at the G7 summit under the existing system of sharing the burden in international institutions.

At the Denver Summit in 1997, the leaders continued to discuss the problem of international financial system reform begun in Halifax and Lyon. This subject was not a central one because the summit took place just before the 1997 Asian financial crisis broke. Nonetheless, the G7 leaders had to look into their collective response to systemic risk and emerging markets because of the great losses incurred at Barings Corporation and Daiwa Bank in connection with derivatives dealing. The leaders concluded there were many technical issues involved and referred the matter to experts to investigate.

The measures for strengthening the international financial system led to the main theme of the Birmingham Summit the following year because of the Asian financial crisis. At this summit, the report entitled 'Strengthening the Architecture of the Global Financial System' was submitted to the G7 leaders and was made public with the following statement from the chair:

> 6. Globalisation has the power to bring immense economic benefits to all countries and people. But the Asian financial crisis has revealed that there are potential weaknesses and vulnerabilities in the global financial system. In particular we are conscious of the serious human and social consequences of such crises when they occur (G7 1998).

The leaders expressed their opinions on the problems of increasing transparency, helping countries throughout the world prepare for global capital flows, strengthening national financial systems, and ensuring that the private sector take full responsibility for its own decisions in order to reduce moral hazard. They told their finance ministers to consider concrete measures in that year. Yet those actions were only to begin the study of accurate and prompt measures for surveying short-term capital flows.

In August 1998, the Asian financial crisis spread to Russia. Long-Term Capital Management (LTCM) failed in September. The financial crisis reached Brazil in January 1999. Such a chain of events made countries all over the world understand that the financial crisis was not caused by special Asian circumstances — crony capitalism — but by a defect hidden in the deregulated financial markets or the risks of global capitalism. In particular, the failure of LTCM received great attention in U.S. meetings and mass media. It thus brought about an opportunity for changing the U.S. government's previous indifference to reform of the international financial system.

At the Cologne Summit, all G8 members shared a philosophy that considered social aspects and support of the weak. The term 'globalisation' meant not only the market mechanism but also humanity, as indicated in a section on strengthening social safeguards in the G8 Communiqué (1999):

> 19. ... We therefore need to take steps to strengthen the institutional and social infrastructure that can give globalization a "human face" and ensure increasing, widely shared prosperity.
>
> 23. We call on the International Financial Institutions (IFIs) to support and monitor the development of sound social policy and infrastructure in developing countries. We commend actions already being taken in this regard. We urge the International Monetary Fund (IMF) to give more attention to this issue in designing its economic programs and to give particular priority to core budgets such as basic health, education and training to the extent possible, even during periods of fiscal consolidation.

With regard to strengthening the international financial system, the Basle Committee on Banking Supervision and the International Organization of Securities Commissions continued to examine ways to manage or regulate banks and securities companies dealing with hedge funds and other financial institutions. The G7/8 played a leading role in establishing the Financial Stability Forum (FSF) in April 1999. This forum set up three working groups on highly leveraged institutions (HLIs), short-term capital flows, and OFCs. The results of their study were presented in the Architecture paper at the Cologne Summit. But even at this stage, plans for improvement, such as methods of direct or indirect supervision of HLIs and disclosure, were not clearly defined. The leaders thus continued to support the establishment of the FSF.

The discussion about the reform of the international financial and monetary system fell into stride from the Halifax Summit in 1995. As far as reform was concerned, Canada consistently took the initiative.[4] If it had not been so, the

G7/8 could not have reached a consensus on reform at Cologne. Canada has already proposed the introduction of a Tobin-like tax as the next step in controlling international short-term capital flows.

Evaluation of the Summit Process

The G7's consensus on reform of the international financial system is based on the following basic framework: first, in principle every country makes the most of the market mechanism, which requires deregulation. Second, everyone who conducts transactions in the market is responsible for their transactions. In other words, one must lie in the bed one makes. Participating economic units in market activity, especially financial institutions, must manage their own risk and disclose their financial information. Third, the authorities should monitor or guard market conditions and the behaviour of participants and try to eliminate destabilising market factors. One of the roles of the IMF, for example, is to detect factors that destabilise the international financial system at an early stage, by way of its surveillance of participating countries and the immediate issuance of recommendations to the country concerned. Therefore, IMF surveillance is a method for preventing financial crises. Fourth, a safety net for the worst-case scenarios. Should a crisis happen, measures such as emergency financing and support must be available.

How can one evaluate the reform of the international financial architecture based on this framework?

The Difficulty of Attaining Consensus among G7/8 Members

Innumerable solutions exist within this basic framework. Discussion may often circulate because it has a recursive structure. For example, countries that attach great importance to the market mechanism and individual responsibility — represented by the U.S. — downplay the need for a safety net. Such countries tend to argue that a safety net can lead to moral hazard and contradict the principle of individual responsibility. On the other hand, the countries concerned about a possible financial crisis place much stress on surveillance and a safety net. The G7/8 summits travelled a hard, long road from Halifax to Cologne on the way to reaching an agreement on strengthening social safeguards.

Some countries may even assert the need for regulation. Japan takes the stand that a curb on capital inflows might be needed in special situations. Japan and Malaysia call for the right to make rules against hedge funds, about the ratio of owned capital to liabilities, and the disclosure of assets. There is, however, a possibility that regulation will touch off some market distortions. Negotiations among the G7/8 governments may return to where they started.

Large differences in interests, philosophy, thought, society, and culture remain among G7/8 countries. At the practical level, it has taken and will continue to take considerable time to reach an agreement on reform.

Who Should Pay?

The second problem is who should pay the costs of stabilising the international financial system. These costs include surveillance and support. Even if the finance surveillance authorities of each country assisted the IMF, surveillance costs would continue to increase as the financial economy diversified and extended. Support entails not only relief to countries facing financial crises but also the costs of debt relief for the Heavily Indebted Poor Countries (HIPCs), financial assistance to developing countries, and country risk management.

None of the G7 countries can afford to spend large amounts of money for IFIs because they must improve their own public finances. Sharing such costs is becoming problematic. Each nation and its national assembly sometimes question why their taxes are spent to shore up the failure of a foreign country's economic management. The U.S. Congress rejected President Bill Clinton's proposal when Mexico was in a difficult situation. Such resistance is apt to make the governments of G7 countries, especially the U.S., overly sensitive to the moral hazard of borrowers.

The quota paid to the international institutions also has much to do with struggles for leadership within them. The current review of the IMF quota mirrors the struggle for leadership among Japan, the U.S., and Europe. As a result, the Japanese government plans to raise the quotas of other Asian countries without any additional burden and to reflect Asian opinions in the IMF's decision making.

A Limit to Surveillance

The third problem is the limit to surveillance. Given the excellent study by Louis Pauly (1997) on the limits to IMF surveillance, this analysis focusses on such limits as an early warning system.

From experience and studies of past financial crises, the international community has learned much: the problems with controls on capital inflows, the speed and volume of capital outflows, the problems of dollarization, the vulnerability of pegged exchange regimes, the establishment of sound financial (banking) systems, the need for consistent macroeconomic policy, the contagion of crisis, and so on.[5] But it cannot predict when and under what conditions a financial crisis will occur. This is a serious shortcoming. There are a number of economists, including this author, who fear that the world economies must live with increasingly frequent crises.

Japan and Malaysia are dissatisfied that there were no regulations concerning hedge funds in the March 2000 report of FSF. The two countries should keep a closer watch on derivative activities. According to statistics compiled by the Bank for International Settlements (BIS), over-the-counter derivatives dealing is concentrated in a few dealer financial institutions that are active internationally, and they take sizeable credit risks. If such a dealer fell into default, the impact would have a domino effect around the world. The derivative market itself contains several unstabilising factors, for example 'positive feedback' and 'hedging overhang'. The BIS and central banks are still searching for ways to manage macroeconomic risks that involve derivative activities.

It is more important to watch over a country with a healthy economy. The collapse of Japan's bubble economy in 1990 and the Asian currency crisis in 1997 showed that there is a possibility that a country with good economic conditions can suddenly break down. The global task at present is to move from unbalanced growth to simultaneous international growth. Can the G7/8 get the U.S. economy to make a soft landing and then help the world economy recover through the IT revolution? From the point of view of securing a soft landing and simultaneous international growth, the most serious matter is whether the G7/8 and the IMF can accurately diagnose the economic situation of the U.S. Is the IMF's surveillance of the U.S. too optimistic? What will G7 co-operation do for a soft landing of the U.S. economy? The world is watching the progress of this situation with interest. The G7 finance ministers and central bank governors did not discuss the U.S. stock market formally in their meeting in April 2000. The next month, U.S. stock prices again plummeted sharply. The impact extended to Japanese and Asian stock markets. It has been clear since autumn 1999 that the U.S. stock market has entered an adjustment period and the U.S. economy has begun to slow down. Its current account deficit in 2000 was expected to be US$40 billion, surpassing the previous year's, which was the largest in history. In contrast, the Japanese economy has begun to recover, and economic conditions are beginning to improve in Europe and Asia. A time lag in the business cycles among countries will lead to a change in international capital flows. There is a possibility of rapid capital outflow from the U.S. in the near future.

Japan and the Asian Economy: The Asian Approach

A movement is stirring in Asia. It is a movement to reflect Asian voices more clearly in the G7/8 process and the IFIs, which are led by European and North American countries, to complement the Bretton Woods institutions with regional co-operation, and to seek reform of the international financial architecture so they might adapt better to each country's circumstances. This section explores this Asian approach, the strengthening of Asian countries' regional co-operation from the Asian crisis to the present, and the issues they raise for reforming the international financial system.[6]

International divisions of labour have appeared within Asia because of foreign direct investment (FDI) made since the 1980s. Judging from the dimensions of trade and finance, Japan has taken a forward-looking attitude toward strengthening relations with Asian countries since 1998. Approval for integrating Asian countries was more forthcoming in 2000. The Japanese government was changing its way of thinking about trade policy, moving away from considering regional or bilateral free-trade agreements as having negative effects on multilateral trade because of discrimination against excluded countries. Since 1998, the Japanese government has been studying the possibility of concluding a free-trade agreement with South Korea and Singapore in order to complement multilateral trade.

Since 1998, co-operative Asian relationships in financial matters have developed more rapidly and tightly. The Asian financial crisis dates from the sudden fall of the Thai baht in July 1997, a fall due to a tremendous outflow of foreign short-term capital. Some countries' foreign currency reserves declined sharply, thus temporarily placing them in very tight positions. They could not avoid calling for emergency support from the IMF. The capital outflows were so huge that the amount of support required was large. The IMF could not meet the expense by itself. A new emergency support scheme involving the World Bank, the Asian Development Bank (ADB), and bilateral aid was needed. Japan and the IMF held a meeting on supporting Thailand in Tokyo in August 1997. Japan stated that it would provide financial support amounting to US\$4 billion to Thailand, which was matched by the IMF; Japan's contribution was the largest. A similar support scheme was made for Indonesia and South Korea. Japan pledged financial support of US\$5 billion for Indonesia and US\$10 billion for Korea. Other Asian countries also co-operated on these support schemes in spite of their tight financial situation.

The Japanese government advocated the establishment of the AMF in autumn 1997. It saw that a sense of solidarity had grown among Asian countries after the combined support of Thailand. The AMF would be a permanent institution that provided multilateral aid within Asia to complement the IMF in terms of both quantity and quality. The AMF's role would be to conduct regional surveillance and to supplement the IMF's support funds. However, the AMF was not established because the U.S., China, and the IMF firmly opposed it. The U.S. maintained that the AMF's easy supply of liquidity would encourage moral hazard and delay structural reforms. The IMF was afraid lest the AMF diminish the function of the IMF due to overlapping roles. China suspected that Japan's real intention was to assert the supremacy of the yen over Asia.

Although the AMF plan fell through, many countries realised the need for a framework for regional surveillance in addition to that of the IMF and for bilateral aid premised on IMF economic adjustment programs. The reasons were the Asian countries' realisation that IMF surveillance had failed to foresee the Asian currency crisis, let alone the gravity of the crisis. In November 1997, 14 countries, mostly Asian, assembled in Manila to discuss regional co-operation. They agreed on the Manila Framework to strengthen regional co-operation in Asia and the Pacific with the goal of securing stable financial systems and currencies.

The next development came when the currency crises changed to a broader financial crisis that, in crisis-afflicted South-East Asian countries, became full-fledged economic crises as a result of IMF programs. Much resistance and criticism grew in response to the IMF programs. The IMF's prescription was the same as the one applied to Latin America in the 1980s and early 1990s: tightened fiscal policy aimed at reducing current account deficits and a high interest-rate policy aimed at maintaining the value of the affected nation's currency. The policy package caused functional disorder in the financial sectors of the affected countries and, as a result, inflicted great damage on the real sectors of their economies.

The IMF concluded that the root cause of the crisis was crony capitalism and strongly pushed for structural reforms. Asian countries felt that the IMF dogmatically imposed Western ideas and forced resulting social costs on Asian peoples. After Russia fell into crisis and the failure of LTCM was reported in August-September 1998, the understanding of the causes of the Asian crisis changed a great deal on the world stage.

The causes were thus clearly not crony capitalism unique to Asia but the globalising international financial system where whimsical short-term capital moves in an instant. In either case, the governments of Asia that had fallen into economic crisis had to restore business activity immediately, to restructure financial systems, and to extend social safety nets to people who had suffered the greatest losses from the crisis. In October 1998, the Japanese government launched the 'New Initiative to Overcome the Asian Currency Crisis: The New Miyazawa Initiative', in order to assist Asian countries in overcoming their economic difficulties and to contribute to the stability of international financial markets. Japan stood ready to provide a package of support measures. The package contained direct and indirect official financial assistance to the amount of US$30 billion to support Asian countries in raising funds from international financial markets, to provide financial support in the form of co-financing with multilateral development banks, and to offer technical assistance. The New Miyazawa Initiative was acceptable to the U.S. and the IMF as well as to Asian countries because it was a bilateral support framework.

Ironically, while the Japanese economy remained stagnant, the real economies of other Asian countries recovered rapidly in 1999. Money from Europe and North America gradually flowed back into Asian stock markets. Yet Asian countries were still confronted with the following problems. First of all, it was necessary for them to reform their economic structures. Second, they had to organise a more robust domestic and international financial system in order to ensure that still-vulnerable Asian economies would not fall into crisis in the future. In particular, they had to reconstruct their banking sectors while breaking up the credit crunch by continuing to dispose of bad loans. The Japanese government thought that measures for the full utilisation of Japanese private-sector capital would be indispensable in settling the problem. From the perspective of Japan, the mobilisation of private sector funds would be helpful in the internationalisation of the yen and the revitalisation of the Tokyo market. Such ideas were written into the 'Resource Mobilization Plan for Asia: The Second Stage of the New Miyazawa Initiative' unveiled at the meeting of Asia-Pacific Economic Cooperation (APEC) finance ministers in May 1999.

The Asian countries then entered a new stage of co-operation. The Joint Statement on East Asia Cooperation was issued by the ASEAN + 3 leaders at their informal meeting in Manila in November 1999. Afterwards, the finance ministers of ASEAN + 3 (including China, Japan, and South Korea) convened their meeting in Chiang Mai to exchange views on economic and financial situations and discuss further co-operation in the East Asian region. The participating countries agreed to strengthen East Asian finance co-operation, an agreement commonly called the Chiang Mai Initiative. More precisely, the joint ministerial statement of the ASEAN + 3 finance ministers meeting stated:

3. ... To further sustain this economic growth, we agreed to strengthen our policy dialogues and regional cooperation activities in, among others, the areas of capital flows monitoring, self-help and support mechanism and international financial reforms.

6. In order to strengthen our self-help and support mechanisms in East Asia through the ASEAN + 3 framework, we recognized a need to establish a regional financing arrangement to supplement the existing international facilities. As a start, we agreed to strengthen the existing cooperative frameworks among our monetary authorities through the "Chiang Mai Initiative". The Initiative involves an expanded ASEAN Swap Arrangement that would include ASEAN countries, and a network of bilateral swap and repurchase agreement facilities among ASEAN countries, China, Japan and the Republic of Korea (ASEAN + 3 Finance Ministers 2000).

China, which had treated the notion of the AMF coolly, joined in the agreement since its admission into the World Trade Organization (WTO) was coming up soon. Now several countries in the Asian region, notably Japan, Malaysia, Thailand, Korea, the Philippines, and Indonesia, were working to create the AMF along these lines. This shows that Japan can act in concert with other Asian countries.

The difficulties confronting the establishment of the AMF are not the only problems of relevance. The first additional problem is that Asian countries must avoid the dollarization of their own debts and ensure a structure where well-balanced, high-quality foreign currency will flow in as well. Control of capital inflows may be needed under certain circumstances. The second difficulty concerns what exchange rate regimes countries should adopt. Asian countries hit with a currency crisis could not maintain pegged exchange rates, so they changed to floating exchange rates. Under the floating system, if the exchange rate in question fluctuated over a broad spectrum, exchange risk could disturb capital inflows. The third difficulty is what conditionality should be imposed by the IMF, especially when Asian countries, including Japan, are wrestling with economic structural reforms. The fourth is the method of surveillance employed for these countries. The fifth is the problem of how best to regulate HLIs such as hedge funds and derivatives. The last is that Asia needs to improve its infrastructure related to IT, which is currently behind that of North America, to promote financial development and economic prosperity. Asian countries have already begun addressing these problems, and recent G7/8 summits have discussed some of them.

The Okinawa Summit and Japan

Seiji Kondo, who served as a Japanese sous-sherpa at the Cologne Summit in 1999, spoke of the results and tasks of that summit immediately after it ended. He noted two points as forming the main theme of the 2000 Okinawa Summit (Kondo 1999, translated by author).

> 1. On going ahead with globalisation with a human face, global governance is the most important problem. That is how we can manage the world without world government or how clusters of sovereign states can manage it successfully by co-operating with each other. The G7/8 summit will have to come up with a new grand design about global management in the twenty-first century at the turn of the century.
>
> 2. A fusion of the two viewpoints of globalism and regionalism is becoming necessary. Regional co-operation will be indispensable to Japan if it is to spread its own agenda in the future. It will also be important to bring about a situation in which Europeans and North Americans will place more value on Asian cultures and senses, namely to infuse the global standard with Asian values. To put the matter more concretely, Japan has not given up the idea of the AMF.

Prime Minister Keizo Obuchi decided to hold the G7/8 meeting of heads of state and government in Okinawa despite the disapproval of his ministers and advisors. But there was a move away from the above two subjects as the central theme. The restoration of economic growth though the IT revolution emerged as the main theme of the Okinawa Summit at the G7 finance ministers meeting in January 2000. U.S. treasury secretary Larry Summers conferred with Prime Minister Obuchi at the same time. Summers advised that deregulation of IT would be key to any economic recovery in Japan. The problem of Asian culture pointed out by Kondo was an item on the agenda. Yet it was impossible to overlook the IT revolution anywhere one went in Japan. It is viewed by the Japanese government and industrial world, thirsty for rapid economic growth and competitive recovery, as a means of survival. The Japanese government picked up the topic at the request of the U.S. government: because Clinton might have otherwise been reluctant to come to Okinawa, the Japanese government yielded to him the right to decide the Summit's centrepiece. The Japanese government easily submits to U.S. pressure. For example, it has maintained a zero interest-rate policy and actual quantitative easing, and has taken additional fiscal actions as the U.S. government has demanded. Finance minister Kiichi Miyazawa formally explained that the AMF was stillborn, so as not to provoke the U.S. government to block its establishment.

The relationship between Japan and the U.S. greatly influences Japan's leadership in Asia. Therefore, this unbalanced relationship becomes the first obstacle to any Asian approach to reform of the international financial system built by Asian countries in recent years. The second obstacle is that some politicians in Japan's ruling party fail to understand Japanese history. In the summer of 1999, the ruling party pushed through a law establishing the national flag and anthem. Hoisting the national flag and singing the national anthem in unison was forced on all schools. Even Prime Minister Yoshiro Mori made a slip of the tongue when he referred to Japan as 'the country of Kami, the Emperor'. This improper remark caused a great sensation in Asia. Such things remind Asian people of Japan's aggressive past and make them uncomfortable about co-operation with Japan. Okinawa bears the heaviest burden of the mistakes of Japan's past. Holding the summit in Okinawa was a good opportunity to reflect on Japanese responsibility, in order for Japan to become a real member of Asia, the Japan of Asia.

Asian countries do not wish to form a closed regionalism. In fact, Asian economies cannot sustain themselves without good economic relations with Europe and North America. They want to shape an appropriate surveillance system and safety net through regional co-operation in Asia even as they deepen relationships with Western countries. The foundation of an Asian approach, therefore, is open regionalism. The Japanese government has attempted to express Asian voices in the debates at the G7/8 summit. It is a mission that Japan, as host, takes seriously as it removes obstacles and promotes reform of the international financial system through an Asian approach.

Conclusion

The meeting of G7 finance ministers held at Fukuoka on 8 July 2000 produced a report called 'Strengthening the International Financial Architecture' (see Appendix D). It includes a chapter on regional co-operation. According to the report, the finance ministers accepted the recent developments in the area of regional co-operation in the Asian region and North America. The report states:

> Regional cooperation through more intensified surveillance can help contribute to financial stability by strengthening the policy framework at the national level. Cooperative financing arrangements at the regional level designed to supplement

resources provided by the IFIs in support of IMF programs can be effective in crisis prevention and resolution.

Furthermore, the finance ministers welcomed monetary union in Europe, which contributes to the economic and financial stability of the global economy. If monetary union succeeds, then regional co-operation in Asia will move toward the formation of a currency bloc with the similar aim of contributing to the economic and financial stability of the global economy. This is consistent with an Asian approach.

The G7/8 should earnestly consider the introduction of the Tobin tax. Global governance makes democracy the rule. This is why the burden of governance should not be covered by the taxes of G7 countries alone. The Tobin tax is one solution. Users of the international financial system should have no objection to paying the costs. The Asian approach and Canadian initiative will have an important influence on future discussions of reforming the international financial architecture in these directions.

Notes

1 The G5 comprises the United States, Britain, Germany, France, and Japan.
2 The material in this section is derived mainly from the reports written by the Japanese sherpa or sous-sherpa on each summit: Sadayuki Hayashi (1995), Kazuo Ogura (1996, 1997), Koichi Haraguchi (1998), and Seiji Kondo (1999).
3 The G10 consists of 11 countries — Belgium, Canada, France, Germany, Italy, Japan, the Netherlands, Sweden, Switzerland, the United Kingdom, and the United States — whose finance ministers and central bank governors meet twice a year.
4 For further details of the Canadian initiative to reform the international financial system, see Kirton 1999.
5 See, for example, Sachs 1998.
6 This section draws heavily on Shuhei Kishimoto (1999) and Toshinori Doi (1999). Fred Bergsten (2000) observed the recent development of regional co-operation in East Asia and pointed out that the most important changes to the world's financial architecture are likely to come from the new regional arrangements being fashioned in East Asia by Japan, China, South Korea, and the ten members of ASEAN.

References

ASEAN + 3 Finance Ministers (2000). 'Joint Ministerial Statement of the ASEAN + 3 Finance Ministers Meeting'. 6 May, Chiang Mai, Thailand. <www.mof.go.jp/english/if/if014.htm> (March 2001).

Bergsten, C. Fred (2000). 'East Asian Regionalism'. East Asian Regionalism. *Economist* 15 July, pp. 23–26.

Doi, Toshinori (1999). 'The Asian Crisis and the Future Measures'. In Japanese. *Finance* October, pp. 17–34.

G7 (1998). 'G7 Chairman's Statement'. 15 May, Birmingham. <www.g7.utoronto.ca/ g7/summit/1998birmingham/chair.htm> (March 2001).

G8 (1999). 'G8 Communiqué Köln 1999'. 20 June, Cologne. <www.library.utoronto.ca/ g7/summit/1999koln/finalcom.htm> (March 2001).

Haraguchi, Koichi (1998). 'Bamingamu Samitto no Seika to Nihon' (The Results of the Birmingham Summit and Japan). *Sekai Keizai Hyoron* August, pp. 8–24.

Hayashi, Sadayuki (1995). 'Harifakkusu Samitto no Seika to Nihon' (The Results of the Halifax Summit and Japan). *Sekai Keizai Hyoron* September, pp. 8–17.

Kirton, John J. (1999). 'Canada as a Principal Financial Power: G7 and IMF Diplomacy in the Crisis of 1997–99'. *International Journal* vol. 54 (Autumn 1999), pp. 603–624.

Kishimoto, Shuhei (1999). 'The Aim of the New Miyazawa Initiative and the Asian Monetary Fund'. In Japanese. *Finance* pp. 31–48.

Kondo, Seiji (1999). 'Kerun Samitto no Seika To Nihon' (The Results of the Cologne Summit and Japan). *Sekai Keizai Hyoron* September, pp. 8–28.

Lindgren, Carl-Johan, G. G. Garcia, and Matthew I. Saal (1996). *Bank Soundness and Macroeconomic Policy*. International Monetary Fund, Washington DC.

Morishima, Michio (1999). *Why Do I Expect Japan to Collapse?* Iwanami Shoten, Tokyo.

Ogura, Kazuo (1996). 'Riyon Samitto wo Migutte' (About the Lyon Summit). *Sekai Keizai Hyoron* September, pp. 6–16.

Ogura, Kazuo (1997). 'Denba Samitto wo Migutte' (About the Denver Summit). *Sekai Keizai Hyoron* September, pp. 8–19.

Pauly, Louis W. (1997). *Who Elected the Bankers? Surveillance and Control in the World Economy*. Cornell University Press, Ithaca.

Sachs, Jeffrey (1998). 'Alternative Approaches to Financial Crises in Emerging Markets'. In M. Kahler, ed., *Capital Flows and Financial Crises*, pp. 247–262. Cornell University Press, Ithaca.

9 Guiding Global Economic Governance: The G20, the G7, and the International Monetary Fund at Century's Dawn

JOHN J. KIRTON

In the rapidly globalising world of the twenty-first century, where will the centre of global economic governance effectively lie? The answer importantly depends on which intergovernmental institutions, each with its distinctive values, mandate, and membership, will prevail in the emerging order. It depends, more precisely, on the impact of newer bodies, led by the G20 and the International Monetary and Financial Committee (IMFC), to set new directions as they struggle to secure a unique role in a world long dominated by the well-established institutions of the G7, the International Monetary Fund (IMF), and the latter's Executive Board.

In this struggle, it is the G20 that faces the greatest challenge. It is one of the newest bodies, born along with the IMFC and Financial Stability Forum (FSF) in 1999 to respond to the failure of the old institutions to deal with the new financial crises and broader challenges of economic governance bred by globalisation. Moreover, unlike the IMFC, which is embedded within the long-established, powerful IMF, and unlike the technically oriented FSF with its close relationship with the Bank for International Settlements (BIS), the G20 lacks an international organisational nest. It thus floats alone as a mere ministerial and deputies forum in a world replete with powerful competitors ranging from entrenched international organisations and jealous national governments to major multinationals and fast-moving markets.

The future influence and ultimate importance of the G20 depend on which of three possible paths the fledgling institution takes in forging its future relationship with these old and new institutions at the centre of global financial governance. In the first instance, the G20 could become, as many thought it was destined to be at its birth, a way of legitimising a G7-bred consensus to a broader influential group of emerging market countries constituting the top tier of the old G77 developing country club. It would thus help G7 positions dominate the new order, either through the appearance or reality of securing broader support from consequential countries drawn from all geographic regions throughout the developing world.

Second, the G20 could fade into a secondary body, destined to decline from being an effective centre for economic governance. This fate would come as it yielded to a new, competing IMFC mobilising the formidable resources of formal organisation possessed by the IMF. These resources are reinforced by the heavy influence of major European powers within the IMF, through the system of voting rights established long ago, the IMFC chair held by Britain, and the support of France. It is further reinforced by the preferences of a weighty United States, which holds a unique veto in all IMF-affiliated forums.

Third, the G20 could become an autonomous and effective centre for defining and delivering new directions in global economic governance in an era of intensified globalisation. It could do so by bringing together G7 members and key developed economies and emerging markets, by empowering the distinctive voices of emerging economies and of the G20's Canadian chair, Paul Martin, by focussing in a broad, integrative and forward-looking way on the central challenge of globalisation, and by charting distinctive and effective responses. Indeed, effectively taking up these larger tasks could be essential to the G20's influence and impact, once the specific issues that caused its creation and initial focus — the 1997–99 Asian-turned-global financial crisis and construction of a new international financial architecture — recede from centre stage. Their retreat will leave the much larger and broader issue of governing globalisation as the primary concern of the international communities in the twenty-first century.

To date, the limited initial analyses of the G20 and the IMFC, based on their design and first year in operation, have provided no conclusive answer to the question of which of these three paths will prevail. Confident optimists argue that the very architecture of the G20 represents a significant turn toward a more inclusive, accountable, and legitimate structure for global financial governance, one that will both replace the U.S.-centricity of the old system and, if it works as envisaged, bring 'tremendous progress' in the 'fight against financial crisis and instability' (Germain 2001, 16). Contingent optimists have also pointed to the G20's institutional potential and initial promise, but believe that its future depends on successfully meeting several large challenges that await (Kirton 2001; Johnson 2000, 2001; Porter 2000). In contrast, sceptics have focussed on a more formidable set of institutional defects to be remedied and future challenges to be met if G20 influence is to come (Culpeper 2000a, 2000b). In addition, harsh critics have charged that the G20 is 'severely flawed' in that it excludes the poorest and smallest developing countries or like-minded Europeans and Nordics, lacks a constituency system, accountability, and transparency, and has a much too narrow agenda (Helleiner 2000, 13–14). In all cases, however, these judgements have not been based on a close examination of the maturing G20's actual work during its second year in operation and how this has compared and related to the ongoing activity of the G20's parent, the G7, the IMFC, and its parent, the IMF.

This chapter conducts such an analysis. It examines in turn the operation of the G7 from its ministerial meetings in Fukuoka in July 2000 to Prague in September 2000, of the IMF and IMFC in the autumn of 2000 at Prague, and of the G20 in its planning for and performance at its second ministerial meeting in Montreal in October 2000. In each case, the chapter focusses on the distinctive agenda, different membership structure, processes of policy consensus, institutional procedure, pressures of inter-institutional competition, and diplomacy of members within each body, and the results achieved by each institution. It further considers the broader global conditions that determine these differences and the overall interrelationship among the institutions that has emerged.

This analysis reveals that at its Montreal meeting the G20 proved to be an effective and legitimate institution that delivered significant achievements. These achievements lay primarily in the new principles and directions it set, supported by some specific decisions reached and institutional processes put in place. These considerable achievements compare favourably with those of its old and new institutional competitors. They flow from the advantages enjoyed by the G20 in its particularly powerful and representative membership, flexible mandate, inclusive procedure, and skilful chairmanship. Together, these features have enabled the G20 successfully to put at the forefront of its work the broad, integrative agenda of globalisation that preoccupies citizens of the global community as the twenty-first century dawns, and to set some genuinely new directions in how the process of globalisation should be governed in this twenty-first century world.

The G7 from Fukuoka to Prague

The G7 at Fukuoka

The tasks of shaping a new international financial system in the wake of the 1997–99 global financial crisis and confronting the broader anxieties about globalisation bred by this crisis were central to the agenda of the G7, the IMF, its new IMFC, and the G20 as the year 2000 began (Kaiser, Kirton, and Daniels 2000; Kirton, Daniels, and Freytag 2001). The G7 was the first to take up the challenge, starting with its finance ministers meetings in January 2000 and April 2000, continuing with preparations for and discussions at the annual G7 summit on 21–23 July 2000 in Okinawa, and culminating in its September 2000 meeting in Prague.

As usual, the leaders' summit dominated the cadence. In the months leading up to the Okinawa Summit, finance deputies and their own deputies in turn worked at an ever-intensifying pace to narrow differences among their countries and ripen the agenda and agreements for their political leaders to endorse. G7 finance ministers met in Fukuoka on 8–9 July to narrow down the finance issues to send on to their leaders in reports on the international financial architecture and on debt relief for the poorest, and on other items that warranted the attention of heads. The G7 leaders themselves met, without Russia, on the afternoon of 21 July in Okinawa to take most of the consequential decisions that remained.

The G7's road through Okinawa was surrounded by several uncertainties — a possible meltdown in stock markets in the U.S. and its contagious impact, financial panics of the sort that gripped the international community in 1997–99, and a Japanese general election on 25 June that endangered the long-serving Liberal Democratic Party and with it veteran finance minister Kiichi Miyazawa. Yet both the G7 and the outside global community could look forward to building on the important advances of the previous three years in constructing a new international financial architecture and doing so amidst a global economy that was growing and free of crisis once again. The lack of drama was itself a testament to the success of the G7 in rescuing the world economy from the crisis of the proceeding years. In the end, the G7 appropriately produced a worker-like effort that made incremental advances across a range of important issues rather than one that delivered new directions or decisions of historic weight.

At Fukuoka, the finance ministers' agenda centred on a review of the world economic situation, the reports to leaders, and Russia. There was little disagreement about the current state of the world economy, and what was required to manage it. The Japanese economy, along with much of Asia, had resumed its growth path and the world economy was moving toward sustained growth. While there was an acknowledgement of poor consumer confidence in Japan, no G7 member wished to emphasise the negatives there. To deal with the future uncertainties identified in the most recent World Economic

Outlook report, the IMF (2000) had hinted that Japan should introduce a supplementary budget for 2000 and continue the Bank of Japan's zero interest-rate policy. Japanese finance minister Miyazawa responded that another budget was not needed at the moment, but might be once growth figures for gross domestic product (GDP) came in early September. Similarly, the Bank of Japan saw the zero interest-rate policy as an exceptional situation that could not continue forever. Yet Japan regarded zero interest rates for very short-term borrowing as a central element of its policy stance and one that would not change too rapidly. Indeed, it reaffirmed its zero interest-rate policy in early June (subsequently raising interest rates only in August). It also remained flexible on its fiscal policy.

G7 members generally shared the view that there were some risks to the world economy, notably a rapid shock to the U.S. stock market. Yet they had confidence in the sound monetary policy of the U.S. and believed that a soft landing was possible. They hoped that the U.S. stock market would continue to do well, and that by the time of a slowdown in the U.S. the Japanese economy would have resumed growth sufficiently strong to absorb the slack. To secure such growth, the key was to restore Japanese consumer confidence and thus domestic demand, rather than have Japan rely on export-oriented growth. To spur domestic demand, the requirement was not for more spending on public works but investment in the information technology revolution and a reduction in some taxes.

There was also general contentment with exchange rates. Japan and its partners were comfortable with a currency level of between 107 and 111 yen to the U.S. dollar. Moreover, although the low value of the Euro posed a problem for the new European Central Bank (ECB), it was advantageous to European business and thus a spur to needed European growth. Currency intervention to manage such rates and ranges was seen as limited in effect, easily accomplished in the largest U.S.-Japanese relationship, but more difficult with a Europe in which it was unclear where real authority for such intervention actually lay.

The questions of whether there had arisen a 'new economy' and what its implications might be receded in significance following the U.S. stock market correction of April. It was discussed in the finance ministers' report to their leaders. This report declared that there was indeed an information technology (IT) revolution, which had made a large difference in the U.S. and which could do so in Europe, Japan, and the developing world. The first item in the report discussed the implications of the IT revolution and what should be done, including a treatment of several items contained in an earlier U.S.-generated thematic paper on what might be termed the 'four electronic freedoms' for the twenty-first century. These centred on the need for lower barriers to and deregulation of electronic commerce, the transportation and telecommunications infrastructure, and the free flow of information. The G7 finance ministers agreed to deal with taxation, patents, financial institutions, and cross-border capital flows, although even here outstanding differences remained. Moreover, the G7/8 leaders were themselves interested in discussing IT, leading to the inevitable tension as to what should be left for leaders to decide.

At Fukuoka, the G7 finance ministers also sought to produce a meaningful agreement on financial crime, including transparency, co-ordination of regulations on financial institutions, and the treatment of offshore tax havens. This issue proved difficult for some G7 members, notably Canada, whose executive director in the IMF represented several Caribbean countries. Their economies could be adversely affected by such G7 action. Others were concerned more generally about the support of developing countries for such a regime. Nonetheless, a workable agreement emerged, based not on opening sovereign territory to outside surveillance but on delegating the issue to the FSF in ways that highlighted the implications of the IT revolution and the need to co-ordinate taxation and regulation. This was an issue that concerned leaders as well.

The finance ministers did not go into detail or offer new initiatives on the emerging new international financial architecture. They discussed reform of IMF facilities following compromise proposals presented by U.S. treasury secretary Larry Summers in response to the U.S. Congress's Meltzer report advocating a major reduction in IMF programs. The finance ministers also discussed the reform of the multilateral development banks (MDBs), notably the respective roles of the World Bank and the regional banks. Earlier the U.S. had proposed that the IMF offer short-term finance and the International Bank for Reconstruction and Development (IBRD) issue long-term development funding, a proposal that had led to a compromise in which few difficult issues remained.

There were discussions about modifying one IMF facility — the recently U.S.-driven and adopted contingent credit lines (CCL). Japan favoured changes so as to permit the use of CCLs and thus reap for the IMF the resources that would come from the highly profitable commissions secured from those countries that used them. Other countries, notably Germany and Canada, remained much more reserved.

Private sector involvement was a major issue, as it had been at the finance deputies forum. Fukuoka moved toward making it routine that the IMF consider private sector involvement when constructing an assistance package and showing markets that it was natural to involve the private sector. The G7 affirmed the need for general guidelines rather than firm principles to accomplish these goals.

Similarly, the G7 agreed to promote codes and standards, but not to make them mandatory, in deference to the concerns of large developing (and Asian) countries such as India and China. It was generally agreed that the absence of such international codes and standards was not the primary cause of the Asian crisis. There were thus no grounds for investing the considerable political resources required to impose them on all countries.

One important issue was the relationship among the various old and new groups working in the field of finance. There were questions of when to table the three reports of the FSF and how the G20 related to it and the IMFC. The G7 saw an obvious need to co-ordinate the work of the G20 and IMFC. Canada called for a clear set of delineated responsibilities about which forum should discuss which issues. It saw the G20 as the central political body that should give a political impetus to work in the FSF, with the IMFC providing political blessing and buy-in. It also saw the G20 as the appropriate forum for discussing the broad, critical issue of the process of globalisation and the benefits and costs brought by it. Canada proved successful in securing G7 support for this conception.

How to advance the initiative on Heavily Indebted Poor Countries (HIPCs) was also an important issue at Fukuoka. At the 1999 Cologne Summit, G7 leaders had agreed to increase debt relief to 90 percent of the amount owed. That target had almost been achieved for those countries currently in the HIPC process. However, only five countries had entered this process, while 35 countries remained outside. At Cologne, the leaders had also agreed that by the end of the 2000 75 percent of countries would be in the process. At the G7 finance ministers meeting in April 2000 in Washington, the effort to get one more country — Uganda — into the process was blocked because German central bank officials objected to the terms of a Ugandan government's lease of a jet of U.S. origin. At Fukuoka and Okinawa, G7 ministers and leaders confronted the question of why their collective will, expressed so clearly at Cologne, had been thwarted, why the process was proving to be so slow, and what could be done to ensure the Cologne commitment was kept.

In host Japan's view, it was largely the responsibility of the debtor countries to secure their entry into the HIPC process. But Japan recognised that a procedure was required to obtain an IMF-debtor negotiation and to ensure that the conditions were not too detailed. At the same time, there was a need to ensure that the funds freed up by debt relief were used for the core task of poverty reduction, rather than to fuel the military conflicts in which 13 of the HIPC countries were then engaged. These views were expressed in a fairly concrete report from the finance ministers to the heads. A further problem with HIPCs was mobilising multilateral financing. At that time, the U.S. budget proposal did not contain sufficient funds to meet U.S. obligations.

The third item for the finance ministers was Russia. Here the G7 finance ministers agreed that while there was uncertainty about the prospects for the Russian economy, the main direction of economic policy and performance under Vladimir Putin's leadership was promising. The outstanding question concerned a G7 response to a possible Russian request for debt reduction in the Paris Club. Russian finance minister Mikhail Kasanov was then canvassing private bankers to ask for such relief in their London Club. The G7 finance ministers stood ready to advise against any request for Paris Club relief on the grounds that Russia was not a HIPC, had abundant natural resources, would not be economically imperilled because of its debt burden, and had a debt that a Debt Sustainability Analysis (DSA) showed was sustainable.

Yet the finance ministers knew this was a card the leaders would keep for their own use. The leaders' inclination was to do something for Russia and send some kind of positive message at the outset of the Putin regime, especially following Putin's successful June summit meeting in Germany. Moreover, the Cologne Communiqué had spoken of the need for a 'comprehensive' approach to Russia (G8 1999). After the IMF program for Russia, Paris Club action would be a logical next step, although the timing was not ripe for an announcement in Okinawa in July. Japan would avoid any temptation to use the prospect of debt relief to advance its desire to have Russia return Japan's Northern Territories.

A final feature of the Fukuoka finance ministers meeting and subsequent Okinawa leaders gathering was their emphasis on the Asian approach to international finance and Asia's re-emerging role as the centre of the future global economy. The day before the Fukuoka finance ministers meeting, Japan hosted a symposium attended by some Asian finance and economics ministers. The discussions on MDBs dealt with building the foundations of Asian development institutions. Yet the larger issue of the Japanese-led move to create the Asian Monetary Fund with clear commitments remained in the background as the globally oriented G7 did its work.

The G7 at Okinawa

At Okinawa a few weeks later, the leaders themselves met in their G7 session on Friday afternoon immediately before the opening of the G8 summit that evening. They had a somewhat broader agenda than their finance ministers had had: it focussed on financial architecture, HIPCs, financial crime, and nuclear safety.[1]

As described by Nicholas Bayne and others in their chapters in this volume, the leaders added relatively little to what their finance ministers had done. They did, however, give the final push to a 15-year quest, launched at the Tokyo Summit in 1986, to close the Chernobyl reactors. It was a task that was finally completed by the end of the year.

The G7 at Prague

When the G7 finance ministers assembled for their first meeting after Okinawa, oil prices had emerged as the main issue.[2] The G7 wanted to find the appropriate wording to take into the subsequent IMFC meeting for broader endorsement. The U.S. in particular wanted and largely secured language welcoming recent Saudi supply increases.

A second issue was the Euro. Here the Europeans said they needed strong statements to prevent markets from driving their currency to ever new lows. The U.S. was reluctant, particularly to act in ways that suggested that the G7 was ready to intervene again in exchange markets.

U.S. reluctance was driven by its unhappy experience with the exchange rate intervention to which it had acquiesced on 22 September 2000.[3] That co-ordinated intervention had been decided weeks in advance when the Europeans, with ECB approval, concluded at their regional summit to intervene. The Europeans were convinced that they needed U.S. support to do so effectively. U.S. treasury secretary Summers was very sceptical. Yet he made it known he was open to being convinced, even though such a move brought no obvious benefit to the U.S. as a presidential election loomed. The Japanese went along, as the Europeans called in a favour from the U.S. What subsequently upset the U.S. and coloured their views on repeating the intervention, was the fact that immediately before the intervention news was leaked to a few European insiders, who were thereby able to benefit from 'front-running' the governments' move.

The September intervention provoked a major debate among G7 finance ministers in Prague, where they discussed the possibility of repeating the move. The Europeans argued that the Euro continued to be too low, trading in a range far outside its fundamentals. Yet the U.S. remained convinced that the solution lay in Europe moving forward on serious structural reform, fiscal consolidation, market flexibility, and restored growth. Summers was very concerned about there being only one engine at work in the global economy, and about the impact if the U.S. economy turned down. He saw Europe as the best hope for providing another engine, as the U.S. had already reached the limit of its expansion. With negative savings, rising unemployment, jittery markets fearing inflation, and interest-rate increases working their way through the system, the U.S. economy was already slowing. An exogenous oil-price rise shock would merely fuel the trend.

On reform of the international financial architecture, there was general agreement. Here the G7 recommended that developing countries rely on private capital markets. There remained a disagreement about private sector involvement in the response to financial crises. Here, the U.S., UK, and Canada were pitted against continental Europe, with Japan leaning to the former camp. The 'Anglos' wanted to deal with the issue on a flexible, case-by-case basis. The 'Continentals' wanted a rule-based approach with a firm framework that would send clear signals to capital markets. The Anglos countered that each case was distinct, that one thus needed flexibility, and that there were advantages to ambiguity as little was known and the markets should be kept guessing. There was no progress on this issue, as the U.S. held firm, knowing its banks and financial services industry did not like the continental approach.

Prague also featured a major dispute over calculating IMF quotas. The Japanese were unusually outspoken, exasperated by the prospect of being held indefinitely at an underweight position in the IMF and World Bank, one only slightly above Germany. They wanted to be substantially above Germany, at a level one half of the U.S., through an increase of between 25 percent and 50 percent of their quota share. The Europeans, knowing this revision would come at their expense, were vehemently opposed. In a clear European victory, the one-line conclusion in the G7 Communiqué merely took note of the effort at quota reform.

Subsequently, at the IMF the Japanese continued to argue that the quotas should reflect the size of a country's economy and its integration into the world economy. But the formula proposed by Japan would also take the U.S. from 17 percent to 23 percent. No one wanted this change. The U.S. knew it would require them to give more money to the IMF and judged that such an increase would not pass Congress. Richard Cooper, head of a consultative group on the issue, offered a simple formula, under which the U.S. and Japan would gain and the developing countries would lose. Indeed, the Africans would lose one of their two seats on the IMF Executive Board. The Europeans continued to advocate delay. It was understandable that the Japanese turned with renewed vigour to a regional approach.

Money laundering was also dealt with by the G7, led by the U.S. and France. On this issue, the G7 served as the engine, with the IMF involved to some extent in Financial Action Task Force (FATF) implementation. The IMF was instructed by the G7 to serve as the arbiter and implementer of the questions of financial transparency, money laundering, tax evasion, and offshore financial centres (OFCs). This item immediately became part of the IMF work programme the day after the G7 Communiqué was issued.

On HIPCs there was little action, as the U.S. had still not provided its share of the necessary funds. A new element was the question of whether the existing sums, when provided, would be sufficient, or whether a 'HIPCs plus' might be required. There was also concern about the speed of the existing program. The UK, supported by four other members, sought to secure a commitment that 20 countries would be brought into the HIPC process by the end of the year. But they were beaten back by the Germans and the Japanese. The G7 Communiqué read only 'as many as 20'. The UK then took the issue to the meeting of the IMFC, which it chaired.

During 2000 then, the G7 displayed a dynamic of U.S. passivity and adjustment and well as impetus. It also showed effective British and Canadian leadership, a new Japanese assertiveness, and a forceful and often successful European resistance to major changes (Kirton 2000; cf. Putnam and Bayne 1987). Compared to earlier years, it took few major steps in building a new international financial architecture that was already substantially constructed, or in moving forward the HIPC Initiative to the targets set at Cologne. It did face a new demand from Japan for a bigger voice for outsiders, particularly Asians, in the governance of the IMF in particular and global finance in general. In addressing this demand and in dealing with other issues such as money laundering, the G7 again showed that it was the centre of control for the formally multilateral IMF. It also further endorsed its 1999 creation, the G20, as the central forum for meeting the demands for broader participation in the governance of global finance and for addressing the central, comprehensive issue of shaping a new order to govern globalisation in more stable and just ways.

The International Monetary and Financial Committee

Prague was also the site of the IMFC's ministerial meeting.[4] It took place amidst large numbers of cobblestone-throwing protestors, whose demonstrations rivalled in their violence those who had disrupted the World Trade Organization (WTO) ministerial in Seattle in late 1999. They showed that globalisation made people feel disenfranchised, alienated, and resentful that decisions were being made far away from their daily lives. They demanded that the international financial institutions (IFIs) be held accountable, that people understand and support what the IFIs do, and that the IFIs learn from ordinary people's concerns.

The new IMF Managing Director, German finance official and G7 veteran Horst Köhler, initially welcomed the demonstrators at Prague, as a way to heighten awareness of the issues the IMF was dealing with. Köhler was nonetheless upset by the level of violence he encountered. He thus declared that the G7 countries must start to defend the IMF's work visibly.

Despite initial hopes that the IMFC would empower members' ministers rather than the IMF's own staff, almost all the work for the IMFC ministerial meeting at Prague had been prepared beforehand. Much was done earlier at the IMFC deputies meeting in London, where the G7 deputies also met. At Prague, the IMFC did feature a new format that proved to be interactive. It opened with a presentation by the IMF Chief Economist, Michael Mussa, on the World Economic Outlook and a discussion of the risks and vulnerabilities to the global economy. Gordon Brown as chair kept the discussion moving. Almost no set statements were read. But with 24 ministers in the room, representing very different points of view, the discussion was somewhat stilted.

The principal issue was the recent oil-price increase. Its negative repercussions were listed in the World Economic Outlook, a move that the ministers appreciated. There was a lively exchange with several very sharp debates between oil-producing and oil-consuming countries on how to describe developments in oil markets in the Communiqué. The oil exporters argued it was fine that prices were increasing, as this was just a normal correction. If industrial countries wanted lower prices they should cut gasoline taxes. Brown in particular did not welcome this position, as the week before there had been a revolt in the UK by consumers asking for such tax cuts. The Saudis led the oil exporters' case. The U.S. carried the case for the consumers, but with strong representation from all G7 members. In the end, Larry Summers pressured the Saudis into accepting language more generous to the oil consumers than to the producers.

Far less time was spent on other issues such as the HIPCs, the ten-year anniversary of the transition economies, and the international financial architecture. Discussion on the latter topic centred on reform of the IMF, a move strongly backed by Köhler. His offered a blueprint for a new and improved IMF, to be constructed in an evolutionary rather than revolutionary way. His approach was to have fewer facilities, programs, and cases, and more restrictions about who would receive loans, about conditions, and about intrusions into the mandates of other institutions. The developing countries resisted this approach, with its emphasis on fewer programs and facilities, and higher charges for their use. A few days before the IMFC meeting, the IMF Executive Board had discussed higher charges during an extremely lengthy and bitter meeting. The G7 had rammed through this program, with the result that others would pay more for IMF loans and that there would be no repeat users. Köhler, Germany, and the U.S. were particularly insistent that IMF resources be used only for short-term emergencies rather than long-term development purposes.

Under this new approach, the IMF mission would be to foster sound monetary, fiscal, and exchange rate policy. It would be responsible for the stability and prosperity of the international macroeconomic system and would venture into structural policy only if such a policy had a significant macroeconomic impact. Labour market restructuring and social policy would be left to others. The IMF would focus its conditionality accordingly.

The IMF would improve its capacity for crisis prevention. It would do so in the first instance through surveillance — the review and monitoring of national economic policies to ensure that they posed no harm to the international economy. It would also identify external and financial sector vulnerabilities, in order to cope with massive and growing capital flows that could not be controlled or regulated. In such a situation, the role of the public sector was to ensure good policies and thus attract capital to the countries and sectors that needed it the most.

To accomplish these tasks, the IMF would act through several instruments. The first was Financial Sector Assessment Programs (FSAP), a joint IMF–World Bank operation with other experts involved. It would internationalise domestic banking supervision by giving countries a 'health check'. It would cull the best practices nationally and bring them to the international level. It would focus on emerging market economies, following the experience with Mexico in 1994.

A second instrument was Reports on Observance of Standards and Codes (ROSCs). Here, the IMF would serve as the arbiter of internationally agreed codes and standards. It would set best practices for domestic policies by examining the work of the International Organization of Securities Commissions, the FATF, the Organisation for Economic Co-operation and Development (OECD), the BIS-Basle Committee, and other bodies, and by encouraging them to devise the best codes. As part of its annual consultations mandated under Article IV of its Articles of Agreement, the IMF would judge how well each country measured up to these standards each year.

In addition, the IMF would strengthen Article IV consultations more generally and secure available and correct data for markets to work rationally. It would obtain the best practices on data for national governments to report to the IMF, to markets, and to their own people.

Finally, the IMF would revise its lending instruments to price incentives into IMF loans, use its own money less often and for shorter terms, and encourage countries to move back to private sector borrowing. Among these instruments, the CCL would be the principal instrument of crisis prevention. It could be used on a day's notice, with unlimited funds for countries following good policy. The standby facility and other instruments would be changed to discourage their long-term use. There would be an escalating surcharge depending on how much was borrowed, so countries would pay back much sooner.

The centrality of the CCL, an instrument pioneered by President Bill Clinton and vigorously opposed by Germany and Canada, represented an apparent victory for the United States. The Germans in particular continued to feel that the CCL would trigger the crisis it sought to prevent, would represent tremendous moral hazard, and would mean spending public money first to bail out the private sector. The Germans secured a rule that the IMF would only disburse one third of what was needed on the Managing Director's authority before having an 'activation review' within a week in order to judge if there was a good case for disbursing the remaining two thirds of the available funds. The failure of the IMF to secure CCL requests from past potential candidates, such as Mexico, or current candidates, such as Argentina, continued to fuel scepticism about the CCL's actual relevance as a tool for crisis prevention.

The one exception to this new approach was the IMF's continuing role in poverty-related issues. The IMF's new Poverty Reduction and Growth Facility (PRGF) would offer extremely inexpensive credit at an interest rate of 0.5 percent and focus this money much more sharply. Countries would be asked to consult with their nongovernmental organisations (NGOs) and civil society to produce a poverty-reduction plan.

The IMF would also fight poverty through the HIPC Initiative, recognising that most potential recipients were genuinely trying to change their societies by investing in health and primary education. It would direct debt relief there and bring 20 countries into the process by the end of 2000. By the time of the G7 Summit in Genoa in July 2001, almost all would be done.

This 'poverty exception' was driven by the UK, Canada, and the U.S., with strong support from France and Italy.[5] Germany and Japan were very sceptical. The UK was the real champion, as it adopted the position of NGOs such as Oxfam and Jubilee 2000. The British convinced the U.S. The full G7 thus came to argue that it could not abandon the poorest countries.[6] Developing countries were also strongly in favour. Köhler's argument, accepted by Summers, was that poverty directly debilitates the macroeconomic stability of the poorest countries and is thus integral to the IMF's core mission.

In this debate, Canada's role was based on its classic stance of being extremely supportive of debt reduction. It was outspoken about the critical need to help poor countries and was a strong proponent of linking debt reduction to improvements in social indicators in great detail for each country. Indeed, Canadian finance minister and G20 chair Martin went to Prague feeling that a new impetus was needed to push HIPCs forward. Hence he proposed a moratorium on debt payments for all HIPCs. This radical proposal was readily rejected, despite Martin's vigorous efforts. The Germans were particularly dismissive.

The debate over HIPCs took place against the continuing lack of U.S. congressional authorisation for the U.S. share of the HIPC Initiative. Others continued to hold back until the U.S. delivered. At Prague Köhler met with musician Bono, the high-profile representative of Jubilee 2000. Köhler agreed to the target of having 20 countries, rather than the eight already in, reach the decision point by the end of the year.[7] At the IMFC, the UK demanded that the number of 20 be set as a hard target. There was no debate over the number, and that view prevailed. The additional 12 countries, almost all in Africa, required the IMF to act in a mad dash to get them approved before year's end.

The IMFC thus proved to be a compatible forum for the U.S. and Germany, which dominated the institution in quota share and occupancy of the IMF Managing Director position, to accomplish their preferred if somewhat conflicting visions of a reformed IMF. Along with the IMF Executive Board, it also proved to be an effective instrument of U.S. hegemonic leadership on issues, notably the CCL, where the U.S. President's personal reputation and the interests of U.S. financial institutions were at stake. To be sure, the IMFC also enabled the UK chair of the IMFC — and through it a broad coalition of civil society organisations, supported by all G7 members save Germany and Japan — to include poverty reduction in the new IMF mandate. Thus the UK accomplished what the Japanese-chaired G7 had failed to do, namely to secure a firm commitment, subsequently fulfilled in a frenzy of action at the IMF, to get 20 countries into the HIPCs process by year's end. Nonetheless, the IMFC proved to be primarily a forum for reinforcing an American, and with it British and European, vision of a new international financial order, rather than one in which a broader array of actors and values had a full and legitimate place.

The G20 at Montreal

The final major thrust during the year 2000 in the ongoing effort to reshape the governance of global finance came through the G20 at its second ministerial meeting, held in Montreal on 24–25 October. Here, with greater success than the IMFC or the IMF at Prague, the G20 moved beyond the narrow, often technical issues of finance to confront the broad *problèmatique* of globalisation. It assured those on the outside of the G7 — as well as many inside — and their civil societies, that their concerns were being heard, understood, and addressed. It thereby took a crucial step in assuring its continuing relevance and legitimacy as a forum and its effectiveness in setting new directions in global economic, social, and ecological governance as a whole (Kirton 2001).

Preparation

The first year of the G20 was marked by the non-G7 members asking how the new forum would work for them and the G7 countries wondering if they would lose control. The members had thus focussed on getting to know one another and deciding to work together on a set of issues. The Group had generated a worker-like approach, a growing consensus about the identification of the problem, and an agreement to co-operate on standards and rules, if not regulations, on international and domestic banking and on private sector involvement.

More broadly, the G20 had generated a growing consensus that it was needed, that there were serious social costs to globalisation that must be addressed through new initiatives, and that new limits must be set. More precisely, a consensus had emerged that the private sector must to some degree accept risk and be involved in the solution of financial crises, that codes and standards were needed, and that they could be shaped by developed and developing countries working together. There was also a growing consensus on exchange rate regimes, with all agreeing that different approaches and mechanisms were required in different circumstances. Yet this emerging G20 consensus had not yet changed what member representatives argued within the Executive Board of the IMF or World Bank.

Along with emerging country members, Canadian chair Paul Martin felt that there was a shared interest in reducing the social costs of globalisation.

Martin wished to involve civil society in the task of determining how this was to be done. The broad topic of globalisation thus formed the centrepiece of the G20's agenda at Montreal.

Among the developed members, the Commonwealth English-speaking countries of Britain and Australia were closest to Canada's approach. France came suspicious of any institution that might detract from the IMF, where it was particularly influential. The U.S. did not want to undermine its privileged veto position at the IMF and World Bank in favour of a forum where it was just one of 20 equal members. But it was comforted by the fact that fellow North American Canada chaired the G20 and was persuaded by intellectual arguments in favour of the Canadian approach. Among the non-OECD members, China was very strong, having just decided on international engagement with its decision to join the WTO. Yet at the preparatory G20 deputies meeting in August in Toronto, Russia was also more energised. South Africa was also very active, Indonesia variable, and the Saudis good team players.

For Montreal, the Canadians sought to have highly interactive sessions, with no time allowed for social activity, caucus groups, G7 meetings on the margin, or scheduled bilaterals. They also sought to secure the future of the forum by identifying its meeting schedule and chair for the following year. Substantively, they sought to secure a concluding recognition that globalisation has two sides — the financial and economic side and the social side, including health, education, welfare, and employment.

On the issue of civil society participation, Martin felt very strongly that civil society organisations (CSOs) were raising real issues. He agreed to meet with representatives beforehand and to bring those views forward to the G20 meeting itself, not as an advocate but as a reporter. Martin personally would have liked to have done more. But there was no consensus among G20 members on involving representatives of CSOs in the G20.

Performance

The Montreal meeting was notable for its spontaneity and the substantive nature of the discussion. It dealt with four items: responses to the challenges of globalisation, the state of the world economy, action on the FSF, and follow-up on means to reduce vulnerability to crises.

The discussion about globalisation was an open, soul-searching exercise on the reasons for the reactions that members were witnessing, and what the G20 could do to engage the opponents more actively. Several speakers pointed to the marginalisation of many countries in the process of globalisation, the insecurity that it bred, and the invisibility of any benefits. Some argued that the system, including technological progress, was increasing the distance between winners and losers, and thus fuelling demand for redistribution and insurance. Yet as globalisation made it more difficult for governments to tax their citizens and corporations, who would otherwise leave, governments had less money to meet these demands. Speakers also pointed to a loss of control, to the feeling that individuals and institutions beyond borders and the electoral process were making decisions that affected them, and to the lack of direct accountability to the populations of sovereign states. Globalisation was infringing on sovereignty and, in the view of one, leading to the victory of the Anglo-Saxon model of economic and social organisation.

The consensus was that there was no simple solution but that the current developments must be put into perspective to show the gains, and more active energetic efforts must be taken to reduce the imbalances created by globalisation. The G20 must deal aggressively with trade, including the impediments to access to markets in developed countries. It must ensure that the rules keep pace with global integration, must deal with poverty, including through increases in official development assistance (ODA), and must speak forcefully on these issues. All agreed that the challenge to globalisation was increasing, would continue to do so, and would require constructive action by the international community.

The discussion on the state of the world economy centred on a presentation on the World Economic Outlook by IMF chief economist Michael Mussa and saw some divergence among the finance ministers and central bank governors about the importance and implications of the U.S. current account deficit. One G7 central bank governor asked how much of a problem the deficit posed in the current world of floating exchange rates, with incoming private investment rather than government deficits now the cause of the U.S. deficit. Two continental European G7 central bank governors countered that the combined European and U.S. deficits and the exchange rates represented undesirable imbalances in the world economy and created important risks. They argued that the flow of world savings was thus moving from developing countries, where they were needed, to the U.S. The U.S. countered that given the inability of G20 ministers to understand why markets were pricing assets as they were, there was no need to assume there would be an abrupt correction. It would thus be far-fetched to consider stabilising exchange rates. The view of the developing countries was that turbulence in G7 exchange markets was a significant problem for their economic growth, and that limitations to the turbulence were required.

Developments in oil markets were discussed. Both sides were concerned about the level of prices, but agreed these were driven by political factors rather than economic ones. The oil exporters argued that producers were producing near capacity, that there was now an expectation of a modest surplus, and that prices should fall once one got through these short-term political driven developments.

Andrew Crockett, General Manager of the BIS, led the discussion on FSF activities. He pointed to its three new interests: market liquidity and volatility; electronic finance, which would be examined by working groups; and the wind-up of complex instruments such as hedge funds, drawing on the work of the G10 deputies on the consolidation of the financial sector. Some argued that the FSF should expand its membership and that if it failed to do so, it should be required to report to the G20.

The last session dealt with reducing vulnerability to crises, discussing once again standards and codes, external liabilities, exchange rate regulation, and private sector involvement. On standards and codes, there was some concern about the process being too rigid, with developing countries arguing that there should be more than one model. One innovative suggestion proposed standards for the delivery of ODA. On exchange rates, there were polar extremes in positions. Yet there was more support for floating exchange rates as the only viable long-range option; because floating involves a concern with exchange rates, some intervention was considered consistent with this approach. The U.S. finally gave a very positive assessment of the prospects for its HIPC budget legislation being passed by Congress, as it subsequently was.

Assessment

The Montreal G20 meeting thus proved to be a gathering of significant achievement. Its importance was grounded more in the new principles and directions it set than in the specific decisions it reached or in the institutional processes it put in place. It offered what Paul Martin called, with some accuracy, the 'Montreal Consensus' on globalisation, featuring the need for shared benefits and social protections for all (Finance Canada 2001). In its broadest terms, the Montreal Consensus consisted of a balanced affirmation of three interlinked principles: that globalisation was good for all, that its benefits must be more broadly shared, and that the poor had to be protected from its costs (see Appendix F). While none of these individual elements was entirely new, having been articulated by the G7/8 in its Cologne Consensus on socially safeguarded globalisation in 1999 (Kirton, Daniels, and Freytag 2001), the

Montreal Consensus did mark a harmony among a representative group of consequential developed and developing countries, and an agreement to move from a singular focus on stabilising the global economy to sharing its benefits and safeguarding its poor.

Montreal was the first time that the enormously diverse and influential countries assembled in the G20 all affirmed that globalisation was the proper direction for them individually and the global community collectively to take. All agreed: 'the economic integration that is at the heart of globalization can continue to be an enormously powerful force contributing to improving the lives of hundreds of millions of people in industrial, transition, and developing countries alike' (G20 2000). Coming in the immediate wake of the 1997–99 global financial crisis and embracing countries such as China and Saudi Arabia, this acceptance was remarkable indeed.

The specific concept of globalisation endorsed by the G20 was also meaningful. It was particularly broad, defined as 'the increasing integration of national economies resulting from the greater international mobility of goods, services, capital, people, and ideas' (G20 2000). It was thus more than the mere economic liberalisation at the heart of the neoliberal consensus of old, notably in its inclusion of the movement of people and ideas. It was very focussed on technology, the acceptance of market-based economic systems, and trade and capital liberalisation. However, it was infused with potential political content, in its celebration of globalisation's generation of 'greater access to ideas'.

An equal and integral place was given to the distributional dimension. Signs that the voices of the emerging economies were heard came in the passages in the news release calling for 'improved access for developing countries' exports to advanced economies' markets' (G20 2000). The G20 affirmed that liberalisation provided the means to 'attack income inequalities and reduce poverty', while noting that it can create 'economic difficulties and social dislocations'. It declared: 'Governments have an important role to play in formulating and implementing policies to promote financial and economic stability and harness the benefits of globalisation'. The process of redefining interests, if not reconstructing identities, had begun (Wendt 1999).

Of less prominence and potency were the specific commitments made at Montreal. Little new was contained in the commitment to improve the effectiveness, transparency, and co-operative spirit of international institutions, although the pledge may have been of some small solace to the few demonstrators protesting on the streets. The steps on the international financial architecture, detailed in an annex to the news release, represented at best small steps forward, although the document's emphasis on implementation was a useful reminder of the work that remained. Of more magnitude, coming from finance ministers with great influence on national budget expenditures, was the recognition that 'emerging market economies should be supported with technical assistance' and the pledge to 'contribute to international efforts to increase the provision of other global public goods to address serious issues such as infectious disease, agricultural research, and the environment' (G20 2000). The passage on HIPCs reaffirmed the need for a sharp focus on poverty reduction and economic reforms, and added a veiled reference to the U.S. contributing its share. The link of financial abuse and 'market integrity' to financial stability was noteworthy. Weak commitments but far-reaching social objectives came in the call for trade liberalisation to benefit the lowest income economies, to 'promote domestic policies that help spread the benefits of integration to all members of society', and to design and implement social safety nets to protect the most vulnerable during liberalisation.

More ambiguous was the legacy of Montreal in forwarding the growth of the G20 as a centre of global economic governance. The breadth of the G20's agenda was striking, as it went well beyond the hard-core finance subjects of crisis response and architecture construction aimed at stability. It embraced debt, development assistance, trade liberalisation, health, agriculture, the environment, and social policy. It thus fulfilled Martin's earlier promise that no area of policy lay potentially outside of the G20's purview. It also, as he noted, would make the conclusions of Montreal the subject of discussion among many other ministers in national governments. Furthermore, it was an agenda whose breadth was appropriate for G20 leaders themselves to address collectively on a future occasion should they so wish.

The institutional depth of the G20 was advanced by the Montreal meeting to a lesser degree. The agreement to have two deputies meetings and one ministerial meeting (time and place to be determined) in the following year represented a continuation of the first-year pattern, rather than a move to a more dense schedule. It did, however, ensure that the G20 had become a permanent body, with an agenda — guiding globalisation — to give it a rationale once the issues of crisis response and architectural reconstruction spawned by the 1997–99 crisis had passed. Moreover, with Paul Martin apparently chairing the body for another full year and thus prospectively hosting the 2001 ministerial, it seemed the body would be guided by an enthusiastic and effective leader as it went through its third year. In addition, the ministerial mandated three follow-on processes. The first was a series of real-world case studies of countries' experiences of being affected by and responding to globalisation, aimed at providing a common diagnosis and balanced evaluation to advance the debate and identify key factors. The second was a G20 seminar on exchange rate regimes, aimed at providing concrete advice to guide real-world decisions. The third, and potentially the most productive, was a study of international institutions, conducted by G20 deputies, to look at the gaps and overlaps and functional responsibilities for global governance. While private sector representatives would be involved in some of these activities, as they had when G20 deputies met in Toronto in August, there were no other real advances in the G20's societal outreach.

Conclusion

As 2000 came to a close, it was clear that the 1997–99 global financial crisis, while rapidly receding into a dim memory in the marketplace, had an enduring legacy in inspiring new directions in the governance of global finance. But each of the old institutions at the centre of the system and the newer institutions created in the immediate wake of the crisis shaped that legacy in very different ways. The G7, having generated a new consensus on the need for socially sensitive and sustainable globalisation at its 1999 Cologne Summit, focussed on the information technology revolution at the heart of the current phase of globalisation and on how its benefits could be magnified and its digital divide diminished by new approaches to governance that involved civil society actors, countries, and institutions outside the G7 circle, and the crucial role of the public sector in addressing distributional concerns. In contrast, the IMF moved toward a much more restrictive concept of its mission, narrowly focussed in banker-like fashion on macroeconomic stability, fewer programs and resources, and more profit incentives, with poverty reduction in the poorest countries the sole acknowledgement of the larger issues at stake.

Similarly, the 1999 crisis-bred progeny of these two competing centres of global financial governance took sharply different paths. The IMFC at Prague concentrated on affirming the U.S. position on the very old issue of oil-price increases, and on securing an endorsement for the new 'lean and mean' IMF and the U.S.-inspired CCL. It proved unable to engage successfully with civil society and its concerns, but did deliver the HIPC commitment that was most consistent with the UK-inspired 'poverty exception' allowed by its parent body. In contrast, at Montreal the G20 focussed on the broad question of globalisation, reached out more effectively to embrace the concerns of developing countries and civil societies, and forged a consensus much different from the divisive fixed positions the same countries still advanced within the IMF. With this foundation, it was able to construct among this broader global constituency a new Montreal Consensus about the governance of globalisation. This consensus built on that of its G7 parent at Cologne, giving the social, ecological, human, and distributional side of globalisation equal weight to the economic fundamentals to which the IMF remained confined. Indeed, only in the G20 was the economic-social balance normatively struck.

The causes of these different paths lay not in the fact of a common global crisis, even if that crisis affected each of the G7 and major developing country members differently. The crisis bred by a globalising financial system did indeed create the impetus for far-reaching transformation. But the degree and direction of the resulting change was determined in important respects by the different international institutions through which the same countries and the international community as a whole reacted to it. These institutions each empowered different values, members, and their interests. The G7, first with its 'red-green' German chair, Gerhart Schroeder, in 1999 and then its Asian Japanese chair, Yoshiro Mori, in 2000, was able to create a more inclusive consensus on socially sustainable globalisation and a process for shaping governance of the new information economy. Only on issues at the core of the IMF, notably quota shares, was Japan thwarted. Similarly, the G20, with its sympathetic Canadian chair of Paul Martin and with its emerging economy members, was able to build on this consensus and in so doing bridge the gap between the developed and developing world that still flourished within the IMF.

In contrast, the IMF responded to the crisis of globalisation by going back to basics and retreating to the core values of its 1945 charter amidst the complexities of the new world. On the broader social and redistributional issues, the Anglo-American leadership coalition made limited headway, and did so only on issues such as HIPCs where the U.S. and France — which the IMF privileged — and many of the rest of the G7 were sympathetic. Similarly, the IMFC, even with its UK chair, remained subject to the heavy confines of its parent body. The governance of global finance in 2000 thus demonstrated that international institutions mattered in ways well embraced within the liberal institutionalist tradition, broadly defined to include a focus on the shifting shared social purposes at their core. They did so even in a rapidly changing world where rampant globalisation led countries and international institutions alike to reconstruct or reaffirm their interests and identities in the aftermath of a crisis that opened up space in which new directions in global goverance could be pursued.

Notes

1   Nicholas Bayne, in Chapter 2 in this volume, provides a detailed account and assessment of the G7's leaders' activity at Okinawa. The current chapter thus focusses on the work of the finance ministers, to render its analysis consistent for comparative purposes with the work of the G20 and IMFC as finance ministers' forums.
2   The resulting assist to the Russian economy temporarily removed the prospect of Russia requesting relief of its Paris Club debt. Russia was later to suspend payments of a large portion of its debt, leading to reports that Germany, which held the largest share of the debt, threatened to exclude Russia from the G7.
3   The intervention itself casts doubt on the argument of those who assert that the G7, imprisoned by a false new consensus, has abandoned co-ordinated exchange rate intervention as a policy instrument (Bergsten and Henning 1996).
4   At Prague, there was a very brief G10 meeting that was very technical and focussed on banking regulation and financial sector supervision. The G10 serves *de facto* as the ministerial meeting of the BIS-Basle Committee on Banking Supervision and the General Arrangements to Borrow (GAB).
5   Indeed, just before the Prague meetings Italy had announced it would write off 100 percent of total debt across the board.
6   This familiar pattern of the UK or Canada, or both, leading and securing U.S. support as the first step in building a winning G7 coalition (Kirton 2000) suggests an 'Anglo-American' leadership model has become as or more prevalent than the 'American leadership' model first specified by Putnam and Bayne (1987).
7   For background, see Dluhosch 2001.

References

Bergsten, C. Fred and C. Randall Henning (1996). *Global Economic Leadership and the Group of Seven*. Institute for International Economics, Washington DC.

Culpeper, Roy (2000a). 'The Evolution of Global Financial Governance'. In North-South Institute, *Global Financial Reform: How? Why? When?* North-South Institute, Ottawa.

Culpeper, Roy (2000b). 'Systemic Reform at a Standstill: A Flock of Gs in Search of Global Financial Stability'. Paper presented at Critical Issues in Financial Reform: Latin-American/Caribbean and Canadian Perspectives, Munk Centre for International Studies, University of Toronto, 1–2 June. Toronto.

Dluhosch, Barbara (2001). 'The G7 and the Debt of the Poorest'. In J. J. Kirton, J. P. Daniels and A. Freytag, eds., *Guiding Global Order: G8 Governance in the Twenty-First Century*, pp. 79–92. Ashgate, Aldershot.

Finance Canada (2001). 'G20 the Ideal Forum to Tackle Problems Associated with Globalization, Says Finance Minister'. 24 January, Ottawa. <www.fin.gc.ca/newse01/01-008.html> (March 2001).

G8 (1999). 'G8 Communiqué Köln 1999'. 20 June, Cologne. <www.library.utoronto.ca/ g7/summit/1999koln/finalcom.htm> (March 2001).

G20 (2000). 'News Release'. Montreal, 25 October. <www.g7.utoronto.ca/g7/g20/ montrealoct252000.htm> (March 2001).

Germain, Randall (2001). 'Reforming the International Financial Architecture: The New Political Agenda'. Paper presented at the annual meeting of the International Studies Association, 20–24 February. Chicago.

Helleiner, Gerald (2000). *Markets, Politics, and Globalization: Can the Global Economy Be Civilized?* United Nations Conference on Trade and Development, Geneva.

International Monetary Fund (2000). *World Economic Outlook 2000*. International Monetary Fund, Washington DC.

Johnson, Pierre Marc (2000). 'Beyond Trade: The Case for a Broadened International Governance Agenda'. *Policy Matters* vol. 1, no. 3 (June), pp. 4–36.

Johnson, Pierre Marc (2001). 'Creating Sustainable Global Governance'. In J. J. Kirton, J. P. Daniels and A. Freytag, eds., *Guiding Global Order: G8 Governance in the Twenty-First Century*, pp. 245–282. Ashgate, Aldershot.

Kaiser, Karl, John J. Kirton, and Joseph P. Daniels, eds. (2000). *Shaping a New International Financial System: Challenges of Governance in a Globalizing World*. Ashgate, Aldershot.

Kirton, John J. (2000). 'The Dynamics of G7 Leadership in Crisis Response and System Reconstruction'. In K. Kaiser, J. J. Kirton and J. P. Daniels, eds., *Shaping a New International Financial System: Challenges of Governance in a Globalizing World*, pp. 65–94. Ashgate, Aldershot.

Kirton, John J. (2001). 'The G20: Representativeness, Effectiveness, and Leadership in Global Governance'. In J. J. Kirton, J. P. Daniels and A. Freytag, eds., *Guiding Global Order: G8 Governance in the Twenty-First Century*, pp. 143–172. Ashgate, Aldershot.

Kirton, John J., Joseph P. Daniels, and Andreas Freytag, eds. (2001). *Guiding Global Order: G8 Governance in the Twenty-First Century*. Ashgate, Aldershot.

Porter, Tony (2000). 'The G7, the Financial Stability Forum, the G20, and the Politics of International Financial Regulation'. Paper presented at the International Studies Association Annual Meeting, Los Angeles, 15 March.

Putnam, Robert and Nicholas Bayne, eds. (1987). *Hanging Together: Co-operation and Conflict in the Seven-Power Summit*. 2nd ed. Sage Publications, London.

Wendt, Alexander (1999). *Social Theory of International Politics*. Cambridge University Press, Cambridge.

Part III
New Directions in
Global Trade Governance

10 The G7 and Multilateral Trade Liberalisation: Past Performance, Future Challenges

NICHOLAS BAYNE

Trade and Finance Compared

The G7 summits have always treated trade very differently from finance. The summits were created by a group of finance ministers promoted to become heads of state or government. The very first summit (Rambouillet 1975, arguably the most successful[1]) was summoned by President Valéry Giscard d'Estaing of France to resolve a monetary and financial crisis. The influence of the first generation of leaders persisted into the 1980s. When none of them survived at the summit, their successors as finance ministers reasserted their authority. They created their own G7 group, got certain topics delegated to them from the summit (such as macroeconomic policy co-ordination), and ensured that others only came to the summit through them. Even the last three summits — Birmingham 1998 to Okinawa 2000 — where the heads have met on their own, have endorsed on each occasion one or more reports sent forward by their finance ministers.[2]

Trade has never been so deeply integrated into the summits. Very few of the heads, over the years, have had a background in trade policy. Trade ministers or negotiators have only twice been directly associated with the summits — at Bonn I 1978 and Tokyo III 1993. Of all the ministerial groups generated by the summit, the Quadrilateral of Trade Ministers, or the Quad, (United States, European Union [EU], Japan, and Canada) has the loosest attachment to the summit itself.[3] On the European side, trade is covered by European Community competence, giving an awkward division of responsibility at the summit between the European Commission and the G7 European members. Since the arrival of the Russians, finance issues have remained reserved for the G7 but trade has been treated in the G8, even though the Russians are not yet members of the World Trade Organization (WTO).

171

Yet trade, as much as finance, brings together issues that require the intervention of heads of state and government. As trade has regularly grown faster than gross national product (GNP), the share of each G7 economy exposed to international competition likewise expands. With this comes greater scope for conflicts between external and domestic policies, which often must be reconciled by leaders. The advance of globalisation since the end of the cold war has shown how trade policy no longer operates at the border, but penetrates deeply into domestic policy-making. Such policy conflicts cannot be resolved by internal arbitration by presidents and prime ministers within their own governments, but must also involve external partners. So trade is an obvious subject for the summits, where the leaders can appreciate the external pressures at first hand and reach international understandings that can be reflected in the decisions they take at home. Among the founding fathers, German chancellor Helmut Schmidt recognised this and regarded international trade issues and the resistance to protectionism as the most important rationale for summitry. He believed that without the summits, 'the greater economies ... could have lapsed into the beggar-my-neighbour policies of the early 1930s' (quoted in Putnam and Bayne 1987, 33–34).

For this reason, trade has seldom been off the summit agenda for long. This chapter reviews the contribution made by the summits so far to strengthening the international trading system and draws some conclusions that may be relevant to the future. It applies the same structure of analysis to trade at the summit as that previously used in regard to finance.[4] There are some differences, however. In finance, the analysis separated the G7's impact on the international system from what the members did among themselves. This allowed a treatment of finance at the summit as a series of discontinuous or overlapping episodes. This separation is not feasible with trade, which is thus treated in a continuous sequence.

On that basis, the summit record on trade matters can be broken down into four stages, related to the General Agreement on Tariffs and Trade (GATT):

- The Tokyo Round, 1975–78
- Between the Rounds, 1979–86
- The Uruguay Round, 1987–93
- From Marrakech to Seattle, 1994–2000.

The stages are determined by whether there are multilateral trade negotiations in progress. Because the WTO ministerial meeting at Seattle failed to start a new round, Okinawa 2000 is still in the fourth stage.

In each stage the summit's performance is judged against a range of criteria. These criteria are the same as used previously for the analysis of the G7's contribution to the international financial system. They are:

- *Leadership.* Did the summit resolve differences that could not be resolved at lower levels?
- *Effectiveness.* Did the summit exercise its talent for reconciling domestic and external pressures?
- *Durability.* Did the agreement reached at the summit provide a lasting solution to the problem?
- *Acceptability.* Was the agreement reached among the leaders readily accepted by the wider international community?
- *Consistency.* Did the trade commitments made at the summit fit in well with policies adopted on other subjects?

As with finance, the judgements against the criteria form the basis for the overall conclusions, as well as for some recommendations for the future. These are summarised as follows.

There are five main lessons from the past. First, the summits showed decisive leadership when they committed themselves to complete international trade negotiations and took steps to make good those commitments. Sometimes they tried to lead and failed — but even this was better than neglect. Second, they were effective when they clearly resisted domestic pressures for protectionism. Their reputation suffered when their summit undertakings did not match their actual policies. Third, to have durable effect, the G7 members had to agree among themselves and ensure their commitments were followed through. Fourth, the results finally achieved in both the Tokyo and Uruguay rounds proved acceptable to the international community, but subsequent dissatisfaction among developing countries raised the standard of acceptability the summits must meet. Fifth, inconsistent macroeconomic or sectoral policies on occasion undermined trade commitments. Conversely, weak trade performance frustrated other summit efforts, for example in development.

Recent summits, including Okinawa in 2000, have not performed well on trade and have thus contributed to the failure to launch a new trade round in the WTO. The summits must exert themselves to regain the initiative. This will require a series of actions: a clear G7 agreement on the agenda for a new round, with greater openness to proposals from developing countries; mobilisation of the Quad under summit direction; resistance to domestic pressures for protection and an end to distracting transatlantic disputes; convincing deadlines to ensure the round, once started, is concluded; full implementation of commitments made to improve trade access and 'capacity building' for poor countries; encouraging the Quad to develop more inclusive consultations; and consistent policies elsewhere, both in economic management and development. This will be a substantial agenda for the Genoa Summit in

2001 and its successors. But the summits need to repair nearly eight years of neglect of trade.

Stage 1: The Tokyo Round, 1975–78

The Tokyo Round of multilateral trade negotiations in the GATT was launched in September 1973, just a month before the Arab-Israeli war provoked the first oil crisis. The round had not got far by the time of the Rambouillet Summit of November 1975, as the *U.S. Trade Act*, which gave the U.S. its negotiating authority, had only been passed late in the previous year. Yet Rambouillet took two simple but highly significant decisions. It set out a position of firm resistance to protectionism, and it fixed a deadline of the end of 1977 for completing the Tokyo Round.

The firm resistance to protectionism could not be taken for granted. The oil crisis had sent all the Western countries into recession and stoked up protectionist pressures just as the round was starting. Among the Europeans, France, Britain, and Italy were all disposed to yield to protectionist pressures, with only Germany (under Schmidt) solid in its resistance. But Rambouillet's clear statement set the pattern for later summits. When British prime minister Harold Wilson (one of the few summit leaders to have a background in trade policy) claimed that the Rambouillet Summit justified some protective measures, his partners were quick to warn him off.

The value of the timetable set by Rambouillet for the completion of the Tokyo Round was that it firmly identified the leaders with the success of the multilateral trade negotiations. While the negotiations were in progress, the leaders could invoke their international obligations to counter domestic demands for protection. This was a crucial factor, which the U.S. perceived very clearly. The 1977 deadline was renewed at Puerto Rico in 1976, but by the time of London I the following year it was clear the deadline could not be met. It was moved back, with the 1978 Bonn Summit identified as the target for major progress. At first, this looked like weakness. But the London I Summit still enabled Robert Strauss, U.S. president Jimmy Carter's energetic special trade representative, to accelerate the tempo of work in the GATT.

Just before the Bonn I Summit in July 1978, a 'framework of understanding' was reached in Geneva, but with many tough issues unresolved. Strauss and the European negotiators went to Bonn and resolved a number of these issues on the margins of the summit. This enabled the summit leaders to promise to complete the GATT negotiations by 15 December 1978, as part of the complex set of economic commitments taken at Bonn. The December deadline was met in substance, although for procedural reasons the Tokyo Round did not formally conclude until April 1979.[5]

The summit record in the Tokyo Round generally scores well against the criteria and is revealing on what these early summits did and did not do:

- The summits from Rambouillet onward showed strong *leadership* in their identification with the success of the GATT round. Setting a deadline for ending the round was innovative and these summits met the deadlines they had set, with only a single extension.
- The summits were *effective* in their resistance to the domestic pressures for protectionism. They maintained this resistance, despite the reluctance of France and even Britain at times.
- The summit agreements were *durable*, since they led to the final conclusion of the Tokyo Round.
- The agreements were also *acceptable* in that the understandings reached on the margins of Bonn I proved the basis for the completion of the round in the GATT five months later. But this outcome was only accepted with reluctance by the developing countries, which felt that the Tokyo Round offered them little.[6]
- The summits' trade commitments were *consistent* with the efforts being made in this period in monetary and macroeconomic co-operation. The undertaking to complete the Tokyo Round fit naturally into the ambitious package of measures agreed at the 1978 Bonn Summit and contributed to the high grading given to this summit.

Stage 2: Between the Rounds, 1979–86

The Tokyo Round was only just completed before the second oil crisis struck. The crisis drove trade off the agenda for the summits of 1979 and 1980. But the new recession provoked by the higher oil prices and prolonged by tight macroeconomic policies greatly strengthened protectionist pressures. These persisted in the United States even after economic growth returned, because President Ronald Reagan's strict monetary and loose fiscal policies widened the external deficit. While the summits continued to condemn protectionism, trade barriers were raised on both sides of the Atlantic, while the very large trade surpluses earned by Japan were a further source of tension.

The absence of trade negotiations in progress made it much harder to keep protectionist demands in check. In an attempt to head off these demands, at the 1981 Ottawa Summit the U.S. pressed the idea for a ministerial meeting in the GATT in 1982 to launch a new trade round. But the French and other Europeans would only agree to a free-standing meeting, hoping that by the next year the revival of growth would make a new negotiating round unnecessary. (The leaders also agreed at Ottawa to set up the informal Quadrilateral of Trade Ministers.) In fact, the 1982 GATT ministerial was held at the trough of the recession and came very close to failure.

The United States continued to press for a new trade round, with growing support from Japan, which actually took the lead at London II in 1984. But the Europeans resisted, essentially because of French fears that new GATT negotiations would undermine the European Common Agricultural Policy (CAP). At Bonn II in 1985, French president François Mitterrand prevented the leaders from agreeing that a new round should begin the following year, despite urgent U.S. arguments that this was essential to restrain protectionist demands back home, especially in Congress. These pressures were diverted by the Plaza Accord of September 1985 to let the dollar fall and thus make U.S. industry more competitive. But that agreement was reached among the finance ministers, not at the summit.

A year later, at Tokyo II 1986, the leaders could endorse the call for a new round after minimal discussion. More important, they had their first serious discussion of agriculture, agreeing that support levels had become self-defeating and that solutions could only be found through joint action. Their intervention helped to ensure that agriculture was firmly on the agenda for the new Uruguay Round of trade negotiations, formally launched three months later.[7]

These summits do not score very highly against the criteria:
- They showed little *leadership*. Most of the impetus for a new trade round was generated elsewhere. The leaders themselves failed to agree and the Bonn II Summit actually discouraged progress. However, these summits were moderately innovative, in launching the Quad and intervening to move agriculture up on the international agenda.
- The summits were not *effective* in checking protectionism. The G7 countries allowed protective measures to gain ground even while condemning them at the summit.
- The proposal for the 1982 GATT ministerial clearly was not a *durable* solution, while the summits came late to backing a new negotiating round.
- After several inconclusive years, the focus on agriculture at the Tokyo II Summit of 1986 was very *acceptable* to other GATT members, especially to the agricultural exporters that had formed the Cairns Group.[8]

- There was a general loss of *consistency* in the G7's economic policies. The macroeconomic policies of the first Reagan administration — hotly disputed at the summits — served to aggravate protectionist pressures by driving up the dollar. In Europe, the growing levels of import protection and export subsidy for agriculture were incompatible with the multilateral trading system.

Stage 3: The Uruguay Round, 1987–93

Although the Venice Summit in 1987 returned to agriculture, trade generally got little attention at the summit in the early years of the Uruguay Round. But the Houston Summit of 1990 was obliged to give it priority.[9] The round was due to end in December of that year, but many issues remained unresolved. In particular, Europe and the United States were far apart on agriculture. Houston focussed on four aspects:
- The *U.S. Trade Act* of 1988 had increased the powers of the U.S. administration to impose unilateral trade measures, which deeply worried the Europeans and others. At Houston, the leaders agreed that all would abide by the multilateral rulings of the GATT, whose dispute settlement mechanism should be strengthened to give it more legal force.
- The Houston Summit also gave the first indication of a new institution to replace the GATT, which later emerged as the World Trade Organization.
- A fragile compromise was reached on the agriculture negotiations.
- All the leaders made a personal undertaking to complete the Uruguay Round on time by the end of the year.

However, the agricultural compromise collapsed. Agriculture was the reason the GATT Brussels ministerial failed and the Uruguay Round ran on into 1991, with the U.S. negotiating authority renewed. The next two summits — London III 1991 and Munich 1992 — again set targets to complete the round by the end of that year, but both times they failed, because of persistent differences between the U.S. and the EU over agriculture.

By 1993, however, the prospect had changed. The Europeans had embarked on an internal reform of the CAP. A deal between the U.S. and the European Community on agriculture was struck in late 1992, as President George Bush was leaving office. The Quad met in Tokyo just before the Tokyo III Summit to work out the tariff deal still missing from the Uruguay Round agreements. All this gave the leaders the confidence to set yet another end-of-year deadline. Thanks to the dynamism of Peter Sutherland, the new Director General of the

GATT, this deadline was met and the round finally concluded in December 1993. It reached an ambitious range of agreements and created a new institution with strong legal powers — all going further than would have been possible in 1990.[10]

This time the summits' performance against the criteria gets a mixed assessment:

- From 1990 onward the summits certainly tried to exert *leadership*, but until 1993 these efforts were largely unsuccessful. The summits were also innovative. They renewed their involvement in agriculture (in which several heads remained active after 1990). They also focussed on the legal force and institutional strength of the new multilateral trade regime, shifting the balance of the Uruguay Round agreements in this direction.
- The summits were *effective* in resisting protectionism in most areas by building up the strength of the GATT (and converting it into the WTO). But until 1993 they failed to overcome the domestic pressures on agriculture, which prevented agreement elsewhere.
- The summits' measures were not *durable* before 1993, as they kept missing their deadlines. But without the deadlines the process might have ground to a halt completely.
- The agreements reached among the G7 during 1993 were largely *acceptable* to others. But there was great frustration among other countries because the G7 took so long to resolve its own problems and then presented the solutions on a 'take it or leave it' basis.
- Lack of *consistency* appeared in the summits' repeated failure to make progress on agriculture and to meet its own deadlines. However, the round was eventually completed, while protectionist pressures were kept in check during the recessions of the early 1990s. The European countries became more attached to the multilateral process, which meshed in with their completion of their own single market. But U.S. support for multilateralism weakened over the period.

Stage 4: From Marrakech to Seattle, 1994–2000

U.S. president Bill Clinton brought to the 1994 Naples Summit an idea for another trade round. But nothing came of it, as the others wanted to see the Uruguay Round agreements brought into effect first. Once the WTO was in operation, from 1995 onward, the holding of regular ministerial meetings seemed to reduce the need for summit attention. The initial ratification and implementation of the agreements went smoothly and, from 1997 on, the WTO proved capable of reaching new agreements, for example on information technology products, telecommunications, and financial services.

This neglect of trade at the summits proved a dangerous mistake. A number of factors, with cumulative effect, contributed to a revival of protectionist pressures and dissatisfaction with the multilateral trading system:

- Although the developing countries had made much wider commitments in the Uruguay Round than ever before, many of them concluded that it brought far more benefit to the richer economies than to themselves. They had to take new measures, for example on intellectual property, while the rich countries contrived to evade their commitments on agriculture and textiles.
- The wide range of agreements and the greater legal impact of the WTO penetrated much deeper into domestic policy even in rich countries and aroused new demands for protection. These went beyond trade into food safety, labour standards, and the environment.
- The United States and the EU, rather than keeping the system in good order, allowed their energies to be diverted into a series of bilateral trade disputes on bananas, hormone-enriched meat, genetically modified foodstuffs, aircraft noise, and the taxation of exports.
- As happened from 1979 to 1986, there were no wide-ranging negotiations in progress to counter these adverse trends or keep them in check.

Although the leaders did not perceive these wider dangers, two factors combined to bring trade matters back to the summits. First, the summits began paying new attention to the problems of developing countries, whether generally, as at Lyon in 1996, or especially in Africa, as at Denver in 1997. The 1998 Birmingham and 1999 Cologne summits focussed on debt relief for poor countries. This gave prominence to improved trade access for developing countries, especially the poorest whose share of world trade was dwindling. Renato Ruggiero, the WTO Director General, proposed at Lyon that G7 countries should admit the products of the poorest countries free of duties and quotas.[11] The idea was accepted in principle, but action was postponed from year to year.

Second, new negotiations on agriculture and services were bound to start in 2000. Leon Brittan, the European Trade Commissioner, proposed that these be enlarged into a new, comprehensive Millennium Round, based, like the Uruguay Round, on a single undertaking. This would enable the Europeans to combine the very difficult issue of agriculture with issues of greater value to them, such as investment and competition. But the Europeans were open to adding subjects of interest to others. This was significant in that it was the first time the EU had ever taken the lead in proposing multilateral trade negotiations. The U.S., however, became very cautious over new negotiations, especially as Clinton had twice failed to secure fast-track negotiating authority from Congress. Reluctantly the U.S. agreed to the idea of a new round, to be launched at a WTO ministerial in Seattle in December 1999. But it wanted a limited agenda, not linked to a single undertaking. It also wanted priority for the nontrade issues of labour and environmental standards, to counter the latest sources of protectionist pressure in the U.S.

At both Birmingham 1998 and Cologne 1999, the leaders had a brief exchange on trade, with Japan backing the European approach and Canada closer to the U.S. On both occasions they failed to reconcile the differences between their two approaches. They regarded the trading system as robust, in that no protectionist barriers had been raised as a result of the Asian financial crisis. But they did not realise how much that crisis had undermined support for liberalisation generally. They ignored the signs that the WTO had become the focus of anti-globalisation agitation among their own peoples. In addition, they did not recognise the mounting discontent with the Uruguay Round regime among developing countries.

The consequence was that the Seattle WTO ministerial was a disaster. Being divided among themselves, the G7 were unable either to defend the open trading system from the attacks of hostile nongovernmental organisations (NGOs) or to respond adequately to the demands of the developing countries. There was no agreement to launch a new round and no clear sign about when or how such agreement could be achieved.[12]

Although this was a period of summit renewal in other areas, the summits' scores for trade against the criteria are low:

- There was little sign of *leadership*. The summit discussions were inconclusive and the G7 failed to reach agreement. The few signs of innovation, for example in trade access for poor countries, were not properly followed through.
- The summits were not *effective* in that the G7 had not reconciled external and domestic pressures on agriculture, food safety, and labour and environmental standards. They had allowed these pressures to fuel bilateral trade disputes, while anti-globalisation sentiment grew in their countries and focussed on the WTO.
- Because they were not agreed among the G7, summit approaches were not *durable*. They contributed to the failure at Seattle to launch a new trade round.

- They were likewise not *acceptable*, especially to the developing countries that were much more active in the WTO than they ever were in the GATT.
- There was a failure of *consistency*, in that the summits' neglect of trade undermined efforts being made elsewhere. The G7 claimed to help the poorest countries, for example by increased measures of debt relief, but offered them too little on trade access. They appeared to humour the NGOs wanting tougher labour and environmental standards, but this further alienated the developing countries, which interpreted such measures as covert protection.

The Okinawa 2000 Summit showed some recognition of these failures, especially in what had been offered so far to the poorest countries. But its message was still inconclusive. In calling for 'a new round of WTO trade negotiations with an ambitious, balanced and inclusive agenda', it gave no sign that the different views over this agenda had been resolved. It made only a weak commitment to 'try together with other WTO members to launch such a round in the course of this year [2000]', as if recognising the difficulty of doing this during a U.S. presidential election year (see Appendix B). As a result, the launch of a new round remained as uncertain as ever, at least until the new U.S. administration had taken office. This put a heavy responsibility on the next summit, in Genoa in July 2001, to put things right.

Lessons from the Past: Stages 1 to 4

The record of the first four stages of summit involvement with trade issues provides some clear lessons on what determines success or failure.

Leadership

The summits have shown effective leadership when they have clearly committed themselves to defending the open multilateral trading system. This was most striking at Bonn I 1978 and Tokyo III 1993, in the final years of the negotiations of the Tokyo and Uruguay rounds, when the leaders mobilised their trade negotiators to ensure that the deadlines they had set for completing the rounds were successfully met. Their attempts to maintain the momentum of the negotiations were more effective from 1975 to 1978 than from 1990 to 1993, when they missed three deadlines in a row. But even unsuccessful leadership was preferable to the inconsistency of the mid 1980s or the neglect of the late 1990s.

From 1986 onward, the summits singled out various trade policy issues: agriculture, dispute settlement, institutional development, and, later, trade access for the poorest. While it was probably a mistake for the Houston Summit to go so deeply into the details of agriculture, the Uruguay Round negotiations would not have gone so far on the first three of these subjects without the involvement of the leaders. Summit innovation should be used sparingly, but can have decisive impact.

Effectiveness

The summits were only effective when they were prepared to resist firmly domestic pressures for protectionism. Their commitments only carried conviction if they matched the policies being implemented by the G7 members. The summits' condemnation of protectionism matched their actions while the Tokyo Round was running. But it became threadbare after trade barriers were raised under pressure from the second oil crisis. During the Uruguay Round, the summits strengthened the general resistance to protectionism — except on agriculture. But the chronic transatlantic trade disputes since 1995 have allowed domestic pressures for protection — on agriculture and food safety in Europe, on labour and the environment in the U.S. — to regain lost ground.

Durability

For durable results, the summit leaders must agree among themselves and their commitments must be properly followed through. This worked well during the Tokyo Round, but much less well in the Uruguay Round. With hindsight, the deadlines missed in 1990–92 can be seen as the price of concluding the Uruguay Round, but they seriously damaged the summit's reputation. Other failures to agree have had even worse consequences. Mitterrand put the Uruguay Round at risk at the 1985 Bonn Summit, while the G7 disagreement over the agenda for a new trade round contributed to the fiasco at Seattle.

Acceptability

The final results of the Tokyo and Uruguay rounds, as promoted by the summits, were broadly acceptable, when judged against the standards of the time. But on both occasions there was dissatisfaction among the developing countries, which felt that the results brought much less benefit to them than to the G7 and other rich nations. Since the end of the Uruguay Round, that dissatisfaction has gathered strength and was the main obstacle to agreement at Seattle. Over the same period, the WTO has become identified with many of the negative aspects of globalisation, especially by the NGOs identified as 'civil society'.[13] Summit commitments must now reach a higher standard of acceptability than in the past.

Consistency

Summit commitments on trade can be reinforced by consistent policies in other economic areas, as was especially clear in 1978. But they can be undermined if macroeconomic or sectoral policies tend to encourage protectionist pressures, as happened with U.S. 'high-dollar' policies and with European support for agriculture in the 1980s. Similarly, weak commitments on trade can frustrate summit efforts elsewhere. This is evident from the limited success of the summits' initiatives on debt relief and development since 1995.

Recommendations for the Future: Getting to Stage 5

The task before the summit is to regain the initiative in international trade. Recent summits' neglect of the subject make this difficult. But it is not impossible, provided the leaders understand how previous summits made progress and avoid mistakes.

The objective must be to launch successfully a new round of trade negotiations and to bring them to a conclusion acceptable to all. The difficulties of launching such a round so far raise the question of whether it is the right course. But the G8 members have the strongest interest in such a round, to achieve the following aims:[14]

- To strengthen the multilateral trading system and engage the developing countries fully in it;
- To continue the process of removing trade barriers, which is incomplete in many areas, including agriculture, basic manufacturing, and services;
- To expand multilateral trade rules so that they cover new methods of trading, such as electronic commerce;
- To resist both old and new pressures for protectionism, which is much easier when negotiations are in progress.

These aims cannot be met by the limited agenda favoured by the United States at Seattle. Nor will the EU's comprehensive agenda achieve them, unless it is changed to reflect far more the aspirations of the developing countries.[15]

The following seven-point plan would build on the summits' earlier successes and help them to regain the initiative:

1. To show *leadership*, the summits must first agree among the G7 members on the scope, agenda, and timing of a new round. Such leadership is expected of them. Other parties, especially developing countries, will not follow such a lead blindly — they have their own objectives. But they are deeply frustrated by the lack of agreement among the G7, since no progress is possible without this.

2. Still in their *leadership* role, the heads should involve their trade negotiators directly in the summit process, through the Quad. This was a key element of the Bonn I 1978 and Tokyo III 1993 summits, which gave backing and credibility to the commitments the leaders made. The Quad has become too detached from the summits; the leaders should engage their own authority in backing their trade ministers, both in 2001 and beyond.

3. To make their commitments *effective*, the G7 members should recognise both the strength of domestic pressures, for example in agriculture, food safety, labour standards, and the environment, and the damage these can do to their external economic objectives and the international system. They should make a new commitment to resist protectionist pressures in any form. To give credibility to such a commitment, the G7 countries should undertake to resolve all bilateral trade disputes among themselves within a certain timetable and to carry out fully the judgements made by WTO panels.

4. To achieve *durable* results, the G7 summit must not only ensure that the new WTO round starts, but must also generate the momentum to carry it through to an acceptable conclusion. The summits in the past made use of deadlines for this purpose and they remain useful; for example, a clear, agreed end-date for the new round will be essential. But the experience of missed deadlines in the 1990s has undermined this method. Any close deadlines — within a year — should be backed up by the policy undertakings required to ensure they are met on time.

5. The summits must meet higher standards of *acceptability* than before. To this end, they should encourage more inclusive methods of consultation, which emerged from Seattle as a major concern of developing countries. The heads should not only mobilise their trade ministers and negotiators in the Quad but also encourage them to widen their contacts in the WTO to the maximum, so as to build up a consensus. The G7 has already moved to more inclusive methods in finance, with the launch of the G20 group of finance ministers. A more flexible and open-ended approach will also be needed in trade.

6. Still under *acceptability*, the leaders must fulfil the commitments they have already taken for the benefit of poor countries and produce concrete results by the time of the Genoa Summit in 2001. The most important of these are:
   - *Trade access for the least of the less developed countries.* The Okinawa Communiqué states: 'We recognise the need to go further with greater urgency in this area. And we will do so' (see Appendix B). The leaders must honour this undertaking with precise commitments on duty- and quota-free access.[16]
   - *Capacity building.* The Okinawa Communiqué commits the G7 'to playing a leading role by strengthening our support ... for capacity building' (see Appendix B). But there is no sense that the G7 has identified either the needs or the resources required. Here, too, firm pledges will be needed in 2001.
7. Finally, to be *consistent*, the G7 must pursue economic policies elsewhere that conform to further trade liberalisation and that respond to problems facing developing countries. Further progress in meeting G8 commitments on debt relief, access to information technology, and fighting infectious diseases will help developing countries take advantage of new trade openings.

All this will provide a heavy agenda for Genoa 2001, but a necessary one. If the new round has not begun by then — as seems likely — the G7 leaders must provide the necessary impetus to get it launched. If it is already under way, measures on these lines will be required to give the new round the momentum it needs to reach a successful conclusion. The Genoa Summit and the summits that follow must all give more attention to trade issues, both in reconciling external and domestic pressures and encouraging the work of the Quadrilateral of Trade Ministers. After eight years of neglect or inconclusive discussion, the international trade regime must return to the centre of the G7 leaders' concerns.

Notes

1   'The Rambouillet summit was an undoubted success, arguably more successful than any which followed' (Putnam and Bayne 1987, 41). Although the Bonn Summit of 1978 scores a higher mark for co-operation achieved, this achievement was not durable.

2   The 1998 Birmingham Summit issued a report from the G7 finance ministers on financial architecture. The 1999 Cologne Summit issued reports on financial architecture and the debt initiative. The reports from the Okinawa Summit in 2000 were on debt and development and on abuses of the financial system. No other ministers have produced reports for issue at the summit.

3   The Quad, although founded at the Ottawa Summit in 1981 (Putnam and Bayne 1987, 131), is not recorded in the Communiqué. This is because the European summit participants did not want a public statement issued until the idea had been endorsed by the rest of the European Community.

4   This chapter follows the same pattern as my chapter, 'The G7 Summit's Contribution: Past Present and Prospective', in *Shaping a New International Financial System* (Bayne 2000a). That chapter already had something to say about trade.

5   For accounts of trade discussions at these first four summits, see Putnam and Bayne 1987, chapters 2 and 4, and de Menil and Solomon 1983, 22–26.

6   See Preeg 1995, 24–27, on the dissatisfaction of developing countries with the Tokyo Round.

7   Accounts of trade discussions at the summits from 1979 to 1986 are in Putnam and Bayne 1987, chapters 6, 8, and 9. For the Geneva meeting, see Preeg 1995, 33–36, and for agriculture see Wolfe 1998, 79–80.

8   The Cairns Group of 18 agricultural exporting countries including Canada, formed in 1986, represents one third of the world's agricultural exports.

9   This section focusses on the trade discussion at Houston Summit 1990 partly because of the author's vivid memories of the event. But, as always, the effect of summit discussion is cumulative.

10   For trade at the summits of 1987 to 1993, see Bayne 2000b, chapters 5 and 7. Assessments of the Uruguay Round results are in Schott 1994 and Preeg 1995 and a complete history in Croome 1995. Jackson 1998 analyses the WTO's legal powers.

11   See Chote and Jonquières 1996 for Ruggiero's initial proposal, which led to a series of imprecise commitments in later summit communiqués.

12   For trade discussions at the summits from 1994 to 1999, see Bayne 2000b, chapters 8 and 10, and Bayne 2000a. An account and assessment of the Seattle meeting is in Bayne 2000c.

13   The role of civil society NGOs is discussed in more detail in Chapter 12, as well as in the separate study by Peter Hajnal in *New Directions in Global Political Governance* (forthcoming).

14   Schott 2000, chapter 1, develops similar arguments for a new round.

15   For a good review of the current demands on trade policy, see 'The Trade Agenda: A Different, New World Order' (2000).

16   For earlier, unsatisfactory G7 commitments in the WTO on trade access for the poorest countries, see Bardacke and Engelhardt 2000 and Williams 2000. Since Okinawa, the European Commission has proposed the removal of barriers on almost all imports from less developed countries ('everything but arms'), but this has provoked resistance among EU member states; see Smith 2000 and Jonquières 2000.

References

Bardacke, Ted and Torsten Engelhardt (2000). 'WTO Aims for Deal with Poor Nations'. *Financial Times*, 14 February, p. 10.

Bayne, Nicholas (2000a). 'The G7 Summit's Contribution: Past, Present, and Prospective'. In K. Kaiser, J. J. Kirton and J. P. Daniels, eds., *Shaping a New International Financial System: Challenges of Governance in a Globalizing World*, pp. 19–35. Ashgate, Aldershot.

Bayne, Nicholas (2000b). *Hanging in There: The G7 and G8 Summit in Maturity and Renewal*. Ashgate, Aldershot.

Bayne, Nicholas (2000c). 'Why Did Seattle Fail? Globalization and the Politics of Trade'. *Government and Opposition* vol. 35, no. 2, pp. 131–151.

Chote, Robert and Guy de Jonquières (1996). 'Tariff Plea to Aid Poor Countries' Exports'. *Financial Times*, 1 July, p. 4.

Croome, John (1995). *Reshaping the World Trading System: A History of the Uruguay Round*. World Trade Organization, Geneva.

de Menil, George and Anthony M. Solomon (1983). *Economic Summitry*. Council on Foreign Relations, New York.

Hajnal, Peter (forthcoming). 'Openness and Civil Society Participation in the G8 and Global Governance'. In J. J. Kirton and J. Takase, eds., *New Directions in Global Political Governance*. Ashgate, Aldershot.

Jackson, John H. (1998). *The World Trade Organization: Constitution and Jurisprudence*. Royal Institute of International Affairs, London.

Jonquières, Guy de (2000). 'Altruism with a Bitter Taste: Brussels Is Being Forced to Rethink Plans to End Trade Barriers for the Poorest Countries'. *Financial Times*, 19 December, p. 23.

Preeg, Ernest H. (1995). *Traders in a Brave New World: The Uruguay Round and the Future of the International Trading System*. University of Chicago Press, Chicago.

Putnam, Robert and Nicholas Bayne, eds. (1987). *Hanging Together: Co-operation and Conflict in the Seven-Power Summit*. 2nd ed. Sage Publications, London.

Schott, Jeffrey J. (1994). *The Uruguay Round: An Assessment*. Institute for International Economics, Washington DC.

Schott, Jeffrey J. (2000). *The WTO after Seattle*. Institute for International Economics, Washington DC.

Smith, Mike (2000). 'EU May End Duty for Poor Nations'. *Financial Times*, 21 September, p. 15.

'The Trade Agenda: A Different, New World Order'(2000). *Economist* 11 November, pp. 141–146.

Williams, Frances (2000). 'Poorest Countries Attack WTO Aid Package'. *Financial Times*, 11 April, p. 14.

Wolfe, Robert (1998). *Farm Wars: The Political Economy of Agriculture and the International Trade Regime*. Macmillan, Houndmills.

11 Securing Multilateral Trade Liberalisation: International Institutions in Conflict and Convergence

THEODORE H. COHN

Scholars and practitioners have often considered the 'global trade regime' to be synonymous with the principles and rules of the General Agreement on Tariffs and Trade (GATT) and, since January 1995, the World Trade Organization (WTO). When 23 governments signed the GATT in 1947 to begin lowering tariffs, they assumed it would only be a temporary agreement. However, the GATT became the permanent global trade organisation by default when the United States Congress failed to approve the creation of an international trade organisation. Although the GATT functioned effectively for almost five decades, its informal origins proved to be a source of weakness. Its members could bypass many of its regulations, and some trade sectors such as textiles and agriculture were largely excluded from the agreement. In the Uruguay Round, the negotiators decided to replace the GATT with a more formal international organisation, the WTO.[1] The GATT/WTO, the International Monetary Fund (IMF), and the World Bank are keystone international economic organisations (KIEOs), because of their role in managing global monetary relations, finance, and trade.[2]

Although the GATT/WTO has been central to the global trade regime, other formal and informal institutions also form an integral part of the regime. Indeed, as early as 1969 the GATT legal specialist John Jackson (1969, 11) noted that the 'regulation of international trade is ... an extraordinarily complex and muddled affair, involving a wide variety of organizations and institutions ... when one considers GATT, it is necessary to relate it to the mosaic and ever-changing picture of other international institutions'.

Despite Jackson's observation, no systematic study has yet been done contrasting the trade-related functions of those 'other international institutions'. This chapter examines the important role played in multilateral trade relations by the Organisation for Economic Co-operation and Development (OECD), the G7, and the Quadrilateral of Trade Ministers (the Quad), and the relationship of these institutions to the GATT/WTO. It covers the period from the GATT's Tokyo Round negotiations in the 1970s to the establishment of the WTO in 1995. It hypothesises that the important role of the G7, the Quad, and the OECD in multilateral trade liberalisation during this period stems from four factors: the dominance of developed countries (DCs) in the North over less developed countries (LDCs) in the South, the decline of U.S. economic hegemony, the variations in expertise among institutions based on a division of labour, and the nature of the GATT/WTO as an international organisation. Institutions such as the G77 and the United Nations Conference on Trade and Development (UNCTAD), which identify with the interests of the LDCs, have been far less important. The LDCs gained some influence in the 1980s and 1990s because they were more involved in the Uruguay Round than they had been in previous GATT rounds. Nevertheless, developed country (DC) institutions such as the G7, the Quad, and the OECD continue to have predominant influence in the WTO and global trade regime. Before tracing the role of these institutions since the Tokyo Round, this chapter explores one of the four factors explaining institutional involvement in global trade policy: the nature of the GATT/WTO as an international organisation.[3]

A Division of Labour among Institutions

A division of labour among institutions results partly from the fact that GATT/WTO officials cannot possibly be the primary experts on all aspects of trade policy. For example, the World Bank, the Food and Agriculture Organization, the International Labour Organization (ILO), and the United Nations Environment Programme have special expertise to offer in areas of trade related to development, agriculture, labour, and the environment, respectively. The work done by these organizations on trade-related issues often complements the negotiations and other functions of the GATT/WTO. The GATT/WTO also has a smaller budget for conducting research and in-depth studies than some other international economic institutions. The OECD as a general-purpose organization, for example, has research and investigatory capacities that have been essential to GATT/WTO negotiations in such areas as agricultural and services trade. Thus, a division of labour is one factor accounting for the wide range of institutions involved with trade-related issues.

The GATT/WTO as an International Organisation

The United Nations (UN) system that developed in the post-war period was based on several key principles, including universality and the sovereign equality of states. However, realists note that the sovereign equality principle does not reflect the hierarchy of power in the international system; some liberals argue that the universality principle is problematic because co-operation becomes more difficult as the number of actors increases (Olson 1965; Oye 1985). The major powers in multilateral institutions have dealt with their concerns about sovereign equality and universality by engaging in 'minilateralism' or '"great power" collaboration within multilateral institutions' (Kahler 1993, 296).[4] One can cite various examples of minilateral processes within the GATT/WTO. For example, the reciprocity principle ensures that the major trading nations are the key actors in GATT/WTO negotiations, because they are the largest importing and exporting countries; that is, they are most able to provide and demand reciprocal advantages. GATT/WTO negotiations are therefore often a pyramidal process, where agreements are 'initiated by the major powers at the top and then gradually multilateralized through the inclusion of other parties in the discussions' (Winham 1986, 376). Unlike the IMF and World Bank, however, the GATT/WTO has not provided minilateral prerogatives for the major trading powers in two major areas: selective membership groups and voting rights.

All GATT/WTO councils and committees are plenary bodies open to every member of the organisation. The GATT/WTO has nothing comparable to the smaller executive boards of the IMF and World Bank, in which the G5 countries (the U.S., Japan, Germany, France, and Britain) have assured membership. The Havana Charter had included a provision for an executive board that was to be responsible for executing the policies of the International Trade Organization (ITO). It was to consist of 18 ITO members including 'the eight Members of chief economic importance'.[5] However, when the ITO was not formed, the GATT never established such an executive board. The closest it came to having a select body was the Consultative Group of 18 (CG18), which first met in 1975. As GATT membership increased, the CG18 was established as a smaller representative group of countries to facilitate discussion of trade issues. The CG18 was purely consultative in nature and has not met since 1987.

Another departure from GATT practice of having only plenary bodies are the informal 'Green Room' sessions, named after a small conference room adjoining the GATT director general's office. These closed-door sessions, which were a favourite of Arthur Dunkel for conducting informal negotiations during the GATT Uruguay Round, were limited to about 25 diplomats from the major countries. Nevertheless, after demonstrators at the November 1999 Seattle ministerial meeting demanded greater transparency, WTO director general Mike Moore 'tried to move away from the Green Room, and thrash out issues in the General Council'.[6] A third departure from GATT/WTO plenaries was a group of 34 WTO members that met during the December 1996 ministerial in Singapore. This group reached a consensus on a range of issues that were then presented to all WTO members for approval. Although the process functioned fairly smoothly, the 94 members not in the core group complained that they had little part in the decision-making process (Blackhurst 1998, 49–50; Preeg 1995, 132).

In addition to lacking an executive body, the GATT/WTO is also a one-nation, one-vote organisation. The IMF and World Bank, by contrast, have weighted voting related to member countries' capital fund contributions and economic power. The voting systems in these three organisations may seem to have little importance, however, because almost all decisions are made by consensus. Consensus decision making has definite value in the WTO, the World Bank, and the IMF, because it can avert divisiveness that may result from vote-taking. Nevertheless, 'the legal structure of potential voting still has a great influence on any organization, no matter how hard the organization tries to avoid voting' (Jackson 1997, 69). Negotiation occurs 'in the context of the participants' knowledge of the likely outcome [of a vote] if the negotiation breaks down'. Thus, the atmosphere surrounding consensus decision making is often more different in the one-nation, one-vote GATT/WTO than it is in the weighted voting of the IMF and the World Bank. Furthermore, consensus decision making requires that no member 'present at the meeting when the decision is taken, formally objects to the proposed decision' ('Marrakesh Agreement Establishing the World Trade Organization' 1994, article IX.1, footnote 1). As the WTO membership becomes larger and more diverse, it may become increasingly difficult to reach a consensus. One reason why the IMF and World Bank have weighted voting is that the major DCs have loaned large amounts of funds through these organisations, and have in return insisted upon special minilateral prerogatives. The DCs have fewer grounds for demanding these prerogatives in the WTO because it is a trade organisation rather than a financing one. Nevertheless, the GATT/WTO's characteristics have often caused the major DCs to turn to plurilateral or limited-membership institutions such as the OECD, the G7, and the Quad.

Each member's contribution to the GATT/WTO secretariat budget is determined by its share of world trade, and the larger DC traders have little incentive to support an increase of WTO secretariat activities when they have no more votes than the smaller traders. Staff in the World Bank, IMF, and OECD secretariats in 1996 numbered 6781, 2577, and 2322, respectively, but the WTO secretariat had only 513 staff members. Although a number of factors such as the sensitive political nature of trade account for the WTO secretariat's limited resources, the major DC trading nations have also been 'reluctant to rely on decisions in GATT reached by majority vote in which a country with $50 *million* of foreign trade has the same vote as a country with $50 *billion* trade' (Atlantic Council of the United States 1975, 58).

The GATT/WTO's lack of executive bodies and its one-nation, one-vote system have resulted in various DC proposals for change. For example, a 1975 Atlantic Council study recommended that the DCs conclude a supplementary agreement among themselves to liberalise trade with tighter trade rules than those of the GATT. The rules of the agreement would be administered on a weighted-voting basis, and LDCs would be encouraged to join as they industrialised. As LDCs would initially not accept the obligations of the supplementary agreement, the GATT would remain in force for DC trade relations with the LDCs. The Atlantic Council recommended that the new DC agreement be administered either by the GATT or the OECD. A 1989 study sponsored by the Twentieth Century Fund similarly recommended that the OECD establish a free trade and investment area, which would be open to other countries that followed democratic principles, had market-oriented policies, and approximated OECD social welfare standards (Atlantic Council of the United States 1975, 6–11, 56–57; Hufbauer 1989, 149–154). In the Uruguay Round, DCs also put forward proposals to form a select executive body within the GATT comparable to the bodies in the IMF and World Bank.[7]

The proposals for a supplementary DC trade agreement and for an executive body within the GATT/WTO were never implemented because of LDC opposition and growing divisions among the U.S., European Union (EU), and Japan. The failure to resolve these issues has sometimes worked to the disadvantage of the WTO. As mentioned, the WTO's 'one nation, one vote' system has deterred the major trading nations from contributing to a larger secretariat. The WTO staff's limited in-house capacity to conduct research forms a marked contrast with OECD staff members, who have exerted considerable influence on trade issues through the quality of their research. Furthermore, major DC traders have been more inclined to turn to the G7, the Quad, and the OECD to discuss in-depth trade policy issues and establish the conditions for trade liberalisation.

In addition to its one-nation, one-vote system and its lack of an executive board, the GATT/WTO's role as a rule-bound organisation has also encouraged members to turn to other institutions. In some circumstances, the major trading powers prefer to deal with institutions that are less legalistic than the GATT/ WTO and have less demanding requirements. For example, in some trade-related areas such as export credits the OECD has negotiated so-called 'gentlemen's agreements', which are not legally binding accords like those of the GATT/WTO. In contrast to the dispute settlement procedures that help to uphold GATT/WTO accords, OECD gentlemen's agreements are upheld only through the commitment of participants to notify others if they deviate from the agreements. In sum, several GATT/WTO characteristics have caused the major trading nations to deal with some trade-related issues in plurilateral institutions. The discussion that follows examines the role of these institutions, and also the role of the two largest trading entities — the U.S. and the European Community (in 1993 the European Community [EC] became the EU). The discussion of the Uruguay Round also focusses on the role of coalition groups and their relationship with the G7, the Quad, and the OECD.

The GATT Tokyo Round

The GATT Tokyo Round began in 1973, in an effort to combat the growing use of nontariff barriers (NTBs), and the negative effects of monetary instability on the global trade regime. The Tokyo Round was a pyramidal process, with the major DC trading countries and the institutions representing their interests having the most influence in the negotiations (Winham 1986; Golt 1974, 5–9). At the apex of the pyramid were the two largest trading entities, the U.S. and the EC; then came the G7 and the OECD.

The United States and the European Community

Changes in global economic relations posed a serious threat to the success of the Tokyo Round. American hegemony was declining more rapidly in trade than in other areas, and in 1971 the U.S. had its first trade deficit in the twentieth century.[8] When Britain, Denmark, and Ireland joined the EC in January 1973, it became the world's largest trading entity, and both the EC and Japan were less willing to defer to U.S. leadership on trade issues. The voluminous literature criticising hegemonic stability theory provides a warning against facile assumptions that U.S. trade hegemony in the 1950s to early 1960s was always conducive to trade liberalisation. In some sectors such as agriculture and textiles, the U.S. in fact contributed to trade protectionism (Cohn 1993).

Nevertheless, U.S. hegemony in the early post-war years was primarily a force for trade liberalisation, since the U.S. provided public goods to promote an open trade regime and economic reconstruction in Western Europe and Japan. In the 1970s, by contrast, U.S. leaders were 'more concerned with specific national economic interests, making their behavior more similar to the behavior of policy makers in other states' (Krasner 1979, 491).

In July 1971, the Williams Commission appointed by President Richard Nixon called for a new round of GATT negotiations to liberalise trade. However, the commission also recognised that the EC had 'overtaken the United States as the most important trading unit', and recommended that the U.S. 'should more than in the past use its bargaining power in the defense of its economic interests' (Commission on International Trade and Investment Policy 1971, 288, 294). In the 1970s, the U.S. was in fact more inclined to adopt policies that circumvented GATT rules such as 'voluntary' export restraints, and to take unilateral actions against 'unfair' traders under Section 301 of the *U.S. Trade Act of 1974*. The EC for its part increased trade protectionism under its Common Agricultural Policy (CAP), and threatened the GATT's nondiscrimination principle by extending its area of preferential treatment to African and European associate states. The 1973–74 oil crisis posed yet another threat to trade liberalisation, when the Organization of the Petroleum Exporting Countries (OPEC) quadrupled oil prices and precipitated a steep recession in the OECD countries.

Despite the protectionist pressures stemming from U.S. hegemonic decline, states that benefited from the global trade regime had the incentive to continue liberalising trade through co-operative efforts. Institutions furnished 'some of the sense of certainty and confidence that a hegemon formerly provided' (Keohane 1984, 183; see also Snidal 1985). Thus, one reason the G7 economic summit became institutionalised in the 1970s was in order to supplement U.S. management of the world economic order with collective management (Putnam and Bayne 1987, 16–18). The degree to which U.S. hegemony declined, however, should not be overestimated. The U.S. continued to have a great deal of influence in the Tokyo Round. Indeed, some of the early initiatives leading to the Tokyo Round came from committees appointed by U.S. presidents, which concluded that negotiations were necessary to combat other countries' restrictions on U.S. exports. The 1971 Williams Commission report indicated that the new talks should deal with NTBs, and that the key trading nations might adopt some 'separate codes or understandings that apply initially only to the members particularly concerned, but are open to accession by other members' (Commission on International Trade and Investment Policy 1971,

297). The Tokyo Round would in fact result in a series of plurilateral NTB codes signed mainly by the OECD states.

As the largest trading entities, the U.S. and EC held informal discussions on contentious issues during the Tokyo Round to avoid the risk of a major confrontation. U.S.-EC co-operation directed the negotiation. When the U.S. and EC did not co-operate, the negotiation became deadlocked because they had effective veto power. When the U.S. and EC adopted a unified position, only the combined efforts of others had any chance of changing the outcome. Thus, the U.S. and EC were at the top of the pyramid in the Tokyo Round negotiations (Winham 1989).

The Organisation for Economic Co-operation and Development

The OECD is a group of 30 mainly industrial states that replaced the Organisation for European Economic Co-operation (OEEC) in 1961. From the time of its creation, the OECD has been committed to liberalising trade and investment flows. It provides its members with reliable data and careful analysis of policy issues, and serves as a forum for DCs to discuss members' economic policies, review common problems, and promote policy co-ordination. Although the OECD has the authority to adopt binding agreements, it usually operates through a system of mutual persuasion, in which governments exert peer pressure on one another to follow compatible policies (OECD 1994, 9; Henderson 1996). In 1972, a high-level group of individuals formed by the OECD Secretary General supported U.S. calls for a new GATT negotiating round and advised that the problem of 'non-tariff measures which directly affect trade must be an essential and priority element' (OECD 1972, 61, 110). OECD 'prenegotiations' also helped prepare the way for the Tokyo Round negotiations. The main function of prenegotiation is to turn 'the problem into a manageable issue susceptible of a negotiated outcome' (Zartman 1989, 246). The OECD prenegotiation process typically involves three phases: defining issues and discussing how to handle them; providing detailed discussion and analysis, mainly on the basis of secretariat documents; and developing a common understanding or consensus that OECD members bring to subsequent GATT/WTO negotiations (Henderson 1998, 127).

Government procurement was one area where OECD prenegotiations laid the groundwork for the Tokyo Round. Formal international talks on government procurement began in 1962, when a working party of the OECD Trade Committee considered a British and Belgian complaint regarding the U.S. *Buy America Act*. The OECD secretariat subsequently produced a summary of government procurement practices and a draft government procurement code. Although OECD members could not reach a consensus on a number of the draft code provisions, the OECD work provided an important basis for the GATT negotiations that resulted in the Tokyo Round Agreement on Government Procurement. Most GATT countries including the LDCs were early participants in the Tokyo Round procurement talks, because the DCs had already identified the key issues and developed the draft code in OECD prenegotiations. Despite the broader participation in the government procurement negotiations, even in this case the U.S. and EC were central actors. U.S.-EC bilateral discussions resulted in a tradeoff, with the U.S. accepting the EC position on tendering procedures, and the EC acceding to U.S. pressure for greater transparency (Winham 1986, 138–141, 189–194; GATT 1986, 27–49).

Although this chapter highlights the role of institutions other than the GATT/WTO, it is important to note that the GATT Secretariat played a critical role in preparations for the Tokyo Round, as did the OECD. A prime example relates to the tariff negotiations. After member countries had implemented the tariff reductions agreed to in the Kennedy Round, GATT conducted a study that recorded for the first time 'the full facts on the tariff structure of each of the major trading countries, together with trade statistics that make it possible to assess the importance of each tariff item' (GATT 1973, 10). The computer tapes produced by the Tariff Study also greatly simplified the problem of storage and recall of information, and facilitated the calculation of simplified measures of reciprocity. As a result, GATT members had to devote far less time to negotiating tariff reductions in the Tokyo Round (Winham 1986, 159).

The G7

The G7 Summits began with six countries (the U.S., Japan, Germany, France, Britain, and Italy) in November 1975; Canada became the seventh member in 1976, and the EC joined in 1977. In a general sense, the summits arose as a result of the increase in economic interdependence, the need for collective management with the relative decline of U.S. hegemony, and the personal inclinations of some Western leaders. Specific events that led to the summits included the collapse of the Bretton Woods system, the enlargement of the EC, the 1973–74 oil crisis, and the 1974 economic recession. Although the G7 summit is not a decision-making forum, the leaders seek to arrive at a consensus on key issues at the highest political level (Bayne 2000, 20–21; Hajnal 1999, 4–5). The summit's agenda 'has expanded well beyond its core concern with macroeconomic policy, trade and north-south relations, and its early interest in east-west economic and global energy issues' to 'a host of microeconomic, environmental, transnational and political-security subjects' (Kirton 1995, 66). Nevertheless, the summits have been consistently concerned with trade.

At the 1975 Rambouillet Summit, the leaders gave some impetus to the Tokyo Round, which was making only slow progress. They set a deadline of 1979 for completion of the round, which had a positive effect in resolving a procedural impasse between the U.S. and EC over agriculture. Although the 1976 Puerto Rico Summit renewed the 1979 deadline for completing the negotiations, this action had little impact on the pace of the round. The Democratic administration of Jimmy Carter that was elected in November 1976 placed a high priority on overcoming the obstacles to negotiation, but divisions were evident at the 1977 London Summit. Although the U.S., Germany, and Japan wanted a commitment to rapid completion of the round, France, Britain, and Italy were concerned that freer trade would increase competition from the U.S. and the newly industrialising countries (NICs). The U.S., Germany, and Japan nevertheless succeeded in getting a qualified commitment to achieve substantial progress in the round, and subsequent meetings held by U.S. trade representative Robert Strauss in European capitals led to a period of intense negotiating activity (Putnam and Bayne 1987 37–43, 67–71; G7 1975, 1976, 1977).

The 1978 Bonn Summit served as an interim deadline for the Tokyo Round, and there was considerable progress in most areas other than agriculture before the Bonn meeting. By publicly setting the interim deadline, the G7 increased pressure on governments to reach a final settlement. Indeed, a framework of understanding on the Tokyo Round was made public on 13 July 1978, three days before the Bonn Summit was to begin. Trade turned out to be the most controversial issue at that summit, showing that major issues still had to be negotiated at a higher political level. Differences among the DCs were substantially resolved when the U.S. offered to downgrade its demands of Europe in agriculture in return for a European agreement to a timetable for rapid completion of the round. However, the pyramidal process of negotiation that the G7 summits represented created major tensions with the LDCs that also required resolution before the Tokyo Round could be completed (Putnam and Bayne 1987, 82–86; G7 1978; Winham 1986, 164–168).

The LDCs were dissatisfied that they had not had any part in developing the Framework of Understanding on the Tokyo Round that the DCs had agreed to in the run-up to the Bonn Summit. They also argued that the DCs had not dealt with the Multifibre Arrangement for textiles and voluntary export restraints that were often aimed at the developing world. To counter frictions, the DCs had to give higher priority to LDC concerns when the Tokyo Round negotiations resumed after the Bonn Summit. The main political difficulty in concluding the Tokyo Round was in fact the LDCs' opposition. They refused to sign the code agreements, and pressed for a delay in concluding the round until an UNCTAD meeting scheduled for May 1979 was convened. Despite LDC objections, the GATT Director General announced on 12 April 1979 that the Tokyo Round had ended. The following month, the UNCTAD secretariat charged that the Tokyo Round agreements 'do little to help poor nations, and only serve to perpetuate a trading system that works more and more against them'.[9] From the time the GATT was formed in the 1940s, LDCs had 'remained bystanders in successive rounds of trade negotiations', and most LDCs refused to sign the Tokyo Round codes and to bind their tariffs (Krueger 1995, 48). In the 1980s and 1990s, however, the foreign debt crisis and the failure of import substitution policies would induce the LDCs to become far more involved in the Uruguay Round.

Between Rounds: 1979–86

Despite its accomplishments, the Tokyo Round resulted in a differentiated trade regime, with some agreements following liberal ideals and others permitting discriminatory behaviour. Two major factors explaining this differentiated outcome were U.S. hegemonic decline and the resulting rise of particularistic interests (Krasner 1979, 524–525). GATT members, however, were reluctant to commit to further liberalisation in the early 1980s because of widespread unemployment and inflation, monetary instability, large payments imbalances, and the LDC foreign debt crisis. In response to its growing balance of payments deficit and the obstacles to multilateral negotiations, the U.S. followed a three-pronged approach: it pressed for a new GATT round to liberalise trade in areas where it had a comparative advantage such as services, high technology, and agriculture; it showed an interest for the first time in joining regional free trade agreements; and it applied unilateral sanctions to allegedly unfair traders. The U.S. regional and unilateral approaches were partly designed as levers to pressure the EC and Japan to agree to a new round of multilateral trade negotiations.

Before detailing the U.S. pressures for a new GATT round, a brief discussion of the formation of the Quad is important, because it was to play a significant role in the Uruguay Round. In the early years of the G7 summits, some government leaders strongly opposed extending the G7 apparatus downward; the resistance to the downward extension of bureaucracy began to decline in the 1980s, and various G7 ministerial groups developed. The first of these groups, the Quad, consists of the U.S., EU, Japanese, and Canadian trade ministers. Even before the Quad was formed at the 1981 Ottawa Summit, the 'Big Three' (the U.S., EU, and Japan) and sometimes the 'Big Four' (including Canada) had exerted the most influence in the GATT Tokyo Round. The Quad usually meets three or four times per year (Bayne 2000, 210–212; Winham 1986, 207). Although 'the groups of "inner participants" were considerably enlarged' in the Uruguay Round, the Quad continues to have considerable influence (Jackson 1997, 70).

U.S. pressure for a new GATT round began at the June 1981 OECD ministerial meeting when the U.S. Trade Representative suggested that the OECD address the newer trade issues. The OECD Secretary General agreed to develop a work program to deal with trade, which was a first step toward forming an agenda for a new GATT round. Since the GATT did not meet regularly at ministerial level, ministers had more opportunity to provide overall political direction in the OECD. OECD ministerials also permitted the major DCs to produce an agenda for trade talks without participation by most LDCs. In addition to its OECD initiative, the U.S. suggested that a GATT ministerial be held in 1982 to develop a work program for a new round. Indeed, a U.S. delegate went directly from the 1981 OECD ministerial to Geneva to confer with GATT officials, and the CG18 subsequently supported the GATT ministerial idea. The 1979 and 1980 G7 summits were preoccupied with the impact of the second oil shock on Western economies and devoted little attention to trade issues, but the 1981 Ottawa Summit strongly endorsed the GATT ministerial proposal (Long 1985, 50–51; Putnam and Bayne 1987, 101; G7 1981; Preeg 1995, 29–30; Croome 1995, 12).

GATT ministerial meetings were infrequent and were usually associated with the beginning of new multilateral trade negotiations. In outlining the purpose of the 1982 ministerial, however, the CG18 tried to satisfy both those who wanted existing GATT rules to be applied more vigorously and those who wanted new negotiations. The vague guidelines provided little direction, and the draft declaration and work program sent by the Preparatory Committee to the 1982 ministerial included many contentious issues that the ministers could not resolve. The global economy had also declined since the end of the Tokyo Round, and there was a deep recession at the time of the meeting. The 1982 ministerial therefore encountered serious problems, which brought the GATT itself near the point of a serious breakdown. The delegates produced a communiqué replete with compromise statements that pleased no one, although it ironically stimulated exploratory work on issues that would become central to the Uruguay Round. GATT director general Arthur Dunkel gave further stimulus to a new round by appointing a panel of nongovernmental experts to report on current trade problems (Dunkel 1987; Preeg 1995, 33–36; Croome 1995, 12–17). In 1985, the panel issued the Leutwiler report, which referred to 'the erosion of the trading rules' and called for a new GATT round 'as soon as possible' (GATT 1985, 19, 47).

Despite the contributions of the CG18 and the Leutwiler report, the GATT played a less important role in building support for a new round than did the G7, the Quad, and the OECD. However, support in these latter fora developed only gradually and it was difficult to reach a consensus, as the results of successive G7 summits demonstrate. The U.S. had pressed for new negotiations since 1981, and at the 1983 Williamsburg Summit it favoured a joint call for a new GATT round. But the G7 leaders would only agree to 'continue consultations on proposals' for another round (G7 1983). At the 1984 London Summit, the U.S. and Japan wanted a 1985–86 target date for preparations and opening of a new round, but the Europeans would only agree to consult GATT partners 'at an early date' on the timing (G7 1984). The U.S. and Japan again pressed for an early target date for the next GATT round at the 1985 Bonn Summit, and this time Germany and Britain gave their support. Before agreeing to a date, however, France's president François Mitterrand wanted assurances that the CAP would be protected and that attention would be given to monetary as well as trade issues (G7 1985). Despite this lack of consensus, the GATT began preparations for a new round. By the time of the 1986 Tokyo Summit, the preparations were already well advanced, and the Declaration from the Tokyo meeting finally endorsed an 'early launching of the new round' (G7 1986). In sum, the G7 summits in the 1980s generally favoured a new GATT round, but the leaders had difficulty agreeing on a timetable, and they were not involved in the technical preparations that were the responsibility of the OECD, the Quad, and the GATT secretariat.

Although support gradually developed for a new GATT round at high-level DC meetings, many LDCs were still disappointed with the outcome of the Tokyo Round and were reluctant to support the inclusion of new areas such as services in which the DCs had a comparative advantage. However, when the U.S. requested a postal ballot of GATT members to force countries to decide whether to exclude themselves from the negotiations, the LDCs backed down and agreed to join in preparations for a new round. During the Preparatory Committee meetings from January to July 1986, most LDCs decided that they would benefit from participation. Through Part IV of the

GATT and the Enabling Clause, LDCs had received special and differential treatment, but this special status had contributed to a lack of LDC influence in GATT negotiations. Thus, the LDCs became more willing to provide reciprocal commitments as a means of increasing their leverage. Canada, the EU, and Uruguay all offered to host the meeting to launch the new round, but the Preparatory Committee selected Uruguay as a show of support for LDC participation (Preeg 1995, 32–34, 55–59, 70–71; Croome 1995, 28–30).

The GATT Uruguay Round

On 14 September 1986, ministers from 96 countries began the week-long meeting at Punta del Este that resulted in the launching of the Uruguay Round. An early warning of divisiveness was the fact that the Punta meeting began with three draft ministerial texts: 48 DCs and LDCs (the G48) issued the main text, which called for an ambitious agenda to liberalise trade and broaden GATT's mandate; 10 LDCs headed by Brazil and India (the G10) provided the second text, which proposed that the negotiations be far more limited in scope; and Argentina supplied a third text. Although the G10 argued that DCs should fulfil previous commitments made to LDCs before negotiating new commitments, the G48's views prevailed and the Punta meeting launched the most ambitious effort ever to strengthen the global trade regime. The agenda included new areas favoured by the DCs such as services, intellectual property, and investment, as well as areas of importance to LDCs such as textiles and clothing, and tropical and natural resource-based products (Winham 1989, 294–295).

Those three texts were an early indication that coalitions would be much more important in the Uruguay Round than in previous rounds. A coalition in trade negotiations is any group of participants 'who agree to act in concert to achieve a common end' (Hamilton and Whalley 1989, 547). Unlike previous rounds, LDCs were active participants in DC-LDC coalitions and in coalitions limited to LDCs. The Uruguay Round coalitions are of interest here because they did not always adhere to the trade agenda of the predominant DCs in the G7, the Quad, and the OECD. In cases of divisions among major DC players, coalitions sometimes shifted the balance in favour of one of the disputants. For example, in the U.S.-EC dispute over agriculture, the Cairns Group strengthened the U.S. position (see below).

In view of the length and complexity of the Uruguay Round, it is important to summarise the stages of the negotiation before discussing the involvement of institutions and coalition groups, as follows.

- *September 1986:* Punta del Este GATT ministerial launches the Uruguay Round with a four-year deadline for completion.
- *December 1988:* Montreal GATT ministerial midterm review produces some results, but continuing U.S.-EC differences over agriculture pose a major problem.
- *December 1990:* Brussels GATT ministerial fails to complete the Uruguay Round, mainly because of the U.S.-EC deadlock over agriculture.
- *December 1991:* GATT director general Arthur Dunkel produces a draft final act.
- *November 1992:* U.S. and EC reach the Blair House Accord, breaking the deadlock over agriculture.
- *December 1993:* Final Uruguay Round agreement reached in Geneva.
- *April 1994:* Ministers sign the final Uruguay Round agreement at Marrakech, Morocco.

Major Coalition Groups in the Uruguay Round

One of the major coalitions was the Cairns Group of 14 (now 13) small-country agricultural exporters that was formed in Cairns, Australia, shortly before the Punta meeting. The Cairns Group added a powerful new voice to the negotiations, ensuring that this time the GATT would have to deal with agriculture. Unlike the OECD, the G7, the Quad, and the G77, which separated the North from the South, the Cairns Group includes one G7 and Quad country (Canada), four OECD countries (Australia, Canada, Hungary, and New Zealand),[10] nine LDCs (Argentina, Brazil, Chile, Colombia, Indonesia, Malaysia, Philippines, Thailand, and Uruguay), and one Eastern European country (Hungary). Although the U.S. had pressed the EC to decrease protectionism under its CAP in the Kennedy and Tokyo rounds, in the end the U.S. had settled for less in agriculture because of its desire to reach agreement in other areas. Agriculture again became a major issue at the Montreal ministerial midterm review of the Uruguay Round, with the U.S. proposing a complete phase-out of trade-distorting subsidies over ten years and the EC only willing to discuss limited, short-term measures. The Cairns Group proposed a compromise solution, but the U.S. and EC would not accept it.

The U.S was more adamant that agriculture be included than it had been in earlier GATT rounds, but it was willing to join the EC in approving the results achieved in other areas in Montreal and have their negotiators resume work on agriculture afterward. However, the five Latin American members of the Cairns Group walked out of the 1988 Montreal meeting, insisting that a midterm agreement must include agriculture. This action served as a warning that the U.S. and EC could no longer shape agricultural issues in the GATT to the same extent as they had in earlier years. Indeed, the Latin American walkout forced the GATT director general to suspend the midterm review until an agreement was achieved on agriculture. In April 1989, the Trade Negotiations Committee finally reached an agreement based on compromises by both the U.S. and EC, and it was possible to resume the round with agriculture still a principal part of the negotiations. Despite this agreement, the divisions on agriculture remained. The Cairns Group position was not far from that of the U.S., calling for a freeze and subsequent phase-out of export subsidies, a decline in the use of trade-distorting domestic policies, and a conversion of all import quotas into tariffs (Canada diverged from its Cairns Group partners on the latter issue).

At the December 1990 Brussels ministerial, which was supposed to complete the Uruguay Round, the EC remained intransigent on agriculture. There was a replay of the events in Montreal. Two Latin American members of the Cairns Group — Argentina and Brazil — refused to negotiate further, and the ministerial was suspended. Meetings did not resume until February 1991, when the EC agreed to make concessions on agriculture. In November 1992, the U.S. and EC finally concluded the Blair House Accord, which broke their agricultural impasse (Higgott and Cooper 1990; Cohn 1993, 29–34; Croome 1995, 172–178, 275–286; Preeg 1995, 84–88).

How influential the Cairns Group was remains debatable. Certainly, it helped to ensure that agriculture could not be bypassed as it had been in previous rounds, because some countries were willing to forgo an Uruguay Round accord without an agreement on agriculture. Nevertheless, even without the Cairns Group, the U.S. was more committed than ever before to ending the GATT agricultural exceptions. The U.S.-EC export subsidy war was imposing huge costs on U.S. taxpayers, and the U.S. viewed agriculture as one area where it could counter its growing balance of payments deficit. In the end, 'the Uruguay Round proceeded at a pace only to the extent it was permitted by the U.S. and the EC negotiators', and although agriculture was included, the Agreement on Agriculture was 'not one of the more solid "achievements" of the [Uruguay] Round' (Jackson 1997, 314).

Another important Uruguay Round coalition was the De La Paix Group, named after the Hôtel De La Paix in Geneva where it often met.[11] Like the Cairns Group, it was a coalition of small and middle-sized DCs and LDCs that began exerting its influence early in the negotiations. Although members did not focus on a specific issue, they all had a general interest in a strong rule-based multilateral trade system that would make a power-based system less justifiable. The group's efforts contributed to the launch of the Uruguay Round in 1986 and played a role in negotiations on dispute settlement, antidumping, tariff and nontariff barriers, and the functioning of the GATT system. The De La Paix Group also pressed the major actors to complete the round successfully. In March 1993, a low point was reached when the GATT Director General indicated the round could not be completed before the expiry of U.S. fast-track negotiating authority. The De La Paix Group responded by sending letters to the U.S. President, the presidents of the EC Council and Commission, and the Japanese Prime Minister urging them to show leadership in completing the round. The group also asked Congress to renew fast-track authority. Subsequently, Congress renewed fast track, the 1993 G7 Summit gave a decisive spur to the negotiations, and GATT members reached the final agreement in December.

As with the Cairns Group, the influence of the De La Paix Group is debatable. Although it helped to stimulate negotiations and reach solutions, ultimately the pace and tempo of negotiation depended on the key players in the G7 and the Quad (Croome 1995, 344–345; Preeg 1995, 158).

Major DC Actors and Institutions in the Uruguay Round

The United States and the European Community

The U.S. had provided strong leadership in earlier GATT negotiations, and it continued to do so in the Uruguay Round. The initial conceptual framework and diplomatic moves that led to Punta del Este came from the U.S., and the U.S. pressed for early results in the negotiations because of its record trade deficit. The U.S. was also a major force supporting the December 1988 midterm ministerial in Montreal, and the successful completion of the Uruguay Round. One essential factor in completing the round was the extension of U.S. fast-track authority; that is, a requirement that Congress cast a single yes or no vote on the final agreement without amendments in 60 legislative days. In view of the protracted nature of the Uruguay Round, Congress had to renew fast track on two occasions — in May 1991 and June 1993. The second extension was long enough to permit completion of the Uruguay Round, but short enough to impose pressure on other countries to avoid further delays in negotiating a final agreement. Although the U.S. was the most important actor, the EC was also critically important. The EC was more regional than the U.S. in its economic outlook, and complex internal decision-making often prevented the EC from taking strong initiatives in the negotiations. Nevertheless, it was evident that resolution of the most difficult political issues in the Uruguay Round would only occur with a settlement between the two largest trading entities. Other countries were dissatisfied because their interests were of secondary concern, but they recognised that a U.S.-EC agreement was necessary if the negotiations were to be concluded (Croome 1995, 287–291; Preeg 1995, 162–165; Winham 1989, 289–290).

Although the U.S. was a major force impelling the Uruguay Round, there were signs of a decline in U.S. ability and willingness to exert hegemonic leadership. In mid 1990, for example, the U.S. and Canada alone opposed the phase-out of the Multifibre Arrangement for textiles, the U.S. opposed a general formula approach for tariff cuts, the U.S. resisted limitations on its ability to use antidumping duties, and the U.S. wanted to exclude air and marine transportation from the services agreement. Even in agriculture, the extreme U.S. position on liberalisation may have helped it avoid implementing specific reductions in its agricultural support programs.[12] During the latter stages of the Uruguay Round, the U.S. leadership role weakened further. Growing U.S. protectionist pressures against some key provisions in the December 1991 Dunkel draft agreement, and initial reluctance by President Bill Clinton to direct U.S. trade policy slowed the moves toward freer trade. The EC stepped in to take a more assertive role, and shifted the final Uruguay Round leadership to a more balanced position between the two largest traders. A stronger role by GATT director general Peter Sutherland also contributed to a broader base of leadership in the last phase of the negotiations (Preeg 1995, 110–112, 189–190).

A specific instance of the U.S. following rather than leading related to its position on the creation of the WTO. The initiative began in the October 1989 Quad discussions. Canada and the EC supported the idea, but the U.S. and Japan did not favour creating a powerful new international organisation for trade. In February 1990, the Italian trade minister voiced the first public support for a new organisation, and in April 1990 Canada's trade minister specifically proposed that the World Trade Organization supersede the GATT. The broad substance of Canada's proposal was derived from a January 1990 study entitled *Restructuring the GATT System* by the American legal scholar John H. Jackson (1990). In June 1990, the EC also proposed that a multilateral trade organisation be formed. The U.S. had several reservations about these proposals. First, the WTO would permanently establish 'one nation, one vote' decision making and the U.S. was concerned that LDCs and centrally planned economies could politicise decision making. Second, the U.S. believed that discussion about reorganising the GATT would take time away from substantive negotiations in the Uruguay Round. Third, U.S. negotiators knew that congressional concerns over loss of sovereignty would be an issue as it had been with the International Trade Organization in the 1940s. Through Sutherland's forceful involvement, a revised text indicated that the WTO would normally seek a consensus and would require a majority of the full membership for decisions interpreting agreements and waiving obligations. This compromise assured the U.S. that the LDCs would not be able to approve major changes over DC objections, and it finally gave its full endorsement to the WTO (Croome 1995, 271–274, 358–361; Preeg 1995, 113–114, 124–126).

Organisation for Economic Co-operation and Development

The OECD helped facilitate the Uruguay Round negotiations in some key areas such as services and agriculture. Services trade had been a concern of the OECD since its creation, through the Code of Liberalisation of Current Invisible Operations and the Code of Liberalisation of Capital Movements. Over the years, the OECD had compiled a large body of information on services in general and on specific sectors. Before the Tokyo Round, a 1972 OECD report had recommended that the DCs should take action 'to ensure liberalization and non-discrimination in the services sector' (OECD 1972, 79; see also Bayne 2000, 52). The *U.S. Trade Act of 1974*, which gave the president authority to negotiate the Tokyo Round, referred to 'trade in both goods and services' (United States 1974, sections 102(g), 135(b), and (c)). There was insufficient time to reach agreement on including services trade in the Tokyo Round, but OECD discussions after the round spurred the DCs to engage in joint efforts to include services trade in the Uruguay Round. The OECD's detailed studies also provided the groundwork for explicitly outlining the objectives of a services agreement at Punta del Este. In view of LDC opposition in the G10 coalition, however, several more years of discussion were needed before a broader consensus developed that services trade liberalisation was a legitimate objective.[13]

As with services, the OECD has been a forum for discussing agriculture since it was established in 1961. Until the 1980s, the OECD produced far more studies on domestic agricultural issues than on agricultural trade. However, the OECD ministerial meeting in May 1982 formally recognised for the first time that domestic agricultural policies have a significant effect on trade and were therefore a legitimate subject of trade negotiations. The meeting also agreed that the OECD should conduct a ministerial trade mandate (MTM) study of member countries' agricultural policies. The MTM study took more than four years to complete. It developed comprehensive measures of a country's support for agriculture, producer subsidy equivalents, and consumer subsidy equivalents. This work demonstrated that agricultural markets were highly distorted and that agricultural protection went far beyond explicit trade measures. The GATT Committee on Trade in Agriculture also spent considerable time on developing guidelines for agricultural trade negotiations. The Punta del Este Declaration therefore provided some detailed discussion of issues to be negotiated in agriculture. Despite the extensive preparatory work done by the OECD and GATT, agricultural trade was to be the issue most responsible for prolonging the Uruguay Round negotiations (Blair 1993, 109–165; Wolfe 1998, 106–146; OECD 1987).

The Group of Seven

The U.S. tried to use the G7 summits to form a consensus on trade issues and increase pressure for completion of the Uruguay Round. For a number of years, however, the summits were better at issuing declaratory statements than at pushing the negotiations to a conclusion. Several factors accounted for the difficulties the summits had in exerting influence: high-level political decisions were not sufficiently attuned to the complex technical decisions that had to be taken in Geneva; the number of key participants had increased in the Uruguay Round; the Uruguay Round agenda included highly sensitive issues such as agriculture, textiles, services, and intellectual property; and the LDCs, with a very different agenda from the G7, were joining coalitions and demanding a greater role in the negotiations.

The Uruguay Round was initially to be completed in December 1990. In June 1990, the International Chamber of Commerce (ICC), representing trade associations and companies in 110 countries, urged the G7 leaders at the upcoming G7 Houston Summit to 'underscore the value of such annual events by agreeing to give firm instructions to their negotiators in the Round to make the necessary decisions for an unequivocally successful result' (ICC 1990). Although the Houston Summit developed a formula for conducting the agricultural negotiations, the agreement did not survive in Geneva and the Uruguay Round had to be extended beyond 1990. The Declaration of the 1991 London Summit stated that 'the aim of all contracting parties should be to complete the Round before the end of 1991' (G7 1991). However, subsequent efforts to resolve outstanding differences were insufficient, and the round had be extended further. The 1992 Munich Summit again concluded with expectations that 'an agreement can be reached before the end of 1992' (G7 1992). Although the November 1992 U.S.-EC Blair House Accord removed major obstacles to an agricultural agreement, France's dissatisfaction with the accord and differences on other issues resulted in another extension of the round. In 1993, the Quad reached a market access agreement on tariff cuts for industrial goods that enabled the Tokyo Summit to fulfil its commitment to complete the negotiations by the end of the year. The Communiqué from the 1994 Naples Summit was then able to express the confident determination of the G7 leaders to 'ratify the Uruguay Round Agreements and to establish the WTO by January 1st, 1995' (G7 1994).

The annual predictions of the G7 communiqués that the Uruguay Round was near completion certainly raised questions about the effectiveness of the summits. Nevertheless, these predictions ensured that there was constant pressure on the GATT negotiators to conclude the round. Furthermore, the G7 leaders limited protectionism and helped keep the negotiations going during recession, supported a strong binding dispute-settlement mechanism, endorsed the formation of the WTO, and pressured the Quad to conclude its market access agreement before the 1993 Tokyo Summit (Bayne 2000, 63).

The Quad

Although the annual G7 summits regularly discussed the GATT Uruguay Round, finance ministers are the top ministerial group influencing the G7 meetings. Thus, G7 leaders normally give more priority to macroeconomic policy and international financial markets than to trade. The Quad is the highest level informal group that focusses specifically on multilateral trade issues. In the Uruguay Round, the Quad was most important during the preparatory period leading up to the Punta meeting in September 1996 and after the Brussels ministerial in December 1990. During 1989 and 1990, the Quad's relative inactivity inspired little in the way of joint leadership. Even then, however, Quad meetings were sometimes useful. For example, the initiative to create a new world trade organisation began in October 1989 in informal Quad discussions among U.S., EC, Japanese, and Canadian officials. After the December 1990 Brussels GATT ministerial collapsed and there was a long U.S.-EC stalemate over agriculture, the Quad gave more serious and detailed attention to institutional reform. A series of Quad meetings largely shaped the final agreement on the WTO before broader-based negotiations were held in Geneva. The Quad was also involved in discussion of other issues related to the Uruguay Round, including intellectual property, trade in services, market access, agricultural trade, and trade and the environment (Preeg 1995, 124–126; Croome 1995, 318).

The most significant Quad contribution to the completion of the Uruguay Round was its market access agreement. In June 1993, the Quad countries engaged in almost nonstop negotiations to reach an access agreement for industrial goods and services before the G7 Tokyo Summit. On the first day of the summit, the Quad ministers were able to announce that 'we have within our reach a far-reaching and comprehensive market-opening package on goods and services ... We look toward a prompt re-engagement of the multilateral negotiating process in Geneva to be concluded by the end of this year' ('The Quad's Initial Market-Access Package' 1993). Differences remained among the Quad members, however, even after the July 1993 agreement was reached. Furthermore, some GATT countries outside the Quad felt that the agreement did not meet their interests; LDCs in particular wanted further market access commitments for tropical and natural resource-based products and for textiles. It was not until the final days of the Uruguay Round that sufficient agreement was reached for U.S. president Clinton to approve a market access agreement by the deadline of 15 December 1993. After that date the Quad was actively involved in working out the details of the Uruguay Round agreements, and in smoothing the transition from the GATT to the WTO ('Administration Floats New Textile Tariff Cut Proposal to EC' 1993; 'Clinton Meets GATT Notification Deadline; Tariff Talks Endure' 1993).

General Agreement on Tariffs and Trade

Although this chapter focusses on the G7, the Quad, and the OECD, it is important to note that several decisions were taken during the Uruguay Round to upgrade the GATT/WTO role in trade policy-making. At Punta del Este, the ministers agreed that the Tokyo Round had been prolonged because of the lack of sufficient high-level political attention and guidance. They therefore established the Trade Negotiations Committee as the senior body to manage the Uruguay Round negotiations. The Uruguayan foreign minister chaired the committee at ministerial level meetings, and the GATT director general chaired when it convened at official level. At the official level, the committee organised the work schedule and established 15 negotiating groups, which accumulated a large volume of material on the issues under negotiation. Regular meetings gave governments the opportunity to express their views of overall progress in the round and to reach agreements on a broad timetable for the negotiations. The body known as the FOGS (Functioning of the GATT

System) negotiating group also adopted two decisions to upgrade the role of the GATT beyond the Uruguay Round. First, it was surprising that an international organisation of the GATT's stature did not convene regularly at the ministerial level. Thus, the FOGS group decided that GATT/WTO ministerial meetings should be held at least every two years. Second, the FOGS group decided that the GATT/WTO should conduct regular reviews of members' trade policies as a means of increasing transparency. This country-review approach was based on long-term practice at the IMF and the OECD, which included peer assessment. LDCs raised some objections to this idea, but it was agreed that the GATT/WTO would conduct more frequent reviews of the most important DCs (Preeg 1995, 68–69; Croome 1995, 261–262).

Conclusion

This chapter has examined the important role of the G7, the Quad, and the OECD in the global trade regime. Four factors explaining the role of these institutions were discussed: the dominance of the DCs in the North over the LDCs in the South, the decline of U.S. economic hegemony, the variations in expertise among institutions based on a division of labour, and the characteristics of the GATT/WTO as an international organisation.

Since its formation in 1961, the OECD has actively promoted trade liberalisation by providing analytical studies of policy issues, serving as a forum for review of common problems and promoting DC policy co-ordination. The OECD has also served along with the GATT as an important venue for prenegotiation. For example, OECD prenegotiations were essential for the Tokyo Round negotiations on government procurement, and OECD studies and discussion facilitated the Uruguay Round negotiations on trade in services and agriculture. Despite the value of such preparatory work by the OECD and GATT, co-operation at higher political levels among the major traders is also essential if the subsequent negotiations are to succeed. For example, despite the extensive OECD and GATT background studies and prenegotiation, agriculture and services became two of the most contentious areas in the Uruguay Round. A minimal level of co-operation between the two largest trading entities — the EC and U.S. — is required if the negotiation is ultimately to succeed. However, the EC and U.S. are not the only important economic actors. The G7 summits were established in 1975 to promote high-level political co-operation during a period of declining U.S. trade hegemony and instability in global economic relations.

The annual G7 summit 'has been neither a continuous success nor continuous failure, but has exhibited a widely varying performance over the years' (Kirton 1995, 65). Studies of G7 members' compliance with their summit commitments generally show that compliance scores for trade are relatively high (Kokotsis and Daniels 1999, 77). The annual G7 predictions that the Uruguay Round was near completion did test the summit's credibility. Nevertheless, the Uruguay Round ultimately resulted in the most ambitious GATT agreement ever achieved. There is evidence that the G7 helped to keep the negotiations going and provided important support for the new dispute-settlement mechanism and the WTO. The role of the G7 summits in the GATT Tokyo and Uruguay rounds generally supports the observation that bargaining sometimes 'needs to be prodded forward at intervals by political decisions taken at a high level' (Shonfield 1976, 172). However, the G7 summits have had an expanding agenda, and in the economic area finance ministers have been far more influential than trade ministers in setting the agenda. Furthermore, the distance between the high-level G7 discussions and the technical discussions required today to negotiate trade agreements in Geneva inevitably affects what the G7 summits can accomplish. Unlike the G7, the Quad discussions, which began in 1982, focus specifically on trade issues. Although the Quad functions at the ministerial level, it decreases the distance somewhat from the G7 summits to the technical negotiations in Geneva. Thus, the Quad, often in conjunction with the G7, has played an important role before, during, and after the Uruguay Round.

One characteristic that the OECD, the G7, and the Quad share in common is that they are primarily composed of DCs. Institutions that more actively support LDC interests, such as the UNCTAD and G77 have had far less influence in the global trade regime. The LDCs have been dissatisfied with this situation and have often demanded that the DCs devote more attention to their interests. For example, the LDCs were dissatisfied that they had no part in developing the Framework of Understanding agreed to by the DCs in the run-up to the 1978 Bonn Summit, and the DCs therefore had to give greater priority to their concerns. In the Uruguay Round, the LDCs were more actively involved in coalition behaviour with DCs and among themselves, which increased the LDCs' influence somewhat vis-à-vis the major DC traders. For example, the LDCs in the Cairns Group insisted that there be no Uruguay Round agreement without an agreement in agriculture. It thus became more difficult for the EC and U.S. to sidetrack agricultural issues as they had in the Kennedy and Tokyo rounds.

Nevertheless, it seems that LDC/DC coalitions such as the Cairns and De La Paix groups could exert only limited influence. The G7, the Quad, and the

OECD continue to have predominant influence in the GATT/WTO and global trade regime. More recently, the DC institutions have had to deal with protests not only from LDCs but also from civil society (for example, see O'Brien et al. 2000). It is evident that these DC institutions will have to share their power with disaffected and disadvantaged groups in the future.

Notes

1 Officially, there was no membership in the GATT, only 'contracting parties'. When the WTO was formed, the GATT reverted to its original status as a trade agreement (now under the WTO).
2 The term 'KIEO' was coined by Jacobson and Oksenberg (1990).
3 This subject is covered in more depth in Cohn, forthcoming.
4 As Kahler (1993) notes, not all liberals support the idea that larger numbers necessarily pose an obstacle to co-operation.
5 The eight seats for members of economic importance were to go to the U.S., Britain, Canada, France, the Benelux customs union, India, China, and the Soviet Union if it joined the ITO. See Wilcox 1949, 154–155; Brown 1950, 228–229.
6 Anne Anderson, Ireland's trade negotiator, quoted in Olson 2000. On the CG18 model see Blackhurst 1998, 49–50; on the green room sessions, see Preeg 1995, 132.
7 For example, Australia proposed the formation of a permanent ministerial steering group similar to the limited but representative official-level CG18 (Croome 1995, 155).
8 Judith Goldstein (1988, 179) has written that 'nowhere is America's hegemonic decline more evident than in changing trade patterns'.
9 Quoted in Preeg 1995, 24; see also Winham 1986, 205–213, 303.
10 Hungary became an OECD member in 1996.
11 The De La Paix Group consisted mainly of Australia, Canada, Colombia, Hungary, Malaysia, New Zealand, the Philippines, Singapore, South Korea, Sweden, Switzerland, Thailand, Uruguay, and Zaire (Hamilton and Whalley 1989, 57).
12 On the complex reasons for the hard-line U.S. position on agriculture, see Paarlberg 1993.
13 The G10, which initially opposed services trade liberalisation, included Argentina, Brazil, Cuba, Egypt, India, Nicaragua, Nigeria, Peru, Tanzania, and Yugoslavia (Hamilton and Whalley 1989, 550–551). For a discussion of the OECD, the UNCTAD, and services trade in the Uruguay Round, see Drake and Nicolaïdis 1992.

References

'Administration Floats New Textile Tariff Cut Proposal to EC' (1993). *Inside U.S. Trade*. 24 September.

Atlantic Council of the United States (1975). 'GATT Plus: A Proposal for Trade Reform'. Report of the Special Advisory Panel to the Trade Committee of the Atlantic Council. Praeger, New York.

Bayne, Nicholas (2000). *Hanging in There: The G7 and G8 Summit in Maturity and Renewal*. Ashgate, Aldershot.

Blackhurst, Richard (1998). 'The Capacity of the WTO to Fulfill Its Mandate'. In A. O. Kroeger with Chonira Aturupane, *The WTO as an International Organization*. University of Chicago Press, Chicago.

Blair, David J. (1993). *Trade Negotiations in the OECD: Structures, Institutions, and States*. Kegan Paul, London.

Brown, William A. (1950). *The United States and the Restoration of World Trade*. Brookings Institution, Washington DC.

'Clinton Meets GATT Notification Deadline; Tariff Talks Endure' (1993). *Inside U.S. Trade*. 17 December.

Cohn, Theodore H. (forthcoming). *Governing Global Trade: International Institutions in Conflict and Convergence*. Ashgate, Aldershot.

Cohn, Theodore H. (1993). 'The Changing Role of the United States in the Global Agricultural Trade Regime'. In W. P. Avery, ed., *World Agriculture and the GATT*, pp. 17–38. Lynne Rienner Publishers, Boulder, CO.

Commission on International Trade and Investment Policy (1971). 'United States International Economic Policy in an Interdependent World'. Report to the President. Government Printing Office, Washington DC.

Croome, John (1995). *Reshaping the World Trading System: A History of the Uruguay Round*. World Trade Organization, Geneva.

Drake, William and Kalypso Nicolaïdis (1992). 'Ideas, Interests, and Institutionalization: "Trade in Services" and the Uruguay Round'. *International Organisation* vol. 46, no. 1 (Winter), pp. 37–100.

Dunkel, Arthur (1987). *Trade Policies for a Better Future: The Leutwiler Report, the GATT, and the Uruguay Round*. Martinus Nijhoff, Dordrecht.

G7 (1975). 'Declaration of Rambouillet'. 17 November, Rambouillet. <www.library.utoronto.ca/g7/summit/1975rambouillet/communique.html> (March 2001).

G7 (1976). 'Joint Declaration of the International Conference'. 28 June, San Juan. <www.library.utoronto.ca/g7/summit/1976sanjuan/communique.html> (March 2001).

G7 (1977). 'Declaration: Downing Street Summit Conference'. 8 May, London. <www.library.utoronto.ca/g7/summit/1977london/communique.html> (March 2001).

G7 (1978). 'Declaration'. 17 July, Bonn. <www.library.utoronto.ca/g7/summit/1978bonn/communique/index.html> (March 2001).

G7 (1981). 'Declaration of the Ottawa Summit'. 21 July, Ottawa. <www.library.utoronto.ca/g7/summit/1981ottawa/communique/index.html> (March 2001).

G7 (1983). 'Williamsburg Declaration on Economic Recovery'. 30 May, Williamsburg. <www.library.utoronto.ca/g7/summit/1983williamsburg/communique.html> (March 2001).

G7 (1984). 'London Economic Declaration'. 9 June, London. <www.library.utoronto.ca/g7/summit/1984london/communique.html> (March 2001).

G7 (1985). 'The Bonn Economic Declaration Towards Sustained Growth and Higher Employment'. 4 May, Bonn. <www.library.utoronto.ca/g7/summit/1985bonn/communique/index.html> (March 2001).

G7 (1986). 'Tokyo Economic Declaration'. 6 May, Tokyo. <www.library.utoronto.ca/g7/summit/1986tokyo/communique.html> (March 2001).

G7 (1991). 'Economic Declaration of the G7 Summit'. 17 July, London. <www.library.utoronto.ca/g7/summit/1991london/communique/index.html> (March 2001).

G7 (1992). 'Economic Declaration: Working Together for Growth and a Safer World'. 8 July, Munich. <www.library.utoronto.ca/g7/summit/1992munich/communique/index.html> (March 2001).

G7 (1994). 'G7 Communiqué'. 9 July, Naples. <www.library.utoronto.ca/g7/summit/1994naples/communique/index.html> (March 2001).

General Agreement on Tariffs and Trade (1973). *GATT Activities in 1972*. General Agreement on Tariffs and Trade, Geneva.

General Agreement on Tariffs and Trade (1985). *Trade Policies for a Better Future: Proposals for Action*. General Agreement on Tariffs and Trade, Geneva.

General Agreement on Tariffs and Trade (1986). 'Agreement on Government Procurement'. *The Texts of the Tokyo Round Agreements*. General Agreement on Tariffs and Trade, Geneva.

Goldstein, Judith (1988). 'Ideas, Institutions, and American Trade Policy'. *International Organisation* vol. 42, no. 1 (Winter), pp. 179–217.

Golt, Sidney (1974). *The GATT Negotiations, 1973–75: A Guide to the Issues*. British-North American Committee, Washington DC.

Hajnal, Peter (1999). *The G7/G8 System: Evolution, Role, and Documentation*. Ashgate, Aldershot.

Hamilton, Colleen and John Whalley (1989). 'Coalitions in the Uruguay Round'. *Weltwirtschaftliches Archiv* vol. 125, no. 3, pp. 547–561.

Henderson, David (1996). 'The Role of the OECD in Liberalising International Trade and Capital Flows'. In S. Arndt and C. Miller, eds., *The World Economy on Global Trade Policy*, pp. 11–28 [Special Issue].

Henderson, David (1998). 'International Agencies and Cross-Border Liberalization: The WTO in Context'. In A. O. Krueger with Chonira Aturupane, *The WTO as an International Organization*. University of Chicago Press, Chicago.

Higgott, Richard A. and Andrew Fenton Cooper (1990). 'Middle Power Leadership and Coalition Building: Australia, the Cairns Group, and the Uruguay Round of Trade Negotiations'. *International Organisation* vol. 44, no. 4 (Autumn), pp. 589–632.

Hufbauer, Gary Clyde (1989). *The Free Trade Debate, Reports of the Twentieth Century Fund Task Force on the Future of American Trade Policy*. Priority Press, New York.

International Chamber of Commerce (1990). 'Statement on the Uruguay Round'. 21 June. International Chamber of Commerce, Paris.

Jackson, John H. (1969). *World Trade and the Law of the GATT*. Bobbs-Merrill Company, Indianapolis.

Jackson, John H. (1990). *Restructuring the GATT System*. Pinter Publishers, London.

Jackson, John H. (1997). *The World Trading System: Law and Policy of International Economic Relations*. 2nd ed. MIT Press, Cambridge, MA.

Jacobson, Harold and Michel Oksenberg (1990). *China's Participation in the IMF, the World Bank, and GATT: Toward a Global Order*. University of Michigan Press, Ann Arbor.

Kahler, Miles (1993). 'Multilateralism with Small and Large Numbers'. In J. G. Ruggie, ed., *Multilateralism Matters: The Theory and Praxis of an Institutional Form*, pp. 295–299. Columbia University Press, New York.

Keohane, Robert O. (1984). *After Hegemony: Cooperation and Discord in the World Political Economy*. Princeton University Press, Princeton, NJ.

Kirton, John J. (1995). 'The Diplomacy of Concert: Canada, the G7 and the Halifax Summit'. *Canadian Foreign Policy* vol. 3, no. 1 (Spring), pp. 63–80.

Kokotsis, Ella and Joseph P. Daniels (1999). 'G8 Summits and Compliance'. In M. R. Hodges, J. J. Kirton and J. P. Daniels, eds., *The G8's Role in the New Millennium*, pp. 75–91. Ashgate, Aldershot.

Krasner, Stephen D. (1979). 'The Tokyo Round: Particularistic Interests and Prospects for Stability in the Global Trading System'. *International Studies Quarterly* vol. 23, no. 4, pp. 491–531.

Krueger, Anne O. (1995). *Trade Policies and Developing Nations*. Brookings Institution, Washington DC.

Long, Olivier (1985). *Law and Its Limitations in the GATT Multilateral Trade System*. Martinus Nijhoff, Dordrecht.

'Marrakesh Agreement Establishing the World Trade Organization' (1994). 15 April. <www.sice.oas.org/trade/ur_round/UR03E.asp> (March 2001).

O'Brien, Robert, Anne Marie Goetz, Jan Aart Scholte, et al. (2000). *Contesting Global Governance: Multilateral Economic Institutions and Global Social Movements*. Cambridge University Press, Cambridge.

Olson, Elizabeth (2000). 'Patching up Morale at the World Trade Organization'. *New York Times*, 31 October, p. W1.

Olson, Mancur (1965). *The Logic of Collective Action: Public Goods and the Theory of Groups*. Harvard University Press, Cambridge, MA.

Organisation for Economic Co-operation and Development (1972). 'Policy Perspectives for International Trade and Economic Relations'. Report by the High-Level Group on Trade and Related Problems to the Secretary General of the OECD. Organisation for Economic Co-operation and Development, Paris.

Organisation for Economic Co-operation and Development (1987). *National Policies and Agricultural Trade*. Organisation for Economic Co-operation and Development, Paris.

Organisation for Economic Co-operation and Development (1994). *The OECD in the 1990s*. Organisation for Economic Co-operation and Development, Paris.

Oye, Kenneth A. (1985). 'Explaining Cooperation under Anarchy: Hypothesis and Strategies'. In K. A. Oye, ed., *Cooperation under Anarchy*. Princeton University Press, Princeton.

Paarlberg, Robert L. (1993). 'Why Agriculture Blocked the Uruguay Round: Evolving Strategies in a Two-Level Game'. In W. P. Avery, ed., *World Agriculture and the GATT*, pp. 39–54. Lynne Rienner Publishers, Boulder, CO.

Preeg, Ernest H. (1995). *Traders in a Brave New World: The Uruguay Round and the Future of the International Trading System*. University of Chicago Press, Chicago.

Putnam, Robert and Nicholas Bayne, eds. (1987). *Hanging Together: Co-operation and Conflict in the Seven-Power Summit*. 2nd ed. Sage Publications, London.

'The Quad's Initial Market-Access Package' (1993). *GATT Focus* no. 101 (August-September), p. 3.

Shonfield, Andrew (1976). 'Can the Western Economic System Stand the Strain?' *The World Today* vol. 32, no. 5 (May), pp. 164–172.

Snidal, Duncan (1985). 'The Limits of Hegemonic Stability Theory'. *International Organisation* vol. 39, no. 4 (Autumn), pp. 579–614.

United States (1974). *U.S. Trade Act of 1974*. <uscode.house.gov/title_19.htm> (March 2001).

Wilcox, Clair (1949). *A Charter for World Trade*. Macmillan, London.

Winham, Gilbert R. (1986). *International Trade and the Tokyo Round Negotiation*. Princeton University Press, Princeton.

Winham, Gilbert R. (1989). 'The Prenegotiation Phase of the Uruguay Round'. *International Journal* vol. 44, no. 2 (Spring), pp. 280–303.

Wolfe, Robert (1998). *Farm Wars: The Political Economy of Agriculture and the International Trade Regime*. Macmillan, Houndmills.

Zartman, I. William (1989). 'Prenegotiation: Phases and Functions'. *International Journal* vol. 44, no. 2 (Spring), pp. 237–253.

12 Stimulating Trade Liberalisation after Seattle: G7/8 Leadership in Global Governance

HEIDI K. ULLRICH[1]

Leadership requires vision. To be effective, however, this vision must be combined with the courage and confidence to promote policies that are not welcomed among some segments of society. The record of the G7/8 in promoting trade illustrates the achievements that co-operative leadership provides *when* this leadership is consistent. With civil society increasingly questioning the merits of multilateral trade liberalisation, it is imperative that the G8 show effective leadership consistently.

The G7/8 has to date shown adequate leadership in the area of multilateral trade through supporting the institutions and activities that encourage liberalisation. This chapter argues that in order to provide the effective leadership necessary to stimulate further trade liberalisation in the post-Seattle multilateral trading system, the G8 leaders must increase their credibility and courage in communicating with their citizens. The G8 leaders should also enter into a structured dialogue with civil society organisations (CSOs), nongovernmental organisations (NGOs), and business/nonprofit and for-profit groups. All such dialogue should be open and transparent, thus allowing for a mutually beneficial exchange of information and opinions.

The G8 summit provides an ideal opportunity for the leaders of eight major industrialised countries, plus the European Union (EU),[2] to speak with representatives of civil society to shape the trade policies that affect them all. This unique opportunity arises from the fact that at these summits trade issues are discussed in an expanded context that includes economic, political, and social factors. As has been the experience of G7/8 heads of state or government over the past 25 years, perspectives broaden when viewed from a summit.

It is clear that the G8 must acknowledge the concerns of civil society. Nonetheless, there is also a pressing need for the G8 to serve as a firm advocate

219

of the benefits deriving from an open trading system. This involves informing their citizens of the merits of trade liberalisation. Additionally, the G8 will need to take the political risk of speaking with a strong and united voice in support of the next round of multilateral trade negotiations if their leadership is to be effective rather than merely adequate. If the G8 leaders are to exercise effective leadership, they must have the courage to promote their vision of the future multilateral trading system.

This chapter explores the role of the G8 in stimulating trade liberalisation in the post-Seattle multilateral trade environment. The first section provides a brief background of G7/8 activities in the multilateral trading system, with particular emphasis on multilateral trade negotiations. Included in this discussion is the evolution of the Quadrilateral of Trade Ministers (the Quad) from the United States, the EU, Japan, and Canada. The second section describes the events leading up to the 1999 World Trade Organization (WTO) ministerial held in Seattle, the sources of the stalemate that occurred there, and what the WTO has done in the aftermath. The third section addresses the newly active civil society participants and the potential for G8 involvement. The chapter concludes with a series of recommendations for how the G8 can stimulate the post-Seattle multilateral trading system and the challenges of the 2001 Genoa Summit.

The G8 and Multilateral Trade Negotiations

Summits and Ministerials

Since the first Western economic summit took place in Rambouillet, France, in November 1975, the leaders have voiced their support for an open trading system. In words that still hold true 25 years after they were first written in the 1975 Rambouillet Declaration, the G7 stated:

> We must seek to restore growth in the volume of world trade. Growth and price stability will be fostered by maintenance of an open trading system. In a period where pressures are developing for a return to protectionism, it is essential ... to avoid resorting to measures by which they could try to solve their problems at the expense of others, with damaging consequences in the economic, social and political fields (G7 1975, section 8).

The G7/8 has consistently supported the role of the General Agreement on Tariffs and Trade (GATT) and, since 1995, its successor, the WTO, in monitoring trade agreements, ensuring the openness of the trading system and as a forum for negotiations.

With respect to multilateral trade negotiations, summits serve four purposes: to call for new rounds, to shape the negotiating agenda, to break impasses through increasing pressure on individual member governments to offer concessions, and to serve as useful deadlines for negotiators. Their impact on multilateral negotiations has been the source of special negotiating terminology, in particular the 'Rambouillet effect', which describes the G7/8's ability to bring about incremental progress during negotiations by having the leaders make the critical political decisions (Bayne 2000b, 21).

However, this effect has not been visible at every summit. The G7/8 has rightly received much criticism for not having a positive impact on the negotiations. This is particularly due to the apparent inability or unwillingness of the leaders to implement their communiqué pledges fully once they have returned home. Summit communiqués called for the completion of the Tokyo Round every year from 1975 through 1978 and urged progress in the Uruguay Round from 1990 through 1993. Given that both rounds were stalled due to bilateral issues between Europe and the United States, the G8 leaders should not be faulted for their lack of success but rather commended for their continued determination in bringing about an eventual agreement. In fact, Bayne (1999, 25) has observed that:

> The summits do not achieve results by flashes of prescient, inspirational decision-making, sparked by the personal chemistry between the leaders. There are a few examples of this, but they are very rare. Nor do they often achieve, at the first attempt, a definitive settlement of issues which can then be handed on to other institutions. Nearly always their achievement comes from dogged persistence, a sort of "worrying away" at the issues until they have reached a solution.

Effective summits for promoting trade liberalisation, specifically the support of multilateral trade negotiations, have been characterised primarily by an agreed agenda prior to the start of the summit. This often requires the discussion of the issue at a previous summit or earlier ministerial meeting of the Organisation for Economic Co-operation and Development (OECD) or the Quad. They are also characterised by the existence of a viable negotiating framework, a personal commitment by each leader, and public political pressure.

Varying Effectiveness of Summits

The following section reviews the factors that may create both effective and ineffective summits. Examples are drawn from the G7 summits that dealt with the Uruguay Round as well as the G8 summits that have discussed the planned Millennium Round. The summits covered are:

- Uruguay Round
  - 1985 Bonn: Members divided on new round (–)[3]
  - 1986 Tokyo: Political impetus for new round (+)
  - 1990 Houston: Political re-commitment (+)
  - 1993 Tokyo: Market access breakthrough due to political pressure (+)
- Millennium Round
  - 1998 Birmingham: Focus on anniversary of GATT, not on new round (–)
  - 1999 Cologne: Members divided on new round (–)
  - 2000 Okinawa: Lack of political leadership and personal commitment (–)

Uruguay Round

Since the 1980s, G7 summits have been used as platforms by individual leaders in calling for new multilateral trade talks. At the 1985 Bonn Summit, U.S. president Ronald Reagan issued a strong call for an early start to a new trade round. However, the leaders were divided, with France refusing to accept a start date of early 1986. Thus, the Communiqué read: 'Most of us think [that the starting date of a new round] should be in 1986' (G7 1985). The U.S., especially Congress, felt rebuffed and initiated protectionist legislation such as the Export Enhancement Program. However, this summit was exceptional for its lack of cohesiveness and that it is one of only two Western economic summits that Robert Putnam and Nicholas Bayne (1987) view to have 'exacerbated international tensions'.

In contrast to the weak and divisive position G7 leaders took in Bonn, the 1986 Tokyo Summit gave political impetus to the Uruguay Round through a strong and cohesive statement in support of a new round. In fact, the leaders even suggested which issues should be included in the negotiations by stating: 'The new round should, *inter alia*, address the issues of trade in services and traderelated aspects of intellectual property rights and foreign direct investment' (G7 1986, section 12). There was an additional paragraph dedicated to the contentious issue of agriculture. The Tokyo II Summit was effective in that the leaders agreed on a common and detailed statement regarding the Uruguay

Round. They also provided the political pressure necessary for certain GATT members to agree to a September start date and pledged to stay involved in the GATT process to ensure the round was successfully launched.

As the host of the 1990 Houston G7 Summit, the United States was eager to make progress on the Uruguay Round negotiations, especially the difficult agricultural discussions. In fact, so critical was the successful outcome of the agricultural negotiations to the heads of state and the representatives of the European Community (EC),[4] that the topic 'dominated proceedings ahead of aid to the Soviet Union; the issue of CAP [Common Agricultural Policy] reform forced itself above the end-game to the Cold War' (Kay 1998, 64).[5]

Houston's final G7 Communiqué sent a clear and firm message to the negotiators that the political leaders had placed the conclusion of the Uruguay Round at the top of their agenda. They pledged to 'take the difficult political decisions' as well as to 'maintain a high level of personal involvement' (G7 1990, sections 19 and 23). The immediate impact of the Houston Summit on agriculture was minimal due to the EC back-peddling on its pledges. However, the long-term impact was more significant as it provided many summit innovations. It was the first time that the leaders had provided negotiators with detailed advice on moving the trade negotiations forward. A critical factor that qualifies the Houston Summit as being effective regarding trade was that for the first time the leaders pledged to become personally involved in the negotiations. This has proven to be a key element in the G7/8 leaders having a positive impact on negotiations both at and between summits.

The expiration of United States fast-track authority on 15 December 1993 provided a critical deadline for the Uruguay Round. Therefore, immense political pressure was placed not only on the host country of the 1993 Tokyo Summit but also the other members of the Quad — the U.S., EC, and Canada. It was reported that in the run up to the summit, the Quad members 'zig-zagged across the world — from Toronto to Paris to Tokyo, back to Toronto and to Tokyo ... in an attempt to hammer out agreement' (Torday 1993).

After marathon talks and a surprise concession from Japan on whiskey and brandy, a significant breakthrough was achieved on 7 July in the form of a substantial market access package. The next day the G7 were able to announce the deal at their summit. A press report stated:

> In what could well end up as the biggest surprise and most important accomplishment of the G7 summit meeting, trade representatives of the world's major economies appear to have succeeded in what some had thought impossible. On [7 July] they gave a new lease on life to moribund world trade negotiations

and a boost to the idea of free trade at a time when the concept is under attack by word and deed (Pollack 1993).

Following the summit, the other GATT contracting parties discussed the Quad's agreement in Geneva. At the same time, the U.S. and EC held several months of intense bilateral negotiations, primarily over agriculture but also financial and audio-visual services. On 6 December 1993, the U.S. and EC announced that they had reached an agreement on agriculture. Japan also agreed to allow foreign rice to be imported. On 14 December, Peter Sutherland, the Director General of the GATT, announced that 'the gavel has fallen on most of the Uruguay Round agreement (Dodwell 1993). The Quad/G7 initiative had clearly paved the way for the successful conclusion to the Uruguay Round.

Millennium Round

The summits leading up to the planned launch of the Millennium Round have shown surprising lack of effective leadership among the G7/8, particularly the U.S. and EU. Their failure to offer solid proposals on contentious issues such as trade and the environment and trade and labour contributed to the difficult and frustrating discussions among WTO ambassadors in Geneva in the last few months before the 1999 WTO Seattle ministerial.

The 1998 Birmingham Summit took place one week prior to the 1998 WTO ministerial held in Geneva, which marked the 50th anniversary of the establishment of the GATT. Thus, the Birmingham Communiqué focussed on a general reaffirmation of the merits of continued liberalisation. As they had done in Lyon in 1986 and in Denver in 1997, the leaders again called for greater participation by developing countries within the multilateral trading system. However, no new initiative was proposed. Notably, the G8 did not address the need for new trade negotiations.

In 1999 at Cologne, the G8 leaders failed to reach a consensus on the issue of the planned Millennium Round. This was a significant failure as it gave their trade ministers no shared political direction in the critical period before the Seattle ministerial. The main points discussed were to pursue an ambitious new trade round, to involve developing countries more widely into the negotiations, to increase the input of civil society, to incorporate environmental and labour concerns into future trade negotiations, and to include biotechnology in their deliberations. However, the U.S. and the EU/EC failed to agree on various elements of the proposed round. The EU insisted on having an ambitious comprehensive round, but the U.S. favoured a more limited agenda. There was also disagreement on the extent that trade-related environmental and labour issues should be discussed.

In the end, the Cologne Communiqué pleased no one by weakly calling for 'a new round of broad-based and ambitious negotiations with the aim of achieving substantial and manageable results' (G8 1999, section 10). More critically, compared to the 1996 Lyon Summit, which offered considerable detail for the upcoming WTO Singapore ministerial, in Cologne the leaders offered little in the way of specific suggestions for Seattle.

Okinawa Summit

Following the failure of the WTO Seattle ministerial to launch the Millennium Round and the weak trade statements coming out of the G7/8 summits in previous years, the Okinawa Summit in 2000 was critical for the issue of trade. In particular, strong political leadership regarding the launch of the Millennium Round was needed.

While there was no meeting of the Quad immediately prior to the summit, trade was high on the agenda at the EU-Japan Summit on 19 July. Japanese prime minister Yoshiro Mori and EU leaders, including French president Jacques Chirac, who held the six-month rotating European Council Presidency, and European Commission president Romano Prodi, stressed their commitment to launch the next round 'during the course of this year'. That round, they said,

> should be designed as a single undertaking and, beyond the negotiations in the built-in agenda on agriculture and services, be comprehensive in that it should reflect the varied interests and priorities of all WTO members in a balanced way (*Daily Yomiuri* 2000).

At a press conference in Tokyo on the same day, United States trade representative Charlene Barshefsky (2000) stated her country's position:

> ... consensus for a new round should be sought and achieved at the earliest possible opportunity including this year. Every country has politics. Every country has elections. The United States is concerned that a vacuum not develop, and that the process of trade liberalization move forward. But the key to the launch of the new round will be the substance. And when that substance will be achieved, whether this year or next, a new round will be able to be launched.

Barshefsky's statement hinted that although the U.S. strongly supported a new round, it would hesitate to support a launch before the agenda was clarified. Therefore, the Okinawa Summit began without a clear consensus, at least among three members of the Quad.

During discussions on the second day of the summit, all G8 participants at one point reportedly expressed their strong support for launching a new round by the end of 2000.[6] However, the leaders agreed that it be left to the sherpas to prepare the final communiqué language.

Similar to Cologne, the Okinawa Communiqué resulted in a relatively weak statement due to a lack both of consensus and of political leadership. In words identical to those issued after the EU-Japan Summit, it stated the leaders pledged to 'intensify our close and fruitful cooperation in order *to try together* with other WTO members to launch such a round during the course of this year' (see Appendix B, section 36; EU-Japan Summit 2000; emphasis added).

However, although the G8's call for a new round was disappointing, the Okinawa Summit did include other current issues relating to the multilateral trading system. The leaders addressed the 'legitimate concerns' of the WTO's developing country members to be better incorporated into the multilateral system. The statement largely reaffirmed the WTO's Framework for Action detailed below. Additionally, the G8 leaders recognised the need for communicating with their citizens on the issue of trade. They stressed the importance 'to establish a constructive dialogue on the benefits and challenges of trade liberalization' (see Appendix B, section 37).

The ineffectiveness of the Birmingham, Cologne, and Okinawa summits in dealing with trade, especially the launch of a new multilateral trade round, is due to several of the factors listed above. In the case of Cologne and Okinawa, the leaders had failed to agree on the issue of trade prior to the start of the summit, the summits all witnessed a clear lack of personal commitment by the leaders, and the leaders did not place trade high enough on the G8 agenda, therefore limiting the public political pressure.

Quadrilateral Ministerials

At the 1981 Ottawa Summit, the G7 endorsed the establishment of the Quadrilateral of Trade Ministers. Known as the Quad, this forum allows the trade ministers of the U.S., EU, Canada, and Japan to discus trade-related issues.[7] According to Bayne (1999, 37), the Quad serves as a pressure group within the WTO and thus its 'summit origins are forgotten'.

This group played a key role during the Uruguay Round. Notably, Winham (1986, 205ff) points out that the Quad played an important part in all stages of the Uruguay Round negotiations. However, Wolfe (1998, 89), notes that the Quad was particularly critical in the final six to eight months of the round.

In 1999, the Quad continued to define the G8's position on trade. At its May meeting immediately prior to the Cologne Summit, the Quad urged the proposed Millennium Round to be broadly based and ambitious, to cover areas such as services, agriculture, non-agricultural tariffs and nontariff barriers, investment, and electronic commerce, and to work toward strengthened capacity building for developing countries. Additionally, it encouraged the WTO to contribute to sustainable development while considering the concerns of civil society.

However, with their political masters unable to give them clear direction in the run up to the Seattle ministerial, the members of the Quad remained at odds with one another over the scope of the proposed round's agenda. This situation remained the same leading up to the Okinawa Summit. The disagreement and lack of leadership among the members of the Quad is elaborated upon in the following section.

Notably, as the number of active members within the multilateral trading system increases, the ability of the Quad to determine the trade policy agenda on its own is declining. A senior WTO official commented:

> Agreement among the Quad is very important, but they are not the critical element that they used to be. Their exclusive position is over. They must now build a consensus (since there are many other participants). The Quad must be pragmatic, realistic and flexible in their position (Rockwell 2000).

However, the members of the Quad still retain a unique ability to present trade packages and formulate acceptable proposals for the other members of the WTO. This is due not only to their combined trading strength but also because of the close trading relations the individual Quad members have with the broader WTO membership.

The Seattle Ministerial

Ingredients of the Impasse

The debacle in Seattle was caused by many factors. Individually, each was a cause for concern; together they were the cause of a catastrophe. However, to the observer of the pre-Seattle activity of the G8, the Quad, and the members of the WTO, the events that transpired in Seattle came as no surprise. They were the ingredients of an impasse.

Lack of Political Encouragement and Leadership

As has been discussed, recent G8 summits did not provide the necessary political encouragement for the Seattle ministerial. Compared to the strong statement issued in Tokyo in 1986 prior to the launch of the Uruguay Round, Cologne was disappointing in its lack of effective leadership. Commenting on the failure of the G8 summits to address trade adequately, Bayne (2000a, 31) notes:

> The Summit has paid a heavy price for their neglect of the trade dossier ... The trade system, which had looked so strong up until then, enters the millennium in confusion and disorder, after the WTO ministerial at Seattle failed spectacularly to launch a new round of trade negotiations. Many factors combined to cause this failure. But the G7 Summit cannot escape its share of the responsibility.

The failure of the G8 to show leadership negatively affected the ability of the Quad to present a united front in the months preceding the Seattle ministerial. Andrew Stoler (2000), Deputy Director of the WTO, attributed the lack of progress in agreeing to the draft ministerial text to the lack of political guidance and the resulting disagreement among Quad members:

> There was an important lack of political will from the Quad. This absence caused shrill voices to take centre stage. The discord between the EU, allied with Japan, and the U.S. hindered progress.

Lack of Information

In addition to showing a lack of effective leadership or the requisite political will, the leaders of the G8, together with other members of the WTO, failed to inform their citizens adequately of the issues, objectives, and institutional procedures that were involved in the agenda-setting stage of the planned Millennium Round. This was primarily due to traditional trade policy processes characterised by limited transparency. Until the recent past, trade issues had been of little apparent concern to civil society. However, as the GATT/WTO has expanded the scope of its responsibility beyond trade in goods to include such trade-related elements as services, intellectual property, the environment, and labour, civil society has accordingly demanded more information and involvement.

The failure of the G8 to address contentious trade-related issues or to promote its vision of the multilateral trading system at the summit level caused discord among the Quad members. This had far-reaching effects. At the same time, the WTO secretariat was slow to make its activities transparent. These factors — in addition to the overwhelming tendency of WTO member governments not to inform their citizens adequately of the issues at stake, address their concerns, or include them in the process of defining their national positions encouraged increased activity by civil society groups opposed to further multilateral trade liberalisation. Based on the arguments and slogans put forth by some of these groups, it was evident that the protestors acted on little, or worse, incorrect information.[8]

Lack of Communication

Closely linked to the lack of information from the leaders was the lack of communication by WTO officials and trade ministers at the Seattle ministerial. This occurred at both the unofficial and official levels. With trade having been placed increasingly in the public domain within the space of a few years, a large turn-out of demonstrators opposed to the WTO and the proposed Millennium Round was expected at the Seattle ministerial.

However, the actual numbers, estimated to have been between 30 000 and 50 000 who marched through the streets of Seattle, surprised many. The violent scenes portrayed by the media gave the impression that these demonstrators were the cause of the failure of the Seattle ministerial. Indeed, certain civil society groups were quick to take the credit (see, for example, ('FP Interview: Lori's War' 2000). However, the reasons for the impasse were much more complex, including a critical lack of consensus among the WTO delegates over the ministerial text.[9]

During the 1998 Geneva ministerial, U.S. president Bill Clinton acknowledged the lack of formal communication between the WTO and representatives of civil society. He called for the WTO to 'provide a forum where business, labour, environmental and consumer groups can speak out and help guide the further evolution of the WTO' (Clinton 1998).[10] Clinton's proposal served as the impetus for the 29 November 1999 'NGO Day' held in Seattle, which was designed to provide a platform both for trade officials as well as for

NGO representatives. This forum brought about a major increase in the number of NGO representatives granted official observer status as compared to the 1996 Singapore ministerial or the 1998 Geneva ministerial. The increase between the Singapore ministerial, at which 235 NGO representatives were present, to the Geneva ministerial with 335 participants present, was relatively small; the numbers jumped to 1500 in Seattle. The large number of environmental and labour NGOs present at the NGO Day differed markedly from the 1996 Singapore ministerial at which business interests represented 65 percent of accredited groups (Scholte, O'Brien, and Williams 1999, 118–119).

Opinions on the effectiveness of the Seattle NGO Day differ, with some noting that 'communication flowed one-way from officials to NGOs rather than two-way' while others thought that the event progressed 'fairly well'.[11] Regardless, this formal NGO session did not prevent tens of thousands from demonstrating.

Recipe for Change

Post-Seattle Actions of the WTO

In the time since Seattle, the WTO has quietly addressed the contentious issues that together were the ingredients of the impasse. Notably, unlike the atmosphere that prevailed among GATT ambassadors after the failed 1990 Brussels ministerial, which had been intended to conclude the Uruguay Round, WTO ambassadors in Seattle have openly searched for solutions to the most problematic issues. WTO director general Mike Moore has described the post-Seattle actions of the WTO as resembling a swan, 'serene on top of the water and paddling furiously under the water' (WTO 2000a).

Consultations

Immediately following Seattle, Moore held consultations in Brussels on 17–18 January and in Washington on 19–20 January in order to find the elements needed to move the stalled talks forward. He also met with James Wolfensohn, president of the World Bank, to discuss how international organisations could incorporate the views of their stakeholders better into WTO and World Bank policies (WTO 2000a).

During the following months, the new chairman of the WTO General Council, Kare Bryn, and the four deputy directors continued to hold consultations with the various WTO member governments. These consultations served to pick up the pieces after the impasse in Seattle. The positive atmosphere among the trade ambassadors as well as from member capitals allowed the development of a framework for action.

Framework for Action

In the aftermath of Seattle, the members developed a four-point framework for action. The elements involved are as follows.

1. *Market access:* Greater market access for developing countries to the markets of developed countries was identified as a key component in creating the environment in which further negotiations may take place.
2. *Implementation:* Another factor recognised as critical to increasing the benefits that developing countries and less developed countries gain from trade liberalisation is to provide them time and assistance to implement the results of the Uruguay Round agreement in full. Of particular concern here are the areas of agriculture, antidumping, customs valuation, subsidies, technical barriers to trade, textiles, trade-related aspects of intellectual property (TRIPs), trade-related investment measures (TRIMs), and services.
3. *Internal transparency:* During the preparation of the draft ministerial text, many members of the WTO voiced their frustration with the seemingly nontransparent internal decision making of the WTO. The director general's use of the infamous 'Green Room', to which selected members were invited to try to formulate compromises, was cited as a prime example of the secretive and elitist nature of the WTO.

   The smaller, informal Green Room discussions are held on an *ad hoc* basis to develop compromises, particularly when a deadline is looming. Moreover, trade delegates are well aware that the WTO is an intergovernmental institution in which all members technically, although arguably not politically, have the same weight, and decisions are taken by consensus in all but a few occasions. Nonetheless, WTO members have acknowledged that increased transparency in decision making is necessary. They have pledged to minimise the use of Green Room techniques and whenever possible to develop texts and hold discussion in the General Council in the presence of all members.
4. *External transparency:* A key criticism of the WTO made by NGOs and members of civil society was the lack of external transparency. This element relates to WTO relations with external stakeholders. Factors such as observer status, readily available WTO documents, and consultations are included

under this point. Among WTO members, there is a growing belief that 'there should be a demystifying of the WTO' (Stoler 2000).

Built-in Agenda

At their February 2000 General Council meeting, WTO members initiated the built-in negotiations in agriculture and services as mandated by the Uruguay Round. While these negotiations are still in their first phase, the areas under discussion will be a critical element of any new comprehensive trade negotiation. There are also plans to implement discussions as called for under the TRIPs agreement.

These post-Seattle activities of the WTO are encouraging as they indicate a sincere attempt by members to address their shortcomings, improve the functioning of the WTO, and get the planned Millennium Round back on track. However, their activities need the support and direction that only the effective leadership of the G8 can provide. Otherwise, there is the danger that the swan will again swim into dangerous waters.

The G8 and the New Actors in the Multilateral Trading System

The scenes of anti-trade and anti-globalisation protestors clashing with police in London as the 1999 G8 Summit took place in Cologne, in Seattle during the WTO ministerial, and in Prague during the September 2000 meeting of the World Bank serve as vivid images of the increasingly active role played by members of civil society in shaping international policies. However, some such groups also present a potential threat to the establishment of a transparent dialogue between government leaders, international organisation representatives, and civil society. The handful of CSOs whose primary means to prevent further trade liberalisation is to disrupt communication among those chosen to represent citizens raises concerns regarding the democratic accountability of all civil society groups.

The activities of the more extreme radical groups, which seek to destroy the existing rules, agreements, and international organisations on which the international system is based, should be held in contrast to the groups wishing to inform and reform current international practice. These latter groups provide not only useful information but also constructive proposals for change. Through holding a dialogue with these groups, the G8 and WTO will be better able to develop viable initiatives on the future multilateral trading system.

Distinguishing Civil Society Organisations and Nongovernmental Organisations

The significant increase in CSOs with various beliefs, objectives, and manners of operation necessitates a clear distinction among them. Such distinction allows politicians, negotiators, officials of international organisations, and other members of civil society to understand the likely aims, objectives, and actions of such groups. Furthermore, it is important that leaders establish the precedent of limiting their interaction to those CSOs and NGOs that follow generally accepted methods of public discourse to change policies rather than acknowledge or legitimise those groups that aim to bring change through destructive demonstrations.

This chapter applies the categorisation of NGOs related to the WTO as developed by Scholte, O'Brien, and Williams (1999) to G8 interaction with both NGOs and CSOs.

Conformists These groups generally support the objectives of trade liberalisation and the basis behind the activities of the WTO. According to Scholte, O'Brien, and Williams (1999, 113), 'Conformers only interrogate the outputs of the existing global trade regime, not its foundations'.

Members of this type of group include business associations such as the Transatlantic Business Dialogue (TABD), the World Economic Forum, and the Commonwealth Business Council; commercial farmers' groups, including the U.S. Dairy Foods Association and the EU's Comité des Organisations Professionnelles Agricoles (COPA); and research institutes such as the Brookings Institution and the Royal Institute of International Affairs.

At their mid-year meeting, TABD business leaders recognised that 'globalization is a positive sum game [in which] all sectors of society can benefit' (TABD 2000, 3). While pledging their commitment to work '*with governments* to dispel the negative myths about trade liberalization', members nonetheless encouraged the WTO to increase transparency and build confidence (p. 3; emphasis added). Additionally, members of the World Economic Forum submitted a report offering suggestions on closing the digital divide in information technology at a roundtable conference with Japanese prime minister Yoshiro Mori.

Reformers Although they generally agree with conformists on the need for a global trade regime, reformists actively work to alter the liberal approach to trade. Additionally, reformist groups seek to transform policies to take into account such aspects as environmental considerations as well as modify WTO operating procedures (Scholte, O'Brien, and Williams 1999, 112).

Members of this group include trade unions, international trade secretariats, human rights associations, environmental groups, and some development advocates. Jubilee 2000 is an example of a reformist group that has been active and effective at the level of the G8 summits. Calling for debt relief of Heavily Indebted Poor Countries (HIPCs), Jubilee 2000 is an international movement active in more than 40 countries. Its objective is the complete cancellation of the debt of the poorest countries from all creditors. At the Birmingham and Cologne G8 summits, Jubilee 2000 organised peaceful demonstrations in the form of human chains made up of 70 000 and 50 000 participants respectively. Jubilee 2000 demonstrated again in Okinawa in 2000 as well as organised a 'virtual chain' across the globe.

In preparation for the Okinawa Summit, Jubilee 2000 worked successfully with other groups, such as the Organization of African Unity and the G77 in Okinawa, to place debt relief high on the G8 agenda. The day before the summit began, President Abdelaziz Bouteflika of Algeria, President Thabo Mbeki of South Africa, and President Olusegun Obasanjo of Nigeria met with several G7 members in order to discuss debt relief. Throughout the summit, Jubilee 2000 representatives were highly visible and gave numerous press briefings and interviews, thereby effectively communicating their message.

Calling for significant progress on the US$100 billion debt relief package announced at the 1999 Cologne Summit, Jubilee 2000 at first seemed hopeful that debt relief had been placed high on the Okinawa Summit agenda. However, representatives expressed disappointment at the results of Okinawa, claiming that the leaders had 'failed to offer any new initiatives' and even 'backtracked' on their Cologne package (Jubilee 2000 Coalition 2000, 1).[12] Nonetheless, Jubilee 2000 immediately set its sights on the September 2000 World Bank meeting held two months later in Prague, at which it called for, among other initiatives, the establishment of an independent mechanism to ensure the increased transparency of debt relief.

Radicals Members of radical groups aim to limit the rule-making powers of the WTO with some fringe groups demanding that world citizens should 'kill the WTO'. Growing from relatively small groups in the mid 1990s, many had united under the loosely organised Peoples' Global Action (PGA) by the time the second WTO ministerial was held in Geneva in February 1998. PGA describes itself as a 'worldwide coordination of resistance against the global market' (Peoples' Global Action 2000b).

Among its principles is the 'very clear rejection of the institutions that multinationals and speculators have built to take power away from people, like the World Trade Organization (WTO) and other trade liberalisation agreements (like APEC, the EU, NAFTA, etc.)' as well as adopting a 'confrontational attitude' (Peoples' Global Action 2000b). Their mode of operation includes the 'simultaneous occupation and transformation of the capitalist social order around the globe — in the streets, neighbourhoods, fields, factories, offices, commercial centres, financial districts, and so on — [which] will strengthen mutual bonds at the local, national, and international levels' (Peoples' Global Action 2000a).

It is ironic that both the PGA and G8 share the goal of meeting to 'strengthen the mutual bonds' between their respective members. However, were the G8 to communicate with the extremist fringes of the radical groups, the danger exists that their destructive mode of operation would be seen as legitimate to the broader spectrum of civil society. Through applying the above categorisation, G8 leaders will avoid the 'danger that [they] accord legitimacy to "civil society" on its own terms and do not differentiate between its component groups' (Bayne 2000b, 215). Additionally, establishing channels of communication with groups that can add to the trade debate by means of coherent arguments and solid information will allow the G8 leaders to educate their own citizens better on trade issues.

Communication with New Actors

As host of the 2000 G8 Okinawa Summit, Japan implemented two important initiatives involving outreach to NGOs and interest group leaders. In a summit first, the Japanese government sponsored an NGO centre located near the international media centre, where various NGOs could work and hold press conferences during the Okinawa Summit. This centre was welcomed by the large number of NGOs in that it allowed a freer interchange between media and NGO representatives than at past summits. Additionally, on 18 July in Tokyo, Prime Minister Mori held a widely covered round-table conference with international business leaders in order to exchange views on how business and government could work together to close the digital divide.

With respect to trade-related issues, the 1999 Cologne Summit concluded that greater participation by civil society in issues concerning the WTO was crucial. The G8 stated that 'given the WTO's vital role, we agree on the importance of improving its transparency to make it more responsive to civil society', but added 'while preserving its government-to-government nature'

(G8 1999, section 9). Indeed, WTO officials support such moves. Early in 2000, Mike Moore stated:

> We all need to be more accountable. Parliaments and Congresses sustain governments. Public opinion sustains governments. Elected representatives are the main expression of civil society. Their support is measured, they are accountable, they need to be more involved. This is a real way in which we can counter some of the anxieties about globalization and public alienation (WTO 2000b).

At Okinawa, there was no official interaction among G8 participants, NGOs, or CSOs on trade-related issues. Instead, between 2 and 9 July, groups of reformist environmental groups from across the world met separately in several locations throughout Japan in a series of forums known as 'WTO Debate Week: Citizen's Forum 2001'.

Stimulating Trade Liberalisation after Seattle: Recommendations

Effective Political Leadership

As the G7 leaders did in Tokyo in 1986, in Houston in 1990, and again in Tokyo in 1993, they may serve as a powerful catalyst for further trade liberalisation if they can show effective political leadership. This leadership must continue beyond the three days of the summit. Effective leadership requires the leaders to provide direction to their respective trade ministers, especially among the members of the Quad. Additionally, they must work to convince protectionist elements in their governments of the benefits of multilateral trade liberalisation.

Pledges of Personal Commitment

Past G7 experience shows that with respect to multilateral trade negotiations, political leadership continues to have significant impact long after the summits end if the leaders pledge to keep personally committed and involved in the progress of the negotiations. This was evident following the 1990 Houston and 1991 London summits. At critical points throughout the year, leaders used their G7 ties to urge concessions from one another in order to break impasses. During the current Millennium Round agenda-setting stage, the G8 leaders need to continue to show personal interest and commitment to the goal of progressive liberalisation.

Structured Dialogue

The G8 must increase their communication with their citizens and NGOs if they are to understand the needs of individuals, various groups including nonprofit, for-profit, and other civil society groups, and promote their vision of the multilateral trading system. This communication must include a two-way exchange of views. The Tokyo information technology forum was a positive start, but such dialogue must include all G8 members as well as a more representative group of interests.

Structured dialogue on the issues of the multilateral trading system between the leaders of the G8 and representatives of CSOs, NGOs, for-profit groups, and nonprofit groups would encourage an exchange of views on trade and its impact on globalisation. As the global trade debate moves beyond discussing trade in industrial goods and moves into trade-related issues, such as services, the environment, and labour as well as food safety, which have historically been within the jurisdiction of national or local authorities, states increasingly will require civil society input, consent, and legitimacy (McGrew 1999, 213–214).

Following the trend of the G8 to support the establishment of separate specialist groups operating within the larger framework of the G8, this new group of civil society representatives could meet throughout the year in order to present the leaders with a set of proposals at the annual summits. Additionally, the director general of the WTO should be invited to attend both the summits as well as the proposed G8/civil society roundtable. A challenge to the Italian hosts of the 2001 G8 Summit in Genoa will be to build on the initiatives of the Japanese and establish a structured dialogue with trade-related groups.

Political Courage

Finally, the G8 must show increased political courage at Genoa. This requires the leaders, both as a group as well as individually in their respective capitals, to face those who oppose further multilateral trade liberalisation. While this is admittedly difficult at times, particularly during election years, the G8 leaders must find the political courage necessary to educate their citizens about the benefits of a transparent, rule-based multilateral trading system. Beyond purely trade-related issues, Bayne (2000b, 215) has called for the G8 to 'become the public advocates of the benefits of globalisation'.

In order for the G8 to show effective leadership in the area of trade, the leaders must stand behind what they say and stand up to opponents of further trade liberalisation. Without such leadership, they will be compelled to stand on the sidelines of the trade debate.

Notes

1   Earlier versions of this chapter were presented at the International Studies Association 20–24 February 2001, at the University of Southampton Cumberland Lodge 2–4 February 2001, and at 'New Directions in Global Governance? The G8's Okinawa Summit', the academic symposium held at the University of the Ryukyus, Okinawa, 19–20 July 2000. The author thanks Nicholas Bayne, George M. von Furstenberg, the staff and students at the University of Southampton, and Jeffrey Hart for their valuable comments.

2   The European Commission represents the EU in the G8, especially the non-G8 members of the EU, and in the WTO. For additional reading on the EU's role in the G7/8 see Ullrich and Donnelly (1998).

3   A minus symbol (–) indicates a G7/8 summit that had little or negative impact on multilateral trade negotiations, while a plus symbol (+) indicates a positive impact.

4   The EU was known as the European Community prior to the enactment of the Treaty on European Union on 1 November 1993.

5   The Bush administration welcomed the conveniently released GATT document known as the De Zeeuw text as a basis for further discussion on agriculture. The De Zeeuw text was agreed by all summit participants as the 'means to intensify the negotiations' (G7 1990, section 23). However, less than one week later, the EC's General Affairs Council declared that the text was only 'one way to intensify' the agricultural negotiations ('Europe Daily Bulletin' 1990). The EC retreat was due to the council feeling that the European Commission, which speaks for the 15 member states of the EU on matters relating to trade, had gone beyond its negotiating mandate.

6   As stated by a UK spokesman during a press briefing at the Okinawa Summit.

7   A unique feature of the Quad is that, unlike the G8 — where the EC is considered a participant rather than a full member — the EC speaks for all member states of the EU on matters of trade.

8   One such slogan, hung from the roof of the WTO in November 1999, declared 'The WTO kills people, kill the WTO'.

9   Andrew Stoler (2000) confirmed that the demonstrations in Seattle were a minor issue compared to the inability to agree on a ministerial text.

10   The legal texts of the WTO address relations with NGOs. WTO Article V.2 states: 'The General Council may make appropriate arrangements for consultation and co-operation with non-governmental organizations concerned with matters related to those of the WTO' (World Trade Organization 1994, 9).

11   The former opinion was stated by Nicholas Bayne while the latter was stated by Andrew Stoler.

12   Representatives noted that the number of HIPCs expected to reach the required 'decision point' necessary for debt relief decreased from 24 to 20.

Bibliography

Barshevsky, Charlene (2000). 'Barshefsky Says Deregulation Is Key to Japan's Recovery'. Transcript, 19 July. *Washington File*. International Information Programs, Washington DC.

Bayne, Nicholas (1999). 'Continuity and Leadership in an Age of Globalisation'. In M. R. Hodges, J. J. Kirton and J. P. Daniels, eds., *The G8's Role in the New Millennium*, pp. 21–44. Ashgate, Aldershot.

Bayne, Nicholas (2000a). 'The G7 Summit's Contribution: Past, Present, and Prospective'. In K. Kaiser, J. J. Kirton and J. P. Daniels, eds., *Shaping a New International Financial System: Challenges of Governance in a Globalizing World*, pp. 19–35. Ashgate, Aldershot.

Bayne, Nicholas (2000b). *Hanging in There: The G7 and G8 Summit in Maturity and Renewal*. Ashgate, Aldershot.

Clinton, Bill (1998). 'Preparing the WTO for the 21st Century'. *Focus* 31 (June), pp. 9–10. <www.wto.org/english/res_e/focus_e/focus31_e.pdf> (March 2001).

Daily Yomiuri (2000). 20 July, p. 3.

Dodwell, David (1993). 'The Gavel Falls on Most of Uruguay Round'. *Financial Times*, 14 December.

'Europe Daily Bulletin' (1990). *Agence Europe*, p. 6.

European Union-Japan Summit (2000). 'Joint Conclusions'. 19 July. <europa.eu.int/comm/external_relations/japan/summit_7_19_2000> (March 2001).

'FP Interview: Lori's War' (2000). *Foreign Policy* Spring, pp. 28–55.

G7 (1975). 'Declaration of Rambouillet'. 17 November, Rambouillet. <www.library.utoronto.ca/g7/summit/1975rambouillet/communique.html> (March 2001).

G7 (1985). 'The Bonn Economic Declaration Towards Sustained Growth and Higher Employment'. 4 May, Bonn. <www.library.utoronto.ca/g7/summit/1985bonn/communique/index.html> (March 2001).

G7 (1986). 'Tokyo Economic Declaration'. 6 May, Tokyo. <www.library.utoronto.ca/g7/summit/1986tokyo/communique.html> (March 2001).

G7 (1990). 'Houston Economic Declaration'. 11 July, Houston. <www.library.utoronto.ca/g7/summit/1990houston/communique/index.html> (March 2001).

G8 (1999). 'G8 Communiqué Köln 1999'. 20 June, Cologne. <www.library.utoronto.ca/g7/summit/1999koln/finalcom.htm> (March 2001).

Jubilee 2000 Coalition (2000). 'Betraying the Poor: The Failure of the G8 to Deliver a New Deal on Debt at the Okinawa Summit'. 26 August. <www.jubilee2000uk.org/reports/dropped0800.html> (March 2001).

Kay, Adrian (1998). *The Reform of the Common Agricultural Policy: The Case of the MacSharry Reforms*. CAB International, New York.

McGrew, Tony (1999). 'The World Trade Organization: Technocracy or Banana Republic?' In A. Taylor and C. Thomas, eds., *Global Trade and Global Social Issues*, pp. 197–216. Routledge, London.

Peoples' Global Action (2000a). 'Global Day of Action; S26'. 19 May. <www.x21.org/s26/calls/s26_en.htm> (March 2001).

Peoples' Global Action (2000b). 'Peoples' Global Action against "Free" Trade and the World Trade Organization'. 2 March. <www.agp.org/agp/en/PGAInfos/about.html> (March 2001).

Pollack, Andrew (1993). 'Summit Breathes Life into World Trade Talks'. *International Herald Tribune*, 8 July.

Putnam, Robert and Nicholas Bayne, eds. (1987). *Hanging Together: Co-operation and Conflict in the Seven-Power Summit*. 2nd ed. Sage Publications, London.

Rockwell, Kenneth (Director of Information and Media Relations of the World Trade Organization), interview with author, 23 June 2000.

Scholte, Jan Aart, Robert O'Brien, and Marc Williams (1999). 'The WTO and Civil Society'. *Journal of World Trade* vol. 33, no. 1, pp. 107–123.

Stoler, Andrew, interview with author, 3 May 2000, Geneva.

Torday, Peter (1993). 'Hurdles Stand in Way of Deal'. *Independent*, 8 July.

Transatlantic Business Dialogue (2000). *2000 Mid-Year Report*. Transatlantic Business Dialogue, Brussels.

Ullrich, Heidi K. and Alan Donnelly (1998). 'The Group of Eight and the European Union: The Evolving Partnership'. *G8 Governance* no. 5, November, <www.library.utoronto.ca/g7/governance/gov5> (March 2001).

Winham, Gilbert R. (1986). *International Trade and the Tokyo Round Negotiation*. Princeton University Press, Princeton.

Wolfe, Robert (1998). *Farm Wars: The Political Economy of Agriculture and the International Trade Regime*. Macmillan, Houndmills.

World Trade Organization (1994). *The Results of the Uruguay Round of Multilateral Trade Negotiations: The Legal Texts*. General Agreement on Tariffs and Trade, Geneva. Reprinted 1995 by the World Trade Organization, Geneva.

World Trade Organization (2000a). 'DG Moore Embarks on Consultations on Future WTO Work'. Press Release 163. 26 January. <www.wto.org/english/news_e/pres00_e/pr163_e.htm> (March 2001).

World Trade Organization (2000b). 'Moore Calls for Closer Parliamentary Involvement in WTO Matters'. Press Release 169. 21 February. <www.wto.org/english/news_e/pres00_e/pr169_e.htm> (March 2001).

Part IV
Conclusion

13 The Challenges Ahead

GEORGE M. VON FURSTENBERG AND JOHN J. KIRTON

At the centre of the international community's effort to govern the far-reaching new processes now underway in global information technology, finance, and trade stands the G7 of major market democracies and its politically oriented institutional twin involving Russia, the G8 (Hodges, Kirton, and Daniels 1999; Hajnal 1999; Bayne 2000). The G8 has a comprehensive array of overlapping and interconnected economic, social-protection, political, and security concerns that each summit now addresses to varying degrees. Economic issues include how best to position a country and the international community in the new economy, the continued liberalisation of international finance and trade for the old economy, and the lessons to be drawn from the major economic and financial crises that have afflicted the world with ever more severity as the era of globalisation intensifies (Kaiser, Kirton, and Daniels 2000). Social initiatives may focus on ways to sustain economic development, for instance through debt forgiveness for the group of Heavily Indebted Poor Countries (HIPCs), and on ways to protect social values and the poor in the face of acute financial crises (Kirton, Daniels, and Freytag 2001). They may also focus on the ecological and social consequences of trade and finance liberalisation, issues of environmental degradation and climate change, or the spread of infectious diseases. Political concerns may relate to rehabilitation and democratisation, as in Russia. Furthermore, security concerns may comprise nuclear proliferation, regional security, money laundering, terrorism, and cyber-crime.

Some summits are absorbed with crisis management or with reacting to recent adverse economic or political developments. Others are more forward looking and proactive, joining in the search for a new technological era's appropriate foundations, defining desirable new directions, and putting in place the international regimes that give them life. This is where an area of increasing engagement at future summits may lie.

This volume does not hew to a single line of argument or drive to a concerted conclusion about what these new directions are, or where the G7/8 can be most effective in defining and delivering these directions at a time of profound global economic change. Yet the various arguments it contains are more complementary than clashing. Several of the contributions, following

Susan Strange (1996), suggest that the role of the state at all levels has been very much diminished and with this, the role of the G7/8 members themselves. Some authors, following Fred Bergsten and Randall Henning (1996), are inclined to attribute this condition merely to a lack of effective leadership in crystallising and exerting the sovereign will, for instance in agreeing on an agenda for a new round of multilateral negotiations on trade liberalisation. Yet many others suggest that the underlying cause lies in profound new technological forces that have now outrun and bypassed the machinery of government, if only temporarily. This chapter adds a historical and analytical perspective to this fundamental point before proceeding to an overall evaluation of summit prospects in light of the individual conclusions of this volume's contributors. It argues that even if the G7/8 was not ready to embrace important specific tasks at the Okinawa 'technology' summit, it could well be on the verge of assuming the foundational role of injecting political and social considerations into the now inherently global, and indeed substantially new, economy.

The New Information Economy: Government Eclipse and Re-emergence at Times of Technological Revolution

Information and communications technology (ICT) and its openness have become new, universal conditioning factors. Hence, the ICT revolution must now be factored into any evaluation of how the global economy unfolds, what governments can accomplish individually or through the G8 process, and how differently they need to proceed in the new environment. But what is new in recent memory — government power eclipsed by a surge in civilian technology — is not unprecedented, nor is it the stable endpoint of the new developments. Several times before in human history it has taken considerable time for public accountability to catch up with major technological leaps that had broad civilian applications. During the twentieth century, from the depths of the Great Depression until the mid 1960s, governments of the leading democracies appeared to acquire a firm grip on the world. They took important initiatives that succeeded in guiding social, economic, political, and military developments. But the G5, which eventually grew into the G7 and then the G8, began in the 1970s, when these governments already commanded far less credit and trust than they had in earlier decades.

Taking an even longer historical view, since the emergence of a market-oriented world economy and the start of the Westphalian system of sovereign states, periods of government activism and confidence have alternated with periods in which the guiding force and the impetus for development have come from outside the public sector. The Age of Exploration, a period covering roughly 200 years from the middle of the fifteenth century, was marked by improvised private/public partnerships and arrangements that gave private parties a very wide berth. Company charters left private partners a free hand to shape the unknown, to extend the horizons of knowledge, and to seize effective control of new territories. The government stepped in, openly at least, only much later. For instance, the East India Company was chartered in 1600 but neither regulated nor subject to British government control of the political aspects of its policy until 1773.

Again, decades passed from the time of the first industrial revolution, which started in Great Britain in the late eighteenth century, until the first labour laws and compulsory education laws were passed well into the nineteenth century. Although statist traditions may have flourished for a time in continental Europe and Japan, there was a powerful conservative political instinct that, while technologically progressive and in tune with the new developments, cannot brook the idea of government interfering with the emergence of a major new capability. In the United States, the impulse was 'to get your stake in the West before letting sheriff, marshal, and surveyor in'. Democratic governments, unless drawn into hostilities with other countries, thus would not engage forcefully until the period of the most intense dynamism of the new development had been exhausted and some of its undesirable features had become apparent. Public action would follow only after the limits of public tolerance of these negative side effects had been reached.

From this historical perspective, as Thomas Lawton and Michele Mastroeni observe, it is not unexpected that the U.S. government, after providing the initial push, has largely stood aside from the teeming young life of the internet. No taxes, little or no government regulation, and 'not to worry' are the guiding principles. As long as the United States retains a large lead in ICT, it sees little benefit from co-operating with other countries on measures that could restrain its high-tech industries in some way. Yet this technology has some of the characteristics of an essential global public good, being difficult to deny and increasingly impossible to do without for a substantial business entity or agency anywhere in the world. For this reason, and because ICT is subject to abuse by those who commit financial crimes and cyber-terrorism from anywhere, there is a growing basis for co-operation, even sharing, with other countries. A technology that is increasingly driven by its end users all over the world and not by its large-cap U.S. progenitors, as George von Furstenberg argues, makes internationally co-ordinated action imperative in those areas where fragility and risks have risen to unacceptable levels.

Countries' Stakes in Risky Ventures and Government Attitudes to Risk

Governments, democratic ones in particular, are responsible for shielding their populations against major risks outside the control of individuals; the protection function is basic to government and enduring. Where the government could exercise some control consistent with agreed individual liberties and rights of property, it would generally be obliged to intervene in order to limit exposure to such risks. To this end, as in the international and domestic financial system, it could regulate, set standards, assign liability, and impose insurance requirements. But although governments differ greatly over how to quantify and weight, say, phytosanitary, genetic, and accidental-release risks, they are unlikely to agree on actions to contain them. What divides the G8 countries, then, are differences in risk aversion and in how governments' political processes weigh a comparatively certain gross return against a far less certain and perhaps improbable — but potentially much larger — eventual cost. Therein lies the large challenge for G7/8 governments, and even for regional partners in North America, to arrive at harmonised environmental and other regulations that would allow for more far-reaching free trade (Rugman, Kirton, and Soloway 1999).

There have been some technological advances, not just in the twentieth century, that were known to carry such high risks that have required governments to be involved early on. Any newly discovered pestilence, deadly poisons to life or environment, and weapons of mass destruction have tended to attract government regulation soon after they were discovered. Indeed, governments may have sponsored the research leading to the discovery of such agents and their delivery techniques. Thus government responsibility was accepted from the start.

In other areas, however, there has been no agreement on the level of risks that would be acceptable for the private sector to take before the government should assert some control over the process of discovery, application, and release. Political myopia and calculation always make it extremely difficult to impose safety standards where there can be no immediate harm and only low-probability scenarios can point to systemic interaction chains that could lead to harm in the future (Cooper 1989).

For example, genetic engineering and genetically modified foods and organisms have divided the G8 into two opposing camps and a middle group unable to bridge the gap. The first of the polar groups treats advances in this area with as much public concern and caution as it treats advances in the application and spread of nuclear technology. Upholding this precautionary principle are continental European governments that see a presumptive, but not fully substantiated, risk of widespread and irreversible damage that is difficult to contain. The second group finds biotechnology to be yet another exciting technology frontier to be pushed back freely and exploited commercially on the presumption of social benefits proportional to market value. At this extreme are countries led by the United States that take the view that little or no action should be taken unless and until a clear threat of systemic proportions has been scientifically identified beyond a reasonable doubt.

Obviously, the G8 can achieve little in areas where some members of the group see the need for concerted government action and regulation while a dominant member is unalterably opposed. In addition, there are basic economic conflicts of interest between countries that benefit from being the leading producers of intellectual property whose applications may convey adverse side effects and other countries that share in these side effects without also benefiting as producers.

Governments at all levels traditionally have assumed a role in fighting the spread of infectious or contagious diseases once their epidemiology began to be understood. Nevertheless, there is often a long lag between steps designed to protect the local or national constituency and steps to protect the world community. Thus, despite earlier efforts (Dittmann 1997), the G8 started to focus on AIDS as an important subject for international assistance only at the Okinawa Summit, almost 20 years after the disease was first described, in 1981, in the United States. The G8's response to the social, political, and security challenges posed by more benign shocks, such as those now presented by ICT, likely will be much slower. However, it is not warranted to assume that the current condition, that of the governments and the G8 having little or no role in shaping the new developments, will persist indefinitely. History suggests otherwise. Indeed, at the technology summit in Okinawa there may have been the first signs of change.

New Constraints and New Opportunities for the G8

There is less and less that governments could achieve at affordable cost if they would need to go against the global pull of existing markets for goods and financial services to have their way. As Nicholas Bayne writes in the first of his two chapters in this volume, globalisation requires more international action on issues formerly considered domestic. Yet even if governments banded together, they might be more constrained by the logic of open markets collectively than they were individually decades earlier when their economies were more closed. It is also not necessarily true that what a state can no longer do alone can be achieved by a critical mass of states acting together. For instance, few believe that the G7 countries could ever agree on a joint approach to the taxation of incomes from capital, and, even if they did, tax shelters could well offer themselves elsewhere in open international capital markets.

Thus some possibilities of control may not only have shifted to different levels of government but may also have slipped out of government hands entirely. The chief task of the G8 might therefore be to adjust their systems of government — from regulation and taxation to legitimacy and participation — down to the new realities rather than the other way around.

Thomas Lawton and Michele Mastroeni have demonstrated convincingly how far the tables have been turned by the ICT revolution in this regard. The radical decentralisation and indispensable utility of the new economy that let it elude most forms of government taxation and control for the time being may be symptomatic of the decline in state-dominated systems. As long as the commitment to open markets is too costly to abrogate individually or collectively, governments are constrained in their choice of both means and ends.

For instance, wealth and incomes from capital become increasingly hard to corral for taxing and redistribution. This has put capital gains taxes, tax withholding on interest and dividends, and inheritance or estate taxes on the endangered list in several advanced countries as tax competition for attracting wealth and the wealthy has intensified. Public choice is constricted, while private choice expands unevenly and, some would say, inequitably. Globalisation pushes out the risk-return frontier, and both risks and opportunities rise. Government is seen as lacking the core competency to tweak the forces of development or to assess risks in a growing number of new areas, including biotechnology. Rather, private industry associations and standing groups of experts increasingly take it upon themselves, or are called upon by government agencies, even in special-topic summits and happenings surrounding the G8, to define the public interest G8 (Hajnal 1999, 60–61; Ullrich and Donnelly 1998).

Does it then follow that the stakes in the game of policy co-ordination among governments have declined so as to make the G7/8 irreversibly less important? Or is it that while governments lose some policy instruments or capabilities, such as capital controls or even an independent monetary policy, they have also acquired new responsibilities and instruments, such as a stake in governance of the new ICT economy, global competition policy, cyber-protection, a multilateral agreement on investment, or the globe's forests and fresh water? In that case, new constraints on both national and international government actions could coincide with the development of new demands for government involvement. Any such demands would have to be addressed with means somewhat different from those available in the past. But they could still be met.

As some of the contributors point out, the competitive realities that now confront countries, for instance in vying for inward foreign direct investment (FDI) or technology transfer, are a not just a product of the spontaneous driving forces of entrepreneurial innovation and technology. They also derive from the incentive aspects and private/public strategies that were adopted earlier on the basis of cultural, legal, and political foundations, as much as on the basis of economic foundations. The public-choice aspect of these evolving foundations gives market institutions a political character even when adjusting to global competitive pressures and participating in the surge of the leading technologies dominate the international agenda. At least some governments and their social philosophies had a hand in the realities that now appear as hard constraints on them and others. Similarly, measures that may have important consequences down the road may have little current relevance or effect. Hence, forward-looking, evolving system thinking is required to make a difference to future security and well-being.

The Summit Agenda and the Emergence of New Functions

Viewed in this way, the summits have dealt to varying degrees with three categories whose dividing lines, of course, are fluid. They are as follows:

- Promoting world-wide appreciation and taking fuller advantage of the current competitive and technological realities;
- Evolving modifications, frequently in response to particular crises, that could gradually change the constraints of tomorrow; and
- Debating and devising the political and economic principles and appropriate regulatory structures to be used in the management of the risks and opportunities associated with emerging technologies.

These three objectives relate to promoting economic development spearheaded by the private sector through the international liberalisation of trade and finance; mitigating the adverse effects of major disturbances, particularly in international financial markets, and analysing their root causes;

and incorporating major new technological capabilities and the global issues they pose into the domestic political and eventually the G8 process of deliberation.

The first objective, promoting globalisation in the spirit of the 'Washington Consensus', calls for reducing opportunities and tolerance for corrupt meddling by politicians and the politically powerful in economic affairs because it undermines economic structures, participation, and development. At the same time, rule-based oversight over, as well as by, regulatory institutions and administrative agencies is to be strengthened so as to establish legal security and accountability in government. At least since the 1996 Lyon Summit, the code word for the entire reform package has been 'transparency'. The continuation of trade liberalisation recommended by Nicholas Bayne, Theodore Cohn, and Heidi Ullrich in the closing chapters of this volume seeks to extend the high degrees of economic freedom already enjoyed by the G7 to more sectors and, in particular, to more of the developing countries outside the group. There is a very conscious attempt to reflect and to build on past successes in the area of trade liberalisation over the post-war period. Ever broader and deeper application of a tried and true formula is the goal.

The second area of summit activity is more remedial and intermittent, but it may stimulate the adoption of new safeguards that have some potential for guiding evolutionary system change. Reform of the architecture of the international financial system has involved experimentation with new, currently still latent, facilities (Kaiser, Kirton, and Daniels 2000; Eichengreen 1999). For instance, as John Kirton discusses in his chapter, when the International Monetary Fund (IMF) established contingent credit lines (CCL) for emerging countries in 1999, it was judged to be pursuing sound policies but was nevertheless at risk from contagion; it was intended to reinforce defences against the spread of a future crisis in emerging markets. At the same time, the moral hazard that arises when parties are shielded from having to bear the full cost of their actions was to be contained by greater contractual involvement of the private sector in international debt workouts and crisis resolution. Sébastien Dallaire, Saori Katada, Kunihiko Ito, and John Kirton cover much of what countries have learned, or failed to learn, from major financial crises. Nicholas Bayne adds international debt relief for HIPCs, trade access for the less developed countries (LDCs), as well as medical and educational assistance for countries and systems overwhelmed by infectious diseases and other calamities to the list of measures called for by the global crisis alleviation and stabilisation function of the G8.

The third area of summit activity is the newest and most tentative. It seeks to position national governments and the G8 in an unfolding dynamic process of great momentum. The contours and future lines of the development propelled by the ICT revolution, by the biotechnology revolution, and perhaps by the climate revolution are as yet dimly perceived. Their social and political processing has only just begun. So governments try to define what are acceptable standards of risk at the margins of developments in ICT, biotechnology, and climate change, and in other areas.

One of the roles of the summit is to take these issues from the realm of scientific discourse and imponderable evidence down to the area of common conversation and deft images through which political preferences can be crystallised. As a result, outlines of a political plan of action may come into full view, or at least be glimpsed, on the summit stage. Governments are not a major factor in driving scientific research or setting the research agenda in these new areas. Lacking the competence that comes from direct participation, governments increasingly contract out for the technology assessments they need. Thus, government is no longer among the first to know and to act.

Rather, the first collective response may be voluntary standardisation, often facilitated by essentially private or tripartite (government, business, labour) organisations or associations in which governments function more as observers than initiators. As detailed by Thomas Lawton, international co-operation is induced among the parties simply by recognising that in some areas agreement on a common operating protocol or network standards is efficient and conducive to reducing everyone's business risk. *Ad hoc* self-regulation and private-law conventions that are respected even by courts of law have proved achievable in several areas where they are convenient for transnational businesses. If the government is brought in early, the main purpose may be to arrange for taxpayers and society at large to assume risks and insurance burdens to backstop business in areas where it wishes to limit liability for any open-ended, as yet incalculable, damages it may cause.

Summit issues that are new in substance and not just in context, application, or degree of concern inevitably involve consequences that are highly uncertain and laden with value conflicts. These conflicts are bound to surface as the G7/8 countries begin to consider facilitation of and adjustment to an as yet unbridled process of innovation for the future. Among new issues that have been moving up to the level of the summit are criminal uses of ICT and the loss of effective privacy protections and the loss of freedom from manipulation on the one hand. On the other, there is the crippling lack of access to ICT in the poorer parts of the developing world. In addition, there are scientific, moral, social insurance, health, and accountability issues that are raised by dramatic advances in biotechnology as they relate to modified organisms, genetic engineering, and food safety concerns.

Concrete achievements in this third area of summit concerns may have been small as yet in the judgement of several contributors to this volume. Yet, if the Okinawa Summit marked an important beginning, it would be found in this area. For this reason, this conclusion has explored what governments and official entities generally have experienced, and then done, when confronted with extraordinary dynamics driven by new technologies developed in the private sector. How has the role of government been diminished initially and restored eventually as popular demands for essential protections and safeguards have mounted? It may well be that what the world is today experiencing is more like a historically 'normal' lag in political recognition and adjustment, even if socially stressful, than part of a new trend progressively diminishing the relevance of government and the G8. In that sense, with the tentative beginnings at Okinawa, the G8 may indeed have begun to set new directions for the governance of the global economy in this new globalising age.

References

Bayne, Nicholas (2000). *Hanging in There: The G7 and G8 Summit in Maturity and Renewal*. Ashgate, Aldershot.

Bergsten, C. Fred and C. Randall Henning (1996). *Global Economic Leadership and the Group of Seven*. Institute for International Economics, Washington DC.

Cooper, Richard N. (1989). 'International Cooperation in Public Health as a Prologue to Macroeconomic Cooperation'. In R. N. Cooper, ed., *Can Nations Agree? Issues in International Economic Cooperation*, pp. 178–254. Brookings Institution, Washington DC.

Dittmann, Sieghard (1997). 'Report on Communicable Disease Surveillance'. Subproject I: Towards a Global Health Network, G8 Global Health Applications Project. World Heath Organization, Copenhagen.

Eichengreen, Barry J. (1999). *Toward a New International Financial Architecture: A Practical Post-Asia Agenda*. Institute for International Economics, Washington DC.

Hajnal, Peter (1999). *The G7/G8 System: Evolution, Role, and Documentation*. Ashgate, Aldershot.

Hodges, Michael R., John J. Kirton, and Joseph P. Daniels, eds. (1999). *The G8's Role in the New Millennium*. Ashgate, Aldershot.

Kaiser, Karl, John J. Kirton, and Joseph P. Daniels, eds. (2000). *Shaping a New International Financial System: Challenges of Governance in a Globalizing World*. Ashgate, Aldershot.

Kirton, John J., Joseph P. Daniels, and Andreas Freytag, eds. (2001). *Guiding Global Order: G8 Governance in the Twenty-First Century*. Ashgate, Aldershot.

Rugman, Alan M., John J. Kirton, and Julie A. Soloway (1999). *Environmental Regulations and Corporate Strategy: A NAFTA Perspective.* Oxford University Press, Oxford.

Strange, Susan (1996). *The Retreat of the State: The Diffusion of Power in the World Economy.* Cambridge University Press, Cambridge.

Ullrich, Heidi K. and Alan Donnelly (1998). 'The Group of Eight and the European Union: The Evolving Partnership'. *G8 Governance* no. 5, November, <www. library.utoronto.ca/g7/governance/gov5> (March 2001).

Appendices

Appendices

A G7 Statement
Okinawa 2000

21 JULY 2000

World Economy

1. Since we last met in Cologne, prospects for world economic growth have further improved, as the underlying fundamentals of the industrial countries and the world economy more generally have strengthened, and as our economies move towards a more balanced and therefore more sustainable pattern of growth. Emerging market economies, including the crisis-affected economies in Asia and elsewhere, continue to strengthen.

2. At the same time, continued vigilance and further action are needed to ensure that sustained, strong and balanced growth is achieved. We agree on the importance of directing macroeconomic and structural policies in all our countries at achieving this objective, with emphasis on taking full advantage of the investment opportunities created by new technologies to raise potential growth rates.

3. More specifically,
   - In the United States and Canada, where growth remains strong with low unemployment and inflation well contained, macroeconomic policies should continue to be directed towards maintaining a sustainable rate of growth and low inflation, and in the United States, national saving should increase.
   - In the euro area, where growth has further strengthened and employment is rising, sound macroeconomic policies and vigorous structural reforms directed towards expanding investment, employment, and productive potential remain important.
   - In the United Kingdom, where growth has strengthened, employment is still rising, and inflation is low, economic policies should continue to aim at meeting the inflation target while sustaining growth and employment.
   - In Japan, where the economy continues to show positive signs of recovery, although uncertainty still lingers, macroeconomic policies should continue to be supportive to ensure domestic demand-led growth.

Structural reform should be continued to promote an increase in productive potential.
- We welcome the recovery in many emerging market economies as well as countries in transition and developing countries, but we stress the importance of further progress in corporate and financial restructuring and the importance of sound underlying fiscal positions and debt structures.
4. We are concerned about the adverse effect on world economic growth of recent developments in world crude oil markets. In this context, we highlight the need for greater stability of oil markets to help ensure sustained growth and prosperity in both oil producing countries and oil consuming countries.

Strengthening the International Financial Architecture

5. Following a series of crises since 1997, the international community has endeavoured to promote greater stability of the global economy through strengthening the international financial architecture, in view of the drastic changes to the global financial landscape, particularly in light of the increasing size and importance of private capital markets.
6. We welcome the progress made thus far and support the further steps set out by our Finance Ministers in the following areas.
7. We will continue to work together with other members of the international community to further strengthen the international financial architecture.

Reform of the International Monetary Fund (IMF)

8. The IMF should continue to play a central role in advancing macroeconomic and financial stability as an important precondition for sustainable global growth and should continue to evolve to meet the challenges of the future. As a universal institution, the IMF must work in partnership with all its members, including the poorest, based on shared interests. In this regard, we attach particular importance to the following measures:
   - Strengthening IMF surveillance to prevent crises: A substantial qualitative shift in the nature and scope of the surveillance is needed in light of globalisation and large scale private capital flows.
   - Implementation of international codes and standards: We are determined to strengthen our efforts to this end, including through their incorporation in IMF surveillance.

- Reform of IMF facilities: To adapt to the globalisation of capital markets, we attach priority to early progress in achieving a streamlined, incentive-based structure for IMF lending as set out by our Finance Ministers.
- Safeguarding IMF resources and post-programme monitoring: It is imperative to implement the strengthened safeguard measures and to enhance IMF's capacity for post-programme monitoring.
- Strengthening governance and accountability: It is important that the IMF's decision-making structure and its operation remain accountable taking into account changes in the world economy.
- Promotion of private sector involvement in crisis prevention and resolution: We welcome that private external creditors have contributed to the financing of recent IMF programmes, confirming the importance of making operational the approach agreed by our Finance Ministers last April based on the framework we laid out in Cologne.

Reform of the Multilateral Development Banks (MDBs)

9. The core role of the MDBs should be accelerating poverty reduction in developing countries while improving the efficiency of assistance and avoiding competition with private financial flows. The MDBs should increase their resources devoted to core social investments such as basic health and education, clean water and sanitation. The Comprehensive Development Framework (CDF) and the Poverty Reduction Strategy Papers (PRSPs) should become the basis for programmes that have strong ownership by the recipient countries.

10. All the MDBs should allocate their support increasingly on the basis of borrower performance. Country assistance strategies should take full account of borrowers' policy environments, including governance issues. The MDBs' own governance and accountability should also be strengthened.

11. We look to the MDBs to play a leadership role in increasing the provision of global public goods, particularly for urgently needed measures against infectious and parasitic diseases including HIV/AIDS, as well as environmental degradation.

Highly-leveraged Institutions (HLIs), Capital Flows, and Offshore Financial Centers (OFCs)

12. We stress the importance of implementing measures recommended by the Financial Stability Forum (FSF) last March.
13. With regard to concerns about the potential consequences of the activities of HLIs, we agree that the recommended measures should be fully implemented and that they will be reviewed to determine whether additional steps are necessary. We note that the FSF considered, but did not recommend, at this stage, direct regulation of the currently unregulated HLIs, but emphasized that direct regulation would be reconsidered, if, upon review, the implementation of its recommendations were not adequately addressing concerns identified.
14. We urge the IMF to conduct quickly assessments of offshore financial centres identified by the FSF as a priority.
15. We agree that it remains essential for each country to strengthen the financial system, choose an appropriate foreign exchange rate regime, and liberalise the capital account in a well-sequenced manner.

Regional Co-operation

16. We agree that regional co-operation through intensified surveillance can help contribute to financial stability by strengthening the policy framework at the national level. Co-operative financing arrangements at the regional level designed to supplement resources provided by the international financial institutions (IFIs) in support of IMF programmes can be effective in crisis prevention and resolution. In this context, we welcome the recent developments in Asia and North America. In a different institutional context, economic and financial integration mechanisms, and monetary unification in Europe are also contributing to the economic and financial stability of the global economy.

Progress of the Enhanced HIPC Initiative

17. The International Development Goal of cutting in half by 2015 the proportion of the world's population living in extreme poverty is an ambitious one. It demands a strategy of economic growth accompanied

by the right social sector policies which can contribute to a virtuous circle of poverty reduction and economic development. Debt relief for Heavily Indebted Poor Countries (HIPCs) is only one part of such a strategy, but it is a crucial part.

18. Last year in Cologne, we agreed to launch the Enhanced HIPC Initiative to deliver faster, broader and deeper debt relief, releasing funds for poverty reduction. We welcome endorsement of this initiative by the international community last autumn.

19. Since then, while further efforts are required, progress has been made in implementing the Enhanced HIPC Initiative. As reported in the annex to our G7 Finance Ministers' report, published today, on "Poverty Reduction and Economic Development," nine countries (Benin, Bolivia, Burkina Faso, Honduras, Mauritania, Mozambique, Senegal, Tanzania and Uganda,) have already reached their Decision Points and are seeing the benefits of the Initiative. Total debt relief under the HIPC Initiative for these countries should amount to more than US$15 billion in nominal terms (US$8.6 billion in Net Present Value).

20. We welcome the efforts being made by HIPCs to develop comprehensive and country-owned poverty reduction strategies through a participatory process involving civil society. We encourage those HIPCs that have not yet done so to embark quickly on the process and thus fully benefit from the debt reduction. We are concerned by the fact that a number of HIPCs are currently affected by military conflicts which prevent poverty reduction and delay debt relief. We call upon these countries to end their involvement in conflicts and to embark quickly upon the HIPC process. We agree to strengthen our efforts to help them prepare and come forward for debt relief, by asking our Ministers to make early contact with the countries in conflict to encourage them to create the right conditions to participate in the HIPC Initiative. We will work together to ensure that as many countries as possible reach their Decision Points, in line with the targets set in Cologne, giving due consideration to the progress of economic reforms and the need to ensure that the benefits of debt relief are targeted to assist the poor and most vulnerable.

21. In this regard, we welcome the establishment of the Joint Implementation Committee (JIC) by the World Bank and the IMF, and strongly urge both HIPCs and IFIs to accelerate their work toward the implementation of the Initiative. IFIs should, along with other donors, help HIPCs prepare PRSPs and assist their financial resource management by providing technical assistance.

22. We reaffirmed our commitment to provide 100% debt reduction of ODA claims, and newly commit to 100% debt reduction of eligible commercial claims. We welcome the announcement made by some non-G7 countries that they too will provide 100% debt relief, and we urge other donors to follow suit.

23. We note the progress made in securing the required financing of the IFIs for effective implementation of the Enhanced HIPC Initiative, and welcome pledges and the initial contributions including those to the HIPC Trust Fund. We reaffirm our commitment to make available as quickly as possible the resources we have pledged. In this context, we recognise the importance of fair burden sharing among creditors.

24. Given the enormous destructive effect of war and crisis, we call upon the OECD to review strengthened measures, including a review of national rules and regulations, toward ensuring that export credits to HIPCs and other low income developing countries are not used for non-productive purposes. We encourage the OECD to complete this work and publish the results as soon as possible.

Actions Against Abuse of the Global Financial System

25. To secure the benefits of the globalised financial system, we need to ensure that its credibility and integrity are not undermined by money laundering, harmful tax competition, and poor regulatory standards.

26. We welcome and strongly endorse our G7 Finance Ministers' report, published today, on "Actions Against Abuse of the Global Financial System," and attach particular importance to the following developments:
    – Money laundering: We welcome the initial work of the Financial Action Task Force on Money Laundering (FATF), which has published its review of the rules and practices of 29 countries and territories and its identification of 15 non-co-operative countries and territories (NCCTs). We note with satisfaction the issuance of advisories to our domestic financial institutions that they should take cognisance and enhance their scrutiny of the risks associated with business and transactions with individuals or entities from the 15 NCCTs. We are ready to give our advice and provide, where appropriate, our technical assistance to jurisdictions that commit to making improvements to their regimes. We are prepared to act together, when required and appropriate, to implement co-ordinated counter-measures against those NCCTs that do not take steps

to reform their systems appropriately, including the possibility to condition or restrict financial transactions with those jurisdictions and to condition or restrict support from IFIs to them.

- Tax havens and other harmful tax practices: We welcome the OECD Report on Progress on Identifying and Eliminating Harmful Tax Practices, which includes two lists: certain jurisdictions meeting tax haven criteria; and potentially harmful regimes within the OECD member countries. We also welcome the public commitments already made by jurisdictions to eliminate harmful tax practices and we urge all jurisdictions to make such commitments. We encourage the OECD to continue its efforts to counter harmful tax practices and to extend its dialogue with non-member countries. We also reaffirm our support for the OECD's report on improving access to bank information for tax purposes and call on all countries to work rapidly towards a position where they can permit access to, and exchange, bank information for all tax purposes.
- Offshore financial centres: Regarding offshore financial centres (OFCs) that do not meet international financial standards, we welcome the identification by the Financial Stability Forum (FSF) of priority jurisdictions for assessment. We consider it essential for OFCs to implement all measures recommended by the FSF with a view to improving weak regulatory and supervisory systems, as well as to eliminate harmful tax competition and to adopt anti-money laundering measures. In this regard, we attach priority to the eight areas identified by our Finance Ministers: international co-operation, exchange of information, customer identification, abolition of excessive secrecy, effective vetting of financial institutions, enhanced resources for financial supervision and anti-money laundering compliance, improved legislation on money launderings and elimination of harmful tax practices. We will take steps to encourage jurisdictions to make the necessary changes and provide technical assistance where appropriate. Where jurisdictions fail to meet certain standards and are not committed to enhancing their level of compliance with international standards, we will also take measures to protect the international financial system from the effects of these failures.
- Role of international financial institutions (IFIs): We urge IFIs, including the IMF and World Bank, to help countries implement relevant international standards, in the context of financial sector assessments as well as programme design and assistance.

27. We stress the urgent need for concrete actions against abuse of the global financial system at both the national and international level. We also strongly urge better co-ordination, further impetus to efforts under way in various international fora, and expeditious follow-up actions.

Nuclear Safety/Ukraine

28. We welcome the decision taken by President Kuchma to close the Chernobyl Nuclear Power Plant (NPP) on 15 December this year. We continue to co-operate with the Government of Ukraine in addressing the problems associated with the permanent shutdown of the Chernobyl NPP.
29. We reaffirm our commitment made at the Cologne Summit to continue our support for the Shelter Implementation Plan (SIP). We welcome the results of the Pledging Conference in July to ensure full implementation of the SIP. We appreciate the contribution of the non-G7 donors.
30. We urge the Government of Ukraine to accelerate its power sector reforms, particularly improvement of cash collection and privatisation, which will attract financially viable investments in the energy sector. We look forward to receiving the report of the European Bank for Reconstruction and Development in this respect. In the meantime, we affirm our commitment in line with the Memorandum of Understanding to assist the Ukraine in the preparation and implementation of energy projects based on least cost principles.

B G8 Communiqué Okinawa 2000

23 JULY 2000

Preamble

1. We, the Leaders of eight major industrialised democracies and the President of the European Commission, met together here in Okinawa for the 26th Summit in the year which heralds a new millennium. We reflected upon the challenges faced and progress made since the First Summit in Rambouillet in working toward peace and prosperity throughout the world, and we discussed the role the G8 should play as it evolves in the 21st century.
2. During the last quarter of the 20th century, the world economy has achieved unprecedented levels of prosperity, the Cold War has come to an end, and globalisation has led to an emerging common sense of community. Driving these developments has been the global propagation of those basic principles and values consistently advocated by the Summiteers-democracy, the market economy, social progress, sustainable development and respect for human rights. Yet we are keenly aware that even now in many parts of the world poverty and injustice undermine human dignity, and conflict brings human suffering.
3. As we make the transition into the new century, we will continue to exercise leadership and responsibility in addressing these persistent problems and squarely face new challenges as they arise. We must tackle the root causes of conflict and poverty. We must bravely seize the opportunities created by new technologies in such areas as information and communications technology (IT) and life sciences. We must acknowledge the concerns associated with globalisation, while continuing to be innovative in order to maximise the benefits of globalisation for all. In all our endeavours we must build on our basic principles and values as the foundations for a brighter world in the 21st century.
4. In a world of ever-intensifying globalisation, whose challenges are becoming increasingly complex, the G8 must reach out. We must engage in a new partnership with non-G8 countries, particularly developing countries,

international organisations and civil society, including the private sector and non-governmental organisations (NGOs). This partnership will bring the opportunities of the new century within reach of all.

5. We hope that our discussions in Okinawa provide a positive contribution to the United Nations Millennium Summit, which we expect to articulate, in the spirit of the Secretary-General's report "We the Peoples", a vision that will guide the United Nations as it rises to the challenges of the new century. To that end, we will continue to work for a strengthened, effective and efficient United Nations and remain convinced that reforms of the United Nations, including the Security Council, are indispensable.

6. A new era dawns. Let us move forward together, with hope, toward a 21st century of greater prosperity, deeper peace of mind and greater stability.

Toward a 21st Century of Greater Prosperity

World Economy

7. The 20th century has achieved unprecedented economic progress. Yet the financial and economic crises of the past few years have presented enormous challenges for the world economy. Together with many of our partners around the world, we have devoted ourselves to alleviating the adverse effects of the crisis, stimulating economic recovery, and identifying ways to help prevent future upheavals, including measures to strengthen the international financial architecture. The world economy will grow strongly this year, and we are particularly encouraged by the strength of recovery in most crisis-affected countries.

8. While the pace of recovery varies across Asia, trade is expanding and indeed some countries have achieved dynamic growth. Reform efforts must now focus on maintaining the momentum behind financial and corporate sector reforms, improving public and private sector governance and transparency, and strengthening social safety nets to ensure strong, sustainable growth and avoid future instability.

9. Despite recent positive developments in the world economy, we recognise that there is no time for complacency as globalisation intensifies and the rapid diffusion of IT brings about fundamental structural changes to our economies. There are encouraging signs of a new reality in the improvement of productivity in the United States and, to a lesser extent, in other G8 economies. But to capitalise on the opportunities before us, we must renew

our unwavering commitment to structural change in our own economies, including greater competition and more adaptable labour markets, underpinned by appropriate macro-economic policies.

Information and Communications Technology (IT)

10. IT empowers, benefits and links people the world over, allows global citizens to express themselves and know and respect one another. It also has immense potential for enabling economies to expand further, countries to enhance public welfare and promote stronger social cohesion and thus democracy to flourish. Access to the digital opportunities must, therefore, be open to all.

11. We clearly recognise that the process of globalisation and the fast pace at which IT is advancing have engendered various concerns. We need to address such concerns so that we can contribute to greater peace of mind for all. Acting in concert, we will maximise the benefits of IT and ensure that they are spread to those at present with limited access. In this regard, we welcome contributions from the private sector, such as those of the Global Digital Divide Initiative of the World Economic Forum and Global Business Dialogue on Electronic Commerce (GBDe).

12. In support of these goals, we commit ourselves to pursuing the aims and ambitions set out in the Okinawa Charter on the Global Information Society. We will set up a Digital Opportunities Task Force (dot force), which will be asked to report to our next meeting its findings and recommendations on global action to bridge the international information and knowledge divide.

Development

13. The 21st century must be a century of prosperity for all, and we commit ourselves to the agreed international development goals, including the overarching objective of reducing the share of the world's population living in extreme poverty to half its 1990 level by 2015. 13. We welcome the Report on Poverty Reduction by Multilateral Development Banks (MDBs) and the International Monetary Fund (IMF) which we requested in Cologne, and we look forward to receiving an annual poverty report as we review progress each year in reducing poverty across the globe. This report shows that progress is possible where the right conditions are created for growth and social development. But it reminds us of the vast challenges

that remain. While the percentage of poor in developing countries declined from 29% in 1990 to 24% in 1998, there are still 1.2 billion people living on less than one dollar a day and there are marked differences both within and between regions. In particular, many developing countries, notably in Africa, are growing too slowly. The HIV/AIDS pandemic aggravates the situation.

14. As the report indicates, many countries have made significant progress in overcoming poverty in the past quarter century, and their example is a beacon of hope for others. From their success, we have learned that poverty can best be overcome in resilient, peaceful, and democratic societies with freedom and opportunity for all, growing and open economies and dynamic private sectors, and strong and accountable leaders and institutions.

15. Robust, broad-based and equitable economic growth is needed to fight poverty and rests on expanding people's capabilities and choices. Government must, in co-operation with the private sector and broader civil society, establish economic and social foundations for broad-based, private sector growth. Small and medium sized enterprises, together with the opportunities presented by IT can be powerful tools for development. We will work with developing countries to put in place policies, programmes and institutions that offer people a fair chance to better their lives. We therefore welcome the constructive discussions of the Tenth Meeting of the United Nations Conference on Trade and Development (UNCTAD X) in Bangkok, and will work in the United Nations and other fora to further reduce poverty, especially in the Least Developed Countries (LDCs).

16. We also welcome the increasing co-operation between the International Labour Organisation (ILO) and the International Financial Institutions (IFIs) in promoting adequate social protection and core labour standards. We urge the IFIs to incorporate these standards into their policy dialogue with member countries. In addition, we stress the importance of effective co-operation between the World Trade Organisation (WTO) and the ILO on the social dimensions of globalisation and trade liberalisation.

17. Trade and investment are critical to promoting sustainable economic growth and reducing poverty. We commit ourselves to put a higher priority on trade-related capacity-building activities. We are also concerned that certain regions remain marginalised as regards foreign direct investment, and that the 48 LDCs attract less than 1% of total foreign direct investment flows to the developing countries. We urge multilateral development organisations and financial institutions to support developing countries'

efforts to create a favourable trade and investment climate, including through the Poverty Reduction Strategy Papers (PRSPs) and the Integrated Framework (IF).

18. We are particularly concerned about the severity of the challenges facing the LDCs, particularly those in Africa, which are held back from sharing in the fruits of globalisation by a debilitating and self-reinforcing combination of conflict, poverty and weak governance.

19. We are committed to mobilising the instruments and resources of the international community to support and reinforce the efforts of these countries to combat and overcome these challenges, with particular priority on promoting equitable distribution of the benefits of growth through sound social policies, including regarding health and education. To this end, as we set out in detail below, we have agreed to:
    - Push forward the Heavily Indebted Poor Countries (HIPC) debt initiative;
    - Provide significantly improved access to our markets;
    - Strengthen the effectiveness of our official development assistance (ODA);
    - Implement an ambitious plan on infectious diseases, notably HIV/AIDS, malaria and tuberculosis (TB);
    - Follow up vigorously the conclusions of the recent Dakar Conference on Education by ensuring that additional resources are made available for basic education;
    - Address the widening digital divide;
    - Implement measures to prevent conflict, including by addressing the issue of illicit trade in diamonds.

20. ODA is essential in the fight against poverty. We commit ourselves to strengthening the effectiveness of our ODA in support of countries' own efforts to tackle poverty, including through national strategies for poverty reduction. We will take a long-term approach favouring those countries where governments have demonstrated a commitment to improve the well-being of their people through accountable and transparent management of resources devoted to development. To achieve increased effectiveness of ODA, we resolve to untie our aid to the Least Developed Countries on the basis of progress made in the Organisation for Economic Co-operation and Development (OECD) to date and a fair burden-sharing mechanism that we will agree with our OECD partners. We believe that this agreement should come into effect on 1 January 2002. In the meantime, we urge those countries which maintain low levels of untying of ODA to improve their

performance. We will also seek to demonstrate to the public that well-targeted ODA gets results, and on that basis will strive to give increased priority to such assistance. Well co-ordinated assistance is helpful for developing countries and we will consider how best to improve such co-ordination.

21. We also agree to give special attention to three issues — debt, health, and education, as a spur to growth.

Debt

22. Last year in Cologne, we agreed to launch the Enhanced HIPC Initiative to deliver faster, broader and deeper debt relief, releasing funds for investment in national poverty reduction strategies. We welcome endorsement of this initiative by the international community last autumn.

23. Since then, while further efforts are required, progress has been made in implementing the Enhanced HIPC Initiative. Nine countries (Benin, Bolivia, Burkina Faso, Honduras, Mauritania, Mozambique, Senegal, Tanzania and Uganda) have already reached their Decision Points and are seeing the benefits of the Initiative. Total debt relief under the HIPC Initiative for these countries should amount to more than US$15 billion in nominal terms (US$8.6 billion in Net Present Value).

24. We welcome the efforts being made by HIPCs to develop comprehensive and country-owned poverty reduction strategies through a participatory process involving civil society. IFIs should, along with other donors, help HIPCs prepare PRSPs and assist their financial resource management by providing technical assistance. We are concerned by the fact that a number of HIPCs are currently affected by military conflicts which prevent poverty reduction and delay debt relief. We call upon these countries to end their involvement in conflicts and to embark quickly upon the HIPC process. We agree to strengthen our efforts to help them prepare and come forward for debt relief, by asking our Ministers to make early contact with the countries in conflict to encourage them to create the right conditions to participate in the HIPC Initiative. We will work together to ensure that as many countries as possible reach their Decision Points, in line with the targets set in Cologne, giving due consideration to the progress of economic reforms and the need to ensure that the benefits of debt relief are targeted to assist the poor and most vulnerable. We will work expeditiously together with HIPCs and the IFIs to realise the expectation that 20 countries will reach the Decision Point within the framework of the Enhanced HIPC Initiative by the end of this year. In this regard, we welcome the

establishment of the Joint Implementation Committee by the World Bank and the IMF. We for our part will promote more responsible lending and borrowing practices to ensure that HIPCs will not again be burdened by unsupportable debt.

25. We note the progress made in securing the required financing of the IFIs for effective implementation of the Enhanced HIPC Initiative, and welcome pledges including those to the HIPC Trust Fund. We reaffirm our commitment to make available as quickly as possible the resources we have pledged in the spirit of fair burden sharing.

Health

26. Health is key to prosperity. Good health contributes directly to economic growth whilst poor health drives poverty. Infectious and parasitic diseases, most notably HIV/AIDS, TB and malaria, as well as childhood diseases and common infections, threaten to reverse decades of development and to rob an entire generation of hope for a better future. Only through sustained action and coherent international co-operation to fully mobilise new and existing medical, technical and financial resources, can we strengthen health delivery systems and reach beyond traditional approaches to break the vicious cycle of disease and poverty.

27. We have committed substantial resources to fighting infectious and parasitic diseases. As a result, together with the international community, we have successfully arrived at the final stage of polio and guinea worm eradication, and have begun to control onchocerciasis.

28. But we must go much further and we believe that the conditions are right for a step change in international health outcomes. We have widespread agreement on what the priority diseases are and basic technologies to tackle much of the health burden are in place. In addition there is growing political leadership and recognition in the most afflicted countries that health is central to economic development. We particularly welcome the success of the recent HIV/AIDS conference held in Durban and the importance attached to tackling HIV/AIDS by African leaders, donors, international financial institutions and the private sector.

29. We therefore commit ourselves to working in strengthened partnership with governments, the World Health Organisation (WHO) and other international organisations, industry (notably pharmaceutical companies), academic institutions, NGOs and other relevant actors in civil society to deliver three critical UN targets:

- Reduce the number of HIV/AIDS-infected young people by 25% by 2010 (UN Secretary-General Report to the General Assembly on 27/3/2000);
- Reduce TB deaths and prevalence of the disease by 50% by 2010 (WHO Stop TB Initiative);
- Reduce the burden of disease associated with malaria by 50% by 2010 (WHO Roll Back Malaria).

30. In order to achieve this ambitious agenda our partnership must aim to cover:
   - Mobilising additional resources ourselves, and calling on the MDBs to expand their own assistance to the maximum extent possible;
   - Giving priority to the development of equitable and effective health systems, expanded immunisation, nutrition and micro-nutrients and the prevention and treatment of infectious diseases;
   - Promoting political leadership through enhanced high-level dialogue designed to raise public awareness in the affected countries;
   - Committing to support innovative partnerships, including with the NGOs, the private sector and multilateral organisations;
   - Working to make existing cost-effective interventions, including key drugs, vaccines, treatments and preventive measures more universally available and affordable in developing countries;
   - Addressing the complex issue of access to medicines in developing countries, and assessing obstacles being faced by developing countries in that regard;
   - Strengthening co-operation in the area of basic research and development on new drugs, vaccines and other international public health goods.

31. We note with encouragement new commitments in these areas. We strongly welcome the World Bank's commitment to triple International Development Association (IDA) financing for HIV/AIDS, malaria, and TB. We also welcome the announcements to expand assistance in this area made by bilateral donors.

32. In addition, we will convene a conference in the autumn this year in Japan to deliver agreement on a new strategy to harness our commitments. The conference should look to define the operations of this new partnership, the areas of priority and the timetable for action. Participation of developing country partners and other stakeholders will be essential. We will take stock of progress at the Genoa Summit next year and will also work with the UN to organise a conference in 2001 focusing on strategies to facilitate access to AIDS treatment and care.

Education

33. Every child deserves a good education. But in some developing countries access to education is limited, particular for females and the socially vulnerable. Basic education not only has intrinsic value, but is also key to addressing a wide range of problems faced by developing countries. Without accelerated progress in this area, poverty reduction will not be achieved and inequalities between countries and within societies will widen. Building on the Cologne Education Charter, we therefore support the Dakar Framework for Action as well as the recommendations of the recently concluded follow-up to the Fourth World Conference on Women, and welcome the efforts of developing countries to implement strong national action plans. We reaffirm our commitment that no government seriously committed to achieving education for all will be thwarted in this achievement by lack of resources.

34. We therefore commit ourselves to strengthen efforts bilaterally and together with international organisations and private sector donors to achieve the goals of universal primary education by 2015 and gender equality in schooling by 2005. We call on IFIs, in partnership with developing countries, to focus on education in their poverty reduction strategies and provide greater assistance for countries with sound education strategies. These strategies should maximise the potential benefits of IT in this area through distance learning wherever possible and other effective means.

Trade

35. The multilateral trading system embodied by the WTO, which represents the achievements of half a century of untiring efforts on the part of the international community to realise rule-based free trade, has provided its Members, developed and developing countries alike, with enormous trade opportunities, spurring economic growth and promoting social progress. In order to extend these benefits to a greater number of countries in a more tangible manner, the system needs to better address legitimate concerns of its developing country members, particularly the LDCs. The adoption of the short-term package in Geneva, regarding implementation of Uruguay Round undertakings, increased market access for the LDCs, technical assistance for enhanced capacity building as well as improvement in WTO transparency, was an important first step in this direction and must be pursued expeditiously. We recognise the need to go further with

greater urgency in this area. And we will do so. In particular, in view of critical importance of trade for the development of developing countries, trade-related capacity building should be substantially expanded, which would be conducive to the more effective participation of developing countries in the system, and especially to fuller utilisation of improved market access in their favour. We also commend bilateral and regional initiatives in this regard. We commit ourselves to playing a leading role by strengthening our support to developing country members for capacity building in line with their individual needs. We also call on international organisations including the WTO, the World Bank, the IMF, the United Nations Development Programme (UNDP), and UNCTAD, to join with us in working collectively toward this objective.

36. We must ensure that the multilateral trading system is strengthened and continues to play its vital role in the world economy. Recognising this responsibility, we are firmly committed to a new round of WTO trade negotiations with an ambitious, balanced and inclusive agenda, reflecting the interests of all WTO members. We agree that the objective of such negotiations should be to enhance market access, develop and strengthen WTO rules and disciplines, support developing countries in achieving economic growth and integration into the global trading system, and ensure that trade and social policies, and trade and environmental policies are compatible and mutually supportive. We agree to intensify our close and fruitful co-operation in order to try together with other WTO members to launch such a round during the course of this year.

37. We recognise that more comprehensive partnership must be developed to help address the challenges of globalisation. In this regard, international and domestic policy coherence should be enhanced, and co-operation between the international institutions should be improved. We also underline the importance of our engagement with our publics to establish a constructive dialogue on the benefits and challenges of trade liberalisation.

38. It is in our common interest to integrate all economies into the multilateral trading system. We therefore welcome the progress made on China's accession to the WTO and support the efforts of other applicants toward early accession.

Cultural Diversity

39. Cultural diversity is a source of social and economic dynamism which has the potential to enrich human life in the 21st century, as it inspires creativity and stimulates innovation. We recognise and respect the importance of diversity in linguistic and creative expression. We welcome the work of relevant international organisations, in particular the United Nations Educational, Scientific and Cultural Organisation (UNESCO), in this field.

40. Increased interaction among peoples, groups and individuals is bringing greater understanding of and appreciation for what is interesting and good in every culture. Promoting cultural diversity enhances mutual respect, inclusion and non-discrimination, and combats racism and xenophobia. We renew our strong support for the work of the United Nations in its preparations for the UN World Conference against Racism to be held in South Africa in 2001. The first steps toward enhancing cultural diversity are the preservation and promotion of cultural heritage. We welcome efforts already made to preserve tangible heritage and call for further efforts toward the preservation and promotion of intangible heritage. We encourage programmes dedicated to protect movable art and archaeological wealth in developing countries, as well as UNESCO's projects on Masterpieces of the Oral and Intangible Heritage of Humanity.

41. Increased encounters between different cultures foster creative cultural interaction. IT opens up unprecedented opportunities for individuals to create and share cultural content and ideas inexpensively and world wide. Experience shows that diversity can arouse interest, engender initiative and be a positive factor in communities seeking to improve their economies, particularly when assisted by the extraordinary means of the IT society. We shall strive to promote the digitalisation of cultural heritage through, for example, fostering international links between national museum systems, with a view to enhancing public access.

42. To maximise the benefits of cultural interaction, we must encourage our peoples to learn to live together by nurturing interest, understanding and acceptance of different cultures. We therefore welcome the results of the G8 Education Ministers' Meeting on the promotion of education that fosters understanding of different cultures and non-mother tongue languages and encourage competent authorities to promote exchange of students, teachers, researchers and administrators with the goal of doubling the rate of mobility over the next ten years.

Toward a 21st Century of Deeper Peace of Mind

Crime and Drugs

43. Everyone deserves a life free from the threat of crime. Rapid globalisation has opened up new opportunities for pursuing more fulfilling lives. But it has also created new room for criminal exploitation, challenging the basic rules of our social, economic and political systems. We reaffirm our support for the adoption by the end of 2000 of the United Nations Transnational Organised Crime Convention and three related Protocols on firearms, smuggling of migrants and trafficking in persons for the establishment of an effective legal framework against transnational organised crime (TOC). We are particularly concerned to fight against those who organise and take advantage of illegal immigration and human trafficking. We appreciate the work undertaken by the Lyon Group in the fight against TOC, and request them to report back to our next meeting. We also endorse the results of the Moscow G8 Ministerial Conference on Combating Transnational Organised Crime.

44. We must take a concerted approach to high-tech crime, such as cyber-crime, which could seriously threaten security and confidence in the global information society. Our approach is set out in the Okinawa Charter on Global Information Society. Taking this forward, we will promote dialogue with industry, including at the joint Berlin meeting in October. We welcome the results and the momentum created by the Government/Industry Dialogue on Safety and Confidence in Cyberspace in Paris, and look forward to the second High-level Meeting on High-tech Crime with industry to be held in Japan.

45. We reaffirm our concern at the increasing global threat posed by the trafficking and use of illegal drugs. We remain committed to reducing demand in our own countries, and to countering the threat from the production and trafficking of illicit drugs globally. We will work with other countries, the UN system and other groups to reduce both supply and demand. We will support regional initiatives to end narcotics production and trafficking. We urge universal implementation of the conclusions of the 1998 UN Special Session on countering the world drugs problem. We are also committed to strengthening international co-operation to:
    - Combat the illicit diversion of precursor chemicals for the production of illegal drugs;
    - Address the growing new threat from amphetamines and other synthetic drugs, and will convene an ad hoc meeting of drugs experts by the end of this year;

- Accelerate the pace of work on asset confiscation;
- Examine, by means of an international conference hosted by the United Kingdom, the global economy of illegal drugs.

46. Financial crime, including money laundering, poses a serious threat to our economies and societies. We hereby declare our commitment to take all necessary national and international action to effectively combat financial crime, in line with international standards.

47. We renew our commitment to combat corruption. We stress the need for transparency in government in this regard, and call for the ratification and effective implementation of the OECD Anti-Bribery Convention by all signatory parties. Working with other countries, we will prepare for the launch of negotiations in the United Nations on a new instrument against corruption, and instruct the Lyon Group to pursue work on this issue. We look forward to the Second Global Forum to be hosted by the Netherlands as a continued response to our call at Birmingham.

48. Enhanced investigation and prosecution of crime requires enhanced judicial co-operation. We direct our experts to find ways to do so.

49. We must assist capacity-building efforts in the more vulnerable jurisdictions to strengthen their criminal justice systems, in order to prevent criminal groups from threatening their social, economic and political structures and exploiting them as loopholes in the global framework to fight crime.

50. We must also protect vulnerable groups and the young in the fight against crime, and provide particular care for the victims of crime. We reaffirm the need for effective co-operation among competent authorities and for measures to be taken in co-operation with civil society.

Ageing

51. The progressive ageing of our populations compels us to rethink the conventional concept of a three-stage life cycle of education, employment and retirement. As the vitality of our societies increasingly depends on active participation by older people, we must foster economic and social conditions, including IT-related developments, that allow people of all ages to remain fully integrated into society, to enjoy freedom in deciding how to relate and contribute to society, and to find fulfilment in doing so. The concept of "active ageing", as articulated at the Denver Summit, remains our guiding principle in this endeavour.

52. The central challenge is to promote a culture that values the experience and knowledge that come with age. To this end, we will:

- Make further efforts to remove inappropriate disincentives for people below retirement age to stay in the labour market;
- Counter age prejudice in employment;
- Encourage life-long learning so that people can remain active through the accelerating transition toward an information society;
- Pursue healthy ageing policies that permit a continued high quality of life;
- Seek to increase relevant cross-national research, including comparable longitudinal surveys;
- Engage with the private sector and civil society in promoting older people's participation in community and volunteer activities.

53. In pursuing these objectives we attach continued importance to international co-operation and policy dialogue, and encourage the OECD to continue its work in this area.
54. We look forward to the upcoming meeting of G8 Labour and Social Affairs Ministers in Italy in November.

Life Science

Biotechnology/Food Safety

55. Maintenance of effective national food safety systems and public confidence in them assumes critical importance in public policy. We are committed to continued efforts to make systems responsive to the growing public awareness of food safety issues, the potential risks associated with food, the accelerating pace of developments in biotechnology, and the increasing cross-border movement of food and agricultural products.
56. The commitment to a science-based, rule-based approach remains a key principle underlying these endeavours. The on-going work in international fora to develop and refine such an approach needs to be accelerated. In particular, we attach strong importance to the work of the CODEX Alimentarius Commission (CAC), the principal standard-setting body in food safety, and encourage its AD HOC INTERGOVERNMENTAL TASK FORCE ON FOODS DERIVED FROM BIOTECHNOLOGY to produce a substantial interim report before completion of its mandate in 2003. We also support the efforts of the CAC's Committee on General Principles to achieve greater global consensus on how precaution should be applied to food safety in circumstances where available scientific information is incomplete or contradictory.
57. Policy dialogue, engaging all stakeholders and including both developed and developing countries, must be intensified to advance health protection,

facilitate trade, ensure the sound development of biotechnology, and foster consumer confidence and public acceptance. The report by the OECD Ad Hoc Group on Food Safety and the work of the Task Force for the Safety of Novel Foods and Feeds and the Working Group on Harmonisation of Regulatory Oversight of Biotechnology represent a useful step in this direction. We welcome the further work agreed by OECD ministers. We note with approval that the OECD will continue to undertake analytical work and to play an effective role in international policy dialogue on food safety, maintaining its engagement with civil society and seeking to share its work in this area with countries outside the organisation's membership. Drawing on its comparative advantages, the work of the OECD will effectively complement the activities of other international organisations, in particular the Food and Agriculture Organisation (FAO) and WHO. We also encourage the FAO and WHO to organise periodic international meetings of food safety regulators to advance the process of science-based public consultations.

58. In pursuing this dialogue we will pay particular attention to the needs, opportunities and constraints in developing countries. We will work to strengthen our support for their capacity building to harness the potentials of biotechnology, and encourage research and development as well as data and information sharing in technologies, including those that address global food security, health, nutritional and environmental challenges and are adapted to specific conditions in these countries.

59. Open and transparent consultation with and involvement of all stakeholders, including representatives of civil society, supported by shared scientific understanding, is a key component of a credible food and crop safety system. We note the proposal to establish an independent international panel put forward at the recent OECD Edinburgh Conference. Building on the success of that Conference, we will explore, in consultation with international organisations and interested bodies including scientific academies, the way to integrate the best scientific knowledge available into the global process of consensus building on biotechnology and other aspects of food and crop safety.

Human Genome

60. Advances in life science continuously improve our quality of life. Opening new medical frontiers points to unprecedented opportunities for the benefit of humankind and will have to be achieved taking account of principles of bioethics.

61. The announcement of the nearly complete mapping of the human genome, a momentous discovery in itself, constitutes a further dramatic and welcome step in this development.

62. We consider this mapping to be critically important for all humanity and call for the further rapid release of all raw fundamental data on human DNA sequences as such. We also emphasise the importance of pursuing the post genome-sequence research on the basis of multilateral collaboration.

63. We recognise the need for a balanced and equitable intellectual property protection for gene-based inventions, based wherever possible on common practices and policies. We encourage further efforts in relevant international fora to achieve broad harmonisation of patenting policies of biotechnological inventions.

Environment

64. We must all work to preserve a clean and sound environment for our children and grandchildren. We welcome the results of the G8 Environment Ministers' Meeting in Otsu. We also welcome the conclusion of the Cartagena Protocol on Biosafety, and encourage the parties concerned to work for its early entry into force.

65. We will endeavour with all our partners to prepare a future-oriented agenda for Rio+10 in 2002. We are strongly committed to close co-operation among ourselves and with developing countries to resolve as soon as possible all major outstanding issues, with a view to early entry into force of the Kyoto Protocol. To that end, we are determined to achieve a successful outcome at the Sixth Conference of the Parties to the Framework Convention on Climate Change (COP6), in order to achieve the goals of the Kyoto Protocol through undertaking strong domestic actions and supplemental flexibility mechanisms.

66. Working together and with existing institutions to encourage and facilitate investment in the development and use of sustainable energy, underpinned by enabling domestic environments, will assist in mitigating the problems of climate change and air pollution. To this end, the increased use of renewable energy sources in particular will improve the quality of life, especially in developing countries. We therefore call on all stakeholders to identify the barriers and solutions to elevating the level of renewable energy supply and distribution in developing countries. We invite stakeholders to join in a Task Force to prepare concrete recommendations for consideration at our next Summit regarding sound ways to better encourage the use of renewables in developing countries.

67. We fully endorse the conclusions of our Foreign Ministers regarding sustainable forest management. In this regard, we attach particular importance to projects that help indigenous and local communities practice sustainable forest management. We will also examine how best we can combat illegal logging, including export and procurement practices.

68. Export credit policies may have very significant environmental impacts. We welcome the adoption of the OECD work plan to be completed by 2001. We reaffirm our commitment to develop common environmental guidelines, drawing on relevant MDB experience, for export credit agencies by the 2001 G8 Summit. We will co-operate to reinvigorate and intensify our work to fulfil the Cologne mandate.

69. Strengthening international maritime safety is vital for the protection of the ocean environment, a global heritage. We will jointly co-operate with the International Maritime Organisation (IMO) to improve maritime safety. We endorse efforts by the IMO to strengthen safety standards, in particular for ships carrying dangerous or polluting cargo, and to verify implementation and enforcement of the application of international standards by flag States. We also endorse efforts by coastal states to enhance safety of navigation and protection of their marine environment through the use, where appropriate, of IMO-adopted routing and reporting measures. We encourage the early achievement of these goals.

70. We welcome the IMO efforts to pursue practical reform of current international regimes on maritime pollution, in particular the 1992 Convention on Civil Liability for Oil Pollution Damage and the 1992 International Oil Pollution Compensation (IOPC) Convention with respect to, inter alia, better compensation.

Nuclear Safety

71. We renew the commitment we made at the 1996 Moscow Summit to safety first in the use of nuclear power and achievement of high safety standards world wide. We agreed to continue to co-operate in promoting a high standard of nuclear safety. We continue to attach great importance to the full and timely implementation of the Nuclear Safety Account Grant Agreement.

Toward a 21st Century of Greater World Stability

Conflict Prevention

72. The international community should act urgently and effectively to prevent and resolve armed conflict. Many people have been sacrificed and injured, many economies have been impoverished, and much devastation has been visited upon the environment. In an ever more interdependent world such negative effects spread rapidly. Therefore, a "Culture of Prevention" should be promoted throughout the global community. All members of the international community should seek to promote the settlement of disputes by peaceful means in accordance with the Charter of the United Nations.

73. We underline the importance of the work done by our Foreign Ministers on conflict prevention since their special meeting in December 1999 in Berlin and the Conclusions of their July 2000 meeting in Miyazaki. We commit ourselves to work for their implementation particularly with respect to economic development and conflict prevention, children in conflict, and international civilian police. We express special concern that the proceeds from the illicit trade in diamonds have contributed to aggravating armed conflict and humanitarian crises, particularly in Africa. We therefore call for an international conference, whose results shall be submitted to the UN, building on the UN Security Council Resolution 1306 and inter alia the 'Kimberley' process launched by the Government of South Africa, to consider practical approaches to breaking the link between the illicit trade in diamonds and armed conflict, including consideration of an international agreement on certification for rough diamonds. The UN Conference on the Illicit Trade in Small Arms and Light Weapons in All Its Aspects next year requires strong support to ensure a successful outcome, including earliest possible agreement on the Firearms Protocol. We invite the international community to exercise restraint in conventional arms exports, and are committed to work jointly to this end. We invite our Foreign Ministers to examine further effective measures to prevent conflicts.

Disarmament, Non-proliferation and Arms Control

74. We welcome the successful outcome of the 2000 Nuclear Non-Proliferation Treaty (NPT) Review Conference. We are determined to implement the conclusions reached at this Conference, including the early entry into force of the Comprehensive Nuclear-Test-Ban Treaty (CTBT) and the immediate

commencement and the conclusion within five years of negotiations for the Fissile Material Cut-Off Treaty. We remain committed to promoting universal adherence to and compliance with the NPT.

75. We look forward to the early entry into force and full implementation of the Strategic Arms Reduction Treaty (START) II and to the conclusion of START III as soon as possible, while preserving and strengthening the Anti-Ballistic Missile (ABM) Treaty as a cornerstone of strategic stability and as a basis for further reductions of strategic offensive weapons, in accordance with its provisions. We welcome the ratification of the CTBT and START II by Russia.

76. The transparent, safe, secure, environmentally sound and irreversible disposition and management of weapon-grade plutonium no longer required for defence purposes remains vital. The agreement on plutonium disposition reached between the United States and Russia, reinforced by their statement of intention concerning non-separation of additional weapon-grade plutonium, marks a critical milestone. The co-operation among the G8 countries has yielded significant results and our next steps should build on this co-operation and related international projects.

77. Our goal for the next Summit is to develop an international financing plan for plutonium management and disposition based on a detailed project plan, and a multilateral framework to co-ordinate this co-operation. We will expand our co-operation to other interested countries in order to gain the widest possible international support, and will explore the potential for both public and private funding.

78. We welcome the reinforcement of global regimes to prevent proliferation of weapons of mass destruction and their delivery systems. We also recognise the need to examine and promote further multilateral measures to curb missile proliferation. In this regard, we strongly support the important work of the Missile Technology Control Regime (MTCR) and will consider the proposal for a Global Monitoring System. We will work to increase the level of international contributions to the Russian chemical weapons destruction programme. We commit ourselves to work with others to conclude the negotiations on the Verification Protocol to strengthen the Biological Weapons Convention as early as possible in 2001.

Terrorism

79. We renew our condemnation of all forms of terrorism regardless of their motivation. We are determined to combat them. We call for the urgent

strengthening of international co-operation, in particular in exchanges of counter-terrorism information, improving measures against the financing of terrorist activities, and working together to bring terrorists to justice. We welcome the adoption of the International Convention for the Suppression of the Financing of Terrorism. We call for all states to become parties to the twelve international counter-terrorism conventions to enhance international co-operation against terrorism.

80. We are deeply concerned at the increased number of terrorist acts, including hijacking and taking of hostages. We express our great concern over the continuing pattern of terrorist activities in many regions. We will continue to raise this in our bilateral contacts, carefully monitor developments and maintain close co-operation between us.

81. In this regard, emphasising the international concern over the terrorist threat emanating from Afghan territory under the control of the Taliban, we call for full implementation of the UNSCR 1267.

Next Summit

82. We have accepted the invitation of the Prime Minister of Italy to meet in Genoa next year. To enhance communications in the meantime, we have agreed to establish an e-mail network among ourselves.

C Okinawa Charter on Global Information Society

OKINAWA, JULY 22, 2000

1. Information and Communications Technology (IT) is one of the most potent forces in shaping the twenty-first century. Its revolutionary impact affects the way people live, learn and work and the way government interacts with civil society. IT is fast becoming a vital engine of growth for the world economy. It is also enabling many enterprising individuals, firms and communities, in all parts of the globe, to address economic and social challenges with greater efficiency and imagination. Enormous opportunities are there to be seized and shared by us all.

2. The essence of the IT-driven economic and social transformation is its power to help individuals and societies to use knowledge and ideas. Our vision of an information society is one that better enables people to fulfil their potential and realise their aspirations. To this end we must ensure that IT serves the mutually supportive goals of creating sustainable economic growth, enhancing the public welfare, and fostering social cohesion, and work to fully realise its potential to strengthen democracy, increase transparency and accountability in governance, promote human rights, enhance cultural diversity, and to foster international peace and stability. Meeting these goals and addressing emerging challenges will require effective national and international strategies.

3. In pursuing these objectives, we renew our commitment to the principle of inclusion: everyone, everywhere should be enabled to participate in and no one should be excluded from the benefits of the global information society. The resilience of this society depends on democratic values that foster human development such as the free flow of information and knowledge, mutual tolerance, and respect for diversity.

4. We will exercise our leadership in advancing government efforts to foster an appropriate policy and regulatory environment to stimulate competition and innovation, ensure economic and financial stability, advance stakeholder collaboration to optimise global networks, fight abuses that undermine the integrity of the network, bridge the digital divide, invest in people, and promote global access and participation.

5. Above all, this Charter represents a call to all, in both the public and private sectors to bridge the international information and knowledge divide. A solid framework of IT-related policies and action can change the way in which we interact, while promoting social and economic opportunities worldwide. An effective partnership among stakeholders, including through joint policy co-operation, is also key to the sound development of a truly global information society.

Seizing Digital Opportunities

6. The potential benefits of IT in spurring competition, promoting enhanced productivity, and creating and sustaining economic growth and jobs hold significant promise. Our task is not only to stimulate and facilitate the transition to an information society, but also to reap its full economic, social and cultural benefits. To achieve this, it is important to build on the following key foundations:
   - Economic and structural reforms to foster an environment of openness, efficiency, competition and innovation, supported by policies focusing on adaptable labour markets, human resource development, and social cohesion;
   - Sound macroeconomic management to help businesses and consumers plan confidently for the future and exploit the advantages of new information technologies;
   - Development of information networks offering fast, reliable, secure and affordable access through competitive market conditions and through related innovation in network technology, services and applications;
   - Development of human resources capable of responding to the demands of the information age through education and lifelong learning and addressing the rising demand for IT professionals in many sectors of our economy;
   - Active utilisation of IT by the public sector and the promotion of online delivery of services, which are essential to ensure improved accessibility to government by all citizens.
7. The private sector plays a leading role in the development of information and communications networks in the information society. But it is up to governments to create a predictable, transparent and non-discriminatory policy and regulatory environment necessary for the information society. It is important to avoid undue regulatory interventions that would hinder productive

private-sector initiatives in creating an IT-friendly environment. We should ensure that IT-related rules and practices are responsive to revolutionary changes in economic transactions, while taking into account the principles of effective public-private sector partnership, transparency and technological neutrality. The rules must be predictable and inspire business and consumer confidence. In order to maximise the social and economic benefits of the Information Society, we agree on the following key principles and approaches and commend them to others:

- Continue to promote competition in and open markets for the provision of information technology and telecommunications products and services, including non-discriminatory and cost-oriented interconnection for basic telecommunications;
- Protection of intellectual property rights for IT-related technology is vital to promoting IT-related innovations, competition and diffusion of new technology; we welcome the joint work already underway among intellectual property authorities and further encourage our experts to discuss future direction in this area;
- Governments' renewed commitment to using software in full compliance with intellectual property rights protection is also important;
- A number of services, including telecommunications, transportation, and package delivery are critical to the information society and economy and improving their efficiency will maximise benefits; customs and other trade-related procedures are also important to foster an IT-friendly environment;
- Facilitate cross-border e-commerce by promoting further liberalisation and improvement in networks and related services and procedures in the context of a strong World Trade Organisation (WTO) framework, continued work on e-commerce in the WTO and other international fora, and application of existing WTO trade disciplines to e-commerce;
- Consistent approaches to taxation of e-commerce based on the conventional principles, including neutrality, equity and simplicity, and other key elements agreed in the work of the Organisation for Economic Co-operation and Development (OECD);
- Continuing the practice of not imposing customs duties on electronic transmissions, pending the review at the next WTO Ministerial Conference;
- Promotion of market-driven standards including, for example, interoperable technical standards;
- Promote consumer trust in the electronic marketplace consistent with OECD guidelines and provide equivalent consumer protection in the

online world as in the offline world, including through effective self-regulatory initiatives such as online codes of conduct, trustmarks and other reliability programmes, and explore options to alleviate the difficulties faced by consumers in cross-border disputes, including use of alternative dispute resolution mechanisms;

- Development of effective and meaningful privacy protection for consumers, as well as protection of privacy in processing personal data, while safeguarding the free flow of information, and;

- Further development and effective functioning of electronic authentication, electronic signature, cryptography, and other means to ensure security and certainty of transactions.

8. International efforts to develop a global information society must be accompanied by co-ordinated action to foster a crime-free and secure cyberspace. We must ensure that effective measures, as set out in the OECD Guidelines for Security of Information Systems, are put in place to fight cyber-crime. G8 co-operation within the framework of the Lyon Group on Transnational Organised Crime will be enhanced. We will further promote dialogue with industry, building on the success of the recent G8 Paris Conference "A Government/Industry Dialogue on Safety and Confidence in Cyberspace". Urgent security issues such as hacking and viruses also require effective policy responses. We will continue to engage industry and other stakeholders to protect critical information infrastructures.

Bridging the Digital Divide

9. Bridging the digital divide in and among countries has assumed a critical importance on our respective national agendas. Everyone should be able to enjoy access to information and communications networks. We reaffirm our commitment to the efforts underway to formulate and implement a coherent strategy to address this issue. We also welcome the increasing recognition on the part of industry and civil society of the need to bridge the divide. Mobilising their expertise and resources is an indispensable element of our response to this challenge. We will continue to pursue an effective partnership between government and civil societies responsive to the rapid pace of technological and market developments.

10. A key component of our strategy must be the continued drive toward universal and affordable access. We will continue to:

- Foster market conditions conducive to the provision of affordable communications services;
- Explore other complementary means, including access through publicly available facilities;
- Give priority to improving network access, especially in underserved urban, rural and remote areas;
- Pay particular attention to the needs and constraints of the socially under-privileged, people with disabilities, and older persons and actively pursue measures to facilitate their access and use;
- Encourage further development of "user-friendly", "barrier-free" technologies, including mobile access to the Internet, as well as greater utilisation of free and publicly available contents in a way which respects intellectual property rights.

11. The policies for the advancement of the Information Society must be underpinned by the development of human resources capable of responding to the demands of the information age. We are committed to provide all our citizens with an opportunity to nurture IT literacy and skills through education, lifelong learning and training. We will continue to work toward this ambitious goal by getting schools, classrooms and libraries online and teachers skilled in IT and multimedia resources. Measures aiming to offer support and incentives for small-to-medium-sized enterprises and the self-employed to get online and use the Internet effectively will also be pursued. We will also encourage the use of IT to offer innovative lifelong learning opportunities, particularly to those who otherwise could not access education and training.

Promoting Global Participation

12. IT represents a tremendous opportunity for emerging and developing economies. Countries that succeed in harnessing its potential can look forward to leapfrogging conventional obstacles of infrastructural development, to meeting more effectively their vital development goals, such as poverty reduction, health, sanitation, and education, and to benefiting from the rapid growth of global e-commerce. Some developing countries have already made significant progress in these areas.

13. The challenge of bridging the international information and knowledge divide cannot, however, be underestimated. We recognise the priority being given to this by many developing countries. Indeed, those developing countries which fail to keep up with the accelerating pace of IT innovation

may not have the opportunity to participate fully in the information society and economy. This is particularly so where the existing gaps in terms of basic economic and social infrastructures, such as electricity, telecommunications and education, deter the diffusion of IT.

14. In responding to this challenge, we recognise that the diverse conditions and needs of the developing countries should be taken into account. There is no "one-size-fits-all" solution. It is critically important for developing countries to take ownership through the adoption of coherent national strategies to: build an IT-friendly, pro-competitive policy and regulatory environment; exploit IT in pursuit of development goals and social cohesion; develop human resources endowed with IT skills; and encourage community initiatives and indigenous entrepreneurship.

The Way Forward

15. Efforts to bridge the international divide, as in our societies, crucially depend on effective collaboration among all stakeholders. Bilateral and multilateral assistance will continue to play a significant role in building the framework conditions for IT development. International Financial Institutions (IFIs), including Multilateral Development Banks (MDBs), particularly the World Bank, are well placed to contribute in this regard by formulating and implementing programmes that foster growth, benefit the poor, as well as expand connectivity, access and training. The International Telecommunications Union (ITU), the United Nations Conference on Trade and Development (UNCTAD) and the United Nations Development Programme (UNDP) and other relevant international fora, also have an important role to play. The private sector remains a central actor driving IT forward in developing countries and can contribute significantly to the international efforts to bridge the digital divide. NGOs, with their unique ability to reach grassroots areas, can usefully contribute to human resource and community development. IT, in short, is global in dimension, and thus requires a global response.

16. We welcome efforts already underway to bridge the international digital divide through bilateral development aid and by international organisations and private groups. We also welcome contributions from the private sector, such as those of the Global Digital Divide Initiative of the World Economic Forum (WEF), the Global Business Dialogue on E-Commerce (GBDe), and the Global Forum.

17. As highlighted by the UN Economic and Social Council (ECOSOC) Ministerial Declaration on the role of IT in the context of a knowledge-based global economy, there is a need for greater international dialogue and collaboration to improve the effectiveness of IT-related programmes and projects with developing countries, and to bring together the "best practices" and mobilise the resources available from all stakeholders to help close the digital divide. The G8 will seek to promote the creation of a stronger partnership among developed and developing countries, civil society including private firms and NGOs, foundations and academic institutions, and international organisations. We will also work to see that developing countries can, in partnership with other stakeholders, be provided with financial, technical and policy input in order to create a better environment for, and use of, IT.

18. We agree to establish a Digital Opportunity Taskforce (dot force) with a view to integrating our efforts into a broader international approach. To this end, the dot force will convene as soon as possible to explore how best to secure participation of stakeholders. This high-level Taskforce, in close consultation with other partners and in a manner responsive to the needs of developing countries, will:
    - Actively facilitate discussions with developing countries, international organisations and other stakeholders to promote international co-operation with a view to fostering policy, regulatory and network readiness; improving connectivity, increasing access and lowering cost; building human capacity; and encouraging participation in global e-commerce networks;
    - Encourage the G8's own efforts to co-operate on IT-related pilot programmes and projects;
    - Promote closer policy dialogue among partners and work to raise global public awareness of the challenges and opportunities;
    - Examine inputs from the private sector and other interested groups such as the Global Digital Divide Initiative's contributions;
    - Report its findings and activities to our personal representatives before our next meeting in Genoa.

19. In pursuit of these objectives, the dot force will look for ways to take concrete steps on the priorities identified below:
    - Fostering policy, regulatory and network readiness;
    - supporting policy advice and local capacity building, to promote a pro-competitive, flexible and socially inclusive policy and regulatory environment;

- facilitating the sharing of experience between developing countries and other partners;
- encouraging more effective and greater utilisation of IT in development efforts encompassing such broad areas as poverty reduction, education, public health, and culture;
- promoting good governance, including exploration of new methods of inclusive policy development;
- supporting efforts of MDBs and other international organisations to pool intellectual and financial resources in the context of co-operation programmes such as InfoDev;
- Improving connectivity, increasing access and lowering cost:
  - mobilising resources to improve information and communications infrastructure, with a particular emphasis on a "partnership" approach involving governments, international organisations, the private sector, and NGOs;
  - working on ways to reduce the cost of connectivity for developing countries;
  - supporting community access programmes;
  - encouraging research and development on technology and applications adapted to specific requirements in developing countries;
  - improving interoperability of networks, services, and applications;
  - encouraging the production of locally relevant and informative content including in the development of the content in various mother tongues.
- Building human capacity:
  - focusing on basic education as well as increased opportunities for life-long learning, with a particular emphasis on development of IT skills;
  - assisting the development of a pool of trained professionals in IT and other relevant policy areas and regulatory matters;
  - developing innovative approaches to extend the traditional reach of technical assistance, including distance learning and community-based training;
  - networking of public institutions and communities, including schools, research centres and universities.
- Encouraging participation in global e-commerce networks:
  - assessing and increasing e-commerce readiness and use, through provision of advice to start-up businesses in developing countries, and through mobilisation of resources to help businesses to use IT to improve their efficiency and access to new markets;
  - ensuring that the "rules of the game" as they are emerging are consistent with development efforts, and building developing country capacity to play a constructive role in determining these rules.

D Strengthening the International Financial Architecture: Report from G7 Finance Ministers to the Heads of State and Government

FUKUOKA, JAPAN, 8 JULY, 2000

A. Introduction

1. Following a series of crises that began in Asia in 1997, conditions in the world economy have stabilized and prospects for expansion have improved. However, in view of the rapid changes occurring in the global financial landscape, and in particular in light of the opportunities and challenges presented by the increasing size and importance of private capital markets, the international community must continue to address the challenge of promoting greater stability in the international financial system as a platform for sustainable world growth and prosperity.

2. We, Finance Ministers of the G-7 countries, submitted a report on strengthening the international financial architecture to the Cologne Economic Summit last year and set out a number of specific proposals toward reform. Since then, we have made substantial progress:

   a. Many developing countries are making efforts to enhance their financial stability by, for example, strengthening financial sectors, adopting appropriate foreign exchange regimes, improving debt management, and adopting internationally agreed codes and standards. Many of them are also making substantial investments in the information they provide to financial markets.

   b. The IMF has taken steps to implement an assessment framework for internationally agreed codes and standards and to make operational our approach to private sector involvement (PSI) in forestalling and resolving crises. Private sector investors and lenders have been more involved in the financing of recent IMF-led programs. In addition, the IMF Executive Board has deepened its discussions on exchange rate regimes, countries' experiences with capital controls, and other important issues. The transparency of the IMF and the Multilateral Development Banks (MDBs) has been significantly improved, including through greater publication of documents.

c. The Interim Committee has been was transformed into the permanent "International Monetary and Financial Committee (IMFC)".

d. The Financial Stability Forum (FSF) was created last year to enhance financial stability, improve the functioning of markets, and reduce systemic risk. As we requested, the FSF examined the issues of, and published reports this spring on highly leveraged institutions (HLIs), capital flows, and offshore financial centers (OFCs). The FSF also carried out work on the implementation of codes and standards on which it recently released a report.

e. The G-20 was established as an informal mechanism for dialogue among systemically important countries within the framework of the Bretton Woods institutional system. The first meeting of G-20 Finance Ministers and Central Bank Governors was held successfully in December of last year in Berlin. The next meeting will be held in October of this year in Montreal.

3. In this report, we discuss how we can further enhance our efforts to strengthen the international financial architecture, carrying forward the reform program that we identified in Cologne. Given the leading role of the International Financial Institutions (IFIs) in implementing a significant part of the Cologne reform program, this report focuses on i) reform of the IMF — especially reform of its facilities, the promotion of the implementation of codes and standards, the enhancement of governance and accountability, and private sector involvement; ii) reform of MDBs; iii) responses to the challenges posed by HLIs, OFCs and cross-border capital movements; and iv) regional cooperation.

4. We are determined to implement all the measures in this report, as well as the broad range of measures endorsed at the Cologne Summit. We will work together with other members of the international community to make steady progress.

B. IMF Reform

5. In view of the changing global financial landscape, and in particular the increasing importance of private global capital markets, we believe it is essential that the international community continues to examine the role and functioning of the IMF and other IFIs. We look forward to exploring this agenda further in Prague this fall at the next meeting of the IMFC and at the next Annual Meetings of the IMF and the World Bank.

Key Principles for Reform of the IMF

6. At our meeting with Central Bank Governors in April, we laid out the following key principles, which reflect our shared understanding of the IMF's role as we move forward:
   a. The IMF should play the central role in promoting macroeconomic and financial stability as an important precondition for sustainable global growth and should continue to evolve to meet the challenges of the future.
   b. The IMF is a universal institution which must work in partnership with all its member countries, based on their shared interests in these goals.
   c. To be effective, the IMF and its activities must be transparent to the public, accountable to its members and responsive to the lessons of experience and external and independent evaluation.
   d. In order to foster strong policies and reduce countries' financial vulnerability to crisis, preventing crisis and establishing a solid foundation for sustainable growth should be at the core of the IMF's work. Surveillance of economic and financial conditions and policies in member countries and the implementation of internationally agreed codes and standards are primary tools for accomplishing these aims.
   e. IMF's financial operations should continue to adapt to reflect the realities of global capital markets while preserving the flexibility to support all member countries, as appropriate, including those with no immediate prospects of market access. They should encourage countries to take preventive measures to reduce vulnerabilities and provide temporary and appropriately conditioned support for balance of payments adjustment, including in cases of crisis, and medium-term finance in defined circumstances in support of structural reform, while avoiding prolonged use.
   f. IMF lending should not distort the assessment of risk and return in international investment. To this end, the IMF should take appropriate

steps to ensure that the private sector is involved both in forestalling and resolving crises, which should help promote responsible behavior by private creditors.

g. While the World Bank is the central institution for poverty reduction, macroeconomic stability - a key tool for the achievement of poverty reduction and growth - is the responsibility of the IMF. The IMF has a crucial role in supporting macroeconomic stability in the poorest countries through the Poverty Reduction and Growth Facility, integrating its efforts with those of the World Bank in working with countries on poverty reduction strategies.

These principles will continue to guide our efforts on IMF reform moving forward in discussions within the IMF Executive Board and the IMFC, and in other fora as we work to implement concrete steps in advance of the Annual Meetings in Prague this fall.

Strengthening Surveillance to Prevent Crises

7. There is consensus within the international community that, as we emphasized in our April meeting, strong surveillance must be at the center of the IMF's efforts to strengthen the world economy and the international financial architecture. In this regard, we reaffirmed the importance of a substantial qualitative shift in the nature and scope of the Fund's surveillance needed in light of globalization, large scale private capital flows, and the emerging framework of internationally agreed codes and standards.

a. The IMF should, in conducting its surveillance work, continue to sharpen its focus on macroeconomic policy, capital flows and structural issues which have an impact on macroeconomic stability, in particular in the financial sector, and on exchange rates with a view toward encouraging countries to avoid unsustainable regimes.

b. The IMF should continue to work to develop and make systematic use of indicators of national liquidity and balance sheet risks as a key part of the surveillance process. We believe that the IMF should begin publishing such indicators regularly together with relevant explanatory material.

c. The IMF has an important role to play in promoting transparency and the flow of information. We support the IMF in its efforts to promote the publication by countries of comprehensive, timely, high quality and accurate information in line with the Special Data Dissemination Standard (SDDS) and welcome the IMF's decision to highlight in a quarterly publication countries' achievement in this respect. We also support further actions to enhance the transparency of IMF surveillance through, inter alia, more general use of Public Information Notices following Article IV consultations and Reports on the Observance of Standards and Codes (ROSCs). In this respect, we support the principle of the release of IMF Article IV staff report, and look forward to the conclusions of the IMF Board review on the pilot project in this area.

Implementation of International Codes and Standards

8. We are determined to strengthen our efforts to promote the implementation of internationally agreed codes and standards as follows.
   a. We confirm the IMF's leading and coordinating role in the assessment of countries' observance of international standards and codes and welcome the IMF's ongoing work in this area through Reports on the Observance of Standards and Codes (ROSCs) as well as through the joint IMF-World Bank Financial Sector Assessment Programs (FSAPs). We also welcome commitments by over 30 countries to undertake ROSC modules and the recent decisions by the IMF and the World Bank to expand the FSAP program. We look forward to consideration of the modalities for voluntary publication of Financial System Stability Assessment (FSSA) reports.
   b. We agree that the assessment process should cover the 12 key codes and standards highlighted in the Financial Stability Forum's Compendium of Standards, and be carried out on a modular basis. The IMF and national authorities, in consultation with the standard-setting bodies where appropriate, should be responsible for identifying priority standards for implementation by individual countries within the framework of a country's overall economic reform agenda. To enhance credibility, we encourage countries to articulate publicly their adoption of standards, announce their plans of action and participate in IMF-led assessment programs. In this regard, we welcome the commitments by the G-20 Ministers and Governors and by the Western Hemisphere Finance Ministers.
   c. We agree on the importance of addressing market and official incentives in promoting observance of codes and standards. In this context, we underscore the need for greater disclosure and transparency about countries' intentions and progress in implementing codes and standards. We call on the IMF to ensure that the results of assessments of observance of codes and standards are published, and to continue its work on

integrating such assessments into its regular Article IV surveillance process. We look forward to the results of further work by the Financial Stability Forum (FSF) on promoting market and official incentives, specifically regulatory and supervisory incentives. We also call on the IMF to explore further ways of promoting compliance with codes and standards. We look forward to further progress on an overall framework for the implementation of codes and standards at this year's Annual Meetings in Prague.

d. We agree that work to implement codes and standards will be most effective if combined with further efforts to foster ownership across a broad range of countries for the codes and standards processes. The IMF and the World Bank should assist countries in the development of action plans for the implementation of codes and standards. We agree to work together and with the IFIs, the FSF, and international regulatory and supervisory bodies to provide technical assistance and training to emerging market and developing countries in this area.

e. In order to facilitate the conduct of consistent and objective assessments of countries' adherence to codes and standards, there must be regular, transparent, and constructive dialogue and cooperation between the institutions and agencies responsible. To this end, we call upon the IMF to chair a meeting of the relevant bodies to determine and report on how best to ensure that inputs from the relevant bodies concerned can be most effectively integrated in the surveillance process managed by the IMF.

Reform of IMF Facilities

9. We reemphasize that the IMF's financial operations should continue to adapt to the globalization of capital markets, while preserving the flexibility to support all member countries, as appropriate, including those with no immediate prospects of market access, in light of their specific circumstances. Therefore, we attach priority to early progress in achieving a streamlined, incentives-based structure for IMF lending that encourages countries to develop stable access to private capital markets on a sustainable basis.

10. The IMF has already begun to simplify its facilities. Going forward, we continue to attach priority to the creation of a more effective structure for IMF lending consistent with this approach that would:

a. provide contingent support and incentives for countries to put in place strong ex ante policies to prevent crises, to observe internationally agreed standards and best practices, and to maintain good relations with private creditors (as is currently the case under the Contingent Credit Line (CCL));

b. address temporary balance of payment imbalances as well as medium-term financing in defined circumstances in support of structural reform, while at the same time encouraging countries to move toward sustainable access to private capital (as is currently the case under the Stand-By Arrangement (SBA) and the Extended Fund Facility (EFF));

c. allow the IMF to respond rapidly and on an appropriate scale to systemic crises with appropriate terms to mitigate moral hazard and encourage rapid repayment (as is currently the case under the Supplemental Reserve Facility (SRF));

d. maintain a strong, focused role for the IMF in supporting sound macroeconomic policies in the poorest countries, integrating its efforts with those of the World Bank given the latter's responsibility for promoting poverty reduction and growth-oriented programs (as is currently the case under the Poverty Reduction and Growth Facility (PRGF)).

11. Specifically, we expect that reform of IMF facilities will be conducted as soon as possible based on the following:

a. The pricing of non-concessional IMF facilities should be fair and reflect their underlying objectives. The new pricing structure should establish more consistent incentives across facilities, encourage access to private capital, discourage prolonged use of, and deter inappropriate large scale access to IMF resources, thus contributing to their more efficient use. For all non-concessional facilities, the interest rate should increase on a graduated basis the longer countries have IMF resources outstanding. The possibility of adding a premium when the scale of financing goes beyond certain thresholds should be explored. In addition, for countries that continuously resort to IMF facilities, the IMF should make more intensive use of prior actions and limit access to its resources.

b. We also look forward to consideration of steps to encourage early repurchases once the IMF borrowers have returned to a sustainable economic and financial path.

c. We call upon the IMF to explore, in the context of the review of its facilities, appropriate uses of any resulting increase in IMF income within the existing framework of the Articles with the objective of targeting support to poorest countries.

12. Concerning specific IMF facilities:

a. The SBA should remain the standard facility to provide short-term assistance.

b. The EFF should be used in well-defined cases where medium-term structural reform is important, and longer-term maturity is appropriate due to the country's structural balance of payments situation and its limited access to private capital. This facility is expected to help countries to carry forward structural reforms necessary to achieve access to private capital over time.

c. The CCL should be reviewed with a view to enhancing its effectiveness without compromising the initial eligibility criteria. Specifically:

  – The commitment fee for the CCL should be abolished.

  – The initial rate of charge of the CCL should be reduced to a level below the initial rate of charge of the SRF. In this context, the progressive structure of the rate of charge of the CCL should be reviewed.

  – The activation of the CCL should move to greater automaticity with regard to the initial drawing and within a predetermined limit, provided that appropriate reviews are conducted and that the ex-ante conditionalities are fully met.

  – After approval of the arrangement committing CCL resources, frequent reviews, at least twice a year, on whether the user country continues to meet eligibility criteria should be conducted. A country should be required to exit the CCL when it becomes clear that eligibility criteria are no longer met. We call on the IMF to develop an appropriate exit strategy for these cases. If a country exiting the facility carries the risk of having a balance of payments problem, it should be encouraged to conclude an appropriate IMF program.

  – In light of the abolishment of commitment fee, the reduction of the initial rate of charge and introduction of greater automaticity, the high standards for qualification should be maintained.

d. The SRF should retain its character as an emergency instrument to respond rapidly and on an appropriate scale to crises of capital market confidence, with appropriate terms to mitigate moral hazard and encourage rapid repayment.

We will work together with other members of the IMF to implement the specific changes proposed and other steps needed to put in place this simplified and incentive-based framework of lending instruments.

13. Going forward, conditions on IMF lending should be focused and address issues of macroeconomic relevance, while adhering to high quality

standards. The IMF should sharpen its focus on macroeconomic policies, capital flows, structural issues having an impact on macroeconomic stability, in particular those in the financial sector, and exchange rate regime with the view toward encouraging countries to avoid unsustainable regimes. Success of IMF-led programs depends on strengthened ownership of borrowing countries.

Safeguarding IMF Resources

14. The IMF's new framework for the conduct of safeguard assessments adopted last spring, strengthened measures to discourage misreporting and a requirement that countries making use of Fund resources publish annual financial statements independently audited by external auditors in accordance with internationally accepted standards should be implemented vigorously to ensure that IMF funds are used appropriately.

Post-program Monitoring

15. It is important that the IMF enhances its capacity to monitor performance while funds are outstanding in order to help ensure that countries maintain strong policies and avoid the need to return to the IMF for financial support. We therefore attach priority to early action by the IMF to strengthen procedures and policies with respect to post-program monitoring.

Strengthening Governance and Accountability

16. We continue to stress that high priority be placed on increasing the transparency and accountability of the IMF.
   a. The IMF should continue its efforts to make its documents public.
   b. We welcome the recent decision to publish quarterly the financial transactions plan and encourage the IMF to take further steps to explore a mechanism for simplifying its financial accounting, in order to make its financial operations and statements more understandable to the public.
   c. The involvement of the IMF Executive Board in the process leading to the formulation of country programs should be further enhanced. The Board should be briefed at an early stage on important and sensitive cases.
   d. We welcome progress made toward establishing a permanent independent evaluation office inside the IMF, and urge that steps be

taken to bring this office into operation by the time of the Annual Meetings in Prague. We look forward to reports on the result of the evaluation by the office to the Executive Board, and regular reports on the activity of the office to the IMFC.

e. For the IMF to maintain its legitimacy, credibility, and effectiveness as a global institution in the international financial system, it is essential that IMF's decision-making structure and its operation remain accountable. We take note of the effort now underway in the IMF to examine the formula for calculating country quotas, which need to be able to reflect changes in the world economy.

We look forward to discussing these proposals constructively and cooperatively with other members of the IMF.

Private Sector Involvement (PSI) in Crisis Prevention and Resolution

17. We welcome that private external creditors, including bondholders, have contributed to the financing of several recent IMF programs of policy reform and recovery. This has confirmed the importance of making operational the framework we laid out in our report to Heads in Cologne.

18. Private sector involvement is crucial for crisis prevention and resolution, and further efforts must be quickly made to implement the following measures;

    a. Emerging market economies participating in international capital markets and their private creditors should seek in normal times to establish a strong, continuous dialogue.

    b. The IMF should also encourage the use of appropriate measures, including collective action clauses, to facilitate more orderly crisis resolution.

    c. The use of collective action clauses in international bonds issued by emerging market economies in our own financial market should be facilitated.

    d. The World Bank and other Multilateral Development Banks are urged to work to have such clauses used in international sovereign bonds or loans for which they provide a guarantee.

19. The approach the international community adopts towards crisis resolution should be based on the IMF's assessment of a country's underlying payment capacity and prospects of regaining market access, informed by the country's economic fundamentals, payment profile, history of market access, and the market spreads on its debts.

20. All IMF programs need to include analysis of the country's medium-term debt and balance of payments profile, including a section explaining the assumptions taken about the sources of private finance.
    a. In some cases, the combination of catalytic official financing and policy adjustment should allow the country to regain full market access quickly.
    b. In some cases, emphasis should be placed on encouraging voluntary approaches as needed to overcome creditor coordination problems.
    c. In other cases, the early restoration of full market access on terms consistent with medium-term external sustainability may be judged to be unrealistic, and a broader spectrum of actions by private creditors, including comprehensive debt restructuring, may be warranted to provide for an adequately financed program and a viable medium-term payments profile.
21. In the case of c) above, where debt restructuring or debt reduction may be necessary, IMF programs should be based on the following operational guidelines.
    a. Put strong emphasis on medium-term financial sustainability, with the IMF determining the appropriate degree of economic adjustment required by the country and the IMF and the country agreeing on a financing plan compatible with a sustainable medium-term payments profile.
    b. Strike an appropriate balance between the contributions of the private external creditors and the official external creditors, in light of financing provided by IFIs. In cases where a contribution from official bilateral creditors (primarily the Paris Club) is needed, the IMF financing plan would need to provide for broad comparability between the contributions of official bilateral creditors and private external creditors. The Paris Club, if involved, should of course continue to assess the comparability desired and achieved between its agreement and those to be reached with other creditors.
    c. Aim for fairness in treatment of different classes of private creditors and for involvement of all classes of material creditors. The IMF should review the country's efforts to secure needed contributions from private creditors in light of these considerations, as well as medium-term sustainability.
    d. Place responsibilities for negotiation with creditors squarely with debtor countries. The international official community should not micromanage the details of any debt restructuring or debt reduction negotiations.
    e. Provide greater clarity to countries at the start of the process about the possible consequences for their programs, including in terms of official financing, of any failure to secure the necessary contribution from

private creditors on terms consistent with a sustainable medium-term payments profile. Such consequences could include the need for a program revision to provide for additional adjustment by the country concerned or the option of reduced official financing, or, conversely, a decision by the IMF to lend into arrears if a country has suspended payments while seeking to work cooperatively and in good faith with its private creditors and is meeting other program requirements.

    f. When all relevant decisions have been taken, the IMF should set out publicly how and what certain policy approaches have been adopted, in line with the Cologne framework.

22. We look forward to further progress at the IMF by this year's Annual Meetings in Prague in making operational our approach, agreed last April, to PSI in the design of IMF programs so as to provide greater clarity to countries and market participants.

C. MDBs Reform

23. We affirm that accelerating poverty reduction in developing countries must be the core role of the Multilateral Development Banks (MDBs). An increased focus on poverty reduction should underpin all aspects of the MDBs' work, including in programs of policy reform, investment projects and capacity-building. MDBs need to adapt their organization and operations in order to fulfill this mission more effectively and consistently in a continuously changing international environment characterized by: a new understanding of the necessary elements of a more effective fight against poverty; growth of private financial markets in the developing countries; new opportunities and challenges arising from globalization; and stakeholders' stronger interest in efficient use of overall aid resources, and higher standards for transparency and accountability of MDBs.

24. Economic growth is the primary determinant of a country's ability to raise incomes and reduce poverty and inequality. Successful and equitable development also depends upon good governance, sound structural and sectoral policies, including social policy and trade liberalization, accountable and transparent institutions, and investment in human capital and public goods. Therefore MDBs should assist poor countries not only to meet such social priority as education and health, but also with economic and social infrastructure support where this has a clear additional impact on poverty reduction.

25. MDBs can also make an important contribution to poverty reduction in emerging market and/or middle-income countries. MDB activities in countries with access to private capital should be more selective in order not to supplant private capital. At the same time, in case of temporary closure of emerging market countries' access to capital markets, MDBs should stand ready to respond quickly by helping to cushion the effects of exceptional shocks on the poorest and most vulnerable groups.

26. In all cases, MDB multi-year operational frameworks should be established and should include clear commitments to increase support for core social investments such as basic health and education, clean water, and sanitation. They should respect appropriate country exposure limits.

27. MDBs should place high priority on good governance and the full commitment to the poverty reduction by recipient countries. They should allocate their support increasingly on the basis of borrower performance. Experience has shown that aid is only effective in reducing poverty where governments are committed to sound policies. In this regard, we stress the importance of the following:

    a. the Comprehensive Development Framework (CDF) and the Poverty Reduction Strategy Papers (PRSPs) should become the basis for programs that have strong ownership by the recipient countries; and

    b. performance-based lending frameworks, such as agreed under IDA-12, should be extended in an appropriate manner to all MDB programs.

28. In addition, MDBs should include support for capacity-building and structural and institutional reform in their broad-based approach to assistance for developing countries. In particular, they should:

    a. strive to enhance the overall financing capacity of recipient countries themselves, including by increasing domestic saving and by helping catalyze private capital flows;

    b. address institutional and structural issues that hamper poverty reduction, to ensure transparency, accountability, the rule of law, and appropriate social and human investments for the poor; and

    c. strengthen the financial sector in recipient countries so as to help them prevent and manage financial crises.

    Since Country Assistance Strategies (CASs) are comprehensive tools for effective and efficient MDB support for developing countries, MDBs should work to improve their quality and broaden their scope. These strategies should take full account of a borrower's policy environment including governance as well as the legal, institutional and regulatory frameworks. Public Expenditure Reviews should be an essential building block of the strategies. Every CAS should provide an assessment of the country's financial sector and governance.

29. MDBs should avoid competition with the private sector, assume a catalytic role and focus their activities more selectively on projects with clear development and/or transition impact. As the private sector increasingly finances projects traditionally funded by MDBs, more public resources are likely to be available for investment in social sector and public goods.

30. MDBs, and especially the World Bank (WB), should take the lead in facilitating the provision of global public goods, by deepening their engagement in global issues such as infectious diseases and environmental problems closely related to development. In this regard, the comparative advantage of various international institutions, including UN agencies (e.g. such as World Health Organization (WHO) and Joint UN Programme on HIV/AIDS (UNAIDS)) and private institutions should be carefully reviewed given the scarcity of concessional resources.

31. MDBs should emphasize a selective, quality-oriented approach rather than a quantity-oriented or profit-oriented one on the basis of clear definition of their roles as public institutions and their development mandates. MDBs which provide resources to private sector should better define their roles, organizations and operations in this respect.

32. It is important for MDBs to look afresh at the instruments available to fulfill their development and poverty reduction mandate in light of the principles described in the preceding paragraphs and in view of the changing international financial environment. In this regard, we call for a prompt initiation of a comprehensive review of loan pricing policy, including the question of price differentiation for the different types of operation. MDBs should also explore the possibility of some separation of lending and non-lending services to enable a wide range of countries to continue to benefit from MDBs' expertise.

33. Concessional lending by MDBs, focused on the poorest countries, has a critical role in poverty reduction. Replenishment of the concessional funds of the MDBs should be based on the principle of fair burden sharing and we encourage new donors to participate actively.

34. The quality of aid may, in some cases, be improved through healthy competition between the WB and some Regional Development Banks (RDBs). It is nevertheless essential that these institutions strengthen collaboration and coordination in order to ensure efficient use of scarce aid resources. The CDF initiated by the WB and PRSP can be useful tools in coordinating of bilateral and multilateral donors. The WB and the RDBs

should conclude Memoranda of Understanding to frame their coordination and closer partnership taking into account circumstances of each RDB. In this regard, we welcome the recent agreement between the WB and the African Development Bank (AfDB). Collaboration in the field is particularly important and, in this respect, a comprehensive review of the progress of the decentralization of the WB operations and the impact of this process on cooperation with the RDBs and on the quality of its projects and its administration would be welcomed.

35. The IMF and the WB have different mandates and need to respect them. Nevertheless, the issues they deal with are increasingly interrelated and in some countries their activities are interdependent. In this respect, they should continue to work closely together to improve efficiency and exchange of information. This would require a clearer definition of their respective responsibilities and activities, and continued development of more effective mechanisms of cooperation.

36. Finally, we call for greater accountability to shareholders and those affected by MDB actions. We therefore support the recent substantial progress that MDBs have made toward this goal. Nevertheless, there is a clear need for additional progress in such crucial areas as information disclosure, public participation and accountability to the shareholders:

   a. A greater range of operational documents should be released to the public, particularly all country strategies and evaluation reports, while paying due attention to the influence on the market.

   b. Independent inspection panels should be in place in an appropriate manner in all institutions.

   c. Each institution should establish a compliance unit to certify full compliance of project proposals with its policies prior to submission to the Executive Boards.

   d. Monitoring and ex-post evaluation function, internal financial controls, procurement policies and practices and auditing procedures of each MDB should be strengthened and all MDBs should have strong and independent evaluation units.

D. HLIs, Capital Flows and OFCs

37. We stress the importance of the implementation of the recommendations set out in the reports of the Financial Stability Forum (FSF) Working Groups on highly leveraged institutions (HLIs), Capital Flows, and

Offshore Financial Centers (OFCs), which were released last March. In this regard, we call on the IMF, World Bank and other bodies to contribute actively to the implementation of the various recommendations by the FSF Working Groups.

38. To respond to concerns about the potential consequences of the activities of HLIs, which may contribute to systemic risks or affect the dynamics of certain markets, it is important to promote the implementation of the following measures:

    a. Better risk management by HLIs and their counterparties.

    b. Better disclosure practices by financial institutions, including enhanced disclosure by HLIs and their creditors. We call on all jurisdictions to consider the adequacy of their own disclosure requirements and introduce, where necessary, appropriate changes to legislation or regulations to ensure that major hedge funds located in their jurisdictions are subject to disclosure requirements. This recommendation should apply, in particular, to offshore centers, since they currently host a significant proportion of unregulated hedge funds.

    c. Enhanced regulatory and supervisory oversight by national authorities of financial institutions which provide credit to HLIs.

    d. Enhanced national surveillance of financial market activity in view of concerns about systemic risk and market dynamics caused by HLIs' activities.

    e. Review by leading foreign exchange market participants of existing good practice guidelines for foreign exchange trading and the articulation of model guidelines for possible adoption by market participants in smaller economies.

    f. Improved market infrastructure We will review these measures and their implementation to determine whether additional steps are necessary. In this light, we note that the FSF considered in March, but did not recommend, at this stage, direct regulation of the currently unregulated HLIs, but emphasized that direct regulation would be reconsidered, if, upon review, the implementation of its recommendations were not adequately addressing concerns identified.

39. It is also important that each country manages debt-related risks appropriately. In this regard, we welcome the work being carried out by the IMF and World Bank, and urge prompt development of guidelines for public debt and reserve management, with special attention to the risk created by short-term foreign currency liabilities, and taking account of countries' vulnerability to capital account crises, including those

vulnerabilities arising from the liabilities of the private sector. The establishment of efficient domestic bond markets is also important. Prudential limitations in the banking system to reduce the risk of excessive exposure to short-term capital flows may be appropriate in some circumstances.

40. Regarding offshore financial centers that do not meet international standards adequately, and therefore, that are potential threats to the international financial system, we welcome the identification by the FSF of priority jurisdictions, and urge the IMF to conduct quickly a specific assessment in these jurisdictions. We urge all the listed jurisdictions to demonstrate their commitment to improve their implementation of standards, for instance, through a public declaration of their intention to implement relevant international standards, completing assisted self-assessments of adherence to these standards, and eventually addressing shortfalls identified through detailed action plans.

41. To respond to risks caused by large and abrupt international capital movements, it will continue to be important for each country to pursue sound macroeconomic policies, proceed with structural reform for the better functioning of the market, strengthen the financial system, choose an appropriate foreign exchange rate regime supported by consistent and credible macroeconomic policies and other measures, liberalize the capital account in a well-sequenced manner, and take other appropriate policies, as needed.

42. Recognizing the crucial role of deposit insurance in contributing to confidence in the financial system, we look forward to further development by the FSF of guidance on deposit insurance schemes.

E. Regional Cooperation

43. As discussed above, IMF surveillance of, and appropriate financing support to, the member countries are important for the stability of the international financial system. In addition, member countries may strengthen, on a regional basis, their cooperation in these areas, in a way which is supportive of the IMF's objectives and responsibilities in the global economy, taking into account their common interests in international trade and investment and shared concerns about the risk of regional contagion. Such regional cooperation can improve regional stability and thus contribute to the stability of the global economy.

44. In this context, we welcome the recent developments in the area of regional cooperation at various levels. In the Asian region, frameworks for regional surveillance and for cooperation in finance including bilateral swap mechanisms have been expanded. In North America, a trilateral swap arrangement is maintained with a process for surveillance and regular consultation on economic matters.

45. Regional cooperation through more intensified surveillance can help contribute to financial stability by strengthening the policy framework at the national level. Cooperative financing arrangements at the regional level designed to supplement resources provided by the IFIs in support of IMF programs can be effective in crisis prevention and resolution.

46. In a different institutional context, economic and financial integration mechanisms, and monetary unification in Europe are also contributing to the economic and financial stability of the global economy.

E Impact of the IT Revolution on the Economy and Finance: Report from G7 Finance Ministers to the Heads of State and Government

FUKUOKA, JAPAN, 8 JULY 2000

1. We, Finance Ministers of the G7 countries, note that the advance of the Information Technology (IT) revolution holds the promise of becoming a major force in the global economy in improving productivity, raising maximum potential output, and promoting higher living standards. In order to ensure that the benefits of IT are promptly reaped by our societies and do not lead to increasing inequalities, countries must put in place appropriate macroeconomic and structural policies.

2. In this report, we focus on the macroeconomic impact of the IT revolution, its policy implications, and issues relating to financial transactions and tax systems.

A. Macroeconomic Impact and Its Policy Implications

Acceleration of Productivity and Increase in Demand

3. We recognize that IT has the potential to increase growth in our economies although the impact of IT is still at an early stage and it is difficult to anticipate its exact timing, nature and strength. The increase in production potential due to IT will not be limited to IT-related industries, but will extend to the overall economy. First of all, the IT revolution can increase the rate of growth of the capital stock by stimulating active IT-related investment. This kind of investment leads to increasingly sophisticated IT technology being built into capital and, accordingly, raises the quality of capital as

well. More importantly, by increasing the speed with which information is disseminated and shared inside and outside corporations, the IT revolution can drastically alter the combination of capital and labor, bring about greater efficiency in conducting business, facilitate corporate restructuring, induce a synergistic effect, and thus lead to productivity increases that cannot be attributed to either capital or labor (total factor productivity). For instance, it can reduce the need for intermediary business, make inventory management more efficient, and enable businesses to procure inputs or conduct outsourcing in the business-to-business (B-to-B) market that is networked globally.

4. In addition to the supply side, the IT revolution will have effects on the demand side through increased IT-related investment, expansion of demand for IT-related services, and the development of new consumer-oriented services, including business-to-consumer (B-to-C) electronic commerce and electronic financial transactions. A two-way flow of information between businesses and consumers made possible through the Internet can generate new types of demand and new business opportunities. IT-related investment and services would involve "network externalities" in which benefits increase dramatically as the number of users increases, and "increasing returns to scale" in which costs are reduced and profits increase as the market grows in size. These are likely to contribute to the further expansion of demand.

5. As a result of this accelerated growth potential on the supply side in parallel with expansion on the demand side, IT can contribute to stronger growth. Like many other technological innovations, IT may bring job losses in certain areas, but create jobs in IT-related businesses. Overall, we can expect a positive impact on employment due to stronger economic growth.

6. Given that the IT revolution has just begun, over the course of time it can have wide-ranging and in-depth effects on our economies, in the same way that important general-purpose technologies had in the past. Already, significant effects on potential growth can be seen in some countries, but there are disparities in the pace at which countries are benefiting from the IT revolution. Indeed, there is nothing automatic about the productivity gains and higher standard of living that come with major innovations such as IT. Deriving the benefits of IT will require sound policies and a robust, but also flexible, open economy as an essential backdrop.

Macroeconomic Policy

7. We agree that the most important role to be played by government, in order to help our economies maximize the potential returns from IT, is to develop an environment that is conducive to private-sector creativity and entrepreneurship. We emphasize that, from this perspective, sound macroeconomic policy continues to be, or is becoming even more, essential. A growth- and stability-oriented macroeconomic environment will stimulate investment and help businesses and consumers to confidently plan for the future and exploit the advantages presented by IT.

8. The IT revolution can make the environment, in which macroeconomic policy is conducted, more complex and uncertain. In the initial stages of the IT revolution, estimating productivity gains and their impact on potential growth becomes more complex. Similarly, traditional yardsticks for gauging financial market performance may appear less applicable, and this has made it more difficult to appropriately assess risk and return on investment decisions. These increased uncertainties can complicate the choices policy-makers face in calibrating macroeconomic policy management and promoting sustained non-inflationary growth. We must remain mindful of these realities in framing our policies.

9. In addition, in an increasingly globalized economy in which capital can be easily and quickly transferred across borders, differences in the degree to which countries adapt to the IT revolution may lead to large capital flows, and widen the divergence in economic performance between countries even further. Such divergences and the ensuing flows may further create challenges for the promotion of stable and balanced macroeconomic conditions. Achieving greater equality in the pace with which countries benefit from the IT revolution will contribute to promoting a balanced pattern of growth among our economies.

10. In the longer term, the IT revolution may have implications for monetary aggregates and their role in the conduct of monetary policy and for the stability of financial system more generally as electronic financial transactions and digital money become major elements of our national economies.

Structural Policy

11. We agree on the importance of structural policy to develop an environment for vigorous private-sector activity for maximizing the results of IT, and

to ensure that people can fairly and widely share benefits from IT opportunities. From this perspective, we emphasize the necessity of:

a) Continuing to remove regulatory impediments in order to promote competition and new entry in key IT-related sectors.

b) Increasing the adaptability of labor markets. Retraining and learning opportunities can help workers successfully transition into new, better-paying jobs.

c) Putting in place appropriate competition and other policies to facilitate dissemination of new technologies and to ensure competition in the new environment.

d) Maintaining an open international trade system.

We note the importance of an efficient and high-quality allocation of our public resources, with the view to contribute to needed structural reforms.

12. It is also crucial that financial markets be designed in a strong, secure and flexible way to channel resources to their most productive uses. A financial system that can properly match the demand for and supply of capital, and diversify and reallocate risks, is essential in order to meet the funding needs for new businesses and investment opportunities. For startup firms that lead in technological innovation and that seek to take the greatest possible advantage of their technology, a highly transparent and deep capital market will be of particular significance from the point of view of risk-taking and corporate governance.

B. Implications for the Financial Sector

13. We observe that the financial sector is undergoing many changes, including the emergence of financial transactions on the Internet. It is important that government provides an appropriate environment for maximizing the efficiency and convenience of this innovation.

Impacts of the IT Revolution on Financial Services

14. As the financial sector deals with information and data that are easily digitalized, this is one of the industries with the most advanced use of, as well as under the heaviest influence of, IT. Specifically, the IT revolution has enabled the following changes in the financial sector:

a) In electronic financial transactions, utilization of the Internet, with its characteristics of speedy, low-cost, and broad communication, can permit a drastic reduction in transaction costs and improvements in customer convenience.

b) By eliminating the limitations of time and distance, electronic financial transactions can make cross-border transactions easier and, thus, make it possible to provide services to customers on a global scale.

c) Electronic financial transactions have enabled new financial services such as the "virtual financial site" that includes services crossing the traditional borders between financial services as well as "aggregation" that allows consumers to obtain consolidated information about their financial accounts in one place.

d) In addition, under the IT revolution, globalization, and resulting competitive environment, we are seeing innovative developments in the unbundling of risks, the evolution of derivative transactions, and the entry of non-financial companies into the financial sector.

15. On the other hand, we note that, since electronic financial transactions, especially those of B-to-C, are being conducted on open networks centered on the Internet, many challenges will arise in terms of transaction security, consumer protection, and privacy.

Financial Regulation and Supervision

16. We recognize that, while financial regulation and supervision should be technology neutral, they should respond to the above-mentioned characteristics of electronic financial transactions. The objective should be to preserve market integrity without inhibiting the initiative of the private sector.

17. It is important that consumers have confidence in the security of electronic financial transactions. We should encourage the development of systems to combat computer hacking, and the use of encryption and electronic signatures to ensure the security of data. In addition, we need to ensure the development of reliable settlement systems on the Internet; the security of existing settlement systems, such as credit cards, will remain important.

18. For consumer protection in electronic financial transactions, it is important to ensure there is no erosion in the level of protection currently enjoyed by customers of financial services. Rules in areas such as disclosure to investors, explanation and information provision at the time of solicitation and purchase, the provision of documents to customers, and dispute resolution, should also apply to business conducted on the Internet, while methods of applications of those rules may need to be adapted. Also, as

the transfer of personal data has become extremely easy, we need to promote strengthening of policies for privacy protection.

19. We should promote international cooperation in establishing as well as implementing principles for financial regulation and supervision, paying due attention to the current rules in each country. From this viewpoint, we welcome the work being done by the Basel Committee on Banking Supervision (BCBS), the International Organization of Securities Commissions (IOSCO), and the International Association of Insurance Supervisors (IAIS) in establishing principles or guidance for the regulation and supervision of electronic financial transactions. We encourage further work by these institutions in line with the following focus:

    a) Consistent regulation and supervision irrespective of the means of transactions, including electronic financial transactions.

    b) Transparent regulation and supervision in a more complicated business environment, and flexibility to continuously review our supervisory activities to reflect new developments.

    c) Fostering the potential of electronic financial transactions within prudent risk parameters without unduly constraining its innovation.

    d) Security of transaction and customer protection pertinent to the characteristics of electronic financial transactions.

    e) Enhanced cooperation among supervisory authorities in response to the increase in cross-border transactions.

20. We welcome the mapping exercise by the Financial Stability Forum (FSF) on electronic financial transactions, including their potential impact on financial safety, as a basis for possible future work.

21. Management and board members of financial institutions must understand the risks and challenges arising from the development of electronic financial transactions. Financial regulators and supervisors must also ensure that they have the necessary knowledge and skills to deal with the new development. From this viewpoint, we encourage our national authorities to promote methods and techniques for training supervisory staff in IT-related knowledge and skills, and ensure that adequate supervisory resources are devoted to this issue. We should also consider providing technical assistance to help developing countries in their efforts to train regulators and supervisors.

Financial Business Patents

22. With the revolutionary changes in technologies through computers and the Internet, patents have been granted to an increasing number of business method inventions, including in the area of financial services. We recognize that, with the development of IT in finance, our policies toward financial business method patents could have implications for innovation and competition in financial markets. This issue needs to be addressed in the context of international cooperation with the view to enhancing common understanding of treatment of business method patents.

23. In this respect, we welcome the joint work already underway among our patent authorities on business method patents, and look forward to further development. We have asked our financial experts to meet with our patent authorities and to discuss whether and how the issues of common interest are being dealt with at the international level and how international cooperation in this field is progressing.

C. Taxation and Customs Procedures

Electronic Commerce and Taxation

24. We recognize that the IT revolution, especially the development of electronic commerce, has important implications for tax systems and their administration, in particular, through the changes discussed below.

   a) Digitalization: IT provides innovative ways of offering "digital" services such as on-line supply of music and images, and for providing information services. Moreover, while broader use of electronic means for recording information improves the efficiency of business activities, it may make it easier to falsify data.

   b) Disintermediation: Electronic commerce often eliminates the need for intermediation and thus reduces the opportunities of monitoring and compliance for taxation purposes.

   c) Further internationalization: Cross-border transactions between parties in different tax jurisdictions can increase substantially through the Internet which is open and borderless.

25. We note the importance of the key elements for addressing issues on electronic commerce and taxation which were identified in the report of the Committee on Fiscal Affairs (CFA) of the OECD, entitled "Electronic

Commerce: Taxation Framework Conditions" and welcomed by OECD Ministers in October 1998 in Ottawa.

a) It is important to provide a fiscal climate within which electronic commerce can flourish, weighed against the obligation to operate a fair and predictable tax system that provides the revenue required to meet the legitimate expectations of citizens for publicly-provided services. In addition, efforts should also be made to improve taxpayer service by making utmost use of information technology.

b) Conventional taxation principles, such as neutrality, equity, and simplicity, should underlie the taxation of electronic commerce. At this stage, existing tax rules can implement these principles for electronic commerce. While there may be cases where some adaptation to the existing rules is required, such adaptation should not discriminate among forms of commerce, be they electronic or traditional.

26. We welcome the OECD's ongoing work on relevant taxation issues, focusing on the following points:

a) How to ensure efficient and effective tax administration: Electronic commerce can be conducted in more invisible and anonymous ways. It is vital, therefore, to secure access for tax administrators to transaction information to the same extent as for traditional forms of commerce.

b) How to apply the existing international rules for direct taxation to electronic commerce: As electronic commerce further facilitates cross-border economic activities, there should be clarification of how the concepts in the OECD Model Tax Convention, such as "permanent establishment" and classification of income, apply to electronic commerce.

c) How to apply consumption taxes to cross-border, on-line transactions: Consumption taxes should be applied where consumption takes place. In order to explore the practical application of this principle, issues, such as the definition of the place of consumption and effective collection mechanisms, are being addressed.

27. We recognize that the CFA of the OECD is taking the lead in the examination of these tax issues related to electronic commerce with contributions from business and non-OECD economies. We support this work and encourage the CFA to make further progress.

Customs Procedures

28. Regarding customs procedures, we endorse our customs experts' report on their efforts to standardize and simplify electronic customs declarations. We urge them to set a timetable for implementation, in which other countries and organizations are invited to participate; take steps to develop "single window" systems to allow traders to report data required by customs and other agencies once when they release goods; and so adopt the principles for the use of IT set out in the revised Kyoto Customs Convention.

F G20 Finance Ministers and Central Bank Governors Meeting, News Release

MONTRÉAL, CANADA
OCTOBER 25, 2000

We, the Finance Ministers and Central Bank Governors of the G-20, held our second meeting today in Montreal, Québec, Canada. We discussed the state of the world economy, particularly the associated policy challenges and ways of addressing potential vulnerabilities. We welcome the continued strengthening of global economic growth, but remain mindful of the importance of sound national economic and financial policies in building an international financial system that is less prone to crises.

Our meeting provided us with an opportunity to engage in a wide-ranging discussion of the opportunities and challenges posed to all of our economies by globalization – the increasing integration of national economies resulting from the greater international mobility of goods, services, capital, people, and ideas. The process of globalization has deep historical roots, but has been accelerated in recent years by unprecedented technological change, the increasing universality and acceptance of market-based economic systems, and the liberalization of international trade and capital movements.

We discussed the benefits of globalization. These include providing people and societies around the world with an unparalleled opportunity to achieve sustained and broad-based improvements in living standards through participation in world trade, further trade liberalization by all countries, including improved access for developing countries' exports to advanced economies' markets, access to cheaper consumption and capital goods, integration into international capital markets, and openness to technological change and innovation. We reaffirm our belief that the economic integration that is at the heart of globalization can continue to be an enormously powerful force contributing to improving the lives of hundreds of millions of people in industrial, transition, and developing countries alike, giving them greater access to goods, capital and ideas – and thus a much greater capacity to achieve rapid and enduring growth in the living standards of their citizens, and to attack income inequalities and reduce poverty.

At the same time, we are in agreement that the process of globalization, like any economic transformation, can also give rise to economic difficulties and social dislocations. Governments have an important role to play in formulating and implementing policies to promote financial and economic stability and harness the benefits of globalization. We agree that putting in place the right frameworks and policies for promoting a globalization process that works well for all of its participants will be the key challenge for the international community in the 21st century.

As G-20 Finance Ministers and Central Bank Governors, we are committed to working together to promote policies that successfully meet this challenge. In particular, we agree to:

1. Commit ourselves to further improve the effectiveness of international institutions, which are fundamental to a strong and stable global financial system. These efforts include increasing the transparency of their activities and decision-making processes, and enhancing co-operation among them.
2. Implement the emerging international consensus on policies to reduce countries' vulnerability to financial crises, including through appropriate exchange rate arrangements, prudent liability management, private sector involvement in crisis prevention and resolution, and adoption of codes and standards in key areas including transparency, data dissemination, market integrity, and financial sector policy. A summary of our conclusions in these areas can be found in the Annex to this statement.
3. Improve integration into the globalized financial world. Emerging market economies should be supported with technical assistance and policy advice by the international financial community in opening their capital accounts in a well-sequenced manner to benefit from international capital flows while minimizing potential risks.
4. Create more favourable conditions for the integration of heavily indebted poor countries into the global economy by urging both bilateral and multilateral creditors to participate fully in the enhanced HIPC Initiative, and, where appropriate, call for those bilateral creditors that have not already done so to consider taking the additional step of committing to 100-per-cent reduction of ODA claims and eligible commercial claims. We further encourage all bilateral donors to improve the effectiveness of international assistance and direct aid to those poor countries that are serious about tackling economic reforms and poverty reduction.

5. Strengthen our efforts to combat financial abuse, including money laundering, tax evasion and corruption, given its potential to undermine the credibility and integrity of the international financial system, cause serious macroeconomic distortions, and jeopardize national financial sectors. Market integrity is an important pre-condition for financial stability, and we look forward to the joint paper by the IMF and World Bank asked for by the IMFC on their respective roles in combating financial abuse and in protecting the international financial system.
6. Contribute to international efforts to increase the provision of other global public goods to address serious issues such as infectious disease, agricultural research, and the environment, which cut across national borders and require concerted global co-operation.
7. Support continued efforts by the WTO to build consensus toward further multilateral trade liberalisation and strengthening of trade rules that would bring broad-based benefits to the global economy, by reflecting the needs and interests of both developed and developing countries, in particular those of the lowest income economies, so that all can realize the rewards of full participation in the global trading system. We also agree to promote domestic policies that help spread the benefits of integration to all members of society.
8. Promote the design and effective implementation of 'social safety nets' that protect the most vulnerable groups of society in the process of liberalization.
9. Ensure that efforts in the areas identified above, and in other areas, take account of a diversity of perspectives.

Annex: Reducing Vulnerability to Financial Crises

At our meeting today, we considered ways to reduce the frequency and severity of financial crises, such as those which in recent years have taken their toll on growth and social conditions in many emerging markets and had significant repercussions for the global economy. We agreed that countries can substantially reduce their vulnerability to crises through sound policies in key areas, including through appropriate exchange rate arrangements, prudent liability management, the development and implementation of international standards and codes, and appropriate involvement of the private sector.

Experience has shown all too clearly that crises originating in one country can have serious repercussions for neighbouring countries and indeed the entire global economy. For this reason, the international community has a strong and legitimate interest in establishing "best practices" in these key policy areas. We agreed that these best practices have the following main elements, which if implemented will help to reduce vulnerability to financial crises in a complementary and mutually reinforcing manner.

1. Exchange Rate Arrangements

We agree that the choice of exchange rate regime must be supported both by appropriate macroeconomic policies and by sound financial institutions if it is to contribute to achieving a country's policy objectives. Foreign exchange crises are felt not only by the countries in which they originate, but can also have spill-over effects on other members in the global community.

There is a spectrum of possible exchange rate arrangements and no single arrangement is necessarily right for all countries all the time. The experience of recent years suggests that countries face a much higher risk of financial crisis if they choose an exchange rate regime that is not backed by consistent macroeconomic and structural policies and appropriate institutional arrangements.

We welcome the movement by many countries toward exchange rate arrangements that are more supportive of financial stability. There is evidence that there may be advantages in choosing either free floating or firm fixing such as a currency board. However, intermediate regimes could be a viable, albeit demanding, option for some economies.

We agreed that it is crucial for all countries, whatever regime they choose, to avoid defending an exchange rate not backed by strong, credible and consistent supporting arrangements and domestic policies.

The IMF plays a key role in advising and supporting countries in this area. It should reinforce its assessment of the compatibility of members' exchange rate regimes with their macroeconomic and financial policies. The IMF should also encourage countries to adapt their policies by giving them advice, and support when appropriate, in order to help avoid unsustainable positions.

2. Prudent Liability Management

We agreed that a comprehensive strategy to reduce vulnerability to financial crises requires attention to liability management including effective management of public-sector liabilities, appropriate consideration of the external financial situation of the private sector, and effective and transparent financial sector regulation and supervision.

In particular, we agreed that effective management of public sector liabilities requires finding an appropriate balance between minimizing financing costs and increasing liquidity risk. Care must be taken to avoid excessive reliance on short-term debt, currency mismatch or the "bunching" of external debt payments. Prudent public sector liability management is also assisted by the development of an efficient and liquid market for long-term domestic currency-denominated government securities.

Prudent liability management is also essential for the private sector, in particular for banks and other financial institutions. Appropriate standards of financial sector regulation and supervision, disclosure, accounting and auditing should be in place to facilitate the monitoring of the external activities of the financial sector. The overall external position of the private sector requires appropriate consideration, subject to the constraints associated with the availability of data.

Our discussions also indicated a clear consensus on the crucial role of the international community in assisting countries to develop and implement liability management strategies. We welcome the work underway at the IMF and World Bank to develop guidelines for public debt management and for the development of domestic public debt markets, developing and as appropriate publishing meaningful indicators of external vulnerability, and promoting the implementation of strong liability management policies and practices through technical assistance and other means.

3. Private Sector Involvement in Crisis Prevention and Resolution

We noted the enormous increase in private capital flows to emerging markets over the past decade, as well as the increasing diversity and sophistication of the means and instruments through which these flows are effected and welcomed the overall impact of this development in fostering more rapid growth and raising the standard of living of hundreds of millions of people around the world. At the same time, the last decade has witnessed a number of severe crises.

In this environment, we agreed that the framework for private sector involvement will benefit both debtors and creditors by promoting more efficient and stable international capital markets, in which financial crises are less frequent and less severe. Efficient international capital markets require that private investors bear the consequences of the risks they take.

We welcomed the agreement reached at the IMFC Spring meeting on a framework of principles and tools, and the progress made at the IMFC annual meeting on the operational framework by which private sector involvement in the prevention and resolution of financial crises can be promoted.

Our discussions indicated a clear consensus on the need to apply the framework flexibly, and in a manner that avoids an overly prescriptive involvement by the international community in the details of any debt negotiation process or that undermines the presumption that borrowers should meet their obligations in full and on time. We reaffirm the importance of the principle of comparability of treatment at the Paris Club, which provides for balance between the contributions of public and private creditors. We also believe that no class of private creditors should in general be treated as privileged relative to others in a similar position.

We believe that encouraging the wider use of mechanisms to improve communications between debtors and creditors will help to ensure that debtor countries and private creditors participate cooperatively in restructurings.

We welcomed the results of the Roundtable held by our Deputies with senior members of the private financial sector in Toronto on August 25. This Roundtable allowed for a structured and constructive dialogue on these issues, including the value of contractual arrangements such as collective action clauses, and an exchange of perspectives on the framework and its application. We have instructed our Deputies to continue this dialogue and report to us at our next meeting as appropriate.

We agreed that the development of a framework for efforts by the official and private sectors in this area must be a continuing process, evolving in a manner that takes account of developments in the global economy and financial markets. We further agreed to monitor experience with the framework to ensure that it will continue to be effective in supporting a stable and efficient international financial system.

4. International Standards and Codes

Finally, we considered the role that weaknesses in financial sector regulation and supervision, in corporate governance, in the disclosure of economic and financial data, and in the transparency of macroeconomic policies have played in contributing to recent financial crises. We agreed on the importance of international codes and standards to address these weaknesses, endorsed the Financial Stability Forum's recommendations, and encouraged continued work on incentives to foster implementation. The G-20, as part of its mandate to promote co-operation to achieve stable and sustainable world economic growth, should play an important leadership role in supporting the continuing implementation of international standards and codes in a manner and at a pace that reflects each country's unique development and reform priorities, and institutional characteristics. Consistent with this objective, we agreed that:

1. Governments should be encouraged to publicly articulate their commitment to adopt key standards and, as appropriate, announce action plans for their implementation. They should also be encouraged to participate in external IMF-led assessment programs, and in the interim conduct on-going self-assessments of progress in observance of standards. In both cases, they should consider ways of disclosing information on progress in implementing standards, to enable more appropriate risk assessments.

2. The official sector should also continue its dialogue with market participants as a way of obtaining their perspective on priorities for countries and the international community in this area, on market incentives for implementation, and on ways of improving the transparency and accessibility of information released.

3. IMF surveillance should be the principal mechanism for monitoring countries' progress in implementing standards and codes, working closely with other international institutions, such as the World Bank, as well as standard-setting bodies and international groups such as the Financial Stability Forum.

4. Governments and the international community should work to ensure that the human and financial resources required for implementation and for assessments of implementation are available to assist countries achieve compliance with international standards and codes.

We reaffirmed our commitment, made at the inaugural meeting of G-20 Ministers and Governors in Berlin in December 1999, to undertake the completion of Reports on Observance of Standards and Codes (ROSCs; formerly "Transparency Reports") and Financial Sector Assessment Programs (FSAPs), within the context of continuing efforts by the IMF and World Bank to improve these mechanisms. In this respect, we are encouraged that FSAPs or ROSCs, or both, have been completed or are underway in a growing number of G-20 countries, in particular Argentina, Australia, Canada, France, India, Korea, Russia, South Africa, Turkey, and the U.K., and look forward to the continued publication of ROSCs on the IMF web site.

Bibliography

Adams, Nassau A. (1993). *Worlds Apart: The North-South Divide and the International System*. Zed Books, London.

'Administration Floats New Textile Tariff Cut Proposal to EC' (1993). *Inside U.S. Trade*. 24 September.

Advisory Commission on Electronic Commerce (2000). 'Report to Congress'. April. <www.ecommercecommission.org/report.htm> (March 2001).

'Ajia Kangeimo Ondosa: G-7 Hejji Fando Kanshi Kyoka ni Goui' (Variation in Asia's Reception: A G7 Agreement on Tightened Regulations on the Hedge Funds) (1999). *Asahi Shimbun*, 19 June, p. 1.

Aldrich, Douglas F. (1999). *Mastering the Digital Market Place*. Wiley, New York.

ASEAN + 3 Finance Ministers (2000). 'Joint Ministerial Statement of the ASEAN + 3 Finance Ministers Meeting'. 6 May, Chiang Mai, Thailand. <www.mof.go.jp/english/if/if014.htm> (March 2001).

Ashley, Richard and R. J. B. Walker (1990). 'Reading Dissidence/Writing the Discipline'. *International Studies Quarterly* vol. 34, pp. 367–416.

Atlantic Council of the United States (1975). 'GATT Plus: A Proposal for Trade Reform'. Report of the Special Advisory Panel to the Trade Committee of the Atlantic Council. Praeger, New York.

Austin, Terry (1998). 'The Personal Computer Supply Chain: Unlocking Hidden Value'. In J. Gattorna, ed., *Strategic Supply Chain Alignment: Best Practice in Supply Chain Management*. Cambridge University Press, Cambridge.

Avi-Yonah, Reuven (1997). 'International Taxation of Electronic Commerce'. *Tax Law Review* vol. 52, no. 3.

Bardacke, Ted and Torsten Engelhardt (2000). 'WTO Aims for Deal with Poor Nations'. *Financial Times*, 14 February, p. 10.

Barshevsky, Charlene (2000). 'Barshefsky Says Deregulation Is Key to Japan's Recovery'. International Information Programs, Washington DC.

Bayne, Nicholas (1999). 'Continuity and Leadership in an Age of Globalisation'. In M. R. Hodges, J. J. Kirton and J. P. Daniels, eds., *The G8's Role in the New Millennium*, pp. 21–44. Ashgate, Aldershot.

Bayne, Nicholas (2000a). 'The G7 Summit's Contribution: Past, Present, and Prospective'. In K. Kaiser, J. J. Kirton and J. P. Daniels, eds., *Shaping a New International Financial System: Challenges of Governance in a Globalizing World*, pp. 19–35. Ashgate, Aldershot.

Bayne, Nicholas (2000b). *Hanging in There: The G7 and G8 Summit in Maturity and Renewal*. Ashgate, Aldershot.

Bayne, Nicholas (2000c). 'Why Did Seattle Fail? Globalization and the Politics of Trade'. *Government and Opposition* vol. 35, no. 2, pp. 131–151.

Bayne, Nicholas (forthcoming). 'The G8 Summit and Global Governance: The Message of Okinawa'. In J. J. Kirton and J. Takase, eds., *New Directions in Global Political Governance*. Ashgate, Aldershot.

Beattie, Alan (2000). 'OECD Meeting Fails to Agree to End Tied Aid'. *Financial Times*, 23 June, p. 14.

Beattie, Alan and Guy de Jonquières (2000). 'Tied Aid Plan at Risk: OECD, France, Denmark, and Japan Seek to Change Terms of Accord'. *Financial Times*, 19 June, p. 3.

Berger, Mark T. (1994). 'The End of the "Third World"?' *Third World Quarterly* vol. 15, no. 2, pp. 257–275.

Bergsten, C. Fred (2000). 'East Asian Regionalism'. *Economist* 15 July, pp. 23–26.

Bergsten, C. Fred and C. Randall Henning (1996). *Global Economic Leadership and the Group of Seven*. Institute for International Economics, Washington DC.

Blackhurst, Richard (1998). 'The Capacity of the WTO to Fulfill Its Mandate'. In A. O. Kroeger with Chonira Aturupane, *The WTO as an International Organization*. University of Chicago Press, Chicago.

Blair, David J. (1993). *Trade Negotiations in the OECD: Structures, Institutions, and States*. Kegan Paul, London.

Bloomfield, Robert and Maureen O'Hara (2000). 'Can Transparent Markets Survive'. *Journal of Financial Economics* vol. 55, no. 3, pp. 425–429.

Braithwaite, John and Peter Drahos (2000). *Global Business Regulation*. Cambridge University Press, Cambridge.

British Foreign and Commonwealth Office (1999). 'Blair Reports on Cologne G8 Summit: Statement by the Prime Minister, Mr. Tony Blair, House of Commons, London, 21 June 1999'. <www.fco.gov.uk/news/newstext.asp?2577> (March 2001).

Broad, William J. (2000). 'The Nuclear Shield: Repelling an Attack; A Missile Defense with Limits'. *New York Times*, 30 June, p. A10.

Brown, William A. (1950). *The United States and the Restoration of World Trade*. Brookings Institution, Washington DC.

Business and Industry Advisory Committee to the Organisation for Economic Co-operation and Development, Global Information Infrastructure Commission, and International Chamber of Commerce. (1998). 'A Global Action Plan for Electronic Commerce: Prepared by Business with Recommendations for Governments'. <www.biac.org/position.htm> (March 2001).

Cerny, Philip G. (1995). 'Globalization and the Changing Logic of Collective Action'. *International Organisation* vol. 49, no. 4, pp. 595–625.

Charles, Carol (2000). *New Global Rules for E-Commerce: Moving the Dialogue Beyond the G8*. Global Information Infrastructure Commission, Washington DC.

Chote, Robert and Guy de Jonquières (1996). 'Tariff Plea to Aid Poor Countries' Exports'. *Financial Times*, 1 July, p. 4.

Cisco Systems (2000). 'Networking the Supply Chain for Competitive Advantage: An Overview of the Cisco Networked Supply Chain Management Solution.' <www.cisco.com/warp/public/779/ibs/solutions/supply/scm_ov.pdf> (March 2001).

Clinton, Bill (1998). 'Preparing the WTO for the 21st Century'. *Focus* 31 (June), pp. 9–10. <www.wto.org/english/res_e/focus_e/focus31_e.pdf>.

'Clinton Meets GATT Notification Deadline; Tariff Talks Endure' (1993). *Inside U.S. Trade*. 17 December.

Cohn, Theodore H. (1993). 'The Changing Role of the United States in the Global Agricultural Trade Regime'. In W. P. Avery, ed., *World Agriculture and the GATT*, pp. 17–38. Lynne Rienner Publishers, Boulder, CO.

Cohn, Theodore H. (forthcoming). *Governing Global Trade: International Institutions in Conflict and Convergence*. Ashgate, Aldershot.

Commission on Global Governance (1995). *Our Global Neighbourhood: The Report of the Commission on Global Governance*. Oxford University Press, Oxford.

Commission on International Trade and Investment Policy (1971). 'United States International Economic Policy in an Interdependent World'. Report to the President. Government Printing Office, Washington DC.

Cooper, Richard N. (1989). 'International Cooperation in Public Health as a Prologue to Macroeconomic Cooperation'. In R. N. Cooper, ed., *Can Nations Agree? Issues in International Economic Cooperation*, pp. 178–254. Brookings Institution, Washington DC.

Cornia, Giovanni Andrea, Frances Stewart, and Richard Jolly (1987). *Adjustment with a Human Face*. Clarendon Press, Oxford.

Council of the European Union (2000). 'Directive on Electronic Commerce'. Interinstitutional file 98/0325 (COD), 28 February, Brussels.

Cox, Robert W. (1987). *Production, Power, and World Order: Social Forces in the Making of History*. Columbia University Press, New York.

Cox, Robert W. and T. Sinclair (1996). *Approaches to World Order*. Cambridge University Press, Cambridge.

Croome, John (1995). *Reshaping the World Trading System: A History of the Uruguay Round*. World Trade Organization, Geneva.

Culpepper, Roy (2000a). 'The Evolution of Global Financial Governance'. In North-South Institute, *Global Financial Reform: How? Why? When?* North-South Institute, Ottawa.

Culpepper, Roy (2000b). 'Systemic Reform at a Standstill: A Flock of Gs in Search of Global Financial Stability'. Paper presented at Critical Issues in Financial Reform: Latin-American/Caribbean and Canadian Perspectives, Munk Centre for International Studies, University of Toronto, 1–2 June. Toronto.

Cutter, Ann Grier and Len A. Costa (1998). 'The Framework for Global Electronic Commerce: A Policy Perspective. Ira C. Magaziner'. *Journal of International Affairs* vol. 51, no. 2 (Spring), pp. 527–538 [electronic version cited].

Daily Yomiuri (2000). 20 July, p. 3.

de Menil, George and Anthony M. Solomon (1983). *Economic Summitry*. Council on Foreign Relations, New York.

Dell, Michael (1999). *Direct from Dell: Strategies That Revolutionized an Industry*. Harper Business, New York.

Der Derian, James and Michael J. Shapiro (1989). *International/Intertextual Relations: Postmodern Readings of World Politics*. Lexington Books, Lexington, MA.

Development Assistance Committee (1999). 'Development Co-operation: Efforts and Policies of the Members of the Development Assistance Committee'. Organisation for Economic Co-operation and Development, Paris.

Development Assistance Committee (various years). 'Development Co-operation: Efforts and Policies of the Members of the Development Assistance Committee'. Organisation for Economic Co-operation and Development, Paris.

Dittmann, Sieghard (1997). 'Report on Communicable Disease Surveillance'. Subproject I: Towards a Global Health Network, G8 Global Health Applications Project. World Heath Organization, Copenhagen.

Dixit, Avinash K. and Barry Nalebuff (1993). *Thinking Strategically: The Competitive Edge in Business, Politics, and Everyday Life*. Norton, New York.

Dluhosch, Barbara (2001). 'The G7 and the Debt of the Poorest'. In J. J. Kirton, J. P. Daniels and A. Freytag, eds., *Guiding Global Order: G8 Governance in the Twenty-First Century*, pp. 79–92. Ashgate, Aldershot.

Dodwell, David (1993). 'The Gavel Falls on Most of Uruguay Round'. *Financial Times*, 14 December.

Doi, Toshinori (1999). 'The Asian Crisis and the Future Measures'. *Finance* October, pp. 17–34.

Doland, Angela (2000). 'AP Report'. 5 July.

Drake, William and Kalypso Nicolaïdis (1992). 'Ideas, Interests, and Institutionalization: "Trade in Services" and the Uruguay Round'. *International Organisation* vol. 46, no. 1 (Winter), pp. 37–100.

Dryden, John (1999). 'The Digital Economy in International Perspective: Common Construction and Regional Rivalry'. Paper presented at the University of California E-conomy Project. Washington DC.

Dunkel, Arthur (1987). *Trade Policies for a Better Future: The Leutwiler Report, the GATT, and the Uruguay Round*. Martinus Nijhoff, Dordrecht.

Economist Intelligence Unit and Arthur Andersen (1997). *Vision 2010: Designing Tomorrow's Organisation*. Economist Intelligence Unit, London.

Eden, Lorraine and Evan Potter, eds. (1993). *Multinationals in the Global Political Economy*. St. Martin's Press, New York.

Eichengreen, Barry J. (1999). *Toward a New International Financial Architecture: A Practical Post-Asia Agenda*. Institute for International Economics, Washington DC.

Eichengreen, Barry, James Tobin, and Charles Wyplosz (1995). 'Two Cases for Sand in the Wheels of Global Finance'. *Economic Journal* vol. 105, no. 1, pp. 162–172.

Elwood, Larry and Sheila Holland-Fox (2000). 'Nortel Networks: Competitive Advantage of Outsourcing'. Irish Academy of Management, annual conference, 7–8 September. Dublin.

Enoch, Charles, Peter Stella, and May Khamis (1997). 'Transparency and Ambiguity in Central Bank Safety Net Operations'. Working Paper WP/97/138-EAWP/97/138. International Monetary Fund, Washington DC.

'Europe Daily Bulletin' (1990). *Agence Europe*, p. 6.

European Union-Japan Summit (2000). 'Joint Conclusions'. 19 July. <europa.eu.int/comm/external_relations/japan/summit_7_19_2000> (March 2001).

Evans, H. P. (1999). 'Debt Relief for the Poorest Countries: Why Did It Take So Long?' *Development Policy Review* vol. 17, no. 3, pp. 267–279.

Evans, Philip and Thomas S. Wurster (2000). *Blown to Bits: How the New Economics of Information Transforms Strategy*. Harvard Business School, Boston.

Evans, Robert and Alister Danks (1998). 'Strategic Supply Chain Management: Creating Shareholder Value by Aligning Supply Chain Strategy with Business Strategy'. In J. Gattorna, ed., *Strategic Supply Chain Alignment: Best Practice in Supply Chain Management*. Gower, Aldershot.

Fidler, Stephen, Brian Groom, and Gillian Tett (2000). 'Charities in Attack on "Obscene" G8 Spending'. *Financial Times*, 22 July, p. 5.

Finance Canada (2001). 'G20 the Ideal Forum to Tackle Problems Associated with Globalization, Says Finance Minister'. 24 January, Ottawa. <www.fin.gc.ca/newse01/01-008.html> (March 2001).

Finnemore, Martha (1996). *National Interests in International Society*. Cornell University Press, Ithaca, NY.

'FP Interview: Lori's War' (2000). *Foreign Policy* Spring, pp. 28–55.

Frost, Ellen L. (1998). 'Horse Trading in Cyberspace: U.S. Trade Policy in the Information Age'. *Journal of International Affairs* vol. 51, no. 2 (Spring), pp. 473–496 [electronic version cited].

G7 (1975). 'Declaration of Rambouillet'. 17 November, Rambouillet. <www.library.utoronto.ca/g7/summit/1975rambouillet/communique.html> (March 2001).

G7 (1976). 'Joint Declaration of the International Conference'. 28 June, San Juan. <www.library.utoronto.ca/g7/summit/1976sanjuan/communique.html> (March 2001).

G7 (1977). 'Declaration: Downing Street Summit Conference'. 8 May, London. <www.library.utoronto.ca/g7/summit/1977london/communique.html> (March 2001).

G7 (1978). 'Declaration'. 17 July, Bonn. <www.library.utoronto.ca/g7/summit/1978bonn/communique/index.html> (March 2001).

G7 (1981). 'Declaration of the Ottawa Summit'. 21 July, Ottawa. <www.library.utoronto.ca/
g7/summit/1981ottawa/communique/index.html> (March 2001).

G7 (1983). 'Williamsburg Declaration on Economic Recovery'. 30 May, Williamsburg.
<www.library.utoronto.ca/g7/summit/1983williamsburg/communique.html>
(March 2001).

G7 (1984). 'London Economic Declaration'. 9 June, London. <www.library.utoronto.ca/
g7/summit/1984london/communique.html> (March 2001).

G7 (1985). 'The Bonn Economic Declaration Towards Sustained Growth and Higher
Employment'. 4 May, Bonn. <www.library.utoronto.ca/g7/summit/1985bonn/
communique/index.html> (March 2001).

G7 (1986). 'Tokyo Economic Declaration'. 6 May, Tokyo. <www.library.utoronto.ca/
g7/summit/1986tokyo/communique.html> (March 2001).

G7 (1990). 'Houston Economic Declaration'. 11 July, Houston. <www.library.utoronto.ca/
g7/summit/1990houston/communique/index.html> (March 2001).

G7 (1991). 'Economic Declaration of the G7 Summit'. 17 July, London.
<www.library.utoronto.ca/g7/summit/1991london/communique/index.html>
(March 2001).

G7 (1992). 'Economic Declaration: Working Together for Growth and a Safer World'.
8 July, Munich. <www.library.utoronto.ca/g7/summit/1992munich/
communique/index.html> (March 2001).

G7 (1994). 'G7 Communiqué'. 9 July, Naples. <www.library.utoronto.ca/g7/summit/
1994naples/communique/index.html> (March 2001).

G7 (1996). 'Economic Communiqué: Making a Success of Globalization for the
Benefit of All'. 28 June, Lyon. <www.library.utoronto.ca/g7/summit/
1996lyon/communique/index.html> (March 2001).

G7 (1997). 'Confronting Global Economic and Financial Challenges. Denver Summit
Statement by Seven'. 21 June, Denver. <www.g7.utoronto.ca/g7/summit/
1997nver/confront.htm> (March 2001).

G7 (1998). 'G7 Chairman's Statement'. 15 May, Birmingham. <www.g7.utoronto.ca/
g7/summit/1998birmingham/chair.htm> (March 2001).

G7 Finance Ministers (1999). 'Report of the G7 Finance Ministers to the Köln
Economic Summit'. 18 June, Cologne. <www.g7.utoronto.ca/g7/finance/
fm061999.htm> (March 2001).

G7 Finance Ministers (2000). 'Actions against Abuse of the Global Financial System'.
Report from G7 Finance Ministers to the Heads of State and Government.
21 July. <www.g7.utoronto.ca/g7/summit/2000okinawa/abuse.htm> (March
2001).

G8 (1997). 'Communiqué'. 22 June, Denver. <www.library.utoronto.ca/g7/summit/
1997nver/g8final.htm> (March 2001).

G8 (1998). 'Communiqué'. 15 May, Birmingham. <www.library.utoronto.ca/g7/
summit/1998birmingham/finalcom.htm> (March 2001).

G8 (1999). 'G8 Communiqué Köln 1999'. 20 June, Cologne. <www.library.utoronto.ca/g7/summit/1999koln/finalcom.htm> (March 2001).

G20 (2000). 'News Release'. Montreal, 25 October. <www.g7.utoronto.ca/g7/g20/montrealoct252000.htm> (March 2001).

G24 (2000). 'Intergovernmental Group of Twenty-Four on International Monetary Affairs Communiqué'. April 15. <www.imf.org/external/np/cm/2000/041500.HTM> (March 2001).

Gardner, Roy (1995). *Games for Business and Economics*. Wiley, New York.

General Agreement on Tariffs and Trade (1973). *GATT Activities in 1972*. General Agreement on Tariffs and Trade, Geneva.

General Agreement on Tariffs and Trade (1985). *Trade Policies for a Better Future: Proposals for Action*. General Agreement on Tariffs and Trade, Geneva.

General Agreement on Tariffs and Trade (1986). 'Agreement on Government Procurement'. *The Texts of the Tokyo Round Agreements*. General Agreement on Tariffs and Trade, Geneva.

Georgantzas, Nicholas C. (forthcoming). 'Self-Organizing Systems (SOS)'. In M. Warner and J. Kotter, eds., *International Encyclopedia of Business and Management*. Thomson Learning, London.

George, Jim (1994). *Discourses of Global Politics: A Critical (Re)Introduction to International Relations*. Lynne Rienner Publishers, Boulder, CO.

Germain, Randall (2001). 'Reforming the International Financial Architecture: The New Political Agenda'. Paper presented at the annual meeting of the International Studies Association, 20–24 February. Chicago.

Gill, Stephen, ed. (1993). *Gramsci, Historical Materialism, and International Relations*ed. Cambridge University Press, Cambridge.

Goldsmith, Arthur A. (1999). 'Slapping the Grasping Hand: Correlates of Corruption in Emerging Markets'. *American Journal of Economics and Sociology* vol. 58, no. 4, pp. 865–883.

Goldstein, Judith (1988). 'Ideas, Institutions, and American Trade Policy'. *International Organisation* vol. 42, no. 1 (Winter), pp. 179–217.

Goldstein, Judith and Robert O. Keohane (1993). *Ideas and Foreign Policy: Beliefs, Institutions, and Political Change*. Cornell University Press, Ithaca, NY.

Golt, Sidney (1974). *The GATT Negotiations, 1973–75: A Guide to the Issues*. British-North American Committee, Washington DC.

Goodman, John B. and Louis W. Pauly (1993). 'Obsolescence of Capital Controls? Economic Management in an Age of Global Markets'. *World Politics* vol. 46, no. 1, pp. 50–82.

Gorbachev, Mikhail (1987). *Perestroika: New Thinking for Our Country and the World*. Collins, London.

Gould, Mark (2000). 'Locating Internet Governance: Lessons from the Standards Process'. In C. T. Marsden, eds., *Regulating the Global Information Society*. Routledge, London.

Gupta, Sanjeev, et al. (1998). 'The IMF and the Poor'. Pamphlet Series, no. 52. International Monetary Fund, Washington DC.

Hajnal, Peter (1999). *The G7/G8 System: Evolution, Role, and Documentation*. Ashgate, Aldershot.

Hajnal, Peter (forthcoming). 'Openness and Civil Society Participation in the G8 and Global Governance'. In J. J. Kirton and J. Takase, eds., *New Directions in Global Political Governance*. Ashgate, Aldershot.

Hamilton, Colleen and John Whalley (1989). 'Coalitions in the Uruguay Round'. *Weltwirtschaftliches Archiv* vol. 125, no. 3, pp. 547–561.

Haraguchi, Koichi (1998). 'Bamingamu Samitto no Seika to Nihon'. The Results of the Birmingham Summit and Japan. *Sekai Keizai Hyoron* August, pp. 8–24.

Hayashi, Sadayuki (1995). 'Harifakkusu Samitto no Seika to Nihon'. The Results of the Halifax Summit and Japan. *Sekai Keizai Hyoron* September, pp. 8–17.

'Hejji Fando Taisaku Kento Shyuyokoku Ga Kinyuu Antei Kyougikai: Ofushoa Shijou Kanshi Mo' (Considering Regulation of Hedge Funds, Key Countries Launch Financial Stabilization Committee Which May Include Surveillance of Off-Shore Market) (1999). *Nihon Keizai Shimbun*, 15 April, p. 3.

Helleiner, Eric (1994). *States and the Reemergence of Global Finance: From Bretton Woods to the 1990s*. Cornell University Press, Ithaca, NY.

Helleiner, Eric (1998). 'Electronic Money: A Challenge to the Sovereign State?' *Journal of International Affairs* vol. 51, no. 2 (Spring), pp. 387–409 [electronic version cited].

Helleiner, Gerald (2000). *Markets: Politics and Globalization: Can the Global Economy Be Civilized?* United Nations Conference on Trade and Development, Geneva.

Henderson, David (1996). 'The Role of the OECD in Liberalising International Trade and Capital Flows'. In S. Arndt and C. Miller, eds., *The World Economy on Global Trade Policy*, pp. 11–28, [Special Issue].

Henderson, David (1998). 'International Agencies and Cross-Border Liberalization: The WTO in Context'. In A. O. Krueger with Chonira Aturupane, *The WTO as an International Organization*. University of Chicago Press, Chicago.

Higgott, Richard A. and Andrew Fenton Cooper (1990). 'Middle Power Leadership and Coalition Building: Australia, the Cairns Group, and the Uruguay Round of Trade Negotiations'. *International Organisation* vol. 44, no. 4 (Autumn), pp. 589–632.

Hodges, Michael R., John J. Kirton, and Joseph P. Daniels, eds. (1999). *The G8's Role in the New Millennium*. Ashgate, Aldershot.

Houlder, Vanessa (2000). 'US and EU Swap Blows on Climate Talks: Some Optimism amid Recriminations for Collapse of Agreement to Combat Global Warming'. *Financial Times*, 27 November, p. 1.

Hufbauer, Gary Clyde (1989). *The Free Trade Debate, Reports of the Twentieth Century Fund Task Force on the Future of American Trade Policy.* Priority Press, New York.

Hughes Hallett, Andrew J. and Nicola Viegi (2000). 'Credibility, Transparency and Asymmetric Information in Monetary Policy'. Prepared at the University of Strathclyde, Glasgow. March.

Ikenberry, John (1993). 'Salvaging the G7'. *Foreign Affairs* vol. 72 (Spring), pp. 132–139.

Ikenberry, John (1998). 'Institutions, Strategic Restraint, and the Persistence of American Postwar Order'. *International Security* vol. 23, no. Winter, pp. 43–78.

Inoguchi, Kuniko (1994). 'The Changing Significance of the G7 Summits'. *Japan Review of International Affairs* Winter, pp. 21–38.

Institute of International Finance (1999). *Report of the Working Group on Transparency in Emerging Markets Finance.* Institute of International Finance, Washington DC.

International Chamber of Commerce (1990). 'Statement on the Uruguay Round'. 21 June. International Chamber of Commerce, Paris.

International Monetary Fund (1995a). 'Presentation of the Fiftieth Annual Report by the Chairman of the Executive Board of the International Monetary Fund'. Summary Proceedings: Annual Meeting 1995. International Monetary Fund, Washington DC.

International Monetary Fund (1995b). 'Social Dimensions of the IMF's Policy Dialogue'. IMF Pamphlet Series 47. International Monetary Fund, Washington DC.

International Monetary Fund (1996a). 'African Prospects Tied to Courageous Adjustment Efforts'. *IMF Survey* vol. 25, no. 15, p. 259.

International Monetary Fund (1996b). 'Concluding Remarks: Statement by the Chairman of the Executive Board and Managing Director of the International Monetary Fund, Michel Camdessus'. Summary Proceedings: Annual Meeting 1996. International Monetary Fund, Washington DC.

International Monetary Fund (1996c). 'Opening Address by the Chairman of the Boards of Governors and Governor of the Fund and the Bank for Chile. Eduardo Aninat'. Summary Proceedings: Annual Meetings 1996. International Monetary Fund, Washington DC.

International Monetary Fund (1997a). 'Annual Meetings: IMF Given Role in Fostering Freer Capital Flows; Quota Increase. SDR Allocation Agreed'. *IMF Survey* vol. 26, no. 18, pp. 289–292.

International Monetary Fund (1997b). 'Managing Director's Opening Address: Camdessus Calls for Responsibility, Solidarity in Dealing with Challenges of Globalisation'. *IMF Survey* vol. 26, no. 18 (6 October), pp. 292–294.

International Monetary Fund (1997c). 'Making the Most of Debt Relief, External Finance'. *IMF Survey* vol. 26, no. 1, pp. 10–11.

International Monetary Fund (1997d). 'La Mondialisation, une Chance à Saisir'. *Bulletin du FMI* vol. 26, no. 10 (2 June), pp. 153–155.

International Monetary Fund (1997e). 'Presentation of the Fifty-Second Annual Report by the Chairman of the Executive Board of the International Monetary Fund'. Summary Proceedings: Annual Meeting 1997. International Monetary Fund, Washington DC.

International Monetary Fund (1998). 'Speech to Economic Club: Participation in the IMF Is an Investment in World Stability and Prosperity'. *IMF Survey* vol. 27, no. 6 (23 March), pp. 88–90.

International Monetary Fund (1999a). 'Code of Good Practices on Transparency in Monetary and Financial Policies: Declaration of Principles'. Adopted by the Interim Committee on 26 September. International Monetary Fund, Washington DC.

International Monetary Fund (1999b). 'ECOSOC Address: Aninat Outlines Ways to Integrate All Countries into Increasingly Globalized Economy'. *IMF Survey* vol. 29, no. 14 (17 July), pp. 227–230.

International Monetary Fund (1999c). 'IMF Annual Report 1999'. International Monetary Fund, Washington DC.

International Monetary Fund (1999d). 'Review of Social Issues and Policies'. IMF-Supported Programs. International Monetary Fund, Washington DC.

International Monetary Fund (2000a). 'Recovery from the Asian Crisis and the Role of the IMF'. Briefs for 2000 by IMF Staff. <www.imf.org/external/np/exr/ib/2000/062300.htm> (March 2001).

International Monetary Fund (2000b). 'Report of the Acting Managing Director to the International Monetary and Financial Committee on Progress in Reforming the IMF and Strengthening the Architecture of the International Financial System'. 12 April. <www.imf.org/external/np/omd/2000/report.htm> (March 2001).

International Monetary Fund (2000c). *World Economic Outlook 2000*. International Monetary Fund, Washington DC.

Jackson, John H. (1969). *World Trade and the Law of the GATT*. Bobbs-Merrill Company, Indianapolis.

Jackson, John H. (1990). *Restructuring the GATT System*. Pinter Publishers, London.

Jackson, John H. (1997). *The World Trading System: Law and Policy of International Economic Relations*. 2nd ed. MIT Press, Cambridge, MA.

Jackson, John H. (1998). *The World Trade Organization: Constitution and Jurisprudence*. Royal Institute of International Affairs, London.

Jacobson, Harold and Michel Oksenberg (1990). *China's Participation in the IMF, the World Bank, and GATT: Toward a Global Order*. University of Michigan Press, Ann Arbor.

Johnson, Pierre Marc (2000). 'Beyond Trade: The Case for a Broadened International Governance Agenda'. *Policy Matters* vol. 1, no. 3 (June), pp. 4–36.

Johnson, Pierre Marc (2001). 'Creating Sustainable Global Governance'. In J. J. Kirton, J. P. Daniels and A. Freytag, eds., *Guiding Global Order: G8 Governance in the Twenty-First Century*, pp. 245–282. Ashgate, Aldershot.

Jonquières, Guy de (2000). 'Altruism with a Bitter Taste: Brussels Is Being Forced to Rethink Plans to End Trade Barriers for the Poorest Countries'. *Financial Times*, 19 December, p. 23.

Jubilee 2000 Coalition (2000). 'Betraying the Poor: The Failure of the G8 to Deliver a New Deal on Debt at the Okinawa Summit'. 26 August. <www.jubilee2000uk.org/reports/dropped0800.html> (March 2001).

Kahin, Brian and Ernest Wilson, eds. (1997). *National Information Infrastructure Initiatives*. MIT Press, Cambridge, MA.

Kahler, Miles (1993). 'Multilateralism with Small and Large Numbers'. In J. G. Ruggie, ed., *Multilateralism Matters: The Theory and Praxis of an Institutional Form*, pp. 295–299. Columbia University Press, New York.

Kaiser, Karl, John J. Kirton, and Joseph P. Daniels, eds. (2000). *Shaping a New International Financial System: Challenges of Governance in a Globalizing World*. Ashgate, Aldershot.

Kapstein, Ethan B. (1994). *Governing the Global Economy: International Finance and the State*. Harvard University Press, Cambridge, MA.

Kay, Adrian (1998). *The Reform of the Common Agricultural Policy: The Case of the MacSharry Reforms*. CAB International, New York.

Keidanren (1999). *Proposal for the Promotion of Electronic Commerce*. Keidanren, Tokyo.

Kenen, Peter B., ed. (1996). *From Halifax to Lyon: What Has Been Done About Crisis Management? Essays in International Finance* no. 200. Princeton University Press, Princeton.

Keohane, Robert O. (1984). *After Hegemony: Cooperation and Discord in the World Political Economy*. Princeton University Press, Princeton.

Keohane, Robert (1989). *International Institutions and State Power: Essays in International Relations Theory*. Westview Press, Boulder, CO.

Kirton, John J. (1995). 'The Diplomacy of Concert: Canada, the G7 and the Halifax Summit'. *Canadian Foreign Policy* vol. 3, no. 1 (Spring), pp. 63–80.

Kirton, John J. (1999a). 'Canada as a Principal Financial Power: G7 and IMF Diplomacy in the Crisis of 1997–99'. *International Journal* vol. 54 (Autumn 1999), pp. 603–624.

Kirton, John J. (1999b). 'Explaining G8 Effectiveness'. In M. R. Hodges, J. J. Kirton and J. P. Daniels, eds., *The G8's Role in the New Millennium*, pp. 45–68. Ashgate, Aldershot.

Kirton, John J. (1999c). 'What Is the G20?' <www.library.utoronto.ca/g7/g20/g20whatisit.html> (March 2001).

Kirton, John J. (2000a). 'The Dynamics of G7 Leadership in Crisis Response and System Reconstruction'. In K. Kaiser, J. J. Kirton and J. P. Daniels, eds., *Shaping a New International Financial System: Challenges of Governance in a Globalizing World*, pp. 65–94. Ashgate, Aldershot.

Kirton, John J. (2000b). 'The G7 and Concert Governance in the Global Financial Crisis of 1997–1999'. Paper presented at the Annual Conference of the International Studies Assocation, 15–19 March. Los Angeles.

Kirton, John J. (2001). 'The G20: Representativeness, Effectiveness, and Leadership in Global Governance'. In J. J. Kirton, J. P. Daniels and A. Freytag, eds., *Guiding Global Order: G8 Governance in the Twenty-First Century*, pp. 143–172. Ashgate, Aldershot.

Kirton, John J., Joseph P. Daniels, and Andreas Freytag, eds. (2001). *Guiding Global Order: G8 Governance in the Twenty-First Century*. Ashgate, Aldershot.

Kishimoto, Shuhei (1999). 'The Aim of the New Miyazawa Initiative and the Asian Monetary Fund'. In Japanese. *Finance* pp. 31–48.

Kobrin, Stephen J. (1998). 'Back to the Future: Neomedievalism and the Postmodern Digital World Economy'. *Journal of International Affairs* vol. 51, no. 2 (Spring), pp. 361–386 [electronic version cited].

Kokotsis, Ella and Joseph P. Daniels (1999). 'G8 Summits and Compliance'. In M. R. Hodges, J. J. Kirton and J. P. Daniels, eds., *The G8's Role in the New Millennium*, pp. 75–91. Ashgate, Aldershot.

'Kokusai Kinyuu Kaikau Oosuji Goui He, Samitto. Sakakibara Zaimukan Kaikenn, Tankishihon No Kokusai Ido, Kanshi Kyouka' (International Financial Reform Leading to General Agreement at the Summit: Vice-Minister Sakakibara Notes Increase in Surveillance on International Short-term Capital Movement) (1999). *Nihon Keizai Shimbun*, 8 June, p. 5.

Kondo, Seiji (1999). 'Kerun Samitto no Seika To Nihon' (The Results of the Cologne Summit and Japan). *Sekai Keizai Hyoron* September, pp. 8–28.

Kopits, George and Jon Craig (1998). 'Transparency in Government Operations'. *Occasional Paper No. 158*. International Monetary Fund, Washington DC.

Krasner, Stephen D. (1979). 'The Tokyo Round: Particularistic Interests and Prospects for Stability in the Global Trading System'. *International Studies Quarterly* vol. 23, no. 4, pp. 491–531.

Krasner, Stephen D. (1983). *International Regimes*. Cornell University Press, Ithaca, NY.

Krasner, Stephen D. (1985). *Structural Conflict: The Third World against Global Liberalism*. University of California Press, Berkeley.

Kratochwil, Fredrich and John Gerard Ruggie (1986). 'International Organisation: A State of the Art on the Art of the State'. *International Organisation* vol. 40, no. 4, pp. 753–775.

Krueger, Anne O. (1995). *Trade Policies and Developing Nations*. Brookings Institution, Washington DC.

Krugman, Paul R. (1994). 'Competitiveness: A Dangerous Obsession'. *Foreign Affairs* vol. 73, no. 2, pp. 28–44.

Krugman, Paul R. (1996). *Pop Internationalism*. MIT Press, Cambridge, MA.

Kuroda, Haruhiko (2000). 'Vice-Minister's Speech on the Future International Financial Architecture and Regional Capital Market Development.' Delivered at the Round Table on Capital Market Reform in Asia, Tokyo, 11 April. <www.mof.go.jp/english/if/if015.htm> (March 2001).

Lairson, Thomas and David Skidmore (1997). *International Political Economy*. Harcourt Brace, Toronto.

Larraín B., Felipe and José Tavares (1999). 'Can Openness Deter Corruption?', Center for International Development, Harvard University, and Department of Economics, University of California.

Lean, Geoffrey (2000). 'World Climate Talks Collapse in Chaos — And We Are All the Losers'. *Independent*, 26 November, p. 1.

Lindgren, Carl-Johan, G. G. Garcia, and Matthew I. Saal (1996). *Bank Soundness and Macroeconomic Policy*. International Monetary Fund, Washington DC.

Long, Olivier (1985). *Law and Its Limitations in the GATT Multilateral Trade System*. Martinus Nijhoff, Dordrecht.

Magretta, Joan (1998). 'The Power of Virtual Integration: An Interview with Dell Computer's Michael Dell'. *Harvard Business Review* March-April, pp. 73–84.

Mangan, John and Kevin Hannigan (2000). *Logistics and Transport in a Fast-Growing Economy: Managing the Supply Chain for High Performance*. Blackhall Publishing, Dublin.

'Marrakesh Agreement Establishing the World Trade Organization' (1994). 15 April. <www.sice.oas.org/trade/ur_round/UR03E.asp> (March 2001).

Martin, Hans-Peter and Harald Schumann (1997). *The Global Trap: Globalization and the Assault on Prosperity and Democracy*. Zed Books, London.

McClure, Charles E. (1997). 'Taxation of Electronic Commerce: Economic Objectives, Technological Constraints, and Tax Laws'. *Tax Law Review* vol. 52, no. 3,

McGregor, Deborah (2000). 'Way Clear For Us — Africa Trade Bill'. *Financial Times*, 4 May, p. 14.

McGrew, Tony (1999). 'The World Trade Organization: Technocracy or Banana Republic?' In A. Taylor and C. Thomas, eds., *Global Trade and Global Social Issues*, pp. 197–216. Routledge, London.

McKenzie, Richard B. and Dwight R. Lee (1991). *Quicksilver Capital: How the Rapid Movement of Wealth Has Changed the World*. Free Press, New York.

Ministry of International Trade and Industry (1997). 'Towards the Age of the Digital Economy: For Rapid Progress in the Japanese Economy and World Economic Growth in the 21st Century'. Draft. Ministry of International Trade and Industry, Tokyo.

Ministry of International Trade and Industry (2000). 'Towards eQuality: Global E-Commerce Presents Digital Opportunity to Close the Divide between Developed and Developing Countries (MITI's Proposal for WTO E-Commerce Initiative)'. Second draft. Ministry of International Trade and Industry, Tokyo.

Mishkin, Frederic S. (1999). 'International Experiences with Different Monetary Policy Regimes'. *Journal of Monetary Economics* vol. 43, no. 3, pp. 579–605.

Moore, Mike (2000a). 'Open Societies Do Better'. Statement by the Director-General of the World Trade Organization at the 11th International Military Chiefs of Chaplains Conference. 9 February. <www.wto.org/english/news_e/spmm_e/spmm22_e.htm> (March 2001).

Moore, Mike (2000b). 'The Post-Seattle Trade Agenda'. Speech Delivered at International Chamber of Commerce — 33rd World Congress, Budapest. <www.wto.org/english/news_e/spmm_e/spmm30_e.htm> (March 2001).

Morishima, Michio (1999). *Why Do I Expect Japan to Collapse*? Iwanami Shoten, Tokyo.

Mukherji, Arijit and David E. Runkle (2000). 'Learning to Be Unpredictable: An Experimental Study'. *Federal Reserve Bank of Minneapolis Quarterly Review* no. Spring, pp. 14–20.

Murphy, Craig (1984). *The Emergence of the NIEO Ideology*. Westview Press, Boulder, CO.

New York Times (1998). 22 February.

'Nichibei Shuno Kaidan, Shushou, "Kinyuu Mondai" Soukishori He — Keizai Saisei Bei Ga Aturyoku' (U.S.-Japan Leaders Meeting: Prime Minister Promised to Have Swift Solution to the 'Financial Problem' — U.S. Pressures Japan on Its Economic Recovery) (1998). *Nihon Keizai Shimbun*, 16 May, p. 1.

O'Brien, Robert, Anne Marie Goetz, Jan Aart Scholte, et al. (2000). *Contesting Global Governance: Multilateral Economic Institutions and Global Social Movements*. Cambridge University Press, Cambridge.

Ogura, Kazuo (1996). 'Riyon Samitto wo Migutte' (About the Lyon Summit). *Sekai Keizai Hyoron* September, pp. 6–16.

Ogura, Kazuo (1997). 'Denba Samitto wo Migutte' (About the Denver Summit). *Sekai Keizai Hyoron* September, pp. 8–19.

Olson, Elizabeth (2000). 'Patching up Morale at the World Trade Organization'. *New York Times*, 31 October, p. W1.

Olson, Mancur (1965). *The Logic of Collective Action: Public Goods and the Theory of Groups*. Harvard University Press, Cambridge, MA.

'Online, of Course' (2000). *Economist* 10–16 June.

Organisation for Economic Co-operation and Development (1972). 'Policy Perspectives for International Trade and Economic Relations'. Report by the High-Level Group on Trade and Related Problems to the Secretary General of the OECD. Organisation for Economic Co-operation and Development, Paris.

Organisation for Economic Co-operation and Development (1987). *National Policies and Agricultural Trade*. Organisation for Economic Co-operation and Development, Paris.

Organisation for Economic Co-operation and Development (1994). *The OECD in the 1990s*. Organisation for Economic Co-operation and Development, Paris.

Organisation for Economic Co-operation and Development (1998). 'A Borderless World: Realising the Potential of Global Electronic Commerce'. Directorate for Science, Technology and Industry, SG/EC(98)14/Final. Organisation for Economic Co-operation and Development, Paris.

Organisation for Economic Co-operation and Development (2000). 'E-Commerce: Impacts and Policy Challenges'. Economics Department Working Papers No. 252 (Jonathan Coppel). Organisation for Economic Co-operation and Development, Paris.

Oye, Kenneth A. (1985). 'Explaining Cooperation under Anarchy: Hypothesis and Strategies'. In K. A. Oye, ed., *Cooperation under Anarchy*. Princeton University Press, Princeton.

Paarlberg, Robert L. (1993). 'Why Agriculture Blocked the Uruguay Round: Evolving Strategies in a Two-Level Game'. In W. P. Avery, ed., *World Agriculture and the GATT*, pp. 39–54. Lynne Rienner Publishers, Boulder, CO.

Pauly, Louis W. (1997). *Who Elected the Bankers? Surveillance and Control in the World Economy*. Cornell University Press, Ithaca.

Peoples' Global Action (2000a). 'Global Day of Action; S26'. 19 May. <www.x21.org/s26/calls/s26_en.htm> (March 2001).

Peoples' Global Action (2000b). 'Peoples' Global Action against "Free" Trade and the World Trade Organization'. 2 March. <www.agp.org/agp/en/PGAInfos/about.html> (March 2001).

Peterson, V. Spike (1992). *Gendered States: Feminist (Re)Visions of International Relations Theory*. Lynne Rienner Publishers, Boulder, CO.

Pollack, Andrew (1993). 'Summit Breathes Life into World Trade Talks'. *International Herald Tribune*, 8 July.

'The Poor Who Are Always With Us' (2000). *Economist*, 1. July.

Porter, M. E. (1985). *Competitive Advantage: Creating and Sustaining Superior Performance*. Free Press, New York.

Porter, Tony (1996). 'Capital Mobility and Currency Markets: Can They Be Tamed?' *International Journal* vol. 51, no. 4, pp. 669–689.

Porter, Tony (2000). 'The G7, the Financial Stability Forum, the G20, and the Politics of International Financial Regulation'. Paper presented at the International Studies Association Annual Meeting, Los Angeles, 15 March.

Preeg, Ernest H. (1995). *Traders in a Brave New World: The Uruguay Round and the Future of the International Trading System*. University of Chicago Press, Chicago.

Putnam, Robert and Nicholas Bayne, eds. (1987). *Hanging Together: Co-operation and Conflict in the Seven-Power Summit.* 2nd ed. Sage Publications, London.

'The Quad's Initial Market-Access Package'(1993). *GATT Focus* no. 101 (August-September), p. 3.

Rhodes, R. A. W. (1996). 'The New Governance: Governing without Government'. *Political Studies* vol. 44, pp. 652–667.

Rockwell, Kenneth (Director of Information and Media Relations of the World Trade Organization), interview with author, 2000.

Rosenau, J. N. and E.-O. Czempiel, eds. (1992). *Governance without Government: Order and Change in World Politics.* Cambridge University Press, Cambridge.

Ruggie, John Gerard (1998). *Constructing the World Polity: Essays on International Institutionalization.* Routledge, London.

Rugman, Alan M., John J. Kirton, and Julie A. Soloway (1999). *Environmental Regulations and Corporate Strategy: A NAFTA Perspective.* Oxford University Press, Oxford.

Sachs, Jeffrey (1998). 'Alternative Approaches to Financial Crises in Emerging Markets'. In M. Kahler, ed., *Capital Flows and Financial Crises*, pp. 247–262. Cornell University Press, Ithaca.

Sanger, David E. (1998). 'U.S. Sees New Villain in Asian Crisis: Tokyo's Leadership'. *New York Times*, 22 February, p. 3.

Schmidt, Vivien A. (1995). 'The New World Order Incorporated: The Rise of Business and the Decline of the Nation-State'. *Daedalus* vol. 124, no. 2, pp. 75–106.

Scheer, Robert (2000). 'Nowhere to Hide'. *Yahoo Internet Life* vol. 6, pp. 100–102.

Scholte, Jan Aart, Robert O'Brien, and Marc Williams (1999). 'The WTO and Civil Society'. *Journal of World Trade* vol. 33, no. 1, pp. 107–123.

Schott, Jeffrey J. (1994). *The Uruguay Round: An Assessment.* Institute for International Economics, Washington DC.

Schott, Jeffrey J. (2000). *The WTO after Seattle.* Institute for International Economics, Washington DC.

Shakow, Alexander (1995). 'A Changing Institution in a Changing World'. In M. ul Haq, R. Jolly and P. Streeten, et al., eds., *The UN and the Bretton Woods Institutions: New Challenges for the Twenty-First Century.* St. Martin's Press, New York.

'Shihon ido No kanshi Kyoka, G7 Zoushoukaigou Kaimakuhe, Gouiann Go Koumoku — Ajia Kiki Saihatsu Boushi' (Strengthening of Surveillance on Capital Movement: G7 Finance Ministers' Meeting Opens with Five Issues to Be Agreed Including the Future Prevention of Asian Crisis (1998). *Nihon Keizai Shimbun*, 8 May, p. 1.

Shonfield, Andrew (1976). 'Can the Western Economic System Stand the Strain?' *The World Today* vol. 32, no. 5 (May), pp. 164–172.

Smith, Mike (2000). 'EU May End Duty for Poor Nations'. *Financial Times*, 21 September, p. 15.

Snidal, Duncan (1985). 'The Limits of Hegemonic Stability Theory'. *International Organisation* vol. 39, no. 4 (Autumn), pp. 579–614.

Solomon, Steven (1995). *The Confidence Game: How Unelected Central Bankers Are Governing the Changed Global Economy*. Simon & Schuster, New York.

Stein, Janice Gross and Louis W. Pauly (1992). 'Choosing to Cooperate: How States Avoid Loss'. *International Journal* vol. 47, no. 2 (Spring/Special Issue).

Stiglitz, Joseph (1998a). 'Boats, Planes, and Capital Flows: Personal View'. *Financial Times*, 25 March, p. 32.

Stiglitz, Joseph (1998b). 'World Bank Conference on Development Economics: Speakers Explore Range of Development Issues and Appropriate Responses to Financial Crises'. *IMF Survey* vol. 27, no. 9 (11 May), pp. 146–148.

Stoler, Andrew, interview with author, 2000, Geneva.

Strange, Susan (1986). *Casino Capitalism*. B. Blackwell, Oxford.

Strange, Susan (1996). *The Retreat of the State: The Diffusion of Power in the World Economy*. Cambridge University Press, Cambridge.

Subcouncil of the Revitalization of the Asian Economy and Financial Markets, Council on Exchange and Other Transactions (2000). 'The Road to the Revival of the Asian Economy and Financial System: Sustainable Growth in the 21st Century and Building a Multilayered Regional Cooperative Network'. (Mimeograph.) Ministry of Finance, Tokyo.

Summers, Lawrence H. (1997). 'Statement of Lawrence H. Summers Deputy Secretary Department of the Treasury before the Committee on Commerce Subcommittee on Communications United States Senate'. <www.treas.gov/press/releases/pr052297a.html> (March 2001).

Summers, Lawrence H. (1998). 'Letter to Speaker of the House', 23 June. <www.treas.gov/cc/062398.htm> (March 2001).

Tayeb, Monir (2000). *International Business: Theories, Policies and Practices*. FT Prentice Hall, London.

Thérien, Jean-Philippe (1999). 'Beyond the North-South Divide: The Two Tales of World Poverty'. *Third World Quarterly* vol. 20, no. 4, pp. 723–742.

Thérien, Jean-Philippe and Sébastien Dallaire (1999). 'Nord-Sud: une Vision du monde en mutation'. *La revue internationale et stratégique* vol. 36, no. Winter 1999–2000, pp. 21–35.

Tickner, J. Ann (1992). *Gender in International Relations: Feminist Perspectives on Achieving Global Security*. Columbia University·Press, New York.

Tinbergen, Jan (1978). *Nord-Sud, du défi au Dialogue? Propositions pour Un nouvel ordre International*. SNED-Dunod, Paris.

Torday, Peter (1993). 'Hurdles Stand in Way of Deal'. *Independent*, 8 July.

'The Trade Agenda: A Different, New World Order' (2000). *Economist* 11 November, pp. 141–146.

Transatlantic Business Dialogue (2000). *2000 Mid-Year Report*. Transatlantic Business Dialogue, Brussels.

Turner, Colin (2000). *The Information Economy: Business Strategies for Competing in the Digital Age*. Kogan Page, London.

Ullrich, Heidi K. and Alan Donnelly (1998). 'The Group of Eight and the European Union: The Evolving Partnership'. *G8 Governance* no. 5, November, <www.library.utoronto.ca/g7/governance/gov5> (March 2001).

Underhill, Geoffrey R. D. (1991). 'Markets Beyond Politics? The State and the Internationalisation of Financial Markets'. *European Journal of Political Research* vol. 19, no. 1, pp. 197–225.

United Kingdom (2000). 'Eliminating World Poverty: Making Globalisation Work for the World's Poor'. British Government White Paper on International Development. <www.globalisation.gov.uk> (March 2001).

United States (1974). *U.S. Trade Act of 1974*. <uscode.house.gov/title_19.htm> (March 2001).

United States (1998). *Internet Tax Freedom Act of 1998* (Reported in the House). H.R.3529.RH. <thomas.loc.gov/bss/d105/hot-titl.html> (March 2001).

United States Department of Treasury (1996). 'Selected Tax Policy Implications of Global Electronic Commerce'. Office of Tax Policy, November. <www.treas.gov/taxpolicy/library/internet.txt> (March 2001).

Vedel, Thierry (1997). 'Information Superhighway Policy in France: The End of High Tech Colbertism?' In B. Kahin and E. Wilson, eds., *National Information Infrastructure Initiatives*. MIT Press, Cambridge, MA.

Von Furstenberg, George M. (2000). 'Transparentising the Global Money Business'. In K. Kaiser, J. J. Kirton and J. P. Daniels, eds., *Shaping a New International Financial System: Challenges of Governance in a Globalizing World*, pp. 97–111. Ashgate, Aldershot.

Wendt, Alexander (1992). 'Anarchy Is What States Make of It: The Social Construction of Power Politics'. *International Organisation* vol. 46, no. 2, pp. 391–425.

Wendt, Alexander (1999). *Social Theory of International Politics*. Cambridge University Press, Cambridge.

White House, Office of the Press Secretary (1998). 'Joint Statement from Australia and the United States on Electronic Commerce'. 20 November.

Wilcox, Clair (1949). *A Charter for World Trade*. Macmillan, London.

Williams, Frances (2000). 'Poorest Countries Attack WTO Aid Package'. *Financial Times*, 11 April, p. 14.

Williamson, John (1990). 'What Washington Means by Policy Reform'. In J. Williamson, ed., *Latin American Adjustment: How Much Has Happened?*, pp. 5–38. Institute for International Economics, Washington DC.

Winham, Gilbert R. (1986). *International Trade and the Tokyo Round Negotiation*. Princeton University Press, Princeton.

Winham, Gilbert R. (1989). 'The Prenegotiation Phase of the Uruguay Round'. *International Journal* vol. 44, no. 2 (Spring), pp. 280–303.

Wolfe, Robert (1998). *Farm Wars: The Political Economy of Agriculture and the International Trade Regime*. Macmillan, Houndmills.

Womack, J.R., D.T. Jones, and D. Roos, eds. (1990). *The Machine That Changed the World*. Ranson Associates, New York.

Wood, Robert Everett (1986). *From Marshall Plan to Debt Crisis: Foreign Aid and Development Choices in the World Economy*. University of California Press, Berkeley.

Wood, Robert Everett (1996). 'Rethinking Economic Aid'. In S. W. Hook, ed., *Foreign Aid toward the Millennium*, pp. 19–37. Lynne Rienner Publishers, Boulder, CO.

World Bank (1996). *Poverty Reduction and the World Bank: Progress and Challenges in the 1990s*. World Bank, Washington DC.

World Trade Organization (1994). *The Results of the Uruguay Round of Multilateral Trade Negotiations: The Legal Texts*. General Agreement on Tariffs and Trade, Geneva. Reprinted 1995 by the World Trade Organization, Geneva.

World Trade Organization (1998). *Electronic Commerce and the Role of the WTO*. World Trade Organization, Geneva.

World Trade Organization (2000a). 'DG Moore Embarks on Consultations on Future WTO Work'. Press Release 163. 26 January. <www.wto.org/english/news_e/pres00_e/pr163_e.htm> (March 2001).

World Trade Organization (2000b). 'Moore Calls for Closer Parliamentary Involvement in WTO Matters'. Press Release 169. 21 February. <www.wto.org/english/news_e/pres00_e/pr169_e.htm> (March 2001).

Zartman, I. William (1989). 'Prenegotiation: Phases and Functions'. *International Journal* vol. 44, no. 2 (Spring), pp. 237–253.

Index

349